SLOW MOTION

SLOW MOTION
Changing Masculinities, Changing Men

Lynne Segal

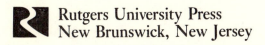

Rutgers University Press
New Brunswick, New Jersey

For Peter

First published in the United Kingdom by Virago Press Limited, 1990
First published in cloth and paperback in the United States of
America by Rutgers University Press, 1990

Copyright © Lynne Segal, 1990

Library of Congress Cataloging-in-Publication Data

Segal, Lynne.
    Slow motion : changing masculinities, changing men / Lynne Segal.
        p. cm.
    Includes bibliographical references and index.
    ISBN 0-8135-1619-6 (cloth)   ISBN 0-8135-1620-X (pbk.)
    1. Men—Psychology.   2. Masculinity (Psychology)   3. Sex role.
I. Title.
HQ1090.S43   1990
305.31—dc20   90-41862
                                                   CIP

Contents

Acknowledgements

As always, I am immeasurably indebted to the many friends and acquaintances who have encouraged and assisted me throughout the writing of this book. Peter Osborne read every draft of every chapter, patiently pointing out the strengths and weaknesses of my argument. Barbara Taylor and Gregory Elliott each painstakingly edited my prose; Ruthie Petrie, Ursula Owen and others from Virago gave advice and encouragement. James Swinson, Bob Connell, Catherine Hall, Stuart Hall, John Fletcher, David Morgan, Sheila Rowbotham, Chris Whitbread and Isaac Julien offered me useful information or assistance on selected chapters. The unstinting affection, generosity and support I have had from Peter Osborne and James Swinson, plus that of my son Zimri, gave me the confidence and desire to embark upon and complete this project (with others, they must also take some of the blame for what optimism there is in the text). I cannot thank enough all those who have steadfastly assisted me over the last few years, and who, even in these depressing times, help sustain my belief in the possibility of enriching the socialist project with a sexual politics of hope, equality and freedom.

Preface

'Women do not write books about men,' Virginia Woolf wrote; at least, not books which end up classified as such.[1] Men do not write books about men either; at least, according to opinions fast becoming fashionable. 'The real man,' Peter Schwenger tells us in his survey of masculinity and twentieth-century literature, 'thinks about practical matters rather than abstract ones and certainly does not brood upon himself or the nature of his sexuality.'[2] He does of course – but more in complacent self-mockery or mournful self-confession than to probe and pin down the specificities of masculinity. In reality, and fortunately for the project of this book, both women and men have written volumes on the male sex. When men have written of themselves, however, they have done so as though presenting the universal truths of humanity, rather than the partial truths of half of it. And even now, when writing of men, women have done so more to expose the evil of their ways than to explore the riddles of 'masculinity' – its relation to, and dependence upon, 'femininity'.

It is certain that men have always preferred to study neither God nor man, but 'woman'. Defined as the particular sex – the different, the difficult, the problematic sex – it is women and not men who have traditionally been the object of scrutiny. But times change, and with them what we read and write. Throughout the 1980s the shifting nature of men's lives, their behaviour, experiences, anxieties, fears and cravings, have been debated with new passion and concern. Books researching fatherhood, men's violence against women and children, male identities and male mythologies now interrogate men, as a sex, in a way until recently reserved for women – as a problem. From the sex-role theories of the fifties to the studies of gender and power of the eighties, the psychology of men has increasingly come to be seen as one fraught with strain and crisis. An emphasis on the divergent, inconsistent and contradictory meanings of masculinity now accompanies most research on men.

Ironically, however, amidst this growing concern with masculinity, the thoughts of those seeking a sexual politics to undermine men's power over women remain consistently gloomy. Feminists and their supporters researching the realities of greater equality between the sexes argue that there is little evidence of significant change, whether in the home, the workplace or in the wider spheres of community, culture and politics. And while there has been some change in some men's behaviour, it is clearly neither on a scale nor of a character seriously to have altered dominant perceptions of gender. Most of the new books on masculinity constantly emphasise complexity and contradiction. Yet they spend little time exploring its specific nature and significance. Despite the explosion of writing on the topic, the category of 'masculinity' remains deeply obscure. As we shall see, it is in fact becoming more obscure.

In this book, I have attempted to approach the problem in a new way by looking not at 'masculinity' as such, but at certain specific *'masculinities'*, in the belief that it is an understanding of the *differences* between men which is central to the struggle for change. The one thing which most of the current literature has not done is locate masculine identities and behaviour in relation to sexual politics – in particular, to the last twenty years of conscious collective struggle to undermine men's power over women, in Britain and elsewhere. Yet, I shall suggest, it is only by making this connection that we can gain any deeper theoretical insight into the problem of just what 'masculinity' is, or might become.

The force and power of the dominant ideals of masculinity, I argue, do not derive from any intrinsic characteristic of individuals, but from the social meanings which accrue to these ideals from their supposed superiority to that which they are not. To be 'masculine' is *not* to be 'feminine', *not* to be 'gay', *not* to be tainted with any marks of 'inferiority' – ethnic or otherwise. It is thus in relation to women's liberation and gay liberation, and to social contexts which either foster possibilities for greater sexual equality or offer continuing obstacles to change, that I will look at competing male identities – macho, Black, gay and anti-sexist – to see how specific male identities and behaviour are constantly produced, reproduced and transformed. <u>Men's attachment to the dominant masculine ideal of power and superiority</u>, which I suggest is necessarily ambiguous, is threatened by other men's assertion of contrasting gay, anti-sexist or Black male identities. Nor are we simply dealing with a multiplicity of masculine styles, for these are always cut across by, and enmeshed within, other, differing relations of power – class, age, skill, ethnicity, sexual orientation, and so on.

In some chapters I will point to areas where change has begun in men's ideals and men's behaviour; or at least where contradictions and strains are most prevalent. Where, I will ask, are men today most vulnerable to pressure for change? How do we undermine their strong resistance to change? From a flashback to the 1950s, for example, I suggest that the relationship of men to home and family has undergone an irreversible transformation over the last three decades. Though domesticity acquired a new salience for men as well as women in the fifties, questions of men's relationship to childcare, housework, violence in the home, were not yet on the conceptual, let alone the political, agenda. In contrast, since the close of the seventies, men's role as fathers, and precisely what they do in the home, have been widely observed and discussed. Most men today desire and have a closer relationship with their children than did their fathers. Reflecting upon the new emphasis on fatherhood, however, suggests that rather than shifting men's power over women and children, there are ways in which men today now have the best of both worlds: they retain power in the public sphere, while having greater access to the satisfactions (often without the frustrations) of family life. Power struggles in the home heighten, however, as conflicts between women and men deepen, strengthening at least the possibilities for further movement.

Having documented one example of change in men's lives, while questioning its precise significance for undermining men's power, I move on to outline and assess the theorizing of masculinity currently available to us. 'Whether we love men or hate them,' Deirdre English has written, 'we – as feminists – have no task more necessary than understanding them.'[3] It is only from psychoanalytic writing, not from the static conformity models of role theory, that we can begin to gain some understanding of the measure of internal conflicts and fragile sexual identities which trouble and torment the minds of men. What we can observe, however, from psychoanalytic studies of the symbolic force of 'masculinity' and the overriding psychic significance of simply being male, we cannot fully explain from within that framework alone. The power and meaning of 'masculinity' derive not just from anatomy or familial interaction, but from wider social relations. They express the cultural reality of women's subordination embodied, not only – as the Lacanians suggest – in language, but in the functioning of the state, industry, and every other source of social, economic and political power. It is the difficulty of moving beyond the pervasive methodological individualism of all psychological thinking (beyond the idea that all explanations of personal and social phenomena can be reduced to facts about individuals) that makes it hard to understand why change is so slow and so contradictory.

The most striking thing about the sexual politics of feminists in the early days of women's liberation was its confidence and optimism. The most striking thing about the progressive spirit – whatever its objectives – in these late days of Thatcherism, is its tendency to cynicism and pessimism. Both hope and despair are always possible in assessing the significance of transformations in the lives of women and men, when change is neither linear nor homogeneous. There has been more movement in the lives of some men than others, and in the lives of some women than others – and it is not, in my view, possible for change to occur for one sex without affecting the other. Nor has the direction and extent of change been arbitrary. Change has occurred where the social as well as the individual possibilities for it have been greatest and, in particular, where women's power to demand it has been strongest.

The idea of men's behaviour as ultimately unchanging and inevitably coercive, if not murderous, has, perhaps unsurprisingly, appeared in much of the writing on men and violence. It is less than helpful, however, to attempt to tie up all forms of aggression, sexual violence, institutionalised heterosexuality, warfare and ecological destruction in one neat package as 'male'. In sifting through the growing literature on men's coerciveness and abuse of women, I suggest that it *is* possible to make distinctions: between men who deploy violence against women and men who do not; between one form of violence and another; and between the structures which foster and maintain different forms of violence and those which help to undermine them. How, for instance, are we to view the reality of both women and men's struggles for new forms of sexual experience and pleasure, in the context of so many men's continuing fear of and contempt for women? Rethinking and reasserting the struggle for 'sexual liberation' helps clarify the possibilities for a new non-repressive sexual agenda for both women and men.

Men's resistance to change is not reducible to their psychic obstinacy or incapacity. Men can and do change. Resistance to change is also bound up with the persisting gender routines which characterise most of the wider economic, social and political structures of contemporary society. But social realities are not static. Future relations between women and men remain open, battles are continuously fought, lost and won; and change, whether the intended outcome of emancipatory activity or the unintended consequence of other agencies, is inevitable. Much of the recent feminist writing on men has seemed to suggest that nothing has changed. But it is more interesting, and certainly more useful, to see how things do in fact change. It *is* possible to steer a course between defeatist pessimism and fatuous optimism. Such, at any rate, is the project of this book.

SLOW MOTION

1. Look Back in Anger: Men in the Fifties

Fatherhood is not yet fashionable. Men are not present at the births of their children, if they can possibly help it. They do not shop, push prams, design the home. Marriage to the unmarried male is a trap, and sex the bait, which by stealth and cunning may yet be won.

Fay Weldon on the fifties[1]

'A new hero has risen among us', wrote Walter Allen in his influential review of Kingsley Amis's first novel, *Lucky Jim*, in January 1954.[2] The new hero is male, the 'intellectual tough' or 'tough intellectual'. He is rude, crude and clumsy, boasts his political apathy, his suspicion of all causes, and he is out to do nobody any good but himself. His heroism consists in the fact that he is honestly self-serving, fiercely critical of all he sees as phoney, pretentious or conformist – a passion which expresses itself most readily in a rejection of what he sees as womanly, or domestic. He exudes a bullying contempt for women.

Explaining the appeal of this young cynic tells us a good deal about the nature of men's lives in the fifties. It also provides a good starting point for reassessing contemporary debate on the changing nature of men and masculinity in the eighties. Back in 1958 the writer and critic Kenneth Allsop was already wondering how someone in 1984 might look back on the fifties: 'I think that he will see a sensitive, emotional, intelligent but wretchedly neurotic society, obedient to protocol beneath the exhibitionist "rebelling", and obsessively class-conscious.'[3] What *he* will not see are public forms of rebellion – exhibitionist or not – from women. It was a woman writer though, Storm Jameson (never of course ranked among the Angry Young Men), who perhaps most clearly expressed what was most refreshing in fifties literary protest. 'What we need now', she argued, 'may be just that insolent irresponsibility, the contempt for safety and comfort and riches, the passionate delight in freedom, the curiosity, the blind hunger for experience and new knowledge, of the mediaeval wandering scholar.'[4]

What was also needed but was largely absent then – for those wishing to shed some light on the existential angst of the new man of mid-century Britain – was some greater understanding of the social and political reality surrounding everyday life in the period. At a conference held in 1987 on the new left of the fifties, Jean McCrindle, one of the handful of women who were part of that movement from its inception, expressed incredulity at the absence of women from the politics of the time: 'I just don't know why women were so absent, so silent – there was a pathological absence of women, silencing of women, in those days.'[5] Exploring the reasons behind the 'pathological silencing' of women in those days can tell us something of the nature of men's lives at the time.

Our most familiar images of the political climate following the defeat of the Labour Party in 1951 conjure up complacency, inertia, illusion. Economic problems were solved, class conflicts dissolved, household harmony restored – so both Labour and Tory politicians declared. By the early fifties, economic growth and Keynesian demand management had yielded full employment and ensured a steady rise in working-class standards of living. Further change, the conventional wisdom ran, was unnecessary. As central as the new myth of classlessness to this cross-party consensus was the myth of sexual equality. 'The feminine sex is a social problem', the eminent sociologist Alva Myrdal had announced a decade earlier.[6] But now women's problems too were solved. Gone for good, it was thought, was the toil and misery of the pre-war working-class housewife, raising too many unplanned, unwanted, underfed and unhealthy children, in dismal poverty and wretched housing. Child benefit, family planning and other forms of welfare provision for mothers and their children did cushion the post-war family from the levels of poverty and ill-health it had often previously experienced. Many women may have returned to the home after the war, with the birth rate soaring and attitudes towards working wives largely hostile – but so too had men. There were many new demands placed upon women as wives and mothers, but, it was felt, women could hardly complain when unlike former times they were no longer alone in their interests and preoccupations.

Man About the House

The man's place was also in the home. Men too, in popular conscious-ness, were being domesticated. They had returned from battlefield to bungalow with new expectations of the comforts and the pleasures of home. Both the popular and the academic writing of the fifties cele-brate a new 'togetherness', domestic harmony and equality between the sexes. The sociological writing of the fifties, for example, applauds the profound changes underway in contemporary family life. The well known community studies of Young and Willmott on working-class families in the early fifties rapidly move on from describing the stereo-typical working-class husband of yesteryear – mean with money, call-ous in sex, harsh to his children, neither helpful nor affectionate towards 'the wife' – to affirming the end of the absentee husband and a new partnership in marriage: 'In place of the old comes a new kind of companionship between man and woman, reflecting the rise in status of the young wife and children which is one of the great transforma-tions of our time.'[7] The influential work of John and Elizabeth Newson reached similar conclusions: 'At a time when he has more money in his pocket, and more leisure on which to spend it, than ever before, the head of the household chooses to sit at his own fireside, a baby on his knee and a feeding-bottle in his hand.'[8]

In some ways the domestication of men was real enough. In his *Anatomy of Britain* (1961) Anthony Sampson wrote of the threat posed by domesticity to professional men's clubs:

> At lunch time they seem confident enough: but it is in the evenings, when the wife and family beckon, that the loyalty of the clubman is tested: and it is then that the crumbling of clubs is revealed. A few defiant masculine clubs like White's, succeed in drinking and gambling till late in the night. But in most clubs, only a handful of bachelors, grass widowers and visitors inhabit the cavernous rooms. No doubt clubs will survive a long time, with their myths, their sites and the convenience: but the old misogynist zeal, which built the Empire and kept wives in their place – that has gone.[9]

The box-office hits of the day and the new Hollywood heroes (in a world now saturated with North American culture) also seemed to reflect a post-war cult of domesticity strong enough to embrace men too. Tough guys were on their way out. As North American film critic Peter Biskind recalls: 'By the fifties, the tough, hard-boiled Hemingway male of the thirties and forties, the man who hid his feelings, if he had any . . . who endured adversity alone with proud, stoical silence or wooden unconcern, had seen his best days.'[10] The new male stars – tough but tender Rock Hudson, slight and sensitive Montgomery Clift, mixed-up and moody James Dean – were a different breed from Humphrey Bogart, James Cagney or Gary Cooper, increasingly portrayed in fifties films as either neurotics or crazies. The new films generally put family before career. And the female stars, whether Marilyn Monroe in *The Seven Year Itch*, Jane Powell in *Seven Brides for Seven Brothers*, Debbie Reynolds in *The Tender Trap* or Elizabeth Taylor in *Giant*, were busy civilising men, and teaching them that their real desires were for matrimony and domesticity.

The new man of Hollywood, like *Homo Sociologicus* of the fifties, may have been putting family first more often, but, as we shall see, his place within it remained decidedly limited. Reviewing the sociological and psychological literature on the family of the fifties two decades later, Elizabeth Wilson suggests:

> To study this body of literature is above all to study how ideology operates by *excluding* whole areas of debate from the very consciousness of readers and authors alike . . . The sexual division of labour, because it was taken for granted, was an *absence* in these works . . . About this conflict [between women and men] there was also silence, for these books are about a myth – a myth of happiness.[11]

But there are ways of seeing through the myth to observe something of what men were actually doing in the home in the fifties, and the conflicts and tensions of family life at the time. 'Man About the House' is a chapter heading from an interesting handbook published in 1958, *The Man's Book*. Aimed at middle-class men – the ones deserting Sampson's clubland – it indicates what they might have been up to in the home: hammers, saws, smoothing tools, gripping tools, boring and drilling tools, scissors, nails, screws and glues are successively illustrated and explained. The book contains not a single reference to children, housework, or any activity traditionally regarded as 'women's work'.[12] Significantly, the topic 'fathers' is rarely listed in the index of fifties books on the family; and when it does appear it is not in connection with childcare.

It is clear from the data on English attitudes in 1950 collected by the anthropologist Geoffrey Gorer that the idea of quite separate roles for husband and wife was completely dominant. Asked which qualities they most desired in husbands, women replied: 'under-standing' (helping in the home was mentioned by less than 5 per cent). What husbands most wanted from their wives was good housekeeping (sharing the husband's interests was mentioned by only 8 per cent). Some wives did comment upon their husbands' unwillingness to participate in any housework or childcare. A 'typical twenty-eight year old working-class wife', for example, complained of husbands who were 'afraid of being thought a cissy; mine hates people to know he helps at all in the house; won't push pram'.[13] Gorer reports that it is the younger married wives 'who are the loneliest members of English society, without even the faint friendliness of pub or cafe'.[14] Taking the sexual division of labour for granted, Gorer does not enquire into the nature or extent of men's participation in housework or childcare – except to ponder whether father or mother is the most appropriate person to punish a very naughty child.

In his influential study of working-class life – *The Uses of Literacy* (1957) – Richard Hoggart also depicts a sharp division between women and men's roles, with men sharing little of women's domestic life. A husband is not really expected to help in the home; '"Oh, that's not a man's job" a woman will say, and would not want him to do too much of that kind of thing for fear he is thought womanish.'[15] Men pushing prams would still be thought 'soft' by most wives, as well as husbands. What women want from men, Hoggart suggests, is not sharing in domestic tasks but a good and steady provider, and one who is not violent. The husband is always 'the boss' in the home, even on the dole. Fathers are not intimate with their children, at least up until the boy leaves school, when 'he is, probably for the first time, close to his father and finds his father ready to be close to him: they now share the real world of work and men's pleasures.'[16] The wife, in Hoggart's view, knows little of her husband's job, and will be working hard 'from getting up to going to bed'. A few younger husbands and wives may, however, be learning from middle-class husbands who, Hoggart feels, are more likely to help their wives, when, with the decline of domestic service after the Second World War, they can no longer afford the paid help they once relied upon. But there are few signs in the literature of the period that the 'togetherness' celebrated in the popular media involved men's sharing of domestic tasks and childcare.

Some of the clearest examples of the separate worlds of women and men, ironically, are to be found in Young and Willmott's own study. Men are around the house more, they suggest: being less overcrowded, the home is a nicer place to be, so 'men do not go to pubs as often as they used to'.[17] But what do they do indoors? As we learn from one woman informant, they go and fetch in a few beers to drink, 'so they can watch the tellie at the same time'. Young and Willmott use occasional washing up ('one or more times during the previous week') as an indication that most men do 'give some regular help to their wives'.[18] Or again, the claim that the sharing of responsibility 'is nowhere more obvious than over childcare' boils down to the report that fathers are not as strict with their children as they used to be. We are given no idea of the real proportion of shared housework or childcare, if such there was, because the interviewers, like the interviewees, do not seriously expect it. The domestic partnership is one in which the separate worlds of men and women are reconstituted inside the home itself:

> When they watch the television instead of drinking beer in the pub, and weed the garden instead of going to a football match, the husbands of Greenleigh have taken a stage further the partnership mentioned in an earlier chapter as one of the characteristics of modern Bethnal Green.[19]

Young and Willmott's stress on the importance of the mother-daughter tie in married life in Bethnal Green, alongside the terrible loneliness of the wives in the new housing estate of Greenleigh ('it was all a misery . . . I sat and cried my eyes out'),[20] unwittingly provides perhaps the most compelling illustration imaginable of the reality of the separate spheres. Husbands, they suggest, are excluded from the world of mother and daughter: women are closer to their mothers than to their husbands. This is precisely why they can proclaim in their conclusion: 'the view which we have found and tested more or less daily for three years is that very few people wish to leave the East End.'[21] But it is only the women who are so lonely in Greenleigh ('It's like being in a box to die out here', confides Mrs Harper); the men, on the whole, like it: 'It's not bad here . . . we've got a decent house with a garden, that's the main thing,' reports Mr Harper.[22]

The most impressive of the 'community studies' of the fifties is the description of Yorkshire miners and their families in *Coal is Our Life*. At odds with the cosy consensus of the time, Dennis, Henriques and Slaughter do perceive the ways in which women remain oppressed by their dependence on their husbands' wages and the organisation of the household around the husband's job. (Significantly, this was one aspect of their analysis which was criticised at the time for its 'morbid preoccupation' with problems of the past.)[23] They also argued that the lives of women and men in the mining villages were not anomalous, but in fact reflected the general pattern of working-class family life, whenever the wife had no prospect of professional or other social interests or activities outside the home. In this situation, they suggest, there can be little genuine sharing between husband and wife.

Once again, unlike their contemporary colleagues, these observers stress the limitations of the new conditions enticing men from the clubs and pubs back into the home: 'Television seems to be making a slight difference in this respect, but it will be recognised that as a "family activity" this is a passive and silent one, a relation between the television screen and each individual rather than between the family members.'[24] Even men's increased involvement in DIY household repairs and improvements, they notice, never seems to demand or encourage the growth of companionship between husband and wife. In the mining villages at least, men remain comparative strangers in the home, distanced from their children (particularly their daughters) and, if not engaged in the almost exclusively male social life outside, spend their non-working time in their gardens or silently pottering about the house.

Husbands and wives are here seen as living separate – almost secret – lives, neither being able to enter properly into the other's world: the wife will know little or nothing of her husband's job and social life, the husband will take no responsibility for the housework or childcare. Few women admitted to satisfaction in their sex lives, while, in the 'almost business-like' arrangements of marriage, husbands too experienced a suppression of affection and desire: 'As the years go by, and any original sexual attraction fades, this rigid division between the activities of husband and wife cannot but make for an empty and uninspiring relationship.'[25] For the husband to maintain his status and prestige in his social life with his peers, he must consciously – and conspicuously – distance himself from his wife and children. Behind this social distance between women and men, it is apparent, as Dennis et al. stress, that women remain inferior and subordinate to men (unlike her husband, a woman spends no money on herself and engages in no activities or amusements without his approval). The husband's relative freedom and power are accepted by women and men alike, reflecting a shared view of his greater importance and responsibilities in a social context in which there is little employment for women, and men's work possesses a peculiarly 'masculine' character (the miner's main source of pride in his job deriving from its arduous and dangerous nature). The passionate conviction that only 'real men' – and certainly not women – could descend down into the dark, dirty dungeons of the coalfields supplies what status there is in a job which, for men, is comparatively poorly paid and hazardous.

Maternity Rules

The depiction of the opposed social spheres of women and men in *Coal is Our Life* accords with other contemporary analyses. Elizabeth Bott, for example, reported that the closer-knit the social network surrounding families, the more segregated the roles of husband and wife, the more isolated the family unit, the more symmetrical the roles.[26] This is consistent with the belief of some contemporary commentators that more traditional sexual divisions might persist in the older working-class areas, but were breaking down in the more isolated family units characteristic of the middle class and the more geographically mobile urban working class. However, a closer look at the assumptions and practices of middle-class family life in the fifties provides a rather different picture. Daughters of these middle-class men have written about fathers who were rarely at home, ill at ease with their emotions, and attuned only to the mysterious demands of 'work', suggesting to Olivia Harris, for example, that English fathers seemed to be 'archetypally absent'.[27] Sheila Rowbotham has recalled how her lower middle-class father, though working from home, was so entirely removed from domestic life that he 'had to resort to creeping up on the kitchen in his carpet slippers to gain access to information . . . To me he was simply a tyrant to be resisted.'[28]

Daughters have often perhaps felt that they received less attention from their fathers than did their brothers. But describing their fathers of this period men today report the same lack of contact throughout their childhood, the same social distance – regardless of their family background:

> When I think of my dad I am overwhelmed with questions . . . . On the surface our life together seemed like a transitory moment. Like we were passing through the same family on separate journeys. But below the surface he's left me with deep sorrow and a sense of loss.[29]

Jonathan Rutherford reports from his men's group in the 1970s that the overriding emotions of men talking of their fathers were of anger and loss. Most men remembered learning to avoid their fathers:

> I was really frightened hearing him come up the stairs, because I thought he might stick his head in.
> I cringed in his presence, especially if he had been drinking. I dreaded that he might come and talk to me.[30]

One man returned from his father's funeral to announce that he really felt nothing other than 'pleased'.[31] There were exceptions, of course. Sara Maitland's father 'bathed his babies, climbed trees, kicked footballs, hugged, kissed and played with his children. Above all he *taught us*.'[32] But in general, it would appear that at home, middle-class men, like their steady-earning working-class equivalent, could expect 'a life well balanced between the TV set and the neatly-tended garden'.[33]

Their wives, meanwhile, were often far from contented. In *Wives*

Who Went To College (1957), Judith Hubback described the dissatisfaction of educated women tied to the home while their children were young. Like the women she interviews, however, she has no solutions to the resentments and frustrations she records: 'I get tired of having very few personal contacts outside my family in which I am anything more than my husband's shadow.'[34] 'Escape', to use their word, can come only, perhaps, when the children have grown up. The problem of combining family and employment was publicly discussed in relation to middle-class women by, for example, Alva Myrdal and Viola Klein in 1956 in *Women's Two Roles*. But they make it clear that they are referring to married women who are childless or have ceased to look after small children. In discussing the positive aspects of women's participation in paid work, they suggest that the prime consideration is how to bring about 'a change of attitudes among women themselves', as well as 'the provision of better services to reduce domestic work'.[35] They do not contemplate change in the services men provide in the home. Indeed, once again, 'fathers' do not even rate a mention in their index.

The absence of any expectations of men's direct participation in childcare or housework, whether in the working-class or middle-class home, is not hard to explain. As Denise Riley argues, the fixing and freezing of women as mothers, and nothing other than mothers, was central to the vision of the fifties.[36] Not even women could yet shift the focus. Policing mothers at all times was the new wisdom, popularised in John Bowlby's bestseller of 1953, *Child Care And The Growth of Love*, which stressed 'the absolute need of infants and toddlers for the continuous care of their mothers'.[37] Bowlby's notion of 'maternal deprivation' was used to explain every conceivable personal and social problem, from educational failure and mental breakdown to delinquency, divorce, promiscuity and general social unrest.

Whatever Bowlby's own intentions (probably to assert and protect the interests of children), his ideas were an important part of the political campaign in the late 1940s to return women to the home and increase the population of Britain. Other writers on the fifties have also commented on the exploitation of 'maternal deprivation' to justify the housebound mother and neglect the needs of 'working' mothers. Peter Lewis, in his book on that decade, suggests 'it took the place in mid-twentieth century demonology that masturbation filled for the Victorians.'[38] The British psychoanalytic literature of the time also emphasised the desirability of separate and distinct male and female spheres for the sake of the child's mental health: the father should remain the more distant and remote visitor from the outside world. He is, in the words of D.W. Winnicott, 'the human being who stands for law and order which mother plants in the life of the child'.[39]

In accordance with expert opinion, the deluge of childcare manuals of the fifties either completely ignored the father's role in parenting, or treated the idea of paternal participation in childcare as a joke. *From Here to Maternity*, for example, restricts itself to warning husbands of the bizarre 'monkey business' they will have to tolerate from their pregnant wives.[40] While *Happy Event*, another light and popular book for new mothers on 'the stark reality' of the first year with baby, has no tips for expectant fathers, but does open with a cautionary poem for mothers to keep baby out of father's way:

> When Baby's cries grew hard to bear
> I popped him in the Frigidaire.
> I never would have done so if
> I'd known that he'd be frozen stiff.
> My wife said: 'George, I'm so unhappy
> Our darling's now completely frappe!'[41]

Women, it seems, knew something about the limitations of men's new domesticity. As Betty Thorne, the wife of a Sheffield steel worker, wrote forcefully to *The Manchester Guardian* in 1960, describing life on her street, 'The husband is an ornament or a nuisance alternately.'[42]

The general social concern with adequate mothering, and the assumed biological imperative dictating women's exclusive responsibility for it, had contradictory effects on women. Ideologically, at least, mothering was accorded new value and importance. Housework or 'homemaking' was portrayed not as a drudgery, but as a 'craft': the 'creative' work of efficient domestic consumption.

Shopping was no longer to be seen as labour, but more as a type of leisure: a symbol of the 'good times' now accompanying and sustaining the golden years of economic growth in Britain. But women also faced new anxieties and accusations – as incompetent carers and selfish slatterns – were they to complain too loudly of the isolation, boredom and strain accompanying their work in the home.

Complain, of course, some of them did. In a sudden public outburst of resentment in the *Guardian* 'Women's Page' in 1959 one woman ('J.B.H.') confessed: 'I love both my sons devotedly, but I suffer the most excruciating boredom in their company'. Another confided:

> I have five children and I found those baby years about which my child-loving friends wax lyrical, full of the most appalling boredom and weariness. It did not get better. It got worse with each one and it is just as bad with my grandchildren.[43]

But for these women, there was no alternative – not even one to ponder on – as the discontented 'JBH' was sharply reminded by another mother of the day: 'Once a woman confesses boredom with any aspect of her God-given role of wife and mother it is a very short step to finding the whole thing intolerable, and to do so J.B.H. must have forgotten the millions of weary, bored women, on whom civilisation was built and depends for its continuance, and whom she has to thank for her position.'[44] (A short step, indeed, but one which it would take women another ten years to make! In the early 1970s a significant number of young mothers were to decide that their position was, precisely, intolerable.)

Meanwhile, the well-nigh obsessive focus on the importance of the mother-child bond in the psychology of the day provoked a backlash: the growth of a youthful rebellion against the oppressiveness of those dutiful mothers attempting to act out the advice so freely heaped upon them. An early warning had appeared in the United States, when *Catcher in the Rye* became a bestseller in 1951. For J.D. Salinger, parents, but in particular mothers, exist to torment and warp the young.[45] Predictably, 'domesticity' came to symbolise 'conformity' in the fifties: the extreme domestication of women – represented as more 'feminine' both in blissful maternity and in the 'New Look' seductive fashions of the fifties – paralleled the mild domestication of men, represented as more home-based (if not more house-trained). Since class differences were now considered surmountable through education and welfare provision, men who felt at odds with their time – bored and dissatisfied – were to turn their anger against the ideals of hearth and home. They turned against women, especially against the 'powerful' mother in the home (powerful because she alone took real responsibility there), displacing onto her all the hatred and resentment they felt towards 'the Establishment'.

Angry Young Men

Many young men of the late 1950s identified strongly with the tough, amoral, anarchic working-class heroes of Alan Sillitoe in *Saturday Night and Sunday Morning* or *The Loneliness of the Long Distance Runner* – men fighting for a sense of freedom and fun against the dreary grey jobs and marriages awaiting them. 'What I want is a good time. All the rest is propaganda,' the Sillitoe hero declares, in rejection of 'the doubled-faced society that really takes no account of him.'[46] In these bestselling books (later made into films) women are never to be trusted. They are part of the system trying to trap, tame and emasculate men. 'Women are all the same,' Arthur Seaton announces in *Saturday Night and Sunday Morning*, 'whores, shrews, fools', enticing the suckers into 'the hell that older men call marriage.'[47] While male protagonists see themselves as opposing all authority – 'fighting every day until I die ... fighting with mothers and wives, landlords and gaffers, coppers, army, government'[48] – in reality the battle is with mothers and wives alone. There is no reflection on women's lot in Sillitoe's celebration of an aggressive, misogynistic masculinity: 'There was something about the whole situation which made him want to hurt her' ... 'all you could do was end up by giving them a smack in the chop'.[49] As Nigel Gray subsequently pointed out in his study of post-war working-class fiction, 'Arthur is against all authority – except the authority of men over women. He fights the authorities with his mouth when they are out of earshot – that's cunning, and saves his muscle for women'.[50]

Sillitoe's individualistic angry young man shares the cynical, self-seeking character and quest of other contemporary heroes, whether created by John Wain, John Osborne, John Braine, Stan Barstow, David Storey or J.P. Donleavy. (The flippant and facetious Kingsley Amis hero – rather like Waterhouse's *Billy Liar* – is less physically aggressive, but no less contemptuous of all he sees as effeminate, sensitive or refined.) By the close of the fifties, similar new working-class idols – Tommy Steele, Marty Wilde and Billy Fury – had appeared on the pop charts to drown out the sugary, suave sentimentality of Frank Sinatra: the yearning for *Love and Marriage* with which the decade had opened had yielded to the new teenage dream *Rock with the Caveman*. It is John Osborne's play *Look Back in Anger*, however, which has been hailed as most representative 'in every nuance' of the context of the mid-fifties.[51] At the time, leading theatre critic Kenneth Tynan welcomed its 'anarchy', its 'instinctive leftishness' and its 'automatic rejection of "official" attitudes'.[52] Writer and critic David Lodge has written of the impact Jimmy Porter, Osborne's young hero, had on his Royal Court audience in 1956: 'I ... remember well the delight and exhilaration its anti-establishment rhetoric afforded me, and the exactness with which it matched my own mood at that juncture in my life.'[53] (Lodge was then a military conscript on weekend leave, and conscription, as we shall see, played a not insignificant role in constructing the masculine mood of the moment.)

Osborne himself was always exceptionally, almost pathologically, hostile to women – witness his great admiration for Tennessee Williams: 'In Baby Doll, Williams has hit off the American Girl-Woman of the last hundred years – spoilt, ignorant, callous, resentful ... Make no mistake about it – this Baby Doll kid is a killer. She would eat a couple of guys and spit them out before breakfast ... The female must come toppling down to where she should be – on her back. The American male must get his revenge sometime.'[54] His revenge is rape. Jimmy Porter speaks for his creator in expressing his fear of his middle-class wife Allison, whom he systematically torments and abuses. He compares her to a gorging python devouring men, and draining them of all vitality: 'She'll go on sleeping and devouring until there's nothing left of me ... Why do we let these women bleed us to death? ... No, there's nothing left for it, me boy, but to let yourself be butchered by the women.'[55]

Life is dull, these rebels roar; life is unheroic – there are no great causes left for men to fight in the 'Brave-New-nothing-very-much-thank-you' fifties world.[56] A stifling domesticity has killed the spirit and ripped out the guts of men, and who is there to blame but women? Who indeed, if, like Osborne and most of the other 'Angries', you are a rebel without a cause and believe that class struggle is obsolete and Marx a fraud? Even Colin MacInnes had bought the fifties myth of classlessness. Though less cynically apolitical than most of his literary peers, in *Absolute Beginners* (1959) MacInnes created yet another scornful, anti-social cult male hero who touched the pulse of contemporary British youth: 'Do try to understand that, clobbo! I'm just not interested in the whole class crap that seems to needle you and all the tax-payers – needle you all, whichever side of the tracks you live on, or suppose you do'.[57] Class hostility, however, was not extinct; rather, in writings like these it is repressed and twisted into new forms of sexual hostility.

In retrospect it is clear that the scorn which the Angry Young Men hurled at 'the Establishment' was a class resentment, but one devoid of any collective class consciousness. As many have since commented, these new writers were mostly university graduate ex-grammar school boys, from lower middle- or working-class backgrounds, climbing quickly – but for them not quickly enough – up the class ladder. They faced a Britain as class conscious as ever – at least, that is, in its upper echelons, where power, authority and prestige still resided, and with it contempt and ridicule for the grant-aided student ('They are scum', as Somerset Maugham blandly pronounced).[58] Life was frustrating for the working-class grammar school boy, as Hoggart – himself from that background – had declared: 'He both wants to go back and yet thinks he has gone beyond his class, feels himself weighted with knowledge of his own and their situation, which hereafter forbids him the simpler pleasures of his father and mother. And this is only one of his temptations to self-dramatization.'[59]

Another temptation was his desire for, yet fear of, middle- and upper-class women. Beware 'the perils of hypergamy', Geoffrey

Gorer warned in 1957, referring to the process of men marrying upwards, he goes on: 'NOW I'M PRACTICALLY SURE OF IT. *Lucky Jim, Look Back in Anger* and all that lot roused my suspicions; the clincher has come with John Braine's *Room at the Top*, which tells much the same story all over again, brilliantly and bitterly. The curse which is ruining, in fantasy if not their own lives, these brilliant young men of working-class origin and welfare-state opportunity is what anthropologists have dubbed hypergamy. It is a new pattern in English life, and apparently a very distressing one.'[60] Displaying the patronising and, inevitably, sexist perspective of the academic elite of his day, Gorer was nevertheless probably right to speculate that these educated sons of the working class felt in especial danger of losing their virility. Having abstained from the money and pleasures available earlier on to their less studious peers, and now perhaps attracted to women they were less sure of being able to dominate, they asserted a particularly pugnacious manliness and heterosexual aggressiveness. One of the main targets of mockery for Amis, Wain or Osborne, in deriding their upper class antagonists, is their effeminacy, as in Amis's constant homophobic references: 'standing rigid with popping eyes . . . they had a look of being Gide or Lytton Strachey'.[61]

Homophobia and the Fear of Unmanliness

Homophobia, coupled with new forms of sexual insecurity and fear of women, was not, however, confined to Angry Young Men like Amis, Braine and Osborne – en route via the political apathy and scepticism of the fifties, to a true-blue conservatism. Such sentiments were the spirit of the times. As others have noticed, there has always been a close link between misogyny and homophobia in our culture.[62] As we shall see many times throughout this book, although the persecution of homosexuals is most commonly the act of men against a minority of other men, it is also the forced repression of the 'feminine' in all men. It is a way of keeping men separated off from women, and keeping women subordinate to men. Craig Owen, for example, has argued that 'homophobia is not primarily an instrument for oppressing a sexual minority; it is, rather, a powerful tool for regulating the entire spectrum of male relations.'[63] The fifties was not only a time when the symbol of the Happy Housewife embraced all women, when Hollywood could portray the career woman, rather than the seductress, as *femme fatale* (as in the celebrated *All About Eve*), it was also a time of intense persecution of homosexual desire.

The social study *English Life and Leisure*, conducted in 1951 by B. Seebohm Rowntree and G.R. Lavers, with the intention of influencing and improving the cultural and spiritual state of the country, attests to the anxieties of the period. After referring to a general awareness of the widespread existence of homosexuality, they add: 'It is only necessary to see a few of the unfortunate persons who have become addicted to it to realize how demoralizing and degenerating an influence it is.'[64] Moreover, they warn, 'sexual excesses are both a symptom of national weakness and a powerful secondary cause of it.'[65] This was a decade when, as Jonathan Dollimore has reminded us in his study of the fiction of the fifties, senior Law Lord Patrick Devlin explicitly associated 'immorality' with treason, demanding the suppression of 'vice' as inherently subversive.[66] Associations of this kind were consolidated in 1951 with the defection of British diplomats Burgess and Maclean to the Soviet Union, and the concurrent McCarthy witch-hunt against Communists and homosexuals in the United States. There was a dramatic increase in police activity against male homosexuality in both Britain and North America, culminating in Britain in the anti-homosexual drive instigated by the authorities in the early 1950s, in which young detectives were employed as *agents provocateurs*.[67] As we will see in chapter six, persecution of homosexuals continued up to and beyond the close of the decade (the homosexual MP Montgomery Hyde, for example, was forced by his constituency association to stand down once his sexual orientation had been revealed).

Amidst this onslaught of persecution, inprisonment and punitive forms of 'treatment' such as aversion therapy, homosexuals themselves came to view their own desire, in the words of Colin MacInnes, as 'a crippled state of being'[68] or, like Quentin Crisp, as 'a fatal flaw in masculinity'[69] or, like Mary Renault in her novels, as an affliction to be endured and overcome.[70] Perhaps the most

moving portrayal of the internalised self-hatred of the male homosexual, unable to conform to the masculine ideal of heterosexuality,
is provided by the Black American writer, James Baldwin.[71] As with
the rage of the Angry Young Man, the plight of the male
homosexual in the fifties tells us much about the contemporary
anxieties over manhood – especially in the area of sex. Colin
MacInnes, as his biographer Tony Gould illustrates, is as aware as
any heterosexual stud of the importance of being manly, delivering
this message in one of his unpublished novels: 'What you must do,
son, is become a fucker, and not become a fucked. It's simple as
that. Boys or girls, up the pussy or the arse, whichever you prefer,
but you've got to remember there's a cock between your legs and
you're a *man*.'[72]

The post-war contrasts between wartime memories and civilian
life, and the maintenance of military conscription marking men's
entrance into adulthood, were both significant aspects of the
tension over 'manhood' in the 1950s. Trevor Royle opens his book
on military conscription between 1945 and 1963, *The Best Years of
Their Lives*, by observing that National Service cast a long shadow
over boys in the 1950s: 'it was simply a part of the fabric of everyday
life.'[73] The writings of David Lodge, Alan Sillitoe and others testify
to the casual brutality and crude insensitivity generated by the futile
monotony of conscript life; while in *All Bull* B.S. Johnson pro-
nounces it 'tedious, belittling, coarsening, brutalising, unjust and
possibly psychologically very harmful'.[74] The daily tedium of army
life was relieved only by the swearing, drinking and boasting
bravado of male bonding. At the same time, however, intensified
male friendship and comradeship were real and lasting joys of
National Service. Those, like Colin MacInnes, who remember
military life with pleasure recall 'the unexpected egalitarianism, the
unlikely friendships, the blissful irresponsibility'.[75] Army training
relies upon intensifying the opposition between male and female,
with 'women' used as a term of abuse for incompetent performance,
thereby cementing the prevalent cultural links between virility,
sexuality and aggressiveness. Such practices serve not only to
discipline men, but to raise 'masculine' morale in the face of a more
typically 'feminine' reality – the enforced servility and conformity

characteristic of army life. 'Effeminacy', as Royle observes, was 'the ultimate soldier's crime' and 'to some people, carrying a gun was like having a permanent hard-on.'[76]

One 'problem' for some of these young male conscripts, therefore, was that they were unlikely to realise their sexualised fantasies of military glory (even if such realisation would have served merely to bring home to them the horrors of war). These were men who were not actually killing anyone, although they were nonetheless taught to kill as the appropriate training for men. Some, like 'Jimmy Porter', were to claim to regret that they had little prospect of ever confronting and defeating an actual enemy. This was a time, it is also relevant to note, of heightened hostilities between East and West, with Western chauvinism kept continually on the boil by US propaganda about the Red Menace, and brand new fears of the Bomb and nuclear extinction. Trained for military action, fed on a Cold War diet of espionage and treason, these men were the first generation to live in a post-imperial Britain and observe the old Empire dismantled – 'given away'. One dramatic exception was the Suez crises in 1956. Ray Gosling, a railway signalman at the time, recalls:

> I can remember the feeling that ran down the line as they 'stood behind Eden', the man who was to show them and the world that the Old Bulldog could bite as well as bark . . . that they were still at the heart of 'the greatest Empire of all time'. They would send a gunboat and show the wogs how the lion still roared. There was not one man who at the time spoke against Eden, yet one could feel in the comments made their knowledge that the Empire was dead; pre-war Britain would never return, Eden would fail.[77]

And he did. (He failed, it is worth noting, primarily because President Eisenhower reminded Britain that their special relationship with the United States involved a subaltern role for Britain.)

The links between army life, masculinity and violence, however, are always more ambiguous than they might at first appear. Actual violence and fighting did not necessarily accompany the near obligatory smoking, swearing, drinking, aggressive sexual boasting and phallic symbolism of military equipment, which permeated the all-male culture of young conscripts. Recollecting his period of National Service in the late fifties, the sociologist David Morgan remembers little actual violence. There was talk of fights, but the reality was more 'an overt disdain for anything that might appear soft or wet' – more 'a taboo on tenderness' than a celebration of violence.[78] In particular, at least in terms of public discussion, there was little room for tenderness in accounts of sexuality. The army did help forge and consolidate certain dominant patterns of masculinity, yet Morgan is cautious in drawing the links: 'It was not that, simply, boys learnt to swear, drink, desire women, favour toughness, rely on their mates and so on . . . It was more a matter of learning to identify masculinity and being a male with these traits and pieces of behaviour'.[79]

These same traits and pieces of behaviour also predominated in the staple literary diet of the fifties. As Ken Worpole reports, the most popular books in Britain in the 1950s, selling in their millions to boys and men – and significant numbers of women as well – were about the experiences of male combatants in the Second World War.[80] Though unquestionably one of the most fainthearted pupils at my all-girls school in fifties Australia, I can remember feeling obliged to read *The Wooden Horse* by Eric Williams. Like *Colditz Story* and others of the genre, it typifies the male adventure story linking masculinity and rugged individualism: men (usually RAF officers) fight for their freedom against the enormous odds of wartime imprisonment. These books were also a powerful influence in the promotion of apparently 'apolitical', but actually intensely conservative, politics and values. Strange as it may seem, although in keeping with the elimination of any political analysis of recent history, not one of these wartime bestsellers, as Worpole notes, ever mention the word 'fascism': the enemy is 'German'.[81] The hero is a man untrammelled by the everyday ties and responsibilities of sexual relationships and family.

In short, there were at least two opposed faces of masculinity in the fifties. There was the new family man, content with house and garden. And there was the old wartime hero, who put 'freedom' before family and loved ones. In the home, men had new responsibilities as husbands, though not yet as fathers. (The marriage guidance literature of the day, for example, was now stressing that men should be able to satisfy their wives sexually.) Men were still seen as necessarily the sexual instigators and educators of women, and one result was the growing visibility of impotence (which I shall be discussing in chapter eight). A literature was developing on the dilemmas of contemporary masculinity, much of it expressing anxieties over male delinquency and educational failure. The rising divorce rates and suppressed reality of family discord similarly stirred up professional anxiety about the popularly celebrated harmonious roles of men and women. Addressing many of these social anxieties, the US sociologist Helen Hacker published a paper in 1957 on 'The New Burdens of Masculinity' in which she outlined the conflicts in 'the masculine role'. Men were expected to be more patient, understanding and gentle in their dealings with others, and yet 'with regard to women they must still be sturdy oaks'.[82] Hacker also characterised what she saw as the increased incidence of homosexuality as an index of men's flight from the new burdens of masculinity.

Whatever the real or imagined burdens on men created by the Janus-face of masculinity, new levels of antagonism in the old 'sex war' are evident in the ubiquitous misogynistic humour of the fifties. If, as Freud has argued, the function of joking is the reduction of anxiety, then male anxiety was running very deep at the time. *The Man's Book* of 1958 referred neither to women nor to children since, as the preface facetiously inquires, 'What really useful advice could one give about women in a twenty-volume encyclopaedia?' It continued by explaining that their final section on humour – 'Wit's End' – was designed to give the last word to men: 'And that in itself makes, as they say, a nice change'.[83] If there was one thing men had in common at the time, as I remember well from my own father's humour, it was the jokey pleasures of insulting women. There are 46 jokes in 'Wit's End', every one of them insulting to women, many expressing violent or destructive fantasies: 'Here lies my wife: here let her lie./ Now she's at rest. And so am I'; 'No man regards his wife with pleasure, save twice: in her bridal bed, and in her grave'; 'A gentleman is a man who never strikes a woman without provocation'; 'But Eve from scenes of bliss/Transported him for life/The more I think of this/The more I beat my wife'. Etc. etc., *ad nauseam*.[84]

We might suggest, as would some feminists, that this pervasive anti-woman humour was simply a weapon used by men to discipline women – a type of propaganda for male dominance and a warning to women of the consequences of challenging it. In later chapters I will be dealing with the difficult question of the relationship between fantasy and actual behaviour. But, whatever the connections we make, there are signs of very high levels of confusion and conflict over male identity in the popular culture of the time. In the late fifties the cartoons of Jules Feiffer began to appear in the American radical paper *The Village Voice*, and were soon to be syndicated worldwide. They portrayed baffled and tortured men confronted by neurotic women in a sad, sick world of non-communication. 'Men Really Don't Like Women' Feiffer confided in an article in *Look* magazine which is pessimistically perceptive about relations between the sexes:

> The American woman is a victim. Her trouble is she is doing comparatively well as a victim. Her problem is not taken seriously. Woman is a second-class victim. And what is her problem? We all know it is man . . . Man has always seen woman as his enemy. But he needs her.[85]

Women and the Left in the Fifties

Amidst this taunting and teasing of women by men in the fifties, few of the 'victims' were writing or speaking publicly and prominently; but those who were, perceived the world in ways which complemented, rather than contradicted, male perceptions. Doris Lessing's ambitious novel *The Golden Notebook* was published in 1962, but is set in the atmosphere of the despair and disillusion experienced by so many on the communist left in the late fifties: 'we have to admit that the great dream has faded and the truth is something else.'[86] It documents its heroine's quest for authenticity and fulfilment, not via the Angries' anarchic (and privately authoritarian) anti-authoritarianism, but through the earlier, more earnest and romantic Lawrentian view of sex as 'the quick of self': Anna Wolf can express herself fully and genuinely only through the love of a *real* man'.

Doris Lessing shared the fifties anxieties over manhood, and an England 'full of men who are little boys and homosexuals and

half-homosexuals'.[87] She does, however, passionately portray the
sufferings of women as mothers and lovers, trying to cope with the
selfishness, dishonesty and aggressive insecurity of men, as well as
the anxieties, embarrassment and self-disgust many women felt
about their own bodies. She is aware of the boredom and depression of women trapped in the home – 'the disease of our time', she
called it.[88] Yet for Lessing, as for the wider world of the fifties,
there is no alternative. We cannot blame men: 'If I were a man I'd
be the same,' she writes.[89] On the contrary, women need to bolster
men up, 'for the truth is, women have this deep instinctive need to
build a man up as a man . . . I suppose this is because real men
become fewer and fewer and we are frightened, trying to create
men.'[90]

Those women who could articulate women's sufferings saw them
as inevitable. Margaret Drabble, for example, reflected in her first
novel in 1963: 'What happens otherwise is worse than what happens
normally, the embroidery and the children and the sagging mind. I
felt all women were doomed . . . born to defend and depend instead
of to attack.'[91] And ironically, if unsurprisingly, when the assault on
the stifling nature of family life in the fifties did finally surface in the
writings of R.D. Laing and David Cooper in the sixties, it took the
form of an attack on women. It denounced the pathological
possessiveness of all those housebound mothers who had had little
option but to live through the lives of their children. It condemned
mothers who could not leave their children alone; who were
denying them autonomy and driving them mad: 'A young man has
only to look a little cross with his manipulative, incestuously
demanding mother to end up on a detention order as "dangerous to
others",'[92] David Cooper accused in 1964. R.D. Laing and his
fellow anti-psychiatrists spread the verdict of maternal guilt.

The left in the fifties was as silent as everybody else on relations
between the sexes, accepting unquestioningly the belief that
women's problems were solved. The same was true even of the
younger, renovating new left born in 1956 out of the twin crises of
Suez and Hungary. As the new left grew rapidly with the rise of the
Campaign for Nuclear Disarmament (CND), the first decisive
break was made with the politics of the Cold War and the politics of

Stalinism. Unlike the bureaucratic and economistic old left, its successor had an exciting, enriching interest in contemporary culture. Yet as Stuart Hall, one of its founding members, recalls: 'We were totally unconscious of questions of gender, totally entombed on that issue – even though we were beginning to think about personal life, even though we realized the boundaries of politics had to be ruptured to bring in those aspects of life seen as important to people.'[93] Another co-founder, Raphael Samuel, has also spoken of the left's anti-feminism:

> We were worse than the Labour Party, who did at least have one-third women members. Like Colin MacInnes we romanticised the working-class male hero as the hope for the future. There was some truth in this, but also a blindness.[94]

Jean McCrindle has written of searching for books 'that would make sense to me as a woman ... There wasn't an awful lot of encouragement from looking at women's actual lives in the 1950s.'[95] Fear and confusion accompanied women's sexual involvement with men outside marriage, with no accessible contraception for single women, no legal abortion, and a crushing stigma attached to unmarried mothers or 'fallen women'. Inside or outside marriage, Jean McCrindle recalls, there was little open discussion of sexual problems, and 'feminism' was utterly scorned as 'bourgeois': 'You were a comrade and wanted to be treated exactly as men were.'[96] '*The Golden Notebook*', she continues, 'describes very brilliantly the kind of women who stayed active in the party and they were often bitter, hard, and certainly didn't identify with the quiet wives sitting in the corner making tea while "the comrades" discussed politics.'[97]

What we can learn from the silence about women on the left goes beyond the ineluctable sexism of the men (however obnoxious they may or may not have been in their relations with women). In what little they did write women were as silent as men about any alternative solutions to the strains placed upon them, whether isolated in the home or, increasingly, going out to work but expected to give complete priority to their families. Discontent was unspoken, unshared: every woman felt she carried her burdens, her fears, boredoms, guilts and anxieties, alone. What was needed was a whole new way – a collective way – of looking at the problem of marriage, childbearing, sexuality and employment. But such thinking was just not available to either women or men at the time, and the consequence, as Jean McCrindle suggests, were relationships 'heavy with boredom and frustration for women, and with guilt for many men.'[98] The solutions, or attempts at them, were, as we shall see, to inform the sexual politics of the sixties, seventies and eighties, when both men and women began in earnest to rebel against conventional respectability, and to go searching for other routes beyond 'the battle of the sexes' and the 'trap' of domesticity.

On the evidence of this flashback to the fifties, it is clear that the relationship of men to home and family has undergone irreversible change over the last three decades. Though domesticity acquired a new salience for men as well as women in the fifties, questions of men's relationship to childcare, housework, violence in the home, were not yet on the conceptual, let alone the political, agenda. Today they have become an essential, if politically often still token, part of it. Nowhere is this change clearer than in the literature on fatherhood in the 1980s. As we shall see, however, the extent and meaning of the change is, as always, contradictory.

2. The Good Father: Reconstructing Fatherhood

Sometimes, in the life of every man, the weight of male tradition must prove burdensome. We are now used to hearing of some of these burdens: men die younger than women; they are more prone to coronary disease; they find it difficult to seek help when they need it – regarding illness, for example, as a sign of weakness: something to be denied. A small but significant number of men have publicly declared their commitment to breaking out of the traditional rules of masculinity – sharing gentler feelings, dedicating themselves to expressing a kinder, more caring, less competitive and aggressive masculinity. But have men generally changed? Is a new *type* of man emerging? One way of throwing light on this question is to look at men as fathers. There is little dispute that fathers have become more involved in at least some aspects of childcare over the last two decades. Yet controversy surrounds the image and reality of the 'new father', ranging from approval and celebration to scepticism and derision.

As we shall see later, this reassertion of fatherhood can create new problems for women. Significantly, the growing stress on fathers has occurred at a time when men's actual power and control over women and children is declining. In the fifties the father *was* essential, but only, it seemed, for financial support, status and legitimacy: his wife and children relied upon him even when he totally ignored them. An alternative way of viewing the emphasis on the importance of fathering today would be to see it as a reassertion of the essential nature, significance and rights of fathers at a time when slight but significant shifts in relations between men and women have meant that some women are better placed to question any automatic assumption of paternal rights. Men's hold on their status as fathers is less firm and secure than ever before.

God the Father: What Fathers Mean to Us

'The very words "my father" always make me smile,' writes Angela Carter.[1] She is lucky. In the same book, *Fathers: Reflections by Daughters*, Eileen Fairweather writes: 'I doubt if my father will ever lose his power to wound me.'[2] My own experiences of my father were more similar to those of Eileen Fairweather. I was, as I remember, never anywhere near my father's knee; it was from some considerable distance that I was to learn that managing to upset my mother and his children was one of his main sources of pleasure. However, it also seems that my father lost his power to wound me very early on. He had filled all the dark corners of my bedroom with frightening, wicked spirits who always wished me harm; and he kept me away from my mother, the one person I thought could protect me from them. Yet, though my fears of the dark would always remain, he himself exerted an ever-decreasing influence upon me from early childhood. I held him, with his rages and his childish tantrums, in contempt. No doubt, at times, we children wounded him: 'father hatred' was what we had all been taught, or so he taunted my mother. He was right, in a sense; but then he never taught us father love. I had to draw upon others' lives, to project my needs into fantasy constructions of strong, loving, caring, protective, sensitive men, in order to create an image of the 'good father'. I have sometimes found men who seem to fit this image in my adult life. In all probability they are more like I wanted my mother to be: my mother who was always absent from my life, out at work nearly all my waking hours. She was the absent 'father', and she identified most strongly with her son.

There is no doubt that the image of 'the father' is a powerful one. 'The life of the father has a mysterious prestige', writes Simone de Beauvoir: 'it is through him that the family communicates with the rest of the world: he incarnates that immense, difficult and marvellous world of adventure; he personifies transcendence, he is God.'[3] These gods that fail us bequeath diverse legacies to their sons and daughters.

The father as God, God the father, may be one of our most powerful mythologies. Yet the father as man, man the father, is a still more mysterious creature. We can never escape the influence of our fathers and mothers – but there are few generalisations we can make about them. Some fathers, like mine, will remain forever strangers in their children's lives, absent from their children's hearts. The very power and authority they were supposed to possess turned against them to create ghosts, so fully and finally did they fail to embody these qualities. A group of feminists in London once began meeting together exclusively to explore their relationships with their fathers. There was little overlap in their experiences. Sheila Rowbotham has described the diversity uncovered: 'Some of the women had fathers who were very obviously dominating men, who, like mine, believed their word should be law. Others had mild-mannered fathers who went into retreat in the family.'⁴ Some had no fathers at all. In discussing their relation to these men, a complex picture of experiences and images of 'fatherhood' and 'manhood' emerged: 'Even within one small consciousness-raising group of feminists, and even within the confines of our restricted understandings of our fathers, these blew open stereotypes of masculinity ... They thus emerged as individuals, not just as "men"; struggling and resistant, vulnerable, trapped, enraged, isolated, cut off.'⁵

Particular dilemmas are created for daughters of fathers battered and demoralised by class and race oppression. Power in the home is often the only prerogative experienced by men daily overworked, humiliated by poverty, facing arbitrary discipline, degrading working conditions, or perhaps racist abuse and the threat of violence from other men. Margot Farnham has written of her conflicts as the daughter of a grey-faced, stooping father, 'unhappy, sick and broken' by his life as a shift worker in a Ford's car plant.⁶ The father's sole site of authority – the home where he bullied his wife and children – was the site of another loss: the lost opportunity to be loved by his children. This father's violence and emotional cruelty produced immense confusion in his daughter: 'I felt all through my teenage years an alarming range of emotions about my father, from hatred to deepest remorse, harbouring at times fantasies about saving his life, and at others day-dreams about speeding his death.'[7] Fatherhood can increase a man's sense of his own failure and vulnerability, when he knows or fears he cannot adequately protect or provide for his wife and children, while at the same time creating a setting in which he can pass on his pain by abusing them. As we will see in chapter nine, because of the particular and contradictory pressures of race solidarity and feminist anger, the attempt to understand, while condemning, the abusive behaviour of violent fathers has been a powerful and eloquent strand of much Black women's fiction by writers like Toni Morrison and Alice Walker in the United States and Joan Riley in Britain[8] But this is only one aspect, although an important one, of a complex and *changing* pattern of behaviours and expectations surrounding fatherhood today.

If the Hollywood of the 1950s was domesticating men, by the 1980s, in films like *Kramer Vs Kramer* and *Ordinary People*, Hollywood was creating men whose tamed domesticity produced fathers who were *more* sensitive, and *more* nurturing, than their self-centred, ambitious wives. After starring in the film *Tootsie* Dustin Hoffman told a reporter: 'There's a lot about being a woman I've felt robbed about, I can't carry children . . . I can't breastfeed.'[9] Yet in his films we are left in no doubt that this man is not only a better 'mother' than women, but also, in virtually every respect, a better 'woman'. Hoffman has even joked that in the sequel to *Tootsie*, he too will give birth.[10] No doubt, he'll do that better, too! In France in 1986, a comedy about three men and a baby by a relatively unknown director was the surprise hit of the year.[11] Subsequently remade in Hollywood the film 'Three men and a Baby' became an even bigger hit, and immediately spawned a sequel. Everywhere, it seems, there is a new interest in fathering and fatherhood. '*Fathers*: for fathers see mothers,' it was possible to read in the index of at least one distinguished book on the family before the re-emergence of fatherhood in the late seventies.[12] But in the new, rapidly expanding literature on 'Fathers', we learn they are 'changing as never before' and that 'the "nurturing" father is steadily taking over new territories of child care'.[13] That fathers are, and ought to be, more involved in childcare is the theme of most of this literature.

In *The Child in Time*, chosen by many critics as the best book of 1987, Ian McEwan transcends the macabre pessimism of his former works to portray the spiritual death and rebirth of his hero through the disappearance of his child and the eventual birth of another. Fatherhood, and matrimony, it would seem, are the only good and meaningful experiences in a world now irredeemably mean and menacing. Without midwife or doctor, the father assists his wife giving birth: 'Then he joined in her panting, making a heavy emphasis on the breathing out, slowing down as the grip on his hand loosened.'[14] The modern father watches and knows how to offer such assistance. The modern father also believes that he should do 'his share' of childcare and housework. He is more affectionate and closer to his wife and children. He feels that he behaves very differently from his own father back in the fifties.

The Heart Is Willing

> If I was critical of anything about my job it's that I spend too much time away from the children. I would like to spend more time with the family. Certainly, men of my age are far more into that way of thinking. It was unknown in the past for a father to be seen with his kids apart from the special treat.[15]

These sentiments are those of David Jenkins, the 35-year-old General Secretary of the Welsh Trade Union Congress (TUC), talking to Yvonne Roberts in 1984. Roberts encounters such sentiments again and again from men she interviews – all 35 years old – but otherwise very diverse. The new right Welsh Conservative candidate, Dennis Jones, tells her he does the household shopping, shares the cooking with his wife, takes his children to school each morning and never leaves the house at night until the children are in bed:

> I want to be very much a part of their growing up . . . I enjoy my family life. I think that the biggest wrench when I do get into the House of Commons, and I *am* going to get in, will be the fact that I will not be seeing the children so much.[16]

Similarly, a detailed study of 75 fathers by the Thomas Coram Research Unit of London University in 1983 found that two-thirds of their sample would have liked to spend more time with their infant children, and 50 per cent would ideally have liked to work fewer hours during their child's first year.[17] Other contemporary research in London conducted by the Institute for Social Studies and Medical Care reported an unexpectedly high level of help with domestic tasks and childcare from a sample of nearly one hundred very young fathers, usually taking the form of shopping, cleaning, washing up, cooking and feeding the baby.[18] And from her extensive work on modern fathers' participation in infant care, Lorna MacKee has described very high levels of paternal interest in and awareness of all the details of their babies' behaviour, enabling fathers to comfort, stimulate and control their infants, and to be sensitive to the areas in which the mothers were most in need of assistance – although fathers' actual level of direct participation in childcare tasks was limited.[19] Graeme Russell reports that 80 per cent of young men from a sample of first-year university students in Australia would like to see social policies developed which would allow them the option of full-time parenting if they had a child.[20] A European attitudes survey found that fewer than three in ten Europeans supported the traditional model of the family – where the man 'works' and the woman runs the home.[21]

It is in the autobiographical reflections of some contemporary fathers, however, that we find the mood of the new fatherhood most directly conveyed. In *A Father's Diary* the writer Fraser Harrison records one year of his experiences as the father of two pre-school children in the Suffolk countryside.[22] Here he conveys the joy and privilege he feels in being able to be at home full time and therefore fully involved in daily childcare. In *An Older Father's Letter To His Young Son* the Canadian Lou Becker confides the intense pleasure he takes in caring full time for his son:

> I've been lucky enough to get to take care of you all day every day . . . I learned that the most important thing I had to do while we were together was to *be* with you and to *do* things with you. Work and play got to be the same thing . . . if when you're big you decide that you'd like to be a daddy, I hope you'll remember that the best part of that is to arrange it so that you can be with your child all day.[23]

Older fathers with second families, or adding another child to their existing family in later years, have been in the forefront of men celebrating their personal conversion to the new fatherhood. One such father writes:

> I never read *The Cat and the Hat* the first time around. I never diapered or bathed

the babies. I just came home after my wife had them all fed and in their pyjamas . . . It wasn't macho to really mother them. Now the rules have changed. Real men take care of the kids. I like that.[24]

As Libby Purves has commented (and Posy Simmonds illustrated), 'Many a balding figure now haunts Mothercare in his lunch-hour to the secret fury, no doubt, of his ex-wife.'[25] Fathers of grown children are also expressing regret that they fathered at a time when it was harder, and they were not expected, to be very close to their children.[26]

Lone fathers have likewise expressed satisfaction with their full-time parenting – although, like Ken Smith from Sussex, they are usually more aware of the isolation and loss of confidence it so often entails: 'you get so used to not meeting people, you don't know what to do when you do.'[27] Other men, like Tony Bradman, deputy editor of the British magazine *Parents*, or Peter Moss from the Thomas Coram Research Unit, have written of their dissatisfaction over the intrusiveness of jobs which deprive them of contact with their children.[28] Graphically describing his anxiety and confusion as a first-time father whose wife was becoming depressed, isolated, bored and hence resentful at being home alone all day, Tony Bradman comes to realise his own resentment over his position and his future: 'a future in which I missed every single important event of my child's life because I was out at work . . . we both felt trapped in roles which were keeping us apart and making us unhappy.'[29] He went on to write *The Essential Father*, offering advice to men on how to share as much as possible with their partners in every aspect of conception, pregnancy, childbirth, childcare and housework – in the belief that many other men and women 'were struggling towards a different idea of parenthood': 'I'm talking about creating a world in which there is a new fatherhood as part of a new way of looking at both men and women.'[30]

In the US in 1986 an article in the *Ladies' Home Journal*, 'A New Kind of Father', saluted today's fathers – 'loving dads who truly nurture their children',[31] reporting that 84.2 per cent of their readers under forty believed men to be just as good as women with children. We can scrutinise this image of the new fatherhood in

Britain in any current Mothercare catalogue, where father stands proudly beside mother, with his own babysling and baby. Today, the hardest of macho male images can combine with the softest portrayals of paternity, like the pin-up of Irish boxer Barry McGuigan, Madonna-like cradling his baby daughter on the cover of a Sunday colour supplement after his triumphs in the ring in 1986. Wherever we look, it seems hard to deny that there has been a remarkable shift in public opinion towards the idea that men should be, and are, more involved in childcare.

This shift in attitude has accompanied the many obvious changes in the lives of women and men since the fifties. Whereas in the fifties it was generally believed that most married women would not choose to work outside the home, except in a very limited capacity, by the seventies it was inescapable that the majority of women, regardless of whether they were married, would not choose to remain at home, except when their children were very young.[32]

The new possibilities and choices available to many women during those decades derived from women's increasing access to education and jobs, alongside the greater availability of contraception, improved welfare provision and, in general, a higher standard of living. These possibilities were, of course, greatly limited by constraints of class, region and race, but nonetheless they were the preconditions for the re-emergence of a feminist movement at the end of the sixties. For the men closest to the mainly white and middle-class core of the women's liberation movement, feminism meant a host of new demands to change their ways. For those more distant from the fray, media stories of the 'antics' of 'women's libbers', meant the message that women were on the move again was no less inescapable.

The Slow Pace of Change

Looking at modern fatherhood, then, we can detect a change in men's *attitudes* towards childcare, a change in their *experiences* of fatherhood, and, as we shall see, a change in psychological perspectives on the importance of the father's role. What proves harder to find is convincing evidence that there has been a change in the amount of practical work men actually do as fathers.

In the fifties, when 'fathering' was defined by expert and popular opinion alike as economic and emotional support for 'mothering', we have little detailed evidence of what men actually did in the home. Indeed, fathers appeared in research prior to the seventies only in response to worries that their total *absence* from the home was a threat to boys' sex-role identity. North American studies of delinquent boys in the fifties and sixties suggested that paternal absence – especially common in Black families owing to discriminatory employment practices – induced a type of hypermasculinity, an insecure but rigid acting out of the masculine role, resulting in delinquent styles and behaviour.[33]

By the early seventies, however, many researchers had begun to question the exclusive fixation on mothers and their role in child-care. New observations of infants and their parents suggested the inadequacy of 'attachment theory' – the idea of an overriding, irreversible bonding between a baby and its mother (or other primary caretaker) from a few days after birth. It was observed that infants could form a variety of attachments, which were not irreversible, with fathers and other carers.[34] By the late seventies research was further demonstrating both desire and capacity in fathers to care for their young children, suggesting that there were – or could be – more similarities than differences in the way fathers and mothers relate to their infants.[35] In the eighties, we could read studies arguing the necessity for paternal participation in childcare, reporting that, for example, mothers with total responsibility for an infant were more likely to feel depressed, while the availability of fathers was correlated with lower depression and anxiety in women.[36]

But the apparently forward march of this new fathering was about to be abruptly halted. The mid-eighties threw up a batch of social surveys, many of them instigated by disillusioned feminists, which questioned what was regarded as the optimism of much recent literature on fathers. The new sceptics quote an American study from Michigan which suggests that men's daily household contribution has risen by a mere one minute over the ten years between 1965 and 1975, averaging around one hour twenty minutes.[37] In his book *Becoming a Father* Charlie Lewis suggests that the changes which have occurred in paternal behaviour are slight. This conclusion is backed up by the research of Kathryn Backett, who concludes that the discovery of highly participant fathers by other researchers has been something of an illusion.[38] A general survey conducted for *Parents* magazine in the mid-eighties revealed that a significant minority of fathers *never* changed nappies (24 per cent), bathed or dressed children (30 per cent and 23 per cent), or attended them at night (43 per cent) – though around 50 per cent of fathers claimed to perform these tasks regularly.[39] An official *Women and Employment* survey published in Britain in 1984, reports that nearly three-quarters of 'working' wives do all or most of the housework, and this remains true even for 54 per cent of the women who work full time.[40] Fathers, the survey indicates, are prepared to participate more in certain childcare activities, particularly when mothers are employed. But this usually involves the more pleasurable aspects of childcare, such as playing with children or taking them out, leaving the routine care of feeding, dressing, washing and so on to wives.[41] Men in general, it seems, select which tasks they are willing to do, leaving mothers with the rest.

What underlies the clash between thought and deed in men's apparently increasing commitment to a more participatory, egalitarian role in childcare and housework? Some, like Tony Bradman, blame society – the inflexible and relentless pressures of men's working lives: 'Men have changed ... But society itself hasn't changed sufficiently to make life easier for fathers (and for families) – and so we have a dilemma.'[42] Others would argue that men have no real wish to change, that they are happy, as a sex, to exploit women by leaving the labour of loving and caring to them. Such critics could point, for example, to the evidence that unemployed men often do less domestic work than men in jobs, even when the mothers in their households have full-time jobs.[43]

We do indeed face a dilemma in our assessment of change and continuity in men's relationship to childcare and housework. The dilemma reflects the greater diversity of contemporary family life: there is evidence of change, and yet the lives of so many women and men seem to continue much the same. As McKee suggests, 'when we scratch the surface of families and penetrate behind closed doors the differences as well as the continuities between fathers are striking.'[44] Many men still do little in the home, or exaggerate what they do do. (A broad survey of fathers' attitudes to paternity leave conducted by the Equal Opportunities Commission in 1983 illustrated the limits of the change in many men; while 91 per cent of fathers-to-be wanted some form of statutory paternity leave, only a tiny fraction of them wanted it to last longer than one or two weeks.[45]) Yet some men are truly committed to sharing equally. Whatever the statistical averages, there is a new 'open-endedness' to fathering today – as many who have struggled with men towards the sharing of children and housework are well aware. It seems foolish to write off the achievements of those women and men who have been able to work together for change. But this is very much a trend in the Britain of the eighties. Increasingly, there is not only a questioning of the optimism expressed in the sudden explosion of books on fatherhood from the close of the seventies, but a shift of mood towards a more smug and complacent dismissal of any change which has occurred, or even the possibility of change. The pre women's-liberation rhetoric of the eternal sex-war has crept back to replace what was, for a while in the seventies, a feminist-inspired, more confident rhetoric on the need and possibility for change in men. It almost seems as if, for some, things which are not completely different, are not different at all.

Over breakfast in April 1987 readers of the *Guardian* were informed that the new man or the new father 'was the man who never was'.[46] Reviewing Charles Lewis and Margaret O'Brien's *Reassessing Fatherhood* Polly Toynbee pronounced that 'researchers and fathers themselves have been fooled by the New Men idea. Every new young father thinks he's quite different to his own father ... Yet in fundamental ways so little changes.'[47] More depressingly, for those interested in promoting change, Toynbee quotes her academic authority Margaret O'Brien (perhaps out of context, or with more emphasis than was intended – I do not know) to the effect that she once saw men and women as fundamentally similar, but now believes 'we must acknowledge that there are fundamental differences.'[48] But what does this mean? These 'fundamental differences', to explain the discrepancies between mothers and fathers, would need to qualify mothers uniquely for changing nappies, cleaning the toilets and mopping the floor, and have less bearing on the pleasanter, more creative tasks of child-care, which are somehow less affected by our anatomical destiny and our gendered fate.

This new conservatism in sexual politics is part of a broader political pessimism. It is part of the retreat and despair of many people formerly active within radical and progressive groupings in the face of what has been the apparently unassailable ascendancy of the radical right. But rather than a return to the cynical embrace of timeless inevitabilities, it might be more illuminating to explore the obstacles impeding change, as well as the forces conducive to it.

Shared Parenting?

Almost all the evidence we possess would seem to indicate that men do take parenting more seriously today, and yet that in the great majority of cases men's participation is far removed from genuine sharing of responsibilities. Which forces promote, and which prevent a more equal sharing of childcare between women and men? They involve external and social as well as internal and psychic factors. They include the shared assumptions which seem to make sense of the way things are. And they all revolve around questions of power.Their diversity makes it all the less surprising that the process of change is slow, the gulf between beliefs and practices wide.

The most obvious impediments to men and women sharing labour in the home, including all the work associated with parent-ing, are economic – the demands of men's paid work. Because paternal employment has never been seen as a problem, little research exists on the link between men's patterns of employment and their participation in the home. But whereas in Britain two-thirds of married women with children have part-time jobs, the majority of men with young children work extremely long hours in paid employment – an average of 50–55 hours a week, with significant numbers employed for over 60 and 70 hours a week.[49] Where women and men both have full-time jobs, men in general are doing paid work for substantially longer hours. As has frequently been noted in recent years, men work longest hours outside the home when they have dependent children; the reverse is true of women. If they have children, one study found, married men under thirty work four times the amount of overtime as childless men of the same age.[50] In their role as financial providers, fathers feel more strongly bound to their jobs.[51] Men with children, especially those in manual and less skilled jobs, are also more likely to work irregular hours or to work shifts.[52] Mothers, on the other hand, are less likely to have irregular hours in their paid work.

The lower wages attached to jobs which are most readily available to women, and seen as 'women's jobs', reinforce the differing parental employment patterns. Only 5 per cent of women with children in full-time jobs in Britain earn as much as or more than their partners.[53] The ever-increasing part-time, casual, sometimes home-based employment of women has reinforced, rather than reduced, economic inequalities between the sexes. These inequalities in employment inevitably undermine the moves towards equality which women's employment might be expected to produce, leaving women still wrestling with the power and status men possess through their higher incomes. Even with jobs, women remain economically dependent upon men – especially when they have children to support.

A number of studies, like those of Rhona and Robert Rapoport in 1971 and 1976, have concluded that when women's jobs are comparable to men's in income and status – in dual-career partnerships for instance – men take greater responsibility for housework and childcare.[54] Other studies have disputed this.[55] Overall, however, research indicates that the greater the income differential between husbands and wives, the less involved husbands are in parenting and housework (as we shall see, this also applies when husbands earn less than their wives, and feel more threatened in their sense of masculinity).[56]

From her North American sample of dual-career families, Rosanna Hertz concluded that careers have more effect on altering the traditional roles of wives and husbands than a conscious commitment to equality. Over and over again, she finds evidence that it is the problems of actually trying to combine two careers, rather than the articulation of a non-sexist ideology, which informs change. This point, she feels, is crucial: 'It is a common misunderstanding that all one needs to do is wish or want another way of life and that somehow marriages, family, work, or even politics will be altered by our dreams and desires.'[57] She finds a markedly greater degree of equality in dual-career families (where partner's jobs are more equal in the status and reward they confer, and the commitment they demand) compared with dual-income families. Though small in number, Hertz sees the dual-career family as an important object of study because it crystallises the contradictions and conflicts provoked when women and men face very similar competing demands between work and family. She concludes that the reward and status of women's careers, as well as the hours worked and the impact of nearly two decades of feminist pressure for equality, do matter in generating confidence and authority in women. However, equality of sharing in these dual-career families is related to the overall reduction in childcare and housework demands through the hiring of domestic help – an individual solution available only to the middle class. This has brought greater equality between women and men for some women, but at the expense of the cheaper labour of other women. And Hertz's optimism about dual-career families also needs qualifying by the observation that these families have the highest rate of divorce.[58] Other studies suggest that men's continuing demands for more traditional wives and their resentment of their wives' career success, added to the frustration of many wives seeking greater equality in the home, can lead to increased family strain and tension.[59]

Hertz's conclusion that employment is a crucial factor shaping domestic change, however, is in agreement with Graeme Russell's research on shared care-giving families in Australia. He found that in such families the majority of mothers had professional or semi-professional jobs, and their occupational status, on average, was higher than the fathers. These families also had fewer and older children, so that overall domestic demands were lower.[60] More than Hertz, however, Russell emphasises the importance of couples' shared ideological commitment to egalitarian relationships as conducive to shared parenting.

Russell also reports that fathers who were centrally involved in childcare tended to encounter negative reactions from their relatives and male peer group, with only a minority finding their men friends or workmates sympathetic to their participation. Elsewhere, an English father has described some of the problems he encountered:

> There seems to be a particular difficulty for men who want to look after their children . . . you get a lot of folklore going up and down the street between women as to how to bring up kids and that, and little technical problems that you need to hear about, but it doesn't come to me . . . there isn't a network for men who've been through it and know about it . . . other women are thinking who's this man with the baby, he's a bit odd, isn't he?[61]

Beliefs about appropriate gender roles and women's innate capacity to mother clearly influence both men's willingness to take on more childcare, and the discouraging responses received by men who do.

The grip of traditional beliefs about gender and parenting may explain why paternal unemployment does not necessarily lead to increased sharing of household responsibilities by men. Unemployment certainly creates a greater involuntary home-centredness. High rates of male unemployment have accordingly been heralded by many as another factor conducive to social change, insofar as they create a growing convergence between the social worlds of men and women. Yet male unemployment also produces low self-esteem, isolation and multiple hardships. Indeed, many studies suggest that it serves more to polarise than to merge the experiences of men and women. Traditional beliefs that men should be the breadwinners, and were being deprived of their rights, would seem to harden, judging from studies like those of Lorna McKee and Colin Bell, who observed a group of mostly young, white, working-class fathers with small children in an area of high unemployment in the West Midlands. Both unemployed men and their wives believed more strongly than ever that a man's pride and self-image, his sense of 'masculinity' and authority, needed to be protected and preserved: 'he likes to be the breadwinner and that's hard on a man', as one woman put it.[62] But then again, few of the women surveyed possessed any real bargaining power – either on the job market or in relation to their husbands. The wives mostly chose to remain unemployed themselves or to give up their jobs – the amount they could earn did not take the family out of poverty, but merely reduced the husband's benefits.

The evidence indicates, then, that when women can command a higher income, when men have already achieved higher levels of personal self-satisfaction and independence (usually when they are older), when there is a more supportive social milieu, or when there are fewer children and household demands are less onerous – in these rare circumstances, men are more likely to accept a primary commitment to home and childcare.

Men's resistance to change, however, not only reflects real economic and social pressures, and both sexes' attempts to shore up a man's sense of self-esteem around a traditional masculinity; it also enables men to remain cushioned and privileged in relation to women. It is quite simply not in men's interest to change too much, unless women force them to. Neither social nor ideological constraints – and certainly not biological priming – can explain why it should be the case that when men do participate in the home, they choose all the more pleasant and rewarding tasks. Women who can manage to, however, also often avoid the grindingly routine tasks, employing someone else to do them instead (it's even becoming fashionable in certain circles to hire a young man for the purpose thereby challenging the tradition of hiring Black, female domestic employees). But most 'working' women have always had to combine the routine tasks of home and jobs. That men for the most part still appear to lack this 'capacity' suggests that what they are lacking is inclination: the inclination to burden themselves with the demanding labours of love and personal maintenance. The consequence, however disguised by other forces, is that most men continue to exploit the labour of women. Women in general work far longer hours overall than men, especially when caring for dependents, and women's career prospects are harmed by their domestic commitments.

I suspect that there is another, deeper psychological aspect to many men's continuing resistance to active parenting, although it rarely appears in the new literature on fathering – not even, as we shall see, in the surveys and experiential reports of men who 'mother'. Just as childbirth is often followed by a period of intense crisis for women (in the form of mild or acute post-natal depression), so too prospective and actual fatherhood can induce an intense crisis in men. In hundreds of articles on contemporary fatherhood, I have come across just three short reflections by men on their ambivalence and fear of fatherhood (we possess far more evidence of women's ambivalence about motherhood, particularly from the early days of women's liberation writing.)[63] Peter Bradbury has written of men's crisis over pregnancy. Not only are men excluded by pregnancy (and even more by the emotional bonding of breast-feeding), but pregnancy can reactivate all the terrors and pleasures of men's early relations to their own mothers.[64] Gavin Smith goes so far as to declare that 'fatherhood is experienced commonly as personal crisis.'[65] The intense emotions aroused in men watching childbirth and handling infants take them back to the emotionality, generalised sensuality and tenderness of childhood so utterly tabooed in most areas of adult masculinity. Fatherhood can thus threaten men's whole perception of themselves as adults, arousing jealousy and anxieties of inadequacy, leaving them feeling tired, confused, vulnerable, insecure and rejected (emotions to which women are likewise prone around childbirth). The most elo-quent statement of these feelings is provided by Jonathan Rutherford, who did care for his son full time:

> When I became a father, I came up against the limits of my masculine
> upbringing . . . It was my lack of emotional resources that stymied me. Far from
> feeling a proud father at his birth, my little son threw me into a crisis. Despite
> reading and talking and wanting to be a different kind of father . . . the reality of
> looking after my baby shattered my fantasies . . . My life as a man left me
> unprepared for the task. My emotional life had been geared around having things
> done for me. Suddenly the tables were turned and I found myself resentful and
> with precious little to give. For the first few months I was angry and self-pitying,
> not only because it was isolating and hard work, but because I was expected to give
> unconditionally . . . Being with my son I was confronted by my own childhood, my
> own insecurity and childish feelings. When men have sons we are faced with all
> that we have lost, but still secretly desire, a mother's love, a boy's sensuality . . .
> Not surprising that we sometimes become like jealous siblings competing for our
> partners' attention.[66]

Nor is it surprising that many men escape into paid work and overtime. I am reminded of Fay Weldon's description in *Female Friends*:

First babies are all blows, make no mistake about it . . . As for him, he's impossible, more of a baby than the baby itself: persnickety (sic) about food, going mad from lack of sleep; he gets drunk, throws tantrums, falls ill, throws baby in the air for fun and fails to catch it when it falls . . . She, the monumental dangerous she, pads about the house, belly and breasts all swollen, desperate, distraught, wondering who this monster is she's married. A baby to cope with, and a madman too![67]

Many women's experiences of the early months of motherhood are captured here: certainly, my own initial despair on the birth of my son. Fatherhood may yield men new confirmation of their importance to, or power over, women and children. Yet it also brings with it many new vulnerabilities – feelings of shame and inadequacy for those men who may lack the capacity to support their families in the desired manner and style.

Men Who 'Mother'

Notwithstanding all the obstacles, however, a small number of men do share fully in housework and childcare. Or at least, as we learn from their personal testimony, and some of us know from personal experience, they attempt to. However much some men have failed to display real signs of change, and others evince only slight change, the fluidity of family life today, in conjunction with the impetus from feminism and the post-sixties counter-culture, has led some men to make the commitment to shared parenting and housework a personal and political project. It is hard to estimate the numbers involved. In Sweden, where government policies allow for paid paternity or maternity leave of up to nine months, it is estimated that around 10 per cent of fathers take on the primary care-giving role at some period of time.[68] In Sydney, Australia, Graeme Russell's random survey at a shopping centre produced 1–2 per cent of father's following this pattern.[69] They remain a small minority, but it is interesting to see what happens in such families.

Studies conducted in the United States, Australia, Norway, Sweden and Israel of families in which men equally shared, or assumed major responsibility for, childcare, have all reported the fathers were pleased with the arrangement.[70] Indeed when men expressed dissatisfaction it was because they were unable to be as involved in childcare as they would like to be. As we saw at the beginning of this chapter, these fathers were particularly enthusiastic about the closer, richer relationship they were able to enjoy with their child or children. Most also expressed a sense of satisfaction and fulfilment that they had come to see themselves as gradually developing a competence in their ability to care for their children equal to that possessed by their wives or partners. In her American study *Parenting Together* Diane Ehrensaft reports the almost ecstatic pleasure which many of her professional middle-class men come to find in very active parenting, as one of the mothers in her study exclaims, 'These men have gone "ga-ga" over their children.'[71] The men love the intense intimacy and tenderness which their parenting experiences allow them to express: 'I just couldn't anticipate the strength of the bond', as one father exclaims. Or another, attempting to explain his love affair with his child, 'Kids are so spontaneous. No layers of social conventions. You can laugh, make silly jokes . . . There's a physical closeness, a spontaneous thing you can't do with adults. With children, you can be a child with them.'[72]

These happily co-parenting fathers, however, all have wives who do at least their share of housework and childcare, as well as access to paid help and provision to ease some of the burdens of childcare. Striking a more realistic note on the joys and difficulties of shared parenting in rather less privileged conditions, an English father, Rob Senior, has written:

> Being a parent involves endless contradictions. Since having Kate I've felt a lot of joy and, at the risk of sounding trite, a profound opening out of my soul and a real connectedness with the world. I've also felt constrained and restricted, bored and angry, and longed for the freedom of the days before she was born.[73]

Like mothers everywhere, men who are actively parenting will find, as Tony Bradman admits, that it can be 'intense hard work'.[74] These English fathers focused more on the importance of collective, rather than purely individualistic, solutions to the constant demands of caring for very young children. Rob Senior, for example, has worked with other like-minded parents (four couples and a single parent) to set up and help run a co-operative crèche for pre-nursery infants:

> I need the creche for the time and space it gives me, free from Kate. At its best it leaves us both energetic and eager to spend time together. At its most prosaic, she

is well looked after . . . It's lovely too to know the other children so well, and to look after them at other times.[75]

However, as Jonathan Trustram, its one full-time worker indicates, the crèche is possible because most of the parents have part-time jobs with reasonably flexible hours.[76] Commenting on his role in the crèche, Trustram writes:

> I get embarrassed when people react in an extravagant way to the fact that I have always looked after Rosie (his child) as much as Sheila (the child's mother) has and that I work in childcare. This seems to me fairly ordinary, if not strictly 'normal', though not without difficulties of course. I feel it is vital for men to be more closely involved in childcare if patriarchy and male violence is to begin to crumble. And that, however bleak our immediate political prospects, one thing that *can* happen now is that men can change.[77]

Trustram, as his sentiments suggest, comes from a left libertarian and feminist milieu which emphasises the importance of personal politics and co-operative lifestyles.

Some men in Russell's study who, unlike their wives, were parenting full time, referred to various of the difficulties of their 'reversed-role' situation. They too were pleased about their intimacy with their children, but, like women at home alone, they felt deprived of adult contact. Many experienced the boredom and repetition of continuous childcare and housework and complained of the lack of support from relatives and friends.[78] A significant number of full-time fathers also bemoaned the loss of status and reduced self-esteem accompanying the absence of paid work.[79] A number were to revert after a few years to more traditional domestic arrangements.[80] Other studies of lone fathering report isolation, rather than feelings of incompetence, as the main problem experienced by men. Indeed, lone fathers often become more isolated than single mothers, without the support network which many single mothers can build up.[81] With children in tow, the personal commitments and priorities of lone fathers tend to shift in a way that makes friendship with other men less reciprocal.

Predictably, men who are less rigid about appropriate gender roles, according to Russell, are the fathers most at ease with, and most likely to engage in, active parenting.[82] Most of the studies mentioned above come to the conclusion that when fathers are primary caregivers from choice, there is very little difference in their capacity to care for children – apart from their inability to breast feed. Parke, for example, after observing fathers with newborn babies concluded that 'I have consistently found that fathers are just as responsive as mothers to infants' signals such as sound and mouth movements.'[83] Russell also reported that fathers who are primary caregivers display the same order of enhanced sensitivity to their infants as full-time mothers, while a mother's more typically greater sensitivity to her baby's needs does not generalise to a greater responsiveness to other people's children. It is the actual experience with particular infants which is crucial.[84]

There is some evidence that in general fathers choose to play with their children in more physical, conventionally 'masculine' ways, while mothers tend to play with them in more verbal, conventionally 'feminine' ways.[85] Ehrensaft also emphasises the somewhat differing spheres of expertise men and women bring to co-parenting, with women more concerned about children's appearance and clothes, tending to worry more than fathers and act more as the general overseer of childcare.[86] Overall, however, there are no studies of men choosing to 'mother' which report any paternal incapacity. Indeed, Russell concludes from his survey of a host of relevant studies that the most remarkable finding about reversed-role parenting with full-time fathers is how little difference it seems to make to children, female or male, *which* parent parents.[87]

Benefits and Costs of the New Fatherhood

I have looked so far at some of the benefits and costs of active fathering for men and for children, but what are the effects on women? From the earliest days of the emerging women's liberation movement at the close of the sixties, feminists had identified women's role in the family as basic to their subordination. At the very first Women's Liberation Conference held in Oxford in 1970 Rochelle Wortis argued: 'If the undervaluation of women in society is to end, we must begin at the beginning, by a more equitable distribution of labour around the child-rearing function and the home ... Men can and should begin to take a more active part in the affective and cognitive interaction with children than they have done until now.'[88] Only by eliminating the sexual division of labour in the family, as well as the accompanying ideologies which restrict women to a narrow range of less valued and rewarded activities, could women be freed from the isolation, dependence and drudgery they experienced in the home, and the secondary status accorded them outside it.

Early women's liberationists, however, not only insisted that men must change their ways, but also that society needed to be transformed in order to allow women a full and equal role within it. In the first major document from the British women's liberation movement, *Women's Liberation and the New Politics*, written in June 1969, Sheila Rowbotham called for a society based on social ownership which would provide the resources to enable maximum personal flexibility to those caring for the needs of others. It would mean, she wrote, 'particular improvements like more nurseries, launderettes, good cheap municipal restaurants in all areas, better housing and imaginative architecture which takes the needs of the people as a prime consideration.'[89]

By the late seventies, however, the emphasis on public provision and resources began to fade as greater stress was placed on the unique significance of men's absence from early childcare: such absence, in itself, being seen as the root of women's oppression. Influenced by psychoanalytic object relations psychology, the feminist sociologist Nancy Chodorow in the US and feminist therapists Luise Eichenbaum and Susie Orbach, then working in Britain, were to point to the overriding significance of exclusive mothering by women in the creation of male dominance and polarised 'masculine' and 'feminine' identities. Developing 'masculine' identities through the repression of their infantile dependence upon, and identification with, their mothers, boy children, in this view, grow into men who fear and devalue all they see as 'feminine', while expecting permanent servicing from women. Girl children, on the other hand, are not required to repress their early identification with their mothers. They remain forever significantly identified with mothers who have themselves identified with their daughters in ways which contrast with their love for their sons. Girls grow into women who experience themselves through their nurturing relations to others, possess a weaker sense of their own autonomy, and have little expectation of being nurtured themselves.[90] The radical implications of this feminist perspective are that men's involvement in early parenting should, over the generations, break down the oppressive nature of 'masculinity' and the self-denial of 'femininity', thereby undermining male dominance. Assessing the benefits of men's active parenting in relation to the interests of women will, then, be bound up with expectations of how change in paternal practices might begin to undermine existing power relations of gender.

Some studies do show that married women with jobs, and mothers of very young children, are happier when their husbands do more in the home and are active in childcare.[91] But Joseph Pleck, a researcher of sex-role changes in the United States, reports that only a minority of women, whether employed or not, seem to desire greater paternal participation in childcare.[92] Together with other writers, he suggests that women fear losing not only their traditional power and domination in the home if they allow men to assume even some of their former responsibilities, but their exclusive importance to children as well. Women, it is suggested, currently dominate in the home, and given that their 'working' lives may be disappointing and provide little sense of power, they are anxious lest they find themselves 'without any arena in which they dominate'.[93]

There are problems with this argument. Women's 'domination' in the home is a limited one – hedged around by the greater economic and social power of their male partners. It is less than obvious that mothers would lose power if men did the ironing, washing and cleaning, leaving women more time to engage in the playful aspects of childcare. Certainly, women may obtain a sense of their self-importance and value from the realisation that the home could not function without them. But it seems to me altogether more plausible that it is women's comparative *powerlessness*, both inside and outside the home, which induces this desire to feel uniquely needed, in some way – if only to scrub the toilet basin. Another crucial constraint upon a woman's expectations of change in men is the tension and turmoil her insistence upon it is likely to provoke. As Kathryn Backett observes from her research, one important coping mechanism for women in the face of unequal domestic burdens is to play down the inequalities and exaggerate the extent of 'sharing', so as to avoid conflict and make life seem more bearable.[94] Both Ehrensaft and Russell point out that even when fathers are actively parenting this creates the potential for conflict and dissatisfaction in couple relationships, with many women – at least to begin with – tending to feel that men are not doing their job as well as they might be – as well as the women themselves would do it.[95]

Finally, while men's sharing of domestic work, where it does occur, may indeéd improve women's career or job satisfactions, as well as their enjoyment of home life, it nevertheless seems unlikely that in isolation, it can do much to undermine overall male dominance. As a strategy for undermining male dominance it is limited, as we have seen, by wider structural constraints outside the family. For the majority of men to engage in primary or equal parenting we would need *already* to have altered existing conditions of employment, career structures and the differential remuneration for jobs defined as 'men's' or 'women's' work. The home is only one site of men's power and privileges *vis-à-vis* women. As some feminists have been arguing – in criticism of others who identify family life as the root of women's subordination – other spheres are equally crucial in the creation of male dominance and forms of masculinity.[96] The workplace plays a significant role in shaping gender difference and establishing and sustaining the power relations between women and men; and as Cynthia Cockburn has indicated, 'It may well cast a shadow on the sex-relations of domestic life.'[97] The cultural and political spheres of contemporary life also consolidate male dominance, notwithstanding the ruptures produced by recent feminist struggle. The contribution which shared parenting can make to modifying established power relations between men and women may therefore be less than one might hope.

The Problem With Reasserting Fatherhood

In an altogether broader perspective, encompassing all contemporary power relations between women and men, there are, as I indicated, real dangers attached to the new emphasis on father-hood. By 1925, when British courts had come to regard the child's welfare as the dominant consideration, fathers had lost their former absolute legal rights over their wives and children.[98] Concern for the interests of children meant that on divorce mothers were usually given custody – a practice which merely ratified existing exclusive maternal care of children. But the crushing stigma attached to 'bastards' and unmarried mothers, the disgrace accompanying divorce, and the limited employment options of women, meant that no woman could consider mothering outside marriage as a positive choice. That situation has now changed – at least for some women. The rise of women's liberation unleashed a fierce attack upon the legal and social subordination of women to men through marriage and the nuclear family. Feminists' insistence on women's right to control their own sexuality and fertility, alongside growing financial independence for women in a context of rising female employment, has meant that some women's choices have expanded.

In Britain, as in most Western countries, it is easier and certainly more common, though not of course without its financial penalties, for women to file for divorce today. It is possible and not altogether uncommon – though by no means easy – for women to choose to have a child without any paternal engagement, or even knowledge. It is also possible for women to obtain abortions if they are unwillingly pregnant. An increasing number of women and men are choosing to have a child outside marriage – a situation in which fathers have few legal rights at present over the child or its mother. With modern methods of artificial insemination by donor (AID), contact with men can be dispensed with altogether if the mother can make suitable arrangements to obtain sperm. The contemporary diversity of households with children includes married couples, co-habiting singles, lesbian couples, women on their own, and women living with friends or other relatives. Men, it seems, can no longer take it for granted that their wives or girlfriends will assume that children need fathers. And men have begun to worry about women's new potential for parenting without them. The penalty of poverty so often suffered by mothers alone with children has proved weaker than many women's desire to escape brutal or loveless marriages, or their desire not to marry at all before having a child or children.

The new emphasis on the importance of fathering has not just been the result of a gradual ideological shift. Significant pressure groups are hard at work seeking legal changes to strengthen paternal rights over children following separation or divorce, and even over foetuses inside women's bodies. As Carol Smart has pointed out, until the mid-1970s the position of the unmarried mother was considered so undesirable that her maternal obligations were seen as little more than her punishment, accompanied as they were, by stigma, discrimination and rejection.[99] Most often, men denied paternity of their illegitimate children so as to avoid having to pay any maintenance costs. But with the greater potential for women's economic and social independence from men, all that has changed. Feminists began to see some advantages to single parenting, outside marriage and men's control. And by the end of the seventies the Law Commission on illegitimacy was recommending the need to strengthen the rights of unmarried fathers. It proposed giving all biological fathers automatic parental rights, similar to those of married fathers. This proposal, as Smart argues, illustrates a new anxiety about the power of some women to exercise a greater degree of choice over motherhood autonomously from men. It was abandoned only because it would allow rapists full paternal rights![100]

The contemporary reinforcement of fatherhood is problematic insofar as it can be used to strengthen men's control over women and children, in a society where men are already dominant socially, economically and politically. The British film *The Good Father*, unlike most of the recent films or writing on nurturing fathers, did begin to explore some of the possible problems. Here two men's anger at their wives' custody of their children becomes a desire for revenge. One of the fathers persuades the other to use his wife's lesbianism to seek custody, and the resulting court case proves grotesque and disastrous for all concerned. It is well known that lesbian mothers have always risked losing their children if the father chose to seek custody, on the grounds that they could not provide a suitable 'father figure'. In their interviews with lesbian mothers in the late seventies Gillian Hanscome and Jackie Forster reported that most of them expressed fear and suspicion of all social and welfare authorities, doctors and law courts.[101] Their most constant fear was that if their lesbianism were officially known they would lose custody of their children. In the many cases they encountered where women had lost custody on the grounds of lesbianism, neither the children's own feelings about their parents and where they wished to live, nor the mother's existing relationship with their children, had been taken into account. Judges simply assumed that the 'normal' father was a more suitable parent than a lesbian mother.[102]

The legal bias against lesbian mothers has been endorsed and sensationalised in media coverage of lesbian mothers. In 1978 the *London Evening News* viciously attacked lesbians seeking motherhood through AID, attempting to stir up further social condemnation of them. On this occasion lesbian feminists fought back, invading the newspaper and obtaining the right of reply.[103] Indeed, lesbian mothers have been organising against the discrimination they face since 1975, at first in Action for Lesbian Parents and more recently in the Lesbian Custody Project – which also seeks the same rights for lesbians to foster and adopt as heterosexuals, and recognition of the rights of lesbian co-parents.[104] It remains true, however, as Lynne Harne reports, that even in the 1980s around 90 per cent of lesbian mothers are losing their custody cases.[105] What they are up against is the myth of the 'normal family', which can only be strengthened by any assertion of the inalienable rights of biological fathers.

The official stress on the importance of a father figure (most strongly argued in custody cases involving sons) is thus becoming even more of a threat to the many women who may choose to mother autonomously from men, or at least from the biological father. The pressure group, Families Need Fathers, formed in 1974 with the claim that paternal rights have been eroded, has argued that children need two parents. (It is referring, of course, to biological parents, not to those more diverse people who may wish to look after and 'parent' a child.) Its adherents maintain that it is always better for children to see their fathers, even fathers who have been denied access because of their physical violence to wives and children: 'We believe it is fair to see much of the physical violence . . . as a final response to violence inflicted in other forms, especially by women, verbal violence.'[106] Families Need Fathers has been pushing, with some success, for joint custody to be granted on marriage break-up. Naturally, this gives the father considerable power over his ex-wife and children since the woman, who is still likely to perform the bulk of the caring, can make few important decisions about children without her ex-husband's consent. Fathers can also try to use their income and status to undermine or interfere with women who have care and control of children.

The case of Families Need Fathers demonstrates that the emphasis on fathering is also another way of asserting the importance of the traditional heterosexual nuclear family: 'good families' are male-headed nuclear families. The new fatherhood thus also serves a rather old pro-family rhetoric, one which has always functioned to shore up men's power and women's dependence. This rhetoric has been under attack for two decades now, not only from feminists identifying the assumptions of male dominance still legally enshrined in marriage, but also from the spiralling divorce rates over that period. It is a rhetoric which denies legitimacy to the choices or circumstances that have led people to live outside nuclear families. Biological fathers may well not be needed in the households where many people with children have chosen to live. Some may wish to live with children – our own or other people's – collectively with friends, as so many early women's liberationists, myself included, did in the seventies. Alternatively, some may wish to live as single parents, as gay couples, or in various other combinations. It is not simply paternal rights but rather carers' rights that need to be considered in relation to children. It seems to me more important than ever today to maintain the possibilities, so passionately sought by some in the early 1970s, for creating a diversity of caring, co-operative households as an alternative to the more traditional family groupings through which women, children and gay people have been oppressed or excluded.

It is a cause for great concern that the new stress on fatherhood can be exploited to bolster the harmful (if, as immigrant British know, frequently hypocritical) pro-family rhetoric of the right. It is a rhetoric which serves to conceal the objectives of politicians out to dismantle the public sector and destroy any notion of collective responsibility for the care and welfare of dependent and needy people. The idea that women today receive more help from their male partners is very convenient as this government returns the full burdens of care to women in the home. Pro-fathers, pro-family rhetoric all too easily unites with the current upsurge in sexual paranoia – a product both of harder times and the threat of AIDS – to feed a moral backlash against non-familial sex and relationships. Sanctions against those living outside the traditional family unit have also been strengthened by Tory legislation in 1988 which removed the mortgage relief formerly available to any individuals buying property jointly. A harsher, more conservative sexual climate has thus been created in which the choices of those seeking alternatives to traditional marriage and the family are being further restricted. The popularity of the stereotyped film thriller *Fatal Attraction* – describing the deadly threat the single woman poses to the healthy, happy, wholesome nuclear family – which enjoyed extraordinary overnight success around the world, is depressing witness to this. Released at the same time, in early 1988, the mirror-image of this film, *The Stepfather* – equally full of suspense and drama, but presenting the more credible scenario of the new husband, in the apparently ideal nuclear family, threatening violence towards his wife and step-daughter – enjoyed no such success.[107]

Strikingly, none of the recent books on fathering have alluded even in passing to men's domestic violence and child sexual abuse, now known to be very much more common than was previously thought. These are fathers whom children not only do *not* need, but from whose fateful attention they may never recover. This secret, for so long concealed behind the closed doors of conventional family life, has come to light only through the determined efforts of incest survivors themselves, and of the feminist movement, which helped give women the confidence to speak out. The pressures to keep child sexual abuse hidden, or to deny its extent, persist. (It was one aspect of the extraordinary media furore surrounding the

Cleveland child abuse cases in 1988). Moreover, current orthodoxy in the professional treatment of child sexual abuse is one so committed to the notion that the healthy family is heterosexual and nuclear that, while recognising the almost invariably male identity of abusers, it nevertheless identifies the 'dysfunctional family' (the unhealthy way of relating within the family as a whole), as the source of the problem. The question of why it is men, and most often fathers or step-fathers, who sexually abuse children is not addressed. Mothers, held responsible for internal family dynamics, are here blamed as both collusive with men's abuse, and culpable – through lack of attention to husband's sexual needs – for its initial occurrence.[108] Siding with the father figure, this literature stresses 'rehabilitation' of the family, rather than support for mothers and children who might want nothing more to do with the abuser.[109] As Mary McIntosh has written, 'this orthodox explanation has led to orthodox solutions: family therapy or removal of the child from both parents.'[110]

The less orthodox thinking and practice with regard to child sexual abuse advanced by feminists sees the problem as directly connected to women and children's powerlessness and vulnerability within the 'normal' nuclear family, combined, as we shall see in later chapters, with the social construction of masculinity around a coercive sexuality. Far from determining the internal dynamics of conventional family life, the dependent status of women within it means that they are often powerless to effect change. And far from criticising women for failing to satisfy men's needs, feminists would question whence these 'needs' derive, and whether these needs themselves should not be seen as the problem – the problem of men. Feminist solutions have centred on support for mothers and children when threatened by men's sexual behaviour, as opposed to keeping the 'normal' family intact.[111] It is frightening to reflect that, as we shall see in more detail in chapter nine, it was only the re-emergence of feminist perspectives and struggle which revealed the prevalence of child sexual abuse, repressed throughout much of the twentieth century – just as it was only feminist concern which focused attention on men's domestic violence as a social problem.[112] Before embracing the importance of fathers, we need to take on board just how readily the abuse of paternal power has been condoned or denied within traditional family life. Given the incidence of violence in the home, it is hard not to agree with Mary McIntosh: 'It is not an extraneous blemish on the social fabric, but part of its warp and weft.'[113]

There is yet another threat for women contained in the recent emphasis on fathers: a threat to the rights women have achieved over the control of their own bodies. In Britain, existing laws do not allow women to choose to have an abortion, but doctors can agree to a termination of pregnancy for medical or social reasons up to 28 weeks. *Abortion Case Father Raises Campus Baby* was the banner headline on a front page article of *The Observer* newspaper in January 1988, at the time of Liberal MP David Alton's bill to lower the foetal age at which abortion is legal. It was placed directly beneath a photo of women demonstrating on behalf of 'a woman's right to choose'. The story, which appeared in every other popular newspaper, concerned an Oxford post-graduate student now combining his studies with raising his seven-month-old baby daughter, having successfully obstructed the baby's mother from having an abortion. Seen by anti-abortionists as a 'shining example' of the justice of their cause, Robert Carver, the father, had taken out an injunction to prevent the baby's mother from having an abortion. Though he lost his case, the publicity surrounding it had compelled the pregnant woman, also a student, to change her mind. She was still absent from her studies trying to recover from the trauma of the case. David Alton, who characterised his bill as but a first move towards the outlawing of all abortion, stated that, 'Robert Carver has shown that abortion is not only an issue for women and that men are prepared to shoulder the responsibility.'[114] What Robert Carver has actually shown is that, in the name of their desire to father, men who have impregnated women are demanding the right to control women's bodies, quite irrespective of women's wishes.

Feminists' fears over men's attempts to use and control women's reproductive capacities have been fanned by rapid developments in new reproductive technologies over the last decade: *in vitro* fertilisation, surrogate motherhood and various forms of embryo research (the first 'test-tube baby' was born in July 1978). These technologies afford new opportunities and constitute new dangers for women. They can serve to end women and men's misery over infertility, but they also increase the potential for medical control over women's bodies – a control still predominantly in the hands of male experts. These practices could be harnessed to eugenic or other political and moral projects, exploited by medical authorities in accordance with their own view of which women are to be accredited as 'suitable' mothers. Most women, surveys have found, do not trust scientists to reveal the truth about such research.[115] We know that the endeavour by women to gain greater control over the conditions in which they either choose, or refuse, to have children, has been a long and difficult one. Women have won the right to assert a greater say in the conditions of childbirth in most parts of Britain since the seventies, despite the arrogance and contempt with which they were so often treated by the overwhelmingly male gynaecological hierarchies. In relation to the new reproductive technologies, women will be obliged to step up their fight to ensure that they will be understood by women and used to increase women's autonomy – not to spawn a breed of technological 'fathers' with powers to select who may or may not bear children.

The Future of Fatherhood

Reflecting upon all the possible dangers involved in reasserting the importance of fatherhood in a context of general male dominance, the anti-sexist writer and campaigner Jeff Hearn has maintained that 'the notion of fatherhood must be smashed or more precisely dropped bit by bit into the ocean.'[116] I share many of his anxieties. But my conclusions would be less drastic.

They would be less drastic if only because I think that the myth of the good father – the strong and protective father – as well as the actual contribution of the caring father, are too powerful for us to smash or drop. Moreover, I believe that feminists were right to identify the importance of men's involvement in childcare and nurturing as a crucial factor (albeit not the only one) in the forging of 'masculinity' into something less coercive and oppressive to women. It is part of the ideological struggle to break down the polarity between 'masculine' and 'feminine' – wherein all that is soft, gentle and tender is all that is, definitively, not 'masculine'. And it is part of a practical struggle by women for greater equality in the home. We need to proceed very carefully in sorting through the rights of active fathers, guided by the principle that it is not biology, but the shouldering of responsibilities, which should determine carers' rights in relation to those they love and nurture. Adoption is only the most obvious instance of a more general need to consider the rights of those who actually parent as legitimate, (in this case, more so than those of biological parents).

Persuading and enabling men to share childcare and housework entails a struggle on three fronts: personal, ideological and social. The last is important, given that the obstacles to change are very real and the conditions of parenting and caring for others are so often appalling – whether it is women, or just occasionally men, who undertake them. We need to break down many of those barriers between the private and the public, to fashion a society in which collective provision for individual needs ensures the maximum choices for those caring and those being cared for alike. The easier and more flexible the conditions of caring, the more women are able to persuade men to undertake it (and begin, at last, to challenge the situation where it has always been left to them to do the persuading).

Meanwhile, the contemporary revalorisation of fatherhood has enabled many men to have the best of both worlds. As Yvonne Roberts discovered, interviewing men of 35 in the early eighties, they are more involved in what was once the exclusive domain of women but, especially in relation to children, they are sharing its pleasures more than its pains.[117] Men's power and privileges in and out of doors can survive this shift. But their survival is no longer so certain: the balance between women's acceptance of men's failure fully to share domestic responsibilities and the pressure on men to change is a delicate one. Recent surveys of undergraduates in the US, for example, show that almost all college women are now seeking high-powered careers as well as husbands and children; while college men accept career goals as normal for women.[118] What neither sex seem able to envisage, however, is how this can be achieved in a society where welfare services fail to provide resources for childcare, or the labour market time off for parenting. While women still seemed more prepared to put future families first, they expected supportive husbands, and careers kept open for them. Reflecting on these findings Anne Machung wonders of these young women:

> Will they, however, after tasting the rewards and opportunities that come with challenging professional jobs, be so willing to give these jobs up, even temporarily, for the sake of their children? Will their own emerging sense of self accommodate itself so easily to the relatively traditional patterns of family life they hope to construct? Will compromises with egalitarian ideals bring them the children, the families, and the careers they want?[19]

The forces which have drawn women into the workforce and ejected men from it, which are bringing women into trade unions and placing 'women's issues' – and more slowly men's behaviour – onto political agendas (as we shall see in chapter ten), which have encouraged the growth of confidence, ambition and creativity in women, are all forces that threaten the traditional sexual contract.

The degree of change in men is related to the demands which women feel able to make of them. But demands will be made, and the image of the 'new man' and the 'good father', however exceptional the reality, will survive. It must be recognised that the struggle for equality between women and men is one which the current wave of political reaction has not succeeded in submerging. Women too *could* have the best of both worlds: but for that to happen the two worlds – the public world of paid work and the 'private' world of the home – would have no longer to be seen as unconnected. Social policies (as in Sweden), backed up by trade union priorities, (which we have yet to see), could be formulated which recognise and uphold the equal rights and responsibilities of women and men in each world. Thus far, however, we have seen little more than the beginnings of a possible journey towards this goal.

3. Shrinking the Phallus: Contemporary Research on Masculinity (I)

> One of the things about being a man in this society is giving away as little as possible.
>
> *Dustin Hoffman[1]*

Until recently the idea of masculinity, to the extent that it was discussed at all, seemed relatively straightforward. What was not written in the genes was, increasingly from the 1940s, understood to be bred in the social expectations of 'sex roles'. Today, however, in the light of the complex input from psychoanalytic thinking and feminism, men and masculinity have become more mysterious, more perplexing and worrying. For some at least, 'masculinity' has replaced 'femininity', as the problem of our time – a threat to civilisation itself. Accordingly, we might well parody fragments of Freud's essay on femininity and his celebrated inquiry 'What is it that women want?', to ask some questions which he never asked of men and their motives – and mourn (in parody also of Jacques Lacan) men's unresponsiveness:

> What is it that men want? If only they could tell us. If only they could communicate at all about their feelings. Throughout history we, who are women, have knocked our heads against the riddle, have been begging men on our knees, and still we cannot learn from them why they present to us such sinister contrasts – the baby and the bully, the rapist and the romantic, the hard and the soft, the terrifying and the ridiculous. Those of you who are men have escaped worrying about this problem – you are yourselves the problem.[2]

It is women who have taken the initiative in beginning to explore what men want, in explaining the ways of man.

Feminist interest in men and masculinity is readily intelligible. It is part of the search for an explanation of men's power over women. But there is still little agreement amongst feminists on any general theory capable of explaining the apparent geographical and historical ubiquity of 'male' power. Debate and dispute among feminists seeking to understand men's dominance have always revolved around whether it attaches to the inherent nature of males, to the distinctive attributes acquired by men through social conditioning, or to the diverse social structures and ideas through which men are invested with power and cultural pre-eminence. Many feminists simply equate 'masculinity' and 'male dominance'. On this view the psychology of men inevitably perpetuates the social structures of male dominance, as a result of certain invariant features of either their biological *or* their social construction. Others distinguish masculinity and male dominance, while nonetheless accepting the existence of connections between the psychologies of men and the social structures of male dominance. We need, therefore, to explore the experience and subjectivity of men in more detail.

Searching for Sex Difference
Despite its many limitations, and in particular its ingrained suspicion of notions like 'experience' and 'subjectivity' (in the search for what was seen as the 'scientific' respectability of the physical sciences), some have turned to academic psychology for knowledge about men and women. From its inception at the turn of the century, modern psychology has framed its empirical studies of sex differences within the 'nature/nurture' debate. Yvette Walczak, for example, begins a recent text, *He and She* (1988) with a summary of the theoretical choices as she sees them:

> Does biology determine destiny and are men and women so very different in every respect: intellectually, emotionally and in terms of their social relationships and careers? Alternatively, are they similar creatures falsely presumed to be ideally biologically equipped for a variety of non-interchangeable sex-linked roles?'[3]

From Cyril Burt in the 1900s, through F.L. Goodenough to Herman Witkin in the 1950s, any cognitive or temperamental differences in behaviour between men and women detected by pscyhologists were usually attributed without further ado to 'nature' or biology.[4] The most consistently reported were women's superiority in verbal skills and men's in spatial skills and abstract reasoning, as well as the latter's greater aggressiveness and dominance behaviour. The impact of feminist thinking from the late 1960s, however, not only intensified the volume of research on sex differences in psychology, but was articulated by many new voices directing us, with equal conviction, to examine social context and the conditioning of sex-role behaviour for the explanation of any observed differences between men and women.[5] Walczak's conclusions are congruent with this new emphasis on the learning of sex roles: 'although differences in behaviour do exist, most of them are induced by environmental pressures and the reality of the social, cultural and economic context.'[6]

A cautious consensus in the nature/nurture debate was established by Eleanor Maccoby and Carol Jacklin in *The Psychology of Sex Differences* in 1974, a book considered authoritative for its exhaustive summary of existing research. They showed that the existence of sex differences in behaviour had been systematically exaggerated, and similarities minimalised. There were no consistent sex differences in traits like achievement motivation, sociability, suggestibility, self-esteem and cognitive styles. However, they did privilege biological explanation over cultural explanation where possible – that is, when it came to explaining the small but 'fairly well established' differences in verbal and spatial ability, mathematical reasoning and aggressiveness.[7] The consensus was compatible, then, with the continued attempts by many psychologists to explain men's dominance as a sex in terms of biology – despite the flimsy (and disputed) nature of their empirical evidence.[8] Indeed in the 1980s there has been a resurgence of stress on innate sex differences, with the popularisation of work like that of Camilla Benbow and Julian Stanley attributing 'male superiority' in mathematics to biology.[9]

Yet researchers like Hugh Fairweather have convincingly criticised the adequacy of any firm conclusions on cognitive sex difference, noting the failure to find any clear sex differences in childhood and the weakness of the majority of studies, which failed to investigate the effects of cultural background, family size, birth order and sex of experimenter.[10] Janet Sayers has similarly pointed to research suggesting that consistent sex differences in aggressiveness (leaving aside, for the moment, the lack of any attention to the complex and varied meanings attached to 'aggressiveness') only occurs among older children, and might as plausibly be explained through the cultural influences of men's currently dominant position as a sex, and boys' greater exposure from an early age to physically boisterous and aggressive behaviour.[11] But the psychological search for innate *difference* between the sexes continues unabated, even though the main finding of some 80 years research has been the massive psychological *similarity* between the sexes in terms of individual attributes.[12]

One new area of research which exemplifies the unflagging quest for biological determinants of existing sex differences – and its many pitfalls – is work on the asymmetry between the two hemispheres of the brain. Roger Sperry pioneered the research in this area, for which he received the Nobel Prize in 1981.[13] He has described the male brain as more asymetrically organised than the female – a feature he linked to claims of men's better overall cognitive performance.[14] Yet, as Fairweather once again indicates, the overwhelming majority of the most relevant experiments (over 80 per cent) failed to provide any corroboration.[15] Indeed, other researchers insist that it is the female brain which is more asymmetrically organised.[16] In general, sheer chaos reigns in the highly contentious and contradictory studies on the effects of hemispherical dominance in the brain. All that is clear is how little is known either about how the brain works or about any reliable sex differences in its functioning. It is equally clear that, despite the inconsistencies, biases and ambiguities of the data, the project of all the research to date had been precisely to seek out sexual difference. Without an ideology of sexual difference we could never have imagined the supposed sex differences in the brain in the first place. As Stephen Katz argues, 'dualism informs the whole project before it even begins.'[17]

The only consistent picture obtained from psychological sex-difference research is one where any sex differences are small, their origins unclear, and the variation within each sex far outweighs any differences between the sexes. Ruth Bleier has summed up the situation as follows:

> The 'sex difference' investigated is a small *statistical* difference between entire groups when it exists and it does not distinguish between the two groups. That is, the two sexes are not different. Knowing a particular score will not predict whether the subject is male or female nor will knowing the gender of the subject predict her or his score.[18]

More fundamentally, however, the whole nature/nurture framework is conceptually inadequate. Not only is the reduction of gender differences to any set of individual attributes theoretically simplistic but, as I have argued elsewhere, human action and experience are not the product of some simple addition or mix of biological and social components.[19] The one always already contains the other. To insist that how we understand and relate to the unfolding and containment of biological potential – that is, how we exist as human beings – is *always* a part of human culture need not, as many critics assert, involve any suppression of the details of biology. What becomes of our bodies has a history determined by human action. We are not dealing with two separate entities. Rather, as the philosopher Kate Soper expresses it, 'Man is naturally social, and his development as man – the process of "hominization" – takes place in and through society.'[20]

Biological sex difference, especially in relation to reproduction, profoundly influences our lives as women and men. Biology affects culture. But *how* it influences our lives is a historical and cultural variable. Biology does affect culture, but not in ways that can be specified independently of that culture; not, as sociobiologists would have it, through some fatality inscribed in our genes. As we shall soon see, but as no psychological test can conceivably 'measure', 'masculinity' and 'femininity' become embodied within us, as part of the way we live as men and women within specific cultures. Biological differences in intellectual and emotional capacities, if they exist, are most certainly not of such a magnitude as to override human culture in explaining existing relationships between women and men. It is time, then, for psychologists to move beyond the nature/nurture debate.

The Power of Sex Roles

The difficulty of finding significant sex differences in cognitive and temperamental capacities led some psychologists to an interest in the sociological category of sex roles. Back in the 1940s Talcott Parsons had written two papers on male and female sex roles, described as 'instrumental' and 'expressive', respectively.[21] These distinctions were originally derived from his studies of small groups and elaborated into an overall perspective on the family and the social system in the 1950s. The socially functional sexual division of labour within the nuclear family, Parsons argued, necessitated these contrasting normative roles for men and women.

The way in which the instrumental/expressive distinction was mapped on to sex differences was, however, always slightly obscure – a kind of sleight of hand, as later sociologists, like David Morgan, have commented.[22] Sociologists were never fully agreed in their definition of 'roles'. Were they what people actually did, or simply what people were expected to do?[23] The assumption underlying role theory, however, is that the social expectations, rules or norms attached to a person's position in society will usually force individuals to conform to them through processes of positive and negative reinforcement. Adopting popularised psychoanalytic notions, sex roles in particular were considered to be internalised through identification with the same-sex parent. Women learned the traits of nurturance, gentleness and the fear of success; men learned to be ambitious, rational and competitive. In Parsonian thinking these roles were seen in terms of complementarity, not in terms of power or dominance.[24] Role theory had a wide appeal in the fifties and sixties, and later seemed useful to feminists, once they had added dominance and oppression to the sex role relationship. As Mary McIntosh has written:

> To see ourselves as players, as hapless victims of a malign scriptwriter, freed us from our past and invited us to embark on writing our own future. It also presented a way of seeing men as redeemable, if only they would break out of their sex roles.[25]

Ironically, it was the problem of men being broken into their sex roles that had troubled social scientists back in the fifties (though this was soon replaced by a focus on women's adjustment to their role requirements, as in the 'problem' or working wives). Father-absence, as we saw in chapter two, was thought to create sex-role anxiety in men, leading to a compensatory 'hypermasculinity', a fear of weakness, and a tendency towards delinquency and educational underachievement.[26] By the seventies, however, both boys and girls were seen as smoothly learning the appropriate sex role. They internalised gender stereotypes from observing the different ways parents and nursery teachers treat girls and boys, through toys, the school curriculum, television, books, comics and countless other sources.[27] Some notes of caution were introduced by findings that, for example, the influence of television seemed to vary with the age, sex and personality of the viewer.[28] In general, however, gender stereotypes were regarded by writers at the time as unremittingly coercive in their effects.[29]

The very notion of 'gender', as we understand it, is a recent one, introduced by Robert Stoller in 1968 to illustrate how 'gender' could differ from biological 'sex'.[30] Popularised by Ann Oakley in the early seventies, the distinction served to highlight the cultural construction of 'gender' as the psychological phenomenon of 'masculinity' and 'femininity', as opposed to the biological construction of 'sex' as the physical reality of genes and genitalia with their differing hormonal states and secondary sexual characteristics.[31] Not surprisingly, psychologists confirmed the ubiquity of gender stereotypes, reporting that their subjects did indeed hold the conventional views of women and men.[32] From these they constructed masculinity/femininity scales designed to measure the strength of a person's gender identity, by requiring subjects to choose between polarised masculine/feminine, rough/gentle, etc., stereotypic self-descriptions. Not only, as critics noticed, do these tests seem *fashioned* to elicit only superficial platitudes from people about how they view themselves as men and women, but they leave no room for conflict, tension and contradiction *vis-à-vis* gender identity.[33]

Intended, at least, to impart some complexity to this approach, the inventory drawn up by American psychologist Sandra Bem was the most popular measure of sex role internalisation by the midseventies. It asked subjects to rate themselves on 'masculine' traits (aggressive, ambitious, analytical, assertive, dominant, independent, etc.) and 'feminine' traits (affectionate, cheerful, childlike, compassionate, gentle, yielding, etc.), but it scored for masculinity and feminity separately so as to allow also for an 'androgynous' score (the combination of both 'masculine' and 'feminine' traits).[3] In line with a dominant strand of the then current feminist thinking, Bem reported that the more androgynous a person's score, the better adjusted and more generally capable they were – as revealed in a variety of test situations.[35] One third of Bem's sample scored as sex-typed ('feminine' women and 'masculine' men), and one quarter as androgynous (high on both scores), with the rest somewhere in between.[36]

The political implication of Bem's work, as she and other feminists saw it, was that it illustrated that people of the same sex vary greatly in the extent to which they conform to gender ideals. But this is hardly surprising. What, sadly, is also hardly surprising is that such results bring us no nearer to understanding anything about people's anxiety, tension, comfort or delight in their experiences as masculine and feminine, or to learning about the pleasures and perils of relations between men and women. What we learn is what we know: people seem to feel there are or ought to be differences between the sexes; sometimes they themselves fit the stereotypes and sometimes they don't. The feminist application of orthodox psychological methods and thinking has not advanced very far beyond the limitations of traditional psychological approaches. Characteristically untroubled by conceptual, linguistic or semantic problems in their search for quantitative response measures, psychologists tell us little of what their tests of masculinity/feminity might be measuring – all we really know is that they are thought to be internally consistent.[37] Bem herself acknowledges today that it was a mistake to imagine that her scales were measuring a masculinity and femininity within us. She now sees them, instead, in line with Kohlberg's cognitive psychology, as measuring the cognitive constructs derived from sex roles which we use to organise our perceptions and our social world.[38]

The continuing problems of role theory are well illustrated in recent work on male sex-role identity, most of it influenced by the politics of feminism and 'men's liberation'.[39] The new sex-role literature of the seventies, unlike that of the fifties, was primarily concerned with the 'hazards of being male' – the title of a book from the period.[40] Paralleling contemporary feminist arguments, men were seen as conditioned into competitive, inexpressive, restrictive masculine roles which were both physically and psychically damaging, inhibiting expression of their authentic selves. (The higher rates of death and illness in men compared to women were also noted in this literature.) Men too were oppressed by their roles, and insecure in their male identities – particularly given the absence of male role models in early life. Men too needed liberating.[41] As Joseph Pleck and Jack Sawyer argued in *Men and Masculinity*, 'Some of us are searching for new ways to work that will more fully express ourselves rather than our learned desire for masculinity.'[42] The source of this conflict between 'self' and 'role' is, however, unexplained – indeed, is incoherent within the sex-role framework. For what is postulated is some essential, pre-social 'self', which must presumably be biological, or, alternatively a merely mystic presence (a soul or *anima*!). The reality of male power also tends to be washed away with the tears shed for men's underlying vulnerability.

Pleck, a social psychologist in the US, has been the most prolific writer to date on the male sex role. In *The Myth of Masculinity* (1981) he attempted an ambitious and critical reassessment of the existing male sex-role literature, offering what he saw as a new version. From an examination of the empirical weaknesses of previous research on masculinity and femininity, Pleck rejected the repeated assertion that sex-role identity is especially difficult for boys (because of the lack of male role models in early life), and that this posed major problems for men. He argued for a tighter 'role' analysis, restricting use of the category to external social expectations, and replacing the notion of 'male sex-role identity' (as some type of internal personality dimension) by the notion of 'male sex-role strain'. Men's problems of adjustment, he claimed, are not due to insecure sex-role identities, but to the constraining, inconsistent and unrealistic or dysfunctional nature of the sex-role expectations themselves. Men who violate these unrealistic or inconsistent demands experience social condemnation – in particular from other men – and in consequence exprience a self-devaluation which leads them to overconform to their roles.[43]

By trying to tighten the role analysis, however, Pleck only highlights its weaknesses. We are not told why non-conformity leads to over-conformity, as opposed to resistance. Without providing any very strong empirical evidence himself, Pleck concurs with the new sex-role literature in claiming that major changes are underway in sex roles.[44] As others have pointed out, however, he regards change as something that simply *'happens'* to sex roles.[45] Like any other role theorist, Pleck fails to locate his 'roles' within actual power dynamics between men and women, or any other concrete social relations. We are no wiser about the actual demands made on men, and certainly no wiser about the emotional and political dynamics of masculinity – why the majority of men not only endure their dysfunctional roles, but display extraordinary resistance to change. As other critics have more relevantly observed, 'we do not speak of "race roles" or "class roles" because the exercise of power in these areas of social relations is more immediately evident to sociologists'.[46]

The whole notion of 'sex roles' and 'sex-role stereotyping', although superficially appealing, has thus been the object of convincing criticism. It assumes a consistent and uniform set of social expectations about men and women universally shared within any society, positing a non-existent homogeneity to social life.[47] It supposes a conformity to social expectations, of the 'nurturing' mother, and the 'responsible' father, positing a non-existent uniformity of individual behaviour. The complex dynamics of gender identity, at both the social and the individual level, disappear in sex role theory, as abstract opinions about 'difference' replace the concrete, changing power relations between men and women. Sex-role theory fails to explain either the passion or the pain of rigid adherence to dominant gender stereotypes of some, resilient resistance to them on the part of others, or confused and contradictory combinations of the two in yet others. We need a fuller picture of the contradictory compulsions and constraints operative at both a social and a psychic level, if we are to get any real grip on the dynamics of sexual identity.

Introducing the Unconscious

In search of a fuller understanding of the complexity and incorrigibility of sexual identity some have turned to Freud to study his account of its origins. To the horror of academic psychology in Britain and the United States, psychoanalysis immediately suggests new layers of ambiguity and contradiction, revealing unconscious mental processes to be the foundation of individual identity, and admitting of no firm boundaries between 'normal' and 'neurotic' aspects of mental life.[48] That said, the potential promise of psychoanalysis on questions of sexual difference has perplexed many who have turned to it and studied Freud's papers on femininity.[49]

Interestingly, as I have already indicated, Freud wrote no formal account of 'masculinity' in its own right, and other analysts have (until very recently) rarely focused on male identity. ('Sexual identity' is the more embodied term which psychoanalytic writing still prefers to the more recent notion of 'gender identity'.) Male development and psychology, it would seem, are equated with human psychology, from which women – the traditional object of study – are seen to deviate.

As is well known, Freud argued that girls and boys in the first few years of infancy and childhood share the same potential desires, gratifications and frustrations. Passing through the sensual comforts and fierce conflicts of oral, anal, phallic and genital eroticism, girls and boys alike desire the mother as their own exclusive love object, passively enjoying and actively seeking the sensual pleasures of her maternal ministrations.[50] Freud saw these active ('masculine') and passive ('feminine') components of libido or sexual drive as constitutive of its inherent 'bisexuality', alongside its capacity to form attachments to people of either sex. These ideas are well illustrated in Freud's case history of the five-year-old boy 'Little Hans', characterised as 'a positive paragon of all the vices', who both wishes to have a baby himself and also to give a baby to his mother.[51] Childhood sexuality is classified as 'polymorphously perverse' in its variety of sexual aims, multiple sources of pleasure, and attachments to people of both sexes.

The child's passionate desire to express and receive exclusive love for and from the mother brings it, however, into a competitive struggle with the father – the Oedipal triangle. The father-son struggle lies at the heart of Freud's own account of 'masculinity', for it is this which arouses the boy's fear of castration by his rival, the father. The anxiety is induced by prohibitions on the boy's expression of his sexuality, and his growing awareness that women 'lack' a penis. The threat of castration challenges the boy's self-loving attachment to his penis (the 'narcissistic cathexis' of the penis). It is sufficiently strong to induce him to renounce his desire for a sexual tie with the mother (his 'libidinal cathexis' of the mother). This occurs through the boy making a powerful paternal identification, effectively choosing the father and hence phallic strength and power in relation to other men, over the strength of the maternal bond.

Freud never saw a person's life history, from the bisexual 'polymorphous perversity' of childhood to a conventional hetero-sexual adult identity, as any straightforward or linear progress. Not only did boys and girls, for different reasons, have to repress their desire for their first love object, the mother; but, Freud argued:

> It has been found that all human beings are capable of making a homosexual object choice and have in fact made one in their unconscious. Indeed, libidinal attachments to a person of the same sex play no less a part as factors in a normal mental life, and a greater part as motive forces for illness, than do similar attachments to the opposite sex.[52]

The boy's powerful paternal identification, though enabling the repression and subsequent revival of a heterosexual object choice, also involves the making of a homosexual object choice – for the father. We could see this as a type of negative Oedipus complex, on which Freud did not elaborate in any detail. The internal conflicts over unresolved active and passive homosexual attachments, and the presence of 'femininity' within men's psychic life, as expressed in a host of sexual fantasies, fears and longings, are what Freud's case histories are all about.[53] One of the most famous of them was the analysis of a Russian aristocrat, known, because of a recurrent dream, as the 'Wolf Man'. When Freud treated this patient, during his second psychotic breakdown, a major component of his

delusions was the belief that he was gradually becoming transformed into a woman, with a woman's type of female voluptu-
ousness. In his late teens he had been promiscuously heterosexual.
However, Freud believed that this masked a passive homosexual
orientation wherein 'few of his psychical trends were concentrated
in his heterosexual object choice'.[54] Early passive homosexual
desire towards the father and identification with women had been
repressed, creating a passive, masochistic sexuality plagued by
anxiety. Freud was in fact frequently to comment upon the
prevalence of pathology due to the repression of homosexual desire,
and upon anxiety in men over passive sexual aims.

In Freud's view, masculinity is neither biologically determined
nor a simple product of social stereotypes and expectations. It is a
complex and difficult process of psychic construction, ineluctably
marked by tension, anxiety and contradiction. It has no single and
consistent set of attributes or essence. As the well-known British
psychoanalyst Donald Winnicott suggested:

> If one takes into consideration the deeper feelings and the unconscious, one may
> easily find a tough male hankering after being a girl . . . In fact every degree of
> cross-identification can be expected, and troubles come mainly from the way these
> awkward things can be truly hidden in the repressed unconscious.[55]

The strength of homophobia, the denial of 'weakness', and the
conscious contempt for women so prevalent in men and ubiquitous
in culture, are all explained in psychoanalytic theory by these
'awkward things' which threaten men's sense of a secure masculine
identity.

Nevertheless, Freud saw the male progress towards normal
'masculinity' as more straightforward than the inevitably more
fraught and difficult female trajectory towards normal 'femininity'.
Albeit in a repressed form, the man can retain his first dominant
heterosexual love object, which he later displaces onto other women
– 'I want a girl, just like the girl, that married dear old Dad'. By
contrast, according to Freud, girls en route to normal femininity
must renounce the mother, the first love object, and turn instead to
the father and to men, at the same time surrendering their more
active clitoral sexuality for the more passive sexual aims of vaginal
receptivity. At the age when both the girl and boy enter the phallic

phase – which is for boys a time of 'of swank and swagger'[56] – the girl's recognition of her 'lack' of any obvious sexual organ like the penis means that, temporarily at least, she feels inferior or maimed. This sense of 'castration' creates a narcissistic wound in the girl and provokes an over-valuation of the penis (or penis envy) which will redirect her desire from mother to father, from active sexual aims to the desire for a penis/baby from the father/male lover.[57]

For several decades, especially after the Second World War, the focus of the psychoanalytic gaze remained firmly upon the vicissitudes of female development. By the late sixties, however, a few papers in mainstream psychoanalytic journals, soon to be supplemented by the popular feminist reappropriation of Freud, were to herald something new in psychoanalytic thinking: a fresh look at the psychology of men. This new perspective developed out of the British and American 'object relations' school of psychoanalysis.

Object Relation: The Fragility of Men?

In 1967 Ralph Greenson from the United States addressed the International Psycho-Analytical Congress on the particular problems involved in the normal development of the boy which interfere with the formation of masculine identity. He traced men's problems to the pre-Oedipal years when, in order to develop his sense of maleness, the boy is obliged to abandon his identification with his mother (at a time when loving and identifying with someone are not yet distinguished) and to identify, instead, with the father: 'Women's certainty about their gender identity and men's insecurity about theirs are rooted in early identification with the mother.'[58] Greenson had been working with Robert Stoller on a study of transsexuals, in the course of which he found that the overwhelming majority of patients unhappy with their own sex were men. This seemed all the more surprising given the prevalence of men's contempt for women and women's envy of men. Men's dissatisfaction with their maleness, and desire to be female, were further confirmed, Greenson argued, in his clinical practice. Though women envy men, men's envy of women is deeper: 'Each sex is envious of the opposite sex; but the male's covert envy underneath his external facade of contempt seems to be particularly destructive with regard to his gender identity.'[59]

The major figures in British psychoanalysis, especially Melanie Klein, had always placed more stress than Freud on the pre-Oedipal phase. From that tradition developed a multi-faceted approach which can be loosely characterised as 'object relations' theory, associated with analysts like Donald Winnicott, Ronald Fairbairn, Harry Guntrip and Alice and Michael Balint. In recent years this school has also become increasingly important in the United States – a prominence reflected in the work and writing of Greenson, Otto Kernberg, Margaret Mahler and others. Object relations focuses upon the mechanisms by which the child in interaction with its environment constructs a mental universe of 'objects' or 'part objects' (the psychic internalisations of people or parts of people) with which s/he comes in contact.[60] The child's developing self or ego is formed very early on from its relations with these 'objects'. Reversing classical Freudianism, Fairbairn, for example, claims that libido is object-seeking rather than pleasure-seeking, and for all these analysts the origin of anxiety and aggression resides in the separation from the first, maternal object.[61] The mother-child bond is of incomparable importance in providing the loving environment which permits the creation within the child of a solid and healthy sense of self – a self which it can then gradually separate off from the maternal imago. Indeed, the tripartite Oedipal scenario more or less disappears in some (although by no means all) of the writings of this school, and the rest of existence is relevant only to the extent that it supports or interferes with the good mothering environment.[62]

The new psychological perspectives focused on the problem of men derive from this very particular psychoanalytic base. The sixteen articles collected in the North American text *The Psychology of Men: New Perspectives in Psychoanalytic Psychology* each address the question: What do men want? Echoing Greenson's thoughts, they all reject or play down the father-son rivalry and castration anxiety in accounting for men's fear and envy of women. Instead, it is argued, these stem from the pre-Oedipal bond with the mother. As one analyst succinctly declares:

At least in the patients with character pathology in analysis today, castration
anxiety serves to defend against more primitive preoedipal terrors, still active
unconsciously and readily activated in the analytic situation.[63]

Men are the vulnerable sex. In bringing, as they see it, the
knowledge of men up to date, these analysts are investigating men's
'often too vulnerable masculinity'.[64] This theme is spelled out in
Gerald Fogel's introduction to the collection, entitled 'Being a
Man':

It is not surprising that . . . for most men the problem is women. Masculinity is
often defined in relation to and in contrast to women; as boys and men we are
dependent upon, threatened by, vulnerable to, and envious of women – in far
more conscious and unconscious ways than we can ordinarily bear. Not only must
men struggle with the real and fantasy-distorted powers of women as objects, but
also with those qualities and impulses within themselves that are perceived as
womanly or womanish. Thus men's view of women becomes further twisted and
confused. If women are not enough of a problem in their own right, they become
so in their role as the bearers or symbolic representatives of various disavowed,
warded off, unacceptable aspects of men.[65]

Rejecting what they variously call the phallocentric or androcentric
bias of traditional psychoanalysis, these analysts, like John Munder
Ross and Ethel Spector Person, emphasise the place of the envied,
powerful mother and the wish for feminine identity in male
psychology.

Ross's contribution explores the prevalence of 'martial masculinity' in our culture, with its sadistic narcissistic fixations. The men he
describes are afraid of intimacy with women and terrified of union
with them ('in and out like a shot', as these men say of sex with
women). They are frightened of fatherhood and the 'soft' sentiments it arouses; either they absent themselves from it, or else they
tyrannise women and children for their own self-aggrandisement.
This is a type of masculinity, Ross believes, related to the unavaila-
bility of the father early on as a libidinal object and figure for
identification. Sons of fathers who are absent emotionally, who act
like oppressors, or are entirely inhibited and ineffectual compared
with a powerful mother (especially in a relationship where the
mother disparages or fears men), are led to create their own
exaggerated, artificial, brittle and aggressive version of manhood as
a protection against their identification with the powerful mother.[66]

This type of analysis seems useful as the (absent) psychological underpinning of the 1950s sex-role literature on the effects of paternal absence.

In an interesting analysis of male sexuality Ethel Spector Person analyses two dominant themes in men's sexual fantasies: the omni-available woman and lesbian sex. She relates the first to men's fears about genital adequacy derived not simply from the threatening Oedipal father and castration anxiety but from the dread of female rejection. Such macho sexual fantasy develops out of the boy's strong sense of sexual rejection and frustration in relation to the mother (and subsequent adolescent female rejection), which threatens his phallic narcissism or self-regard. The fantasy denies and reverses the reality of female sexual rejection, and assuages sexual anxiety through the further reversal evident in the common male fantasy of the penis which is 'two feet long, hard as steel, and can go all night'.[67] The fantasy of the sexually available woman also camouflages intense oral and dependent needs – the desire for the pre-Oedipal 'feeding' mother – under the guise of sexual demands. By the same token, the lesbian fantasy is linked to residual incestual impulses *vis-à-vis* the mother, and to an unconscious female self-identification stemming from envy or separation anxiety or both.[68]

There are many useful insights in these articles (usually backed by detailed case studies), especially for understanding men's attitudes and behaviour towards women. At the same time, however, there is something very puzzling about this new psychoanalytic approach to masculinity – even within the small circle informed by feminism. No mention is ever made of men's power in the outside world. No sustained analysis of male violence, or of child sexual abuse, is attempted. Indeed, there is a disturbing and, for feminists, provocative tendency in object relations psychoanalysis, as in Kleinian and most mainstream forms of analysis, to suggest that 'women are the powerful sex', but they 'give away' their power to men.[69] This claim, whilst demonstrably false on any objective perspective, is advanced because men's power in every sphere of existence disappears in the psychoanalytic focus on the psychic – the fantasy creations of the mind – and the familial. But, although operating in ways which are autonomous from, and certainly irreducible to, the social relations of public life, psychic dynamics – and even more so familial dynamics – are not unaffected by wider social relations. In fact, as well as in fantasy, mothers obviously do have a certain 'power' over children. However, it is an odd sort of power, restricted, precisely, to children: existing in inverse proportion to the supposed power of adults to control their own lives and organise them in accordance with their personal needs. Habitually constrained by dependence on men, regulated by the state, medical and other professional bodies, typically isolated from meaningful adult contacts, motherhood, in our society, most often results in women's greater sense of powerlessness as an adult person.

Ignoring the material constraints, however, Kleinian therapist Jane Temperley, argues that women are 'their own worst enemies' when it comes to shifting the balance of power and privilege between the sexes: 'we need to examine very carefully how far our perception of men's aggression may be overlaid by our own projection onto them of our own hostility towards the role and function of women.'[70] I certainly do not dismiss some of what Temperley has to say about the 'investment women can have in being subordinate and disadvantaged', in terms of projecting one's own aggression and hostility onto men in a 'manoeuvre virtue'.[71] But I do find provocative the psychoanalytic reconstruction of the dramas of everyday life as examples of eternal interpersonal conflicts unfolding outside of time, place, culture, and in particular, the power relations of gender. When Joyce McDougall, who writes so compellingly of adult conflicts and violence between men and women stemming from 'infantile objects of desire, of frustration and of terror',[72] alludes to the need for all of us to accept as adults 'the power and sexual attributes of both parents', it is as if that 'power' is in fact equivalent (whatever may have been the young child's perception of the all-powerful mother, or the older child's perception of the all-powerful father). We are presented with a psychic reductionism which neglects, where it does not deny or invert, the relevance of men's social power and (except in the case of childcare) the sexual division of labour and its dynamics.

I have only come across one contemporary analyst who is

seriously troubled by the uncritical acceptance or denial of the power relations of gender in psychoanalytic discourse – the New York radical, Joel Kovel. With characteristic passion Kovel addressed the problem in his book, *The Age of Desire*:

> Why did so much psychoanalytic writing, even the most seemingly abstract theory, read like a string of complaints directed by a boy against his mother: the subject always a "he", the offending parent, who does too much or too little, a "she". It is not enough to pass off such usage as a necessity imposed by language or reflective of actual social structure. The analysts were always trying to do this . . . what they never began to consider was the active aspect of language and society. For them these were givens . . . they saw social practice as an automatic fixed structure, not as a dialectical play of forces within which their own activity and the choices they made sustained one side or another. And one side that analysts always seemed to support was patriarchy: the vector of their work invariably pointed to a "nature" represented by woman who nourishes the human represented by the male and against which he is to struggle and eventually dominate.[73]

Kovel points out that while most contemporary analysts have been sufficiently influenced by bourgeois feminism to oppose women's subordination, the logic of their approach makes it difficult for them even to support day-care.

This indifference to, or denial of, the wider realities of gender relations is particularly stark in most of the new writing on the psychology of men: 'We men,' writes George Stade, studying the Dracula myth, 'nowadays have all the ontological insecurity we can handle.'[74] 'What men want,' John Munder Ross tells us, from his re-reading of psychoanalytic case histories, is not infrequently 'to bear, suckle and rear babies'.[75] It is the phallocentric bias of psychoanalysts in the past, 'their womb and breast envy', he adds, which has suppressed such anxiety-laden wishes – conflicting as they do with men's efforts to maintain their masculinity.[76]

Perhaps all Don Juan ever did want was to be the Virgin Mary (hence his obsessive pursuit). But there is something missing here. The riddle remains. What is the extraordinary pull of the masculine? What accounts for men's overwhelming fear of the feminine, the maternal? (Women too have powerful, engulfing and rejecting mothers: what is it that distinguishes the boys' experiences from the girls?) These are crucial questions, if we wish to understand the 'vulnerabilities' of men. And yet, they are not really addressed in these papers on men's psychology. There is nothing exclusive to the mother/son bond in itself – absent, destructive and ineffectual fathers notwithstanding – which can answer them. Quite the reverse. The actual power of men and the symbolic power of the phallus have not only shrunk in these accounts: they have disappeared.

There is now, however, a specifically feminist approach within object relations theory, which does take the question of men's power very seriously. It too emphasises the overriding importance of the mother – but criticises the institution of mothering. (The traditional approach, in contrast, romanticises the institution of mothering, while almost always, in every case study, condemning the individual mother.) In *The Mermaid and the Minotaur* Dorothy Dinnerstein maintains that female-dominated childcare guarantees antagonism towards women by children of both sexes. She concludes: 'The universal exploitation of women is rooted in our attitudes towards early parental figures and will go on until these figures are male as well as female.'[77] In her influential book *The Reproduction of Mothering*, the sociologist Nancy Chodorow likewise argues that exclusive female mothering is a major factor in both the creation and perpetuation of male domination.[78] And this because, in accordance with traditional object relations theory, the boy must repress and deny the intimacy, tenderness and dependence of the early symbiotic bond with the mother if he is to assume a 'masculine' identity.

Paternal absence from early childcare means, Chodorow stresses, that masculinity is always defined negatively as that which is not feminine. Though overvalued in society, masculinity remains forever precarious, insecure, and 'becomes an issue in a way femininity does not'.[79] Boys create their own fantastical idealisation of masculinity by inverting their earlier identification with the mother into a fear and abhorrence of femininity: 'A boy represses those qualities he takes to be feminine inside himself, and rejects and devalues women and whatever he considers to be feminine in the social world.'[80] This explains the prevalence of male violence and of men's profound inability to sustain equal and caring relationships with women. All men, Chodorow seems to suggest, develop a neurotic form of masculinity. In a sense *all* boys are fatherless children, like those who troubled the sex-role theorists back in the fifties – the tradition to which Chodorow belongs.

Thus it is that men acquire the impersonal, self-assertive and aggressive psychology necessary for male domination, which in turn is, or has been, functional for society. For, according to Chodorow, men thereby acquire the psychology required for success in a competitive capitalist world or a mass bureaucratic one.[81] Boys achieve their separation from the mother, and a more autonomous sense of self, because from the outset a mother experiences and loves a boy child differently from a girl; her relationship with her son is 'anaclitic' – one in which she loves and experiences him as someone separate from herself. The daughter is experienced and loved 'narcissistically' by the mother, as someone just like herself. The girl therefore remains forever more attached to, and identified with, the mother, more secure in her gender identity, defining herself more in relation to others, with a weaker sense of her own individuality, competence and autonomy than men. (Clearly, there is little room for fantasy here in the mother's perceptions of her child. Mothers do not, for example, confuse the sex of their children according to their own projected desires.) It follows from this account that one central way of undermining male dominance (and, it would seem, capitalism as well), is through the practice of shared childcare. This 'would leave children of both genders with the positive capacities each has, but without the destructive extremes these currently tend towards'.[82]

Not surprisingly, feminist object relations theory, and the view that masculine identity and male dominance grow out of the repression of maternal identification, has appealed to many men, particularly anti-sexist men. Informed by this approach, the fragility of male gender identity and the conflicts and contradictions underlying the fraught, unrewarding nature of much of male sexuality, is the theme of the British collection of anti-sexist men's writing *The Sexuality of Men*. Men's power over women is not denied in these articles. But it is something *not worth having*: women, despite their relative powerlessness, are more secure in their gender identity and closer to psychic health and happiness.

For their own good, as Andy Metcalfe writes in the introductory essay, men must acknowledge their need to change, to abandon a masculinity which is destructive both 'towards women, and towards our own natures'.[83] 'A fear of intimacy has held men in terrible isolation and loneliness', writes Vic Seidler.[84] The solution, therapist Tom Ryan suggests, lies in the active presence and participation of men in childcare, which may 'lessen the need for the defensive posturing inherent in masculinity'.[85] Men's greater involvement in reproduction, in conjunction with learning to express their needs and feelings more directly and openly, are ways of creating the conditions for male sexuality to 'mature out of its infancy', another article concludes.[86]

Involving men in childcare is, for many reasons, an important step in undermining the oppression of women. Despite the insights of this approach into men's fears of intimacy and of female power, it cannot, however, carry the weight of explaining male domination. Men's absence from childcare, as we saw in the last chapter, is as much a product of other institutional practices of male dominance as their cause. Indeed, detailed study of such transformations as have occurred over recent decades suggest that it is more a product of external, than internal, constraints. As we saw in the last chapter, when shared parenting does exist, it is neither as difficult, nor as dramatic in its effects upon children, as these men maintain.

Nor can such an approach fully account for the nature, power and privilege of masculinity. Chodorow's explanation of gender differences, like the analogous approach of Luise Eichenbaum and Susie Orbach, relies upon the effects of a mother's actually contrasting relationship with boys and girls, and upon her actually performing her maternal functions according to the conventional script.[87] But real families do not correspond to this familial ideal quite so closely. Some men are present and caring fathers; while some mothers are absent, absorbed in jobs, identify with their sons, are not defined through their relationship to children, or are in other respects distanced from the conventional maternal role – without this either threatening patriarchy or, as yet, undermining conventional patterns of masculinity and femininity.[88]

Feminist object relations theory, like its more orthodox parent, has no grip on the symbolic power and meanings attached to 'men' and 'masculinity'. The violent repudiation of women and femininity, the determination of the boy to embark on the painful separation from the mother, cannot be understood primarily through the dyadic bond of mother and son, however 'anaclitic' the mother's love for her son. As I have argued elsewhere, there is a circularity in the reasoning: for mothering to create, in Chodorow's words, 'the psychology and ideology of male dominance', we need to presuppose a society where femininity is already devalued and masculinity already more highly valued.[89] Moreover, it is surely rather odd that 'masculinity', understood here as fragile, insecure and primarily a defensive reaction to 'femininity' – rather than any type of creative or positive contrast – is nevertheless the exciting identity, linked with success, power and dominance in every social sphere. It is more plausible, surely, to argue that masculinity 'becomes an issue' precisely because it is so valued and desirable. Rejecting phallocentrism as the product of a defensive sexist imagination, rather than exploring it as a cultural reality, leaves much of the mystery of masculinity concealed. The relationship to the father's phallus remains, as Jessica Benjamin has written, 'the indissoluble lump in the batter for a feminist version of psychoanalysis'.[90]

4. Asserting Phallic Mastery: Contemporary Research on Masculinity (II)

There is no doubt that the image of the phallus as power is widespread to the point of near-universality, all the way from tribal and early Greek fertility symbols to the language of pornography, where the penis is endlessly described as a weapon, a tool, a source of terrifying power.

Richard Dyer[1]

It is within the journals and texts of cultural studies, rather than those of psychology, that the 'phallus' has been most tirelessly tracked down as the ubiquitous symbolic representation of the penis, and hence of male power. One of the predominant influences on this work has been the writings of Jacques Lacan.

Linguistic Law and Phallic Order

Lacan was the controversial author of some of the most perplexing and obscure rereadings of Freud, as well as the autocratic and peremptory founder of a French psychoanalytic school contemptuous of all procedural orthodoxies – downgrading the importance of training therapists, occasionally shrinking the session to a matter of minutes, permitting a studied, even disdainful silence from the analyst, dismissing clients who were silent.[2] He was the brilliant orator who liked to mock and deride his spellbound audiences, and the inventor of a tangled fragmented text of punning word games, jokes, metaphors, irony, contradictions and puzzling digressions designed to mime the ways in which the unconscious operates. For the unconscious, in a celebrated phrase, is structured like a language – a language which Lacan came increasingly to describe as the language of mathematics, of topology. Up to his death in 1981,

Lacan seemed to be the quintessential phallocentric analyst: the analyst who reduced the mystery of Woman to what She lacks, Her existence as Not-man. Such a position, it might be presumed, would be anathema to feminists.

Clarifying her own interest in this thinker, however, North American feminist scholar Jane Gallop declares in *Feminism and Pscyhoanalysis:* 'If feminism is to change a phallocentric world, phallocentrism must be dealt with and not denied.'[3] In Britain, Juliet Mitchell, Jacqueline Rose and other feminist writers introducing Lacan to their readership have felt the same: 'No phallus, no power – except those winning ways of getting one', Mitchell declared.[4] The symbolic significance of the phallus must be studied, and Lacan, it is argued, can act as our guide.

At the heart of Lacan's 'return to Freud', as he regarded it, is the outright rejection of the biological in the study of human consciousness. His goal was the depiction of how subjectivity is constituted through its insertion into the symbolic order. As one of the founders of French structuralism, what needs to be explained for Lacan is precisely how the human subject is constructed in and through language, and its complex systems of meanings and representations. Human subjectivity and human sexual identity, it is argued, are produced simultaneously, as the child enters language: the symbolic order. Freud had maintained that it was only recognition of the presence or absence of the penis which created the child's awareness of sexual difference, and hence the girl's sense of lack (penis envy) and the boy's fear of loss (castration anxiety). Lacan insists that Freud's usage of the term 'penis' always refers not to the biological organ, but to its symbolic representation – the 'phallus'. Drawing on structural anthropology and post-Saussurean linguistics, Lacan proceeds to assert that the reduction of sexual difference to the presence/absence of the phallus is a symbolic law which in turn is a product of patriarchy, or the Law of the Father: 'it is in the *name of the father* that we must recognise the support of the symbolic function which, from the dawn of history, has identified his person with the figure of the law.'[5] It is this law which dictates the legal assignation of father's name to the child, and the exchange of women by men, from father to husband. (Here, especially in his early work, Lacan draws upon Lévi-Strauss' analysis of kinship in which women are defined as objects of exchange.)[6]

The subject, Lacan thus argues, can only assume its identity through the adoption of a sexed identity, and the subject can only take up a sexed identity with reference to the phallus, for 'the phallus is the privileged signifier'.[7] Lacan exploits Saussure's general linguistics to insist upon the primacy and independence of the signifier, 'no signification can be sustained other than by reference to another signification'.[8] A signifier, in Saussurean linguistics, obtains its meaning not through any correspondence between language and the real world, but only through its difference from other signifiers. Where Lacan departs from Saussurean linguistics, however, is in his search for primal or privileged signifiers.[9] The phallus, as symbol of anatomical difference, is *the* mark of division, and 'the organ actually invested with this signifying function takes on the value of a fetish': 'the penis sublime', as Stephen Heath quips.[10]

Lacan offers various reasons for the role of the penis as privileged signifier. These have been summarised by Mandy Merck as follows: '(1) the role of the male genitals in copulation (*Ecrits*); (2) the epistemological supremacy of vision – and thus of the most visible organ (*Seminaire II*); and (3) the physical origin of the signifier (*Seminaire XI*): "it is through sexual reality that the signifier came into the world."'[11] In general, however, as Benvenuto and Kennedy conclude in their lucid introduction to Lacan, it is the visibility of the male organ which is crucial: 'the visibility of the phallus predominates over the black hole of the female genitals.'[12] The woman thus enters the symbolic order as the 'not-whole', reinforcing the privileged function of the phallus in representing human identity. Willy-nilly, it would seem, phallic meanings and representations inhabit individual consciousness. There are not two sexes, in Lacanian writing, but only one: one and its Other – *'Woman does not exist (La femme n'existe pas')*.[13]

Before assuming its place in the symbolic world, by 'lining up on one side or the other' of the phallus, the infant of *in-fans* (without speech), the *hommelette* (moving off in all directions), has no sense of fixed self or sexual difference, but begins life as a tumultuous array of unlimited drives. Between the age of six months and eighteen months, during the pre-symbolic 'mirror stage', the child begins building an identity. The 'helpless' infant, as yet lacking any sense of bodily unity, becomes aware of its own body as a totality by seeing it reflected in the mirror (or the mother's gaze). The child thus gains an illusory sense of itself as whole (often accompanied by great jubilation), as it begins to 'recognise' itself in this external image.[14] The subject now graduates from fragmentation to illusory unity, and commences a series of identifications with other human images, such as the face and the gaze of the mother. This, however, is not the beginnings of a 'true self', but of an inevitably alien and constraining ego, a self-for-others, always 'referential to the other', and therefore distanced from the child's inner drives and desires.[15] A false or mistaken self-identification, based upon these reflected images, thus provides the first (illusory) bodily unity on the Lacanian interpretation – in contrast to the object relations account of the mother, who ideally reflects back the child's true self. Any notion of a unified, 'healthy' individual is always false: 'In Lacan's view, the ego's mastery of the environment is always an illusory mastery, as a result of the way it is formed at the mirror stage, and the human subject will continue throughout life to look for an imaginary "wholeness" and "unity".'[16]

At this stage, the boy, like the girl, does not *have* the phallus, but he (or she) wishes to be the object of the mother's desire. Identifying with the object of the mother's desire, the child *is* the phallus: the mother possesses the phallus in having the child. Yet the child, whether boy or girl, is forbidden to be the exclusive desire of the mother: the duality of mother and child is broken by the place of the father. (There does not have to be a real forbidding father, for the child to learn the place of the father as the omnipotent figure; if not through direct intervention, then via the mother's discourse.) The child perceives that the mother's desires are organised in terms of the symbolic father, who is regarded as a rival phallus. At this point the child becomes aware of both its own and the mother's lack of the phallus – its own lack because it cannot be the phallus for the mother. The child becomes aware of castration. Only the father is seen as complete and the source of his own desire

– the one who has the phallus.[17] The boy child now knows he is not the phallus for the mother, and abandons his former desires, hoping, instead, that by loving and identifying with the father who has the phallus, he too will come to possess it. But this desire for possession of the phallus is itself the product of a loss, of castration. The boy can no longer be the phallus. The assumption of identity in relation to the phallus is thus itself a loss and a castration for both sexes, and an index of the precariousness of sexual identity. As Jacqueline Rose indicates, quoting Lacan, 'the phallus stands at its own expense and any male privilege erected upon it is an imposture "what might be called a man, the male speaking being, strictly disappears as an effect of discourse . . . by being inscribed within it solely as castration".'[18]

From the mirror stage to the external symbolic positioning of the subject in language, there is never any unique or authentic self to determine meanings and desires, but only an alienated being which in shifting from the Imaginary to the Symbolic becomes subject to the primacy of language:

> The effect of language is the cause introduced into the subject. Because of this effect he is no longer the cause of himself and he carries with him the worm of the cause that splits him. But this subject is what the signifier represents, and it cannot represent anything except to another signifier: it is to this that the subject who listens is reduced.[19]

Observing the position of the woman, Lacan proclaims: 'There is for her something insurmountable, something unacceptable, in the fact of being placed as an object in a symbolic order to which, at the same time, she is subject just as much as the man.'[20] Lacan also insists, however, that the idea of the phallus, which constitutes women in terms of a lack, and men in terms of the threat of a lack, creates a sense of difference from a power which is *illusory* – the fantasised possession of the phallus. For the phallus is not the penis, but its representation as symbol of power and desire – less a product of biological possession, than of patriarchal discourse. The phallus is not something men possess, but a seemingly timeless symbolic order, representing sexual difference and the law of the father, which holds women and men alike in its thrall.

It is the place of language within Lacan's theory that has seemed to some to suggest ways of exploring the connection between the psychic life of the unconscious and the social realities of male domination. As I have indicated, it has inspired a host of work in cinema, literature and cultural studies more generally, best illustrated by *Screen*, a British journal of film and television studies which was particularly influential in the 1970s. Many of the appropriations of Lacan in cultural studies, however, do not depend to any great extent on the deeper structure of his theory, but rather use it as a starting point for the exposure of a universal and ubiquitous cultural phallocentrism. Images of men and masculinity are displayed, explored and exposed, as in, for example, Richard Dyer's study of the male pin-up, which illustrates the symbolic association of male power and the phallus. Dyer draws attention to the empirical research of the psychologist Nancy Henley, which reveals that in any distanced and public situation men tend to stare at women, women to avert their eyes. In one to one conversation, however, men more often avoid eye contact, while women watch men attentively. Both dispositions confirm male power. Staring is used to assert dominance; not looking while listening is a denial of importance ('Look at me, when I talk to you,' the authority demands.)[21]

This creates special tensions in images of men available to women – whether publicity photos, portraits, drawings, paintings, sculptures or pin-ups. Men being looked at by women violates the code that men do the looking in public places; accordingly men subjected to the inquiring gaze will be presented as though unaware of the viewer. As Margaret Walters has shown in her study *The Male Nude*, male poses more often than not look away from the viewer, suggesting not (as in images of women) that the man is modestly avoiding the eyes of the viewer; but rather that his interest lies elsewhere.[22] As Dyer's graphics confirm, when focusing on the viewer the male gaze appears to stare straight back, through and beyond him or her, whereas the female looks invitingly at the viewer. In accordance with the Lacanian motif, the male look is made to appear active, able to penetrate, and not passive, susceptible to penetration. It conveys the phallic function. Disavowing passivity, images of men are often images of men in action – playing sport, at work – or at least tightening the muscles ready for action.[23]

Sport provides the commonest contemporary source of male imagery, and not only of sportsmen. The acceptable male image suggests – in its body's pose, its clothes and general paraphernalia – muscles, hardness, action. Dyer is clear that it is precisely because the penis isn't a patch on the phallus, can never live up to the mystique implied by it, that we find such excess, even a 'hysterical quality' in so much male imagery: 'The clenched fist, the bulging muscles, the hardened jaws, the proliferation of phallic symbols – they are all straining after what can hardly ever be achieved, the embodiment of the phallic mystique.'[24] The strain and instability of a masculinity which must forever remain tough, hard and active, even in repose, as the object of our gaze, is almost comical. Dyer displays for us, for example, a 'hysterically phallic' portrait of Bogart, pipe in hand, staring firmly into space, and surrounded by hound dog, tennis racket, trophies, grizzly bear's head, sailing boat, tripod and more. But is he, even so, male *enough*?

It is only too easy to present the dominant male image which saturates our culture, from Westerns to Y-fronts, as one which portrays and appeals to men as active, tough, desiring, omnipotent. It seems inevitable that these ruling, invasive images of the 'male', with the 'female' as their subordinated object, form part of the construction of our identities. They provide the meanings which tell us what it is to be a man – or not a man. And yet, thus informed by Lacan, are we any nearer to knowing how the male symbol – active, powerful, desiring – gains its force in the first place? If language is to be our guide, can Lacanian semiotics, with its transhistorical, universal Law of the Father, provide a convincing explanation?

The Limits of Lacan

The first problem, characteristic of all psychoanalytic thinking, but most extravagant in the Lacanian version, is its indifference to any particular historical processes. Not only does Lacan neglect the significance of the realities and constraints of material factors as they might affect the role and behaviour of actual fathers and mothers; but he offers a completely ahistorical account of how meanings and identities are produced in language. The second problem, consequently, is that the primacy Lacan attributes to language in its determination of psychic forces is itself unconvincing. As Francoise Gadet has shown, Lacan's use of Saussurian linguistics to indicate the primacy of the signifier is a misinterpretation – for Saussure the signifier and the signified are of equal significance.[25] Most importantly of all, the phallus as transcendental signifier renders all differences other than genital literally insignificant. The considerable, specific contribution of class, age, race, region and sexual orientation to sexual identity is inconsequential in Lacanian analysis. The deeper movement of Lacan's thought operates at a level which is neither psychological, sociological nor political so much as metaphysical – a largely Hegelian-derived metaphysics of consciousness, influenced by the 'existentialist' thought of Heidegger, and then wedded to structuralist methodological principles.[26] And there are problems with Lacanian thought even as a metaphysics.[27]

For the purposes of this book, however, the most problematic feature of Lacanian analysis is that it does not address the possibility of transformation in the construction of masculinity, or display any interest in the power relations of gender: the Law of the Father and the negative definition of woman as 'not-whole', the 'object' of the phallus, are simply our eternal birthright – endlessly rediscovered in the analysis of all systems of representation. This is not, of course, to deny the centrality of the idea of cultural phallocentrism – far from it. Nor is it to deny the importance of language, which, as Lacan asserts, is not a neutral vehicle for communication, but already contains and thus symbolically erects the hierarchies of phallocentric culture. It is rather to suggest that Lacan gets us little further than the identification of the problem. But then, for Lacan, the identification of the problem is as far as we can get.

Lacan sees the symbolic order, with its single privileged signifier, as the transcendental ground of all meaning; the concrete specificity of particular material relations of personal life, labour, power and political struggle, do not impinge upon the manifestations of this single symbolic relation. (Indeed, women influenced by Lacan, like Antoinette Fouque of the *psych et pol* group, have frequently used his ideas to dismiss as 'feminist illusion' women's search for equality with men.[28] In contrast to Freud's careful tracing of the precarious construction of sexual identity in his case studies, we find no reference in Lacan's writing to the empirical data of particular case histories. The efficacy of the phallus in constructing sexual hierarchy rests solely on the power of the symbol: 'All legitimate power,' Lacan argues, 'like any kind of power, is always based on the symbol.'[29] But while it is true that power always has a symbolic dimension, this is not its only dimension: Lacan's account of the absolute primacy of the symbolic is scarcely convincing.

Peter Dews illustrates its implausibility in discussing Lacan's own example of symbolic primacy – the power of the police. Contrary to policemen's own beliefs, this, according to Lacan, is not based upon sheer force:

> Like all other powers, [it] also rests on the symbol. As you have seen for yourself in periods of unrest, you would have let yourselves be arrested like little lambs if a guy had said to you *Police!* and showed a card, otherwise you would have punched him in the face as soon as he laid a finger on you.[30]

But this is simply wrong. As Dews retorts, there is no unbreakable pact between police and students. As Lacan should have seen for himself, the production of such ID might as readily invite aggression as enforce submission: *vive Mai '68!*[31] Symbolic power does not operate in splendid isolation from other social forces.

Others too have criticised the type of linguistic determinism found in Lacan.[32] Lacan treats language as a whole, because of its founding role in sexual difference, as limiting the inherent fluidity of meaning. And he treats language as the only domain of power. Yet language also interacts with other power relations in social life. We can at least *conceive* of routes beyond the continuous reproduction of phallic power in systems of representation. As I have argued elsewhere, however, we do not find these routes in the French feminist appropriations of Lacan, which, in my view, also fail to take us through and beyond Lacan's linguistic determinism and cultural phallocentrism.[33] Accepting Lacan's basic dualism and the absolute primacy of the symbol of the phallus, they merely invert it to celebrate a pre-symbolic, inchoate, oppositional sense of female difference – infantile disorder as a new order disruptive of the phallic regime.

Writers like Irigaray, for example, have attempted to move

beyond Lacan to explore a type of 'women's speech' based upon the construction and celebration of a 'feminine imaginary', which would exist outside phallocentric discourse and be linked with women's distinctive bodily experiences. The feminine imaginary, for Irigaray, is an expression of the genital morphology of the female body. Because women's 'sexe' is formed 'of two lips in continual contact', women's sexual pleasure is in every way more subtle, diversified and complex than is commonly imagined: 'women have sex organs more or less everywhere.'[34] However, the words to express the female body, to enable women to 'speak of their sex', are not part of existing phallocentric language, but pertain to a language yet to be invented.

The importance of Lacan's work lies in his perception that 'masculinity' (like 'femininity'), is irreducible to any fixed internal essence or any set of attributes (however sophisticated our conception of them may be as stable feminine, or as inverted masculine, internalisations of maternal features). It is not something which can be pinned down inside the personality. Nor can it be summed up in terms of any assigned set of roles. 'Masculinity' can only be illuminated through study of the relation of language and meanings to subjectivity and consciousness. In my view, however, what we need to explore is how meanings – especially the significance accorded to the phallus – intersect with the historically specific and changing power relations between women and men within the wider social structures and practices that produce them. Masculinity is more complex, though fortunately less abstract, than Lacan would have us believe. Masculinity and femininity cannot be understood separately from the wider concept of gender, which I would define, along with Mary McIntosh, 'as the individual, cultural and institutional ways in which biological sex is given social existence in any particular context and period.'[35]

The influence of Lacan but, more centrally, that of Michel Foucault, also appears in 'discourse theory', another contemporary strand of post-structuralist thought dealing with the question of sexual difference. Like Lacan, discourse theorists emphasise that masculinity and femininity refer neither to any collection of traits, nor to some set of stereotypical roles, but rather to the effects of discursive practices – conventional ways of conceiving and representing reality which serve to produce sexual difference in specific contexts of knowledge. These writers, like the feminist psychologists, Margaret Wetherall and Valerie Walkerdine, have been concerned to stress that various types of discourses set up contradictory positions for women and men, and thus undermine any unitary or coherent sexual identities, while nonetheless providing sites for resistance and struggle.[36] Discourse analysis thus seeks to substitute for Lacan's universal and eternal symbolic order a less ambitious emphasis on historically specific discourses.[37] Exploring specific discourses, these writers once again expose the male position as generally the dominant, active, authoritative one, the female as its object – but not without certain contradictory placings. Wendy Hollway, for example, dissects the 'male sex drive discourse', the 'have/hold discourse' and the 'permissive discourse', all of which serve to structure gender differences in contemporary discussions of sexuality. Women cannot be subjects in the first, and still dominant, discourse. They may assume an active, if often deviously active (out to 'trap' their man), role in the second. They are addressed as active, but may have trouble seeing themselves as such, in the third. The third discourse denies the meanings sexual experience carries for women as objects of the coercive and aggressive practices connected with the first discourse.[38]

Although more socially and historically grounded than orthodox Lacanianism, the idea of sexual difference in discourse theory has also been linked with an anti-realist epistemology. In the now defunct feminist journal *m/f*, one of its former editors Parveen Adams argues that 'as long as feminist theories of ideology work with a theory of representation within which representation is always a representation of reality, however attenuated a representation that may be, the analysis of sexual difference cannot be advanced.[39] For there are, apparently, no 'real', concrete reference-points outside systems of representation – in this case, outside those producing sexual difference. In contrast, I would argue for the importance of a form of realism wherein we must analyse the structures which generate the discourses and practices of phallocentrism and male power – while accepting that these structures cannot be identified independently of the way they manifest themselves in discourse. Reality is symbolically mediated, but we can nevertheless try to reconstruct that reality. Once we ask what social processes underlie gender relations and representations, we must move towards a complex integration of psychoanalytic accounts of family dynamics and unconscious motivations, on the one hand, and sociological analysis of social structures, practices and relationships, on the other. But outside of the feminist writing on mothering – which fails to place maternal practices within specific, historical contexts, instead reducing them to a single timeless institution – such an integration has rarely been attempted.

Gender and Power

Back in 1977 Andrew Tolson set out to discover the manner in which masculinity is institutionalised.[40] Drawing upon his interviews with different groups of men, he emphasised the significance of class differences in masculinity, and a work-based (rather than primarily family-based) culture of masculinity. Competitiveness, personal ambition, social responsibility and emotional restraint were described as the main ways whereby masculinity is patterned in middle-class families and other institutions of middle-class life – in particular, in public schools. The working-class boy, in contrast, is directed towards physical toughness, endurance and male bonding. Tolson drew upon a rather simplified Freudian Oedipal theory to suggest that the boy's ambivalent identification with the father as 'worker' was responsible for the ways in which the different contexts of labour affected masculinity:

> To the boy, masculinity is both mysterious and attractive (in its promise of a world of work and power), and yet, at the same time threatening (in its strangeness and emotional distance) . . . This simultaneous distance and attraction is internalized as a permanent emotional tension that the individual must, in some way, strive to overcome.[41]

The macho solidarity of the 'culture of work' of the working-class father produces a masculinity which not only provides compensations for men socially subordinated to other men, but also enables collective resistance and self-respect – forming the basis, for example, of trade union consciousness. Tolson gives the vivid example of the long-distance lorry driver, badly paid, never able to relax, who has to take some pride in his job just to be able to keep going: a pride based only upon the exclusion of those who are not up to the job – women, and 'soft' men. The bureaucratic masculinity linked to a middle-class work culture, on the other hand, emphasises duty and self-discipline. It is more a lonely inner struggle to achieve and assert one's will and authority over others. Tolson thus emphasises the links between the identifications of domestic life and the social system of work in capitalist society (through positing a somewhat over-simplified link between personality and social milieu reminiscent of role theory), and suggests two distinct types of masculinity (though again, he does not dwell on the contradictions within these contrasting masculine identities.) The same year as Tolson's book appeared, the sociologist Paul Willis published a rather similar account of how the acquisition of a positive working-class identity for men is synonymous with the embodiment of a type of masculine power:

> Manual labour is suffused with masculine qualities and given certain sensual overtones for 'the lads'. The toughness and awkwardness of physical work and effort . . . takes on masculine lights and depths and assumes a significance beyond itself.[42]

It is the work of the Australian sociologist Bob Connell, however, that provides the most ambitious attempt to date at some synthesis of a depth-psychological approach and a historically grounded account of social context and systems of representation. In embarking on a similar project here, I shall draw upon his structural framework, adding my own examples and reflections. *Gender and Power* ranges over a wide area, seeking to elaborate a social theory capable of weaving together personal life and social structure – something altogether more complex than the static conformity models of role theory.[43] Connell produces what he calls a 'theory of practice': a practice-based approach to personality whereby human agency is contextualised within the personal, intersubjective, discursive and broader structural dynamics of particular social groupings at particular moments. He draws primarily on psychoanalysis (with its rejection of any fixed sexual identity and its awareness of internal conflict), on sociology (with its emphasis on structures of labour and power), and on sexual politics (with its emphasis on the ongoing struggle between women and men). His goal is to explain the 'sheer intractability' of gender relations, while seeing that concrete relationships and practices do change. Reconstruction is possible – all the more so if we identify the central crises and conflicts in sexual identities and gender relations and construct appropriate strategies in response.

Connell identifies three main structures underlying relationships between women and men: labour, power and desire. These overlap and interconnect. The central institutions through which these structures operate – family, workplace, state, and all the rituals of public places and the street – each have their own 'gender regimes' for maintaining male authority. The maintenance of men's power over women, and related understandings of masculinity, are, on this account, not reducible to any single or primary cause. They are instead attributed to an overarching, historically rooted system which interlinks, and changes, along with the similarly historically grounded system of capitalist class divisions.

The first structure of this gender system, familiar from sociological writing, concerns divisions of labour. Here Connell lists housework, childcare, job segregation, unequal training, promotion and wages, and the relation between paid and unpaid work.[44] It was feminists, in the early seventies, who first argued that women's role in childcare is basic to the sexual division of labour, and the root cause of men's overall power over women – giving men greater freedom to participate in economic, cultural and political activity.[45] Like Tolson and Willis, or the more detailed investigations of Cynthia Cockburn, however, Connell makes it clear that different patterns of dominant masculinities and subordinated femininities are also produced in the workforce. Technical knowledge and expertise, for example, form one type of work-related masculinity, requiring total absorption in the development of skills uninterrupted by the demands of personal life. Unequal training – with various mechanisms for the exclusion of women – works together with women's workplace vulnerability (due to the constraints of their domestic routines), and men's unthinking assumptions of superiority (which express themselves in sexual put-downs and harassment of women) to create a less assured and less confident work-related femininity.[46]

These divisions of labour, however, do not operate without resistance, usually individual, but sometimes – as with feminist struggles – collective. The routines of, and resistance to, male power in domestic and paid work are themselves affected by changing technologies and labour processes, which shake up old divisions of labour in the capitalist search for profit. Male unemployment and the restructuring or dismantling of old industries create new crises in traditional patterns of male authority. Such disruption connects up in turn with cultural struggles over the meanings of 'masculinity' – meanings which are embedded in the habitual authority, technical expertise, sexual assertiveness and economic advantage of men in the day-to-day functioning of institutions like the workplace and trade unions, as well as the family.

Male dominance and the meanings of masculinity also interconnect with other power relations and patterns of emotional attachment outside divisions of labour. The second structure basic to gender relations which Connell identifies, here strongly in agreement with most contemporary feminist analysis, is that of power. This involves all the institutions of authority, control and coercion: the state and business hierarchies, institutional and interpersonal violence, sexual regulation and control, and domestic authority and its contestation. The way in which the state operates to institutionalise men's power has been widely discussed within feminist writing, including explorations of how welfare, taxation, benefits, and so on are all premised upon assumptions of female dependance on men.[47] It is men, often only men, who are to be found at the top of every state bureaucracy, just as it is overwhelmingly men who are 'captains' of industry. The murkier rituals of Masonic Lodges are not the only ones which serve to exclude women from business and state hierarchies. Men can also rely upon the exclusively male rituals of almost any club or society catering for the power élites of public life.[48]

The state institutions licensed to use violence – the military and the police – gain much of their legitimacy through appeals to heightened gender ideologies: strong,   protective' males must defend weak, passive, vulnerable females. Military training for men, for example, is explicitly designed to promote a particular type of aggressive masculinity – 'woman', 'cunt', 'queer' being the ubiquitous insults hurled by sergeant majors at each new recruit to 'toughen' him up for military manhood. As I have argued elsewhere, men's control over military technology and their role as professional fighters are concrete manifestations of the ideology and ritual of male dominance.[49] Military training of men, and its representation in cultural celebrations of a 'Top Gun', 'Rambo' masculinity, feed both a generalised misogyny and many men's acceptance (or use) of everyday violence against women – and other men.[50]

State and cultural regulation and control of sexuality has, as feminists have argued, been another central way in which men have asserted and maintained power over women. The denial of access to sex education, contraception and abortion facilities, the stigma and difficulties of mothering outside marriage – these have all served to inhibit, primarily, women's access to sexual pleasure free from accompanying anxieties. In Britain women's continuing battle, forever re-fought and only ever partially won, to secure the right to control their own fertility, is emblematic of their attempts to contest the overwhelmingly masculine state and medical regulation of female sexuality – a regulation in which dominant definitions of women's sexuality and women's bodies as reproductive vessels remain embedded.[51]

The state also plays a decisive role in regulating a hegemonic heterosexual masculinity. As we shall see again in chapter six, male homosexuality has been severely controlled and policed since the late nineteenth century – particularly in moments of panic over dominant forms of Western manhood, as we saw in the 1950s, and now once again in the 1980s, with official and unofficial attacks on homosexual people and practices. The state may no longer criminalise all forms of homosexuality in Britain (except in the armed services), yet through legislation on the age of consent, welfare practices as regards adoption, and in all forms of taxation and benefit arrangements, it denies legitimacy to homosexual relationships. The labelling and policing of gay men is one obvious way of constructing a compulsory and dominant heterosexual masculinity: a masculinity defined through difference from, and desire for, women; a masculinity depicted as sexually driven and uncontrollable in its relentless pursuit of women – in perpetual contrast to the depiction of the passive and restrained sexuality of the 'gentle sex'. Pointing to the historically variable nature of this production and policing of masculinity, however, Carrigan, Connell and Lee contrast the experiences of Chevalier d'Eon, who enjoyed an active political career dressed as a woman, with the martyrdom of Oscar Wilde a century later.[52]

Men's position at the top of all state and business hierarchies has not, however, gone entirely unchallenged in recent years. Over the last decade, the number of women enrolling in law schools, in medicine, business and other professional fields has steadily risen.[53] Some women have moved into central positions in local government and risen up trade union hierarchies. Culturally, at least, a feminist challenge to the inevitability of male élites governing public life, and regulating 'private' life, has been issued.[54] Strategically, mechanisms for positive discrimination, female quota systems and other means of chipping away at the male face of authority have been studied, and occasionally implemented.

Maintenance of men's power in the family is arguably the most diverse in its forms, and the most strongly contested. While still upheld and partially reinforced by the state, that institution seems less able than ever to provide a stable base for male authority, riven as it habitually is by tension and turmoil between men and women, parents and children. It has been clear for several decades now, from divorce statistics alone, that the time is out of joint with conventional family life: the only family form which is growing in numbers is one-parent (female-headed) households.[55] As ever more married women leave the home to work, men, it seems, feel neglected and threatened by 'working' wives. Andrew Cherlin reported from several studies in the United States that the 'greater the wife's annual earnings ... the greater was the probability that the family would separate.'[56] As Andrew Hacker suggests, wives who work 'are not the cause of divorce so much as their husbands who still expect to hold center stage.'[57]

Yet, however inflexible their needs and demands, it remains the case that men's advantages in family life are only gradually eroding. Divorced men are more likely than their wives to remarry (twice as likely if in their forties) and, usually unencumbered by the children, their financial prospects are far superior to their wives. The gender and generational conflicts of contemporary family life, nevertheless, are here to stay. Placed alongside and interacting with changing labour markets and challenges to men's monopoly of state and cultural authority, they constitute one of the central crises of contemporary masculinity. The capitalist economy itself increasingly sets the individual against traditional family arrangements. Today, as more men can openly be seen to choose a homosexual way of life, and more women can more openly be seen to choose to live outside the once necessary 'protection' of male-headed households, traditional notions of masculinity are undermined. The dominant idea of a fixed and pure heterosexual masculinity, to which women and children are inescapably subordinated, once so securely grounded in the nuclear family, is, if not in crisis (as is often glibly claimed), at least a little less hegemonic than it has ever been before.

The shifting power men and women can wield over partners and children intermeshes with the third structure identified by Connell as underpinning gender relations: desire or the psychodynamics of emotional life. The nuclear family, by law and custom affirming a heterosexual male authority over women and children, is the institution regarded as primarily responsible for the immediate regulation of desire. Patterns of desire, desirability and object choice moulded within the family extend beyond that institution to permeate the wider world of labour and authority. Connell examines the construction of, and connections between, heterosexuality and homosexuality, the antagonisms of gender (man-hating, woman-hating and self-hatred), and the emotional dynamics of marriage, sexual relationships and childrearing.[58] The patterning of desire concerns the prohibitions and incentives which surround it: the incest taboo, age of consent, sanctions against homosexuality and the laws on rape, on the one hand, the ideologies of family life, romance and pleasure, on the other.

Desire, as we have already seen and will see again throughout this book, plays a central role in constructing 'masculinity' and affirming or subverting men's power and authority. The polarities of male and female, heterosexual and homosexual, are the pivot of contemporary Western thinking on sex. Sex is about sexual difference, the desire for the 'opposite' sex. When North American gay novelist Edmund White declares, in his semi-autobiographical story of a homosexual boy, 'It was men, not women, who struck me as foreign and desirable',[59] he knows he is a sexual outcast: 'I never doubted that homosexuality was a sickness; in fact, I took it as a measure of how unsparingly objective I was that I could contemplate this very sickness.'[60] At other times, in other places, as we now know from historical research on homosexuality, he would have thought differently.[61] And, at whatever historical moment, desire must always be located within the more general patterns of male dominance – men's place in the workforce, their higher pay and superior training, their visibility in positions of power, their role in legitimate state violence and the learning of physical skills embedded in muscular bodies, their regulation of women's sexuality, and so on. These are the social and historical realities through which sexual difference, and along with it desire, acquire their meaning and significance.

Writing up his experiences from nearly twenty years as a psychiatrist and psychoanalyst, and seeking an approach which is broader than the psychological and yet encompasses it, Joel Kovel provides us with a case history of 'Curtis' – a rich and powerful investment banker. Curtis is heterosexual, 'fiendishly' interested in money for its own sake, a workaholic, desperate for power, and desperately unhappy. Like a neurotic (rather than psychotic) 'Wolf Man', Curtis's fantasies (which he recognises as fantasies) are beset by demons, in the form of powerful men, who would nail him to a rack and pull his insides out. Kovel uncovers Curtis's wish to be assaulted anally and subdued by a powerful man, alongside a desire to be that powerful man and penetrate his victim. Kovel links both wishes to his patient's impoverished relationship with his father, who became ill and died when Curtis was in his teens. But Kovel departs from psychoanalytic discourse to insist that Curtis's repressed wishes for his father, and the demons that trouble him, exist in the form they do because of the hierarchical estrangements of the bank and the public sphere Curtis inhabits:

> It was not the father that did this . . . Curtis would not suffer neurotically, work like a fiend, repress his lovingness, twist his bodily experience into knots, and be constantly depressed were he not in a situation which makes him constantly estranged from others . . . The demon resides at the bank too, as it is the real world of work and current associations that perpetually structures the infantile complexes initially established in the family.[62]

Writers like Kovel and Connell have – from opposite directions – begun to pioneer ways of thinking about the links between the psychic and the social, without undermining the autonomy of the two spheres. There are, however, certain problems with Connell's analysis of the three dimensions of gender hierarchy as three distinct types of *'structures'*, since each refers to a different type of category. It is not just that these three aspects of social relations interconnect, but power and desire would appear to be dimensions or aspects of all structures, whereas labour seems to refer to a specific structure – as does the state and language and representation. (These three specific structures, however, would take us back to the Althusserian framework of the economic, political and ideological, which Connell wants to move beyond.) The solution is perhaps to avoid any tripartite structural divisions for a more flexible naming of the central dynamics of gender hierarchy. Power, surely, is everywhere – in the economic, the political and the interpersonal; desire, and its opposites, fear and loathing, are similarly ubiquitous.

Reflecting upon the polarities of desire – heterosexual and homosexual – it is immediately clear from psychoanalytic work that the creation of heterosexual desire, heterosexual masculinity, is far from preordained. Masculinity is never the undivided, seamless construction it becomes in its symbolic manifestation. The promise of phallic power is precisely this guarantee of total inner coherence, of an unbroken and unbreakable, an unquestioned and unquestionable masculinity. Deprived of it, how can men be assured of 'natural' dominance? The antagonisms of gender coalesce with the strains of affirming and maintaining sexual polarities. That, at least, is the case for men. And it is clear that the cultural expression of misogyny eclipses any equivalent discourse of man-hating: indeed, 'misanthropy' refers to humanity in general, there is no female linguistic counterpart to it. Man-hating, devoid of institutional backing, cultural representation or social significance, is reduced to an amusing, pitiable, individual quirk.

The constant pressure to confirm masculinity in its difference from femininity may also explain why it is only when men are seen at their most unquestionably masculine – as soldiers in combat, as footballers in action – that they can embrace, weep, display what Western manhood depicts as more feminine feelings and behaviour. (On the football terraces a rather more hysterically macho masculinity prevails.) Intimacy with other men can also represent a threat to masculinity. It is common for men to have few, or no, intimate male friends, and to treat men in general with suspicion, despite the spaces provided for male bonding; too close, men become their own potential enemies.[63]

I have argued that it is only with the insights of psychoanalysis that the intensities of men's paranoia over masculinity, their endemic violence towards women, and the cultural fear and hatred of women become comprehensible. But it is also only by placing the psychology of men within the social context of those broader patterns of existence which maintain and disrupt male domination that we can understand the contemporary dilemmas of masculinity. Therein we also discover clues to the difficulties of the struggle to establish and maintain a hegemonic, heterosexual masculinity. Masculinity is surrounded by its enemies, as Antony Easthope illustrates in his survey of the masculine myths of popular culture: 'Within, femininity and male homosexual desire must be denied; without, women and the feminine must be subordinated and held in place.'[64] These are far from easy tasks to accomplish.

5. Competing Masculinities (I): Manliness – The Masculine Ideal

'Masculinity' and 'femininity' are constructs specific to historical time and place. They are categories continually being forged, contested, reworked and reaffirmed in social institutions and practices as well as a range of ideologies. Among these conflicting definitions there is always space for negotiation and change although often differing interpretations are covered by a seemingly unified 'common sense'. Violations of gender boundaries by either men or women were, and are, subject to sanctions ranging from ridicule to violence.

Leonore Davidoff and Catherine Hall[1]

'Being a man,' we learn from Norman Mailer, 'is the continuing battle of one's life.'[2] Like the Arthurian knight at arms, forever at war, with oneself, with women, with honour, the contemporary guardians of true manhood still believe that living one's life as a man involves toughness, struggle and conquest. Man is forever at war because, as Mailer once again informs us, he 'can hardly ever assume he has *become* a man'.[3] To understand men's contemporary anxieties over manliness, it helps to locate them historically. The interplay between power, labour and desire, which we looked at in the last chapter, are themselves historically constructed and historically changing. Recently, Western historians have begun to show a new interest in charting the history of modern concepts of 'manhood', looking back to the nineteenth century as 'the crucible in which our contemporary understandings of masculinity and femininity were forged'.[4]

On the rise from the eighteenth century, the triumph of bourgeois culture in the nineteenth century brought with it a new moral and religious enterprise.[5] Bourgeois ideals of 'Christian manliness' stressed spiritual, cerebral and moral precepts, as well as the dignity of labour and the importance of manly independence and autonomy. Competing with the Christian manliness of the early nineteenth century, however, an increasing stress on sport and physical strenuousness was to produce the celebration (and occasional condemnation) of a more spartan, athletic and conformist 'muscular manliness' by the close of the century.[6]

Learning about Manhood: Historical Reflections

The cultural ascendency of the English middle-class throughout the nineteenth century was accompanied by a continuous restructuring of familial and sexual relations. The new middle-class family, as Leonore Davidoff and Catherine Hall illustrate so well in *Family Fortunes*, had its own idyll of domestic harmony: a vision of the home as a haven of domestic comfort and moral strength.[7] The home would provide the requisite moral strength to make the monogamous bourgeois family the foundation of a stable, industrious society: 'The goal of all the bustle of the market place was to provide a proper moral and religious life for the family.'[8] Together with an ideology of hard work and thrift (alongside a critique of aristocratic hedonism, sensuousness, idleness and effeminacy), this entailed a far greater emphasis on psychological differences between men and women, and an ever-widening gulf between the private 'feminine' sphere of the household and the public 'masculine' world of the market. Within families it meant increased economic dependency for the wife, greater stress on the significance of marital – as opposed to extra-marital – sexuality (though with the wife's sexuality always seen in terms of the husband's sexual needs), and more emotional investment in children (reflecting also the growing concern with population and the production of young men trained for the demanding world of industrial capitalism).

In his prose and poetry Matthew Arnold gave expression to the high moral, emotional and intellectual seriousness and sensibility of Christian manhood acquired from the teachings of his father, Dr Thomas Arnold, headmaster of Rugby in the early nineteenth century. A somewhat mocking sister captured his style: 'Matt is stretched at full length on one sofa, reading a Christian tale of Mrs Gaskell's which moves him to tears, and the tears to complacent admiration of his own sensibility.'[9] Whereas 'masculinity' for the old aristocracy had signified sporting and military honour, bourgeois Christian manhood was initially more attuned to the articulation of a type of tenderness and intellectual earnestness. As this new ideal spread through provincial England from the late eighteenth century, 'to become the triumphant common sense of the Victorian age', the new man of his day was trained to be clean, modest, neat, restrained in voice and physicality.[10]

This Arnoldian emphasis on intellectual and emotional earnestness, influenced as it had itself been by the works of men like Samuel Taylor Coleridge, was soon competing with far harsher versions of nineteenth-century, middle-class masculinity. Thomas Carlyle, the Grand Old Man of English letters, played a major role in articulating the notion of English manliness based upon 'toughness of muscle' and 'toughness of heart' in mid-Victorian England. Scorning the 'wisdom of philosophers', Carlyle declared: 'Man is created to fight.'[11] His praise for a pugilistic English masculinity was echoed and preached by the Reverend Charles Kingsley. Like Carlyle, who celebrated strong and inarticulate heroes, Kingsley rejected 'morbid introspection' and emotional display to praise physical strength, courage and health.[12] It was Kingsley's Christian manliness, verging at times on brutality, which was derided by its critics – like Leslie Stephen (the father of Virginia Woolf) – as mere 'muscular Christianity'.[13] But it was immortalised by Kingsley's friend, and fellow Christian socialist, Thomas Hughes, whose classic *Tom Brown's Schooldays* (1857) was to become mandatory reading for every British and American schoolboy:

> After all, what would life be without fighting, I should like to know? From the cradle to the grave, fighting, rightly understood, is the business, the real, highest, honestest business of every son of man.[14]

While we cannot neatly periodise early and late-Victorian ideals of manhood (nor those of any other epoch), it is nevertheless evident that competition between competing ideals intensified with the increasing glorification of a more muscular, militaristic masculinity, in alliance with British imperialist expansion in the late Victorian era. According to Norman Vance in his study of Christian manliness in Victorian literature:

> After *Tom Brown's Schooldays* the history of manliness in Victorian public schools and public-school literature crucially involves the issues of games and militarism, while Christianity gradually drops out of the picture. But the terms in which these are discussed owe more to contemporary circumstances than to the perennially interesting but increasingly out-of-date adventures of Tom Browne.[15]

Shelley, Keats and even Shakespeare, were to be attacked as weak, morbid and effeminate – along with most other manifestations of artistic or intellectual activity – by the late-Victorian storm-troopers of a new aggressive masculinity. Darwin's theory of evolution, also popularised during the late nineteenth century, seemed to establish the 'scientific' basis for the necessary elimination of the weak by the strong. It served, as we shall see in chapter seven, to strengthen British racist and imperialist ideologies at home and abroad, all premised upon the continual assertion of the 'natural' superiority of English manhood.

The rigid athleticism dominant in late nineteenth-century ideals of manliness in Britain and America has been explained by most historians, like James Walvin, in terms of public concern about men's physical weakness at a time of expanding imperial conquests and increasing demands on the defence of existing colonial territories.[16] Other studies of this period, like that of the North American historian, Jeffrey Hantover, have pointed to a crisis of masculinity in Britain and the United States fuelled by the very success of the bourgeois vision – the intensely feminine atmosphere of the middle-class home.[17] As well, in both Britain and North America (though with somewhat different class and gender nuances in the two countries), there was a move to salvage some of the open-air life of the countryside in the new and less healthy urban environments.[18] With the 'feminine' increasingly associated with physical weakness and emotionality, the 'masculine' with physical strength and self-reliance, 'Men,' as Jeffrey Weeks comments, 'no longer dared embrace in public or shed tears.'[19] To be a man in the late nineteenth century, as contemporary dissenters, like Edward Carpenter complained in *Love's Coming of Age*, was 'to conceal all signs of love or tenderness of affection', and to cultivate, instead, an outwardly brutal masculinity.[20]

This new ideal of manhood, based on physical fitness, courage and audacity, was instilled most directly in the public schools, especially after the great expansion of the education system for middle-class boys in the mid nineteenth century.[21] As Christine Heward illustrates from her study of English public schools, rigid conformity and discipline were effected through compulsory team games, military training, poor food and spartan conditions. The harshness of this school regime reached its peak before the First World War and entered into a decline, though far from disappeared, after the 1920s.[22] Former Arnoldian ideas of scholarship and morality had been replaced by a near ubiquitous insistence on physical fitness, courage and the suppression of emotion, invariably making a boy's life in the public schools 'a physical and psychological struggle for survival against hunger, cold and callousness in one form or another'.[23] As Henry Salt, the headmaster of Eton, declared on his resignation in 1885, his boys had learnt to be 'irretrievably unintellectual'.[24] His successor, Edmund Warre, was a fanatical sportsman, as was Edward Thring at Uppingham and G.E.L.Cotton at Marlborough during the same period.[25] From 1870 to 1914, educational historian Brian Simon concludes, originality and creativity of thought were being stifled in the English public schools, producing a 'loyal, honest and self-confident' manhood, contemptuous of imagination, sensibility and critical reflection.[26] (A parallel emphasis on organised athletics was introduced by American educational theorists for middle-class boys in the late nineteenth century.[27]

We have many descriptions of the effectiveness of this toughening regime in men's autobiographical writing, along with its pain and destructiveness. Leonard Woolf, for example, describes how public school imposed on him a carapace to conceal his inner intellectual and emotional life:

> I suspect that the male carapace is usually grown to conceal cowardice . . . . It was the fear of ridicule or disapproval if one revealed one's real thoughts or feelings, and sometimes the fear of revealing one's fears, that prompted one to invent that kind of second-hand version of oneself which might provide for one's original self

the safety of a permanent alibi . . . it was this vulnerable inhabitant of our bodies over which the irresistable steam-roller of society pounded in whatever private or public school to which our parents happened to have sent us, flattening us all out in the image of manliness or gentlemanliness which our parents or lords and masters considered appropriate.[28]

Similar thoughts are echoed by the writer Gerald Brennan, who concludes:

Let me give the school its due. It shot me out into the world in a frame of mind to discover bearable conditions anywhere. Even in the worst moments of war I comforted myself that anyhow I was no longer at Radley. For those shells and bullets whose noises filled the air were inanimate objects discharged by an impartial hand; they did not come at me dressed in the malignancy of the human face.[29]

Today the games-cult of British public schools no longer enjoys the exalted status it once had, but, as Vance tells us, it took a long time to die: 'Perhaps it lingers still'.[30] The rigours of public-school life may have declined since the 1920s, but old Etonians right up to the 1970s recall the appalling cold, terrible food, constant bullying and terrible beatings they had to endure as young pupils. As Derek Malcolm testifies: 'I was endlessly cold and endlessly miserable, and endlessly frightened among my peers.'[31] At the same time they almost all express the sense of 'effortless superiority' acquired at Eton, and in particular the confident, arrogant wielding of total power and control over the lives of other boys experienced by so many of them in their senior years: 'You will never, ever in your whole life, be in a position of such unchallenged superiority and control as you are if you're a boy in Pop [the most prestigious group of senior boys at Eton],' writes David Thomas, a pupil there in the 1970s.[32] In short, hierarchy and competition have remained the prevailing ethos, and, as of old, a continued emphasis on sport, along with 'a battening down of any emotional response,' David Thomas also affirms.[33]

Outside the middle-class world of schooling, attempts were also being made in Victorian times to promote the ideals of bourgeois manhood within the working class. The pride of the respectable working-class man lay in his entrance into a decent job with the prospect of being able to provide for his dependants. Entrance into an apprenticeship, seen as a 'time of servitude' when adolescent 'lads', particularly at first, would be subjected to various humiliations from the older men, was a necessary but never sufficient guarantee of future economic security, and hence the transition to manhood.[34] For, as we shall see in chapter ten, the status of the respectable working man (still a small minority of the English working-class in the late nineteenth century) rested upon the exclusion of women from skilled jobs – to counter employers' strategies for cheapening labour-power – and upon female dependency in the household.[35] Christian socialists like Thomas Hughes worked with the early working men's associations of the struggling trade-union movement in the 1860s and 1870s promoting his version of public-school manliness: strenuous physical work and co-operative team spirit, within a rhetoric of universal brotherhood.[36]

The strategies for survival for most of the working class, however, could not rest upon a man's ability to maintain his family through his own labour – wives and daughters would all need to seek whatever work they could get. But attempts to promote middle-class ideals of manliness amongst the labouring poor were nevertheless pursued through settlement houses, boys' clubs and Boy Scouts from late Victorian and Edwardian into modern times. Lower-middle-class and aspiring working-class parents did encourage such pursuits, but for the majority of young working-class men manliness remained synonymous with what their would-be educators described as 'hooliganism': 'the manly was to be reached through swaggering, brawling and the oblivion produced through alcohol or violence'.[37] The term 'hooligan' made its appearance in English newspapers in the late 1890s, with reference to street gangs and troublesome male youth.[38] Seen as essentially un-English (as the Irish name Houlihan, from which hooligan derives, implies), these were the young men whose 'manly' pugnacity was channelled not into subduing the 'barbarian' abroad, but into manifesting the 'barbarian' spirit at home. Baden-Powell always believed, as he wrote in 1910, that his scouting movement was the one force which could redeem the enemy within: turn working-class 'hooligans' into 'fellows of character . . . instead of being absolute waste material, fit only to be buried'.[39] It could do this, that is, by following the codes of the public school – by placing youths in the right uniform, by instilling discipline through organised drill and sporting activities. Male working-class youth was less convinced, occasionally hurling stones at the Boy Scouts and mocking their uniform.[40] However, Baden-Powell was not altogether wrong to perceive in the rough, tough pugnacity necessary for survival on the streets of London at the turn of the century something analogous to the muscular, militaristic, masculinity then being promoted in the English public schools, or their equivalent in America.

The period 1870 to 1914 has come to be seen as a turning point in Anglo-Saxon ideologies of manhood. Baden-Powell in Britain, and Theodore Roosevelt in North America exemplified the sporting, hunting, patriotic and conformist 'virtues' of the new imperialistic, all-conquering, white manhood. It was a heritage young Ernest Hemingway, for half-a-century the self-conscious possessor of the most popular image of Western manhood, was to live out to the full.

Tough Guys: The Pursuit of Heroism

For Norman Mailer, as for most mid-twentieth century Americans (indeed for a whole post-war world increasingly in the thrall of North American cultural imperialism), Ernest Hemingway was the man who both embodied and fictionalised true virility. As John Updike commented in the early seventies, 'An entire generation of American men learned to speak in the accents of (his) stoicism.'[41] His work – the action-packed, concrete, laconic prose – and his life – the boxing, big-game hunting, shooting, fishing, drinking, swearing, whoring champion of any and every manly pursuit – were both crafted to teach the world the meaning of manhood: tough, patriotic, North American masculinity. In dedicating his life and work to the legend of his own masculinity, 'Papa' Hemingway (as he liked to be called from the age of twenty-seven) provides us with the measure of its limitations. His chronic depression, insomnia, habitual lying and self-deception, self-dramatisation, ferocious envy, bullying competitiveness and vicious humiliation of friends and foe alike, were always present for the discerning eye to behold. Increasingly, full-blooded masculinity assumed the form of full-blown paranoia, self-destruction, and fear of, yet longing for, death – culminating in break-down and suicide.

Just a few of his contemporaries, like Gertrude Stein and Zelda Fitzgerald, had seen from quite early on that the Hemingway style of life and prose protested its masculinity just a little too much not to convey an underlying insecurity. He had spawned a whole school of fiction writers in his image, but it was 'a literary style', the critic Max Eastman suggested, 'of wearing false hair on his chest'.[42] However, it was not until long after his violent death (described by Mailer as 'the most difficult death in America since Roosevelt's', because it called into question the 'bravery' of the life)[43], that the evidence of 'Papa's' savagely subdued passivity and 'feminine' longings were to be fully revealed. In the posthumously published *The Garden of Eden* (extracted from the interminably long manuscript its author had worked on for fifteen years without nearing completion), the signs of pleasure in sexual passivity and cross-sexual identification – not entirely lacking in the earlier writing – are allowed full play. Here, in the most erotic writing he ever produced, the hero, David Bourne, is persuaded by his strong-willed and increasingly wild young wife – who has always wanted to be a boy – into occasionally pretending to be a girl. The wife crops her hair like a boy's, declares herself a boy, and makes love to David as though he is a girl, while David – joyfully conscious of 'the weight and strangeness inside' – is told and feels:

> You are changing . . . Oh you are. You are. Yes you are and you're my girl . . . Will you change and be my girl and let me take you?[44]

This scene, according to Hemingway's latest biographer Kenneth Lynn, is reminiscent of Hemingway's diary accounts of his own happiest sexual engagements with his fourth wife, Mary. As he recorded in 1948, she:

> Has always wanted to be a boy and thinks as a boy . . . loves me to be her girls (sic), which I love to be, not being absolutely stupid . . . I loved to feel the embrace of Mary which came to me as something quite new and outside all tribal law. On the night of December 19th we worked out these things and I have never been happier.[45]

Yet for Hemingway this male passivity and 'feminine' identification were usually rapidly transformed from eroticism into aggression –

leading him to treat each of his verbally abused and humiliated wives, in Mary's words, in 'the role of a whipping boy'.[46] These conflicts, Lynn states, tormented him throughout his life, threatening his self-proclaimed seamless masculinity. Hemingway's sexual vulnerability and anxieties over his own manhood underlay his incessant theatrical bragging, lying bravado – bordering at times on the lunatic – and his incessant accusations of sterility, impotence and homosexuality against others, friends and foes alike. They were the hidden truth behind Hemingway's prevailing nightmare that he was, at some level, just a coward – 'the worst luck any man could have'.[47]

Lynn's explanation of Hemingway's torments looks to his child-hood: 'Thanks to the manipulations of his mother, Hemingway did not enjoy a normal childhood.'[48] His mother, Grace Hemingway, put her son in frocks until the age of two, and liked to dress and treat Ernest and his older sister as though they were twins of the same sex, sometimes little girls, sometimes little boys. Moreover, this mother dominated a sport-loving, hard-working husband, who, facing old age and illness, would shame his son with the 'cowardice' of committing suicide. But Lynn's insistence on Hemingway as a man 'whose own sexual integrity had been tampered with' by a dominating, manipulative mother from whose influence he could never feel free (and whom he certainly did claim to hate throughout his adult life), seems to me overstated.[49] After all, it was not so unusual for mothers at the turn of the century to dress their infant sons in frocks, or for that matter, to have more forceful personalities than their husbands.

It is undeniable that Hemingway feared and repressed his own more passive, 'feminine' emotions. It is scarcely surprising, how-ever, that such contradictory emotions should be present in this tough-as-nails man; unless we are attached to some theoretically simplistic bioligical theory of gender, we would surely expect this to be the case, at least in some degree. Perhaps there was an unusually extreme psychopathology behind Hemingway's relentless search for proof of manhood, as his final decline into paranoia and suicide suggests. But if so, the 'abnormal', as ever, reveals truths about the 'normal'. What interests me about Hemingway's living out his life as a man is what it reveals about our ideal of 'normal' masculinity. The cultural pressures of becoming a legend in his own lifetime forced Hemingway to enact the normal stereotype. Taking it literally and to the extreme, his life exposes the inevitable abnormality of such a position. It could be that, having decided to live out his own legend as archetypal male hero (which did, after all, bring him fame, fortune and the love of beautiful women), he was haunted by the sheer impossibility of actualising the myth in a manner free from deception and pretence. 'He has the most profound bravery that it has ever been my privilege to see,' Dorothy Parker had proclaimed in her profile of him in the *New Yorker* in 1929, where she confessed that she felt towards him the type of reverence a tourist feels at the majestic sight of a Grand Canyon sunset![50] Not being, as he tells us, absolutely stupid, he could not but be at least partially aware that his self-dramatisation was theatrical charlatanism. But not being, as his writing also tells us, prone to deep self-reflection, he could not see – as he opened jammed doors with his head, 'won' his boxing matches by playing 'dirty', and lied his way to Hell and back – the ineluctably mythic quality of the masculinity he represented. No man could be 'as male as all that', Zelda Fitzgerald observed of Hemingway, feeling also that there was something ambiguous about his relationship with her husband – even suspecting (wrongly, according to the biographers) that they could have been lovers.[51]

Hemingway's struggles with his male identity highlight a real dilemma: a 'pure' masculinity cannot be asserted *except* in relation to what is defined as its opposite. It depends upon the perpetual renunciation of 'femininity'. No one can be 'that male' without constantly doing violence to many of the most basic human attributes: the capacity for sensitivity to oneself and others, for tenderness and empathy, the reality of fear and weakness, the pleasures of passivity – all, of course, quintessentially 'feminine'. So while the 'feminine' may be dispatched in the insouciant bravado of masculine endeavour, it will always return to haunt the conquering hero. Hence, Hemingway's life-long fear of his mother, 'the bitch'; hence Norman Mailer's fictional (and once attempted) murder of the 'great bitch,' woman[52]; hence, finally, the furious search for manhood by Japanese homosexual writer, self-styled general and right-wing fanatic, Yukio Mishima, which engendered his desire to purge the self of all awareness in order to become a wholly masculine object, a whole man – something possible, he concluded, and acted out, only at the moment of self-extinction, the moment of death.[53]

'Martial Men': the Appeal of Fascism

'There is a certain gesture of virility, be it one's own or someone else's,' the cultural critic and philosopher Theodore Adorno noted back in 1944, 'that calls for suspicion.'[54] Attuned to cultural contradiction as he was, the presence of such contradiction in the assertion of masculinity seemed obvious: 'In the end the tough guys are the truly effeminate ones, who need the weaklings as their victims in order not to admit that they are like them ... the opposites of the strong man and compliant youth merge in an order which asserts unalloyed the male principle of domination'.[55] Adorno and the other members of the Frankfurt school were among the first to analyse the growth and triumph of Nazism in Germany, in studies of the authoritarian family begun in the 1930s. Fascism, they argued, appealed to the authoritarian personality type: people who, having been harshly disciplined by parental figures in child-hood, repressed both their own sexual impulses and their hostility towards their parents, to project sexuality and displace aggression onto anyone who could be seen as weak or powerless.[56]

Using psychoanalytic reasoning, and in-depth interviews (bizarrely mixed with quantitative, largely transparent, behaviouristic questionnaire techniques of measurement), *The Authoritarian Personality*, when it finally appeared during the Cold War era in the US in 1950, took a more anodyne form than that of the original research. It identified nine traits of the authoritarian character thought to underlie a predisposition to fascism: rigid adherence to conventionalism, authoritarian submission, authoritarian aggression, opposition to subjective and imaginative reflection, superstition and rigid stereotyping, preoccupation with power and toughness/dominance and submission, generalised destructiveness and cynicism, projection of dangerous impulses onto others, and an exaggerated concern with sex.[57]

The work of Adorno *et al* did not address the issue of gender, but the authoritarian character has since been characterised as quintessentially masculine – the masquerade of power concealing weak and dependent feelings through the assertion of strength and the rejection of everything gentle, spontaneous, soft, relaxed, chaotic (seen as intrinsically connected to the body, rather than the mind). It has been frequently alleged in consequence that 'fascism, fully revealed, is the extreme, exquisite expression of masculinism . . . the natural enemy of femininity, its quintessential opposite.'[58] Fascism, on this reading, is the product of men living masculinity to its logical extreme.[59] Such an analysis can be found in Klaus Theweleit's compendious and enormously influential book *Male Fantasies*, which became a bestseller in Germany, where he explores fascism in terms of a style of masculine identity based upon the dread of women, sex and the body.

Theweleit opens his book – enlivened by photos, posters, poetry, and paintings – with a detailed textual analysis of the memoirs, letters and novels of a group of men who were part of the *Freikorps*. These were German officers and soldiers who did not return to civilian life at the close of the First World War, marked by the collapse of the Imperial Reich and the emergence of the Weimar Republic, but roamed the country to be hired by different authorities to suppress workers' uprisings and murder their leaders (the Spartacist uprising of 1923, for example, and the killing of Rosa Luxemburg). Many of them joined the National Socialist movement, and played a crucial role in its success. Their writings, Theweleit suggests, not only evince the real fears and obsessions of the proto-fascist, but perhaps also the inner motivation of masculine identity in general: 'Is it true, as many feminists claim, that fascism is simply the norm for males living under capitalist-patriarchal conditions?'[60]

The memoirs of these men are distinctive for their lack of any intimacy with women. Wives and lovers are almost entirely absent. Even in their accounts of their own marriages wives are not referred to by name, but presented as mere shadows of men.[61] The women who do make an appearance in these autobiographical writings and novels, many of which became bestsellers, are sharply contrasted:

the stiff and lifeless 'white' women (sisters, nurses, virgins, dead women) – ascetic, aristocratic, angelic; the warm and sexual 'red' women (communists, workers, rebels) – wanton, working class, wicked. Images of flooding and streaming – whether blood, women or the masses – pervade the *Freikorps* literature and appear to be linked with fears of communist chaos – the 'Bolshevik Wave', seen as overwhelming and destructive of Imperial Germany. The Bolshevik flood is also, however, associated with the female, for femininity symbolises emotion, sexuality, chaos. Intense obsession with, and fear of, the contaminating female body (with the continual use of categories like 'slime', 'dirt', 'pulp', 'the mire', 'the morass') are thus related to the threat of communism, arousing murderous anger in these crusading soldier males and dictating a total, violent cleansing to prevent their own annihilation and destruction.

The 'upright individual', *Freikorps* imagination suggests, must stand firm with the ruling class and its phallic culture of order and authority as a barrier against the anarchic working-class 'swamp'. Caught in between, the middle-class male must aspire upwards, identifying with army, nation and race. These identifications alone can fend off the fascist's anxieties about the absence of boundaries to the male body, and the threatening world beyond. Drawing upon Elaine Morgan, Michel Foucault and others, Theweleit suggests that the obsession with the symbols of water and flowing reveals a fixation upon, and fear of, the material reality of free-flowing desire, located, at least since the fifteenth century, in female bodies.[62] 'Could it be,' he asks (in one of the tantalising rhetorical questions typical of his style), 'that the fear of dissolution through union with a woman actually causes desire to flee from its object, then transforms itself into a representation of violence?'[63] He explains such fear in terms of his subjects '*general* difficulty of establishing any object relations', causing the desire to love to mutate into the desire to kill – 'where the man pushes the woman far away (takes her life), and gets very close to her (penetrates her with a bullet, stab wound, club etc.)'.[64] This murderous rage in *Freikorps* soldiers is in turn seen as deriving, in the first instance, from a failed relationship with the mother in infancy.

Theweleit argues that in what he refers to as 'the bourgeois family', women are often fed up with their infants and secretly reject them, and yet alternate this with displays of overwhelming sentimentality. In consequence the (male) infant may be exposed to contrasting waves of hatred and concern in response to his physical needs.[65] With his needs unmet, the male infant fails to experience his own body as a separate whole entity with 'a pleasure-filled periphery'. (The female infant never appears in Theweleit's account.) This early lack of bodily boundaries or any coherent ego development means that male identity only gradually emerges through the harsh military training and discipline instilled in various punitive institutions. The lack of boundaries is replaced by integration into totalising 'molar machines' like school, army, nation. The body is now armed and strengthened, discovering in military discipline and war a murderous discharge for blocked sexual energies and fears of loss of identity. Echoing Wilhelm Reich's approach to the psychological study of fascism, Theweleit concludes that the key to understanding the obsessions, fears and violence of the literature he analyses, is what happens to human bodies when they cannot function 'in a manner consistent with their sexual needs and potential'.[66] His suggestions as to how the fascistic, murderous and misogynistic masculinity he depicts might be changed, are equally Reichian – or sub-Reichian: 'For the martial man, locked up within his armoured totality, it is perhaps a question . . . of bringing him to some acceptance of his bodily orifices and his entrails, so that a pleasurable stimulation of his physical periphery no longer engulfs him in fear of disintegration.'[67]

Despite its popularity, and the chilling force of the primary texts it assembles, Theweleit's analysis of the *kind* of men these were, and of their relevance to the question of mass support for fascism, seems both inadequate and confusing. All the more inadequate, in fact, given the implications which its author (and many of his readers) seem to want to draw – as in Theweleit's (for once) firm assertions:

> I don't want to make any categorical distinction between the types of men who are the subjects of this book and all other men. Our subjects are equivalent to the tip of the patriarchal iceberg, but it's what lies beneath the surface that really makes the water cold.[68]

All the more confusing too, when, as Lutz Niethammer points out in a succinct critique, not all of the *Freikorps* men whose writings Theweleit records became Nazis (at least one became a resolute resistance fighter against Nazism) and most ordinary Nazis were not drawn from the *Freikorps*.[69] Nor are we given any biographical studies of the childhood of any *Freikorps* soldiers in support of the claim that such 'martial men' were the products of a type of ambivalent mothering which prevented the development of any pleasurable sense of their own bodies, or capacity to form object relationships. As Barbara Ehrenreich notes in the book's introduction – a point not reflected in its text – we are reading about a very particular group of 'warrior' men, in a very particular time and place – men who were engaged in almost continuous and uninterrupted war for over thirty years, between 1914 and 1945. 'It may be helpful to recall,' Ehrenreich – again unlike Theweleit – emphasises, 'that it is not only men that make wars, but wars that make men . . . each war deforms the human spirit and guarantees that survivors – or some among them – will remain warriors.'[70]

Another remarkable silence in Theweleit's work on the psychosocial creation of a fascistic type of masculinity is the complete absence – in this text, as in those he studies – of any mention of actual women. Though the author suggests that men and women ought always to be seen in relation to each other, we learn nothing of what women were doing or thinking in the period under study. Women only appear in the thoughts of men, and then only as victims. Indeed, in Theweleit's analysis a woman never does become an agent in history or an agent of her own desire. He explains:

> This is achieved by teaching her to make demands on others (as opposed to taking action herself), demands that are addressed not to society or to life, but to men. Her demands for adequacy in a man are security, money, a home, a job, children.[71]

She is not a sexually active person, for the young girl, we are told, 'is not sexualised as part of her education'.[72] 'No one,' he continues, absurdly (contrary to the evidence of Gothic and Romantic literature, mass and élite culture more generally), 'paints a wonderfully mysterious yet horrifying picture of male sexuality for a young woman.'[73] (Heathcliff, where are you hiding?) Woman, as commodity, 'is finally forced to love the customer paying the highest price – or promising to pay the highest price.'[74] Yet, of course, actual women, being more than captive creatures, fantasy images or commodities, are not 'trained' or 'forced' quite so easily – even were Theweleit less ridiculous about the cultural pressures confronting them. And, painful as it is to face up to, one thing many women did in that tragic period was to become active and passionate Nazis: a reality which receives not even a passing mention in Theweleit's book, questioning as it does conventional assumptions about the roots of fascism in specifically *male* fantasies, *male* bodies and *male* actions.

There is a gender analysis to be made of the appeal of fascism, but it is more complex than Theweleit's. In her study, *Mothers in the Fatherland*, Claudia Koonz attempts to document the role of women in Nazi life, looking in particular at the women – over eleven million of them – eventually drawn into active membership of Nazi organisations.[75] Hitler, like the *Freikorps* soldier, had spent his young manhood entirely in the company of men and had often boasted that 'the Nazi revolution will be an entirely male event'.[76] It was not. From the outset women were among his most zealous and fanatical supporters, and crucial to his success. (Almost half the votes cast for Hitler in 1932 were women's.) They were not, Koonz indicates, the simple dupes of men; nor were they masochists attracted to jackboots. Despite the male-supremacist goals and the contempt for women inscribed in Nazi ideology, they were attracted to its emphasis on women's separate sphere and the significance it assigned them as – and only as – mothers and homemakers. Some were also able to enhance their own power and influence, organising what was seen as the necessarily separate sphere of female education and 'spiritual' development. The belief in separation afforded these Nazi women greater autonomy from men than was enjoyed by women in other political parties. Many shared Hitler's intense nationalism and authoritarianism. They too were inspired by his rhetoric of racial renewal and military glory: 'Motherly love in its separate sphere, far from immunizing women against evil, fired women's dedication to the Fuhrer's vision of an "Aryan" future and expanded opportunities for women to reign in their own *Lebens-raum*.'[77]

Nor were the closest and most odious deputies of the vegetarian, non-smoking, teetotal Hitler, in any sense Theweleit's hardened woman-hating killers. Goering and Eichmann could not bear the sight of blood; Himmler screamed and almost fainted witnessing the execution of two women.[78] The men chosen to supervise the routine killing of children, women and men in the Auschwitz, Treblinka and Dachau camps were often, Koonz suggests, those with the closest relations with their wives and children: men who could separate off 'doing their duty' from their love for wives and children.[79] Highlighting the contradictory nature of gender identities, Koonz points out that aspects of what we see as 'feminine', rather than 'masculine', emotions provided the ideal model for Hitler's followers, who were to be, and became, blindly obedient, passionate and weak: 'Hitler released men from society's emotional straitjackets and rendered them "feminine" in their obeisance and even obsequiousness.'[80] Moreover, Hitler himself was aware that his rhetoric was directed at what he called 'the intrinsically feminine character of the masses', confiding the secret of his terrifyingly successful oratorial tactics to an old comrade: 'The Crowd is not only like a woman, but women constitute the most important element in an audience. The women usually lead, then follow the children and at last . . . follow the fathers.'[81]

There is currently a widespread debate over the role of women in Nazi Germany, and other women historians have argued that women in general *were* more resistant to Nazi propaganda than were men, and that women were not a major force in attacking Jews in Germany.[82] Nevertheless, against Theweleit, it does seem clear that it was not merely a type of basically insecure, woman-hating martial 'masculinity' which was deeply attracted to fascism – and hence that could provide a satisfactory explanation of its appeal, or that of right-wing ideology more generally.

It is true, as Koonz makes clear, that there existed intense anxiety over the erosion of traditional gender arrangements throughout the whole of German society after the First World War; and this was fundamental to the rise and success of Nazism. German women were the first in Europe or the US to obtain the franchise. More women were being educated, were in jobs in which they remained as the Depression began to destroy male employment, and were active in politics and cultural life generally, than in any other Western country. But women's comparative emancipation was a product of military defeat: economic chaos, deprivation (if not starvation), social dislocation, humiliation and despair were affecting the bulk of the German people. 'The Woman Question', as Erich Fromm found in a survey just before the Depression, was one of the most controversial topics of the day.[83] Men, and women as well, blamed women's employment and 'emancipation' for most of the social problems as they saw them: falling birth rates, the rapid rise in male unemployment, the 'emasculation' of men, the 'selfishness' of women, and sexual depravity everywhere. For the most part poorly paid in the workforce, or unable to feed families at home, women too desired their 'liberation' from an unsatisfactory emancipation, longed for retreat to a mythical, idealised past where they were secure in hearth and home.

The Nazi promise to restore women to their place in the home, men to their place outside it, appealed to both sexes. Times of extreme deprivation, in conjunction with erosion and change in traditional roles, have often served, as they do today, to enhance the appeal of conservative movements. All the more so as progress for women is never free from problems and set-backs – dividing women from women as well as increasing the tension between women and men. I don't think we can understand that appeal exclusively, or even primarily, in terms of the psychologies of men or of women. The bond between the psychic and the social, though always important and in need of exploration, is never as straightforward as analyses like Theweleit's suggest. Nor can we understand the commitment to militarism simply as some form of hyper-masculinity. When Yvonne Roberts interviewed the British bomber fighter, David Morgan in 1984, just back from his 'heroic' role blowing up more planes than any other fighter in the Falklands, she was looking to see if he displayed some particular idea of manliness or desire for the camaraderie of an all-male society. She found a man completely without bravado, who had been close to his father ('more like a brother'), who was modest and, above all, simply pleased to be back home once again and able to spend as much time as possible with his wife and children: 'I'm very conscious of the fact now that if I don't sit back and enjoy the family to the full then I'm actually wasting something. I was certainly very aware of that down there.'[84] This man who enjoyed his job as a fighter pilot, and 'wouldn't have missed a single day' of the war, seemed distinguished only by a very ordinary lack of imagination: 'Death doesn't bother me . . . you pay your money and you take your chance . . . I've no qualms now at all (about using his bombs).'[85] When he thought he was facing death, he resolved only to worry less about the bills, in the event of his survival. We seem to see here a mild but unimaginative man who wants, in his own words, to 'do what you've been trained to do'.

Making It: Masculinity as Power

The closer we come to uncovering some form of exemplary masculinity, a masculinity which is solid and sure of itself, the clearer it becomes that masculinity is structured through contradiction: the more it asserts itself, the more it calls itself into question. But this is precisely what we should expect if, as I suggested at the close of the last chapter, masculinity is not some type of single essence, innate or acquired. As it is represented in our culture, 'masculinity' is a quality of being which is always incomplete, and which is equally based on a social as on a psychic reality. It exists in the various forms of power men ideally possess: the power to assert control over women, over other men, over their own bodies, over machines and technology.

If we look more closely at some contemporary models of exemplary masculinity, the sporting man, the politician, the man who is successful with women, we uncover once again the instabilities of 'masculinity': dependent as it is upon the steady confirmation of power from what can prove unstable social institutions and practices, dependent also upon its hierarchically understood difference from what can prove insubordinate 'others'. Today's most prominent models of masculinity – used to promote and sell a myriad merchandise of manliness – are, in the old public-school tradition, mostly drawn from the world of sport. In Britain, Daley Thompson, Viv Richards and Ian Botham, all embody the putative ideal of a dominant and successful masculinity. One such all-round sporting champion from Australia – swimmer, runner, surfer (collecting $100,000 a year from prizes, sponsorships and endorsements) – was interviewed for a masculinity project underway in that country. This sporting hero (referred to in the interview as 'Steve'), from an affluent, white, middle-class background, serves the media as its perfect example of the masculine. His interview, however, reveals how hard he must work to produce this effect:

> You're up at 4.30 to go training and that goes most of the day. And you are too tired to go out anyway and you've got to get your rest. It's like being in jail.[86]

The interview also illustrates the constraints and contradictions of this type of masculinity. It entails restraint in sexual life, in commitment to others and in any general pursuit of pleasure. As Bob Connell comments, 'Steve the exemplar of masculine toughness, finds his own exemplary status prevents him from doing exactly what his peer group defines as thoroughly masculine behaviour: going wild, showing off, drink driving, getting into fights, defending his own prestige.'[87] Steve knows that to stand still he must 'keep winning, keep winning and keep rolling in the money'. Yet he is neither an aggressive nor a particularly competitive person. His competition is with himself, to 'control the pain' and 'make my body believe that I am not hurting it as much as I am'. With enormous work and sacrifice, then, Steve can force his body to become an archetype of masculinity, he can literally *embody* the masculine ideal. In doing so, however, his ideal masculinity becomes a saleable commodity for promoting other commodities. He can be used as an object in the way it is more customary for women to be used. In tending to his body – a pursuit which keeps him in a homosocial environment, with little time for any other serious activity or relationship – Steve remains within an adolescent world. Asked what it means to be a man, this paragon of manliness finds the question very hard to answer (he knows it has something to do with being 'strong', and 'not to be a gay'). Present in the practice of his successful competition with other men, his control over women (who must agree to put his training first), and his command of body and surfboard, 'masculinity' still seems somewhat elusive to this manly man.

Another forum for publicly promoted, tough-minded masculinity is 'the normal rough and tumble of politics', which, to quote self-proclaimed people's hero, Derek Hatton, 'is no place for the faint hearted'.[88] Derek Hatton was deputy leader of Liverpool Council for three and a half years in the early eighties, during which period, he believes, he secured a place in history for 'the names of Militant and Derek Hatton'.[89] (Militant is a highly disciplined, backward-looking, Trotskyist organisation, which operates within the British Labour Party.) Hatton's autobiography – its cryptic sentences seeking out the shortest route between one boast and the next – provides us with another glimpse of an apparently successful ideal of masculinity embedded in a very traditional political milieu, in this case that of the left. Hatton is a man who, in his own impersonal, action-packed language, likes to view himself, as he likes to treat all others, as an object. The self-object must be tirelessly promoted; the objects that are others are to be manoeuvred and manipulated by Hatton and his team. As a man who not only desired, but was able to flaunt, his taste for expensive suits (Pierre Cardin), cars (BMWs) and women (the heiress Katie Baring, among many others), he self-consciously acts out other men's dreams of manhood.

'The first fight he ever won', we learn, was in schoolboy boxing at the age of eight. Boasting his lack of academic talent, at school he was interested – again the same old manly refrain – only in sport: 'I lived for playing football and cricket.' Henceforth football became his model for successful life as a man; he played to win. From a childhood in which, we are told, the mother controls home, money and Dad 'with a rod of iron' (which usually means that the men of the family play little role in domestic life), Hatton imbibed masculinity from his father – 'powerfully-built, six-foot, ex-Coldstream Guards, boxing champion and an ex-English Schoolboys footballer'.[90] Leaving school, Hatton is also taught toughness by his training, again in the footsteps of his Dad, in the fire service. It is, or was, an all-male job, where men must always be on their heterosexual macho guard.

Once, he recalls, having worked all night, he fell asleep on the shoulder of a fellow workmate – 'They didn't stop ribbing me about it for weeks and neither did Dad.'[91] And from his job Hatton learned other manly values which he took with him into politics – his belief that, no matter what other people may think, the end justifies the means: 'you have to be absolutely ruthless in order to take people with you . . . I've been prepared to push people on one side and say "Get on with it – I don't give a damn what you think."'[92] (In a bizarre and horrific tale, Hatton tells us that he learned this lesson from the hard-headed humour of a fireman hosing down the remains of a young student 'pulped' to death in a road accident.) His instructions in this type of cool, authoritarian, coercive, insensitive masculinity, silencing all opposition, create the macho climate that discourages all but the most aggressive and competitive from engaging in politics.

For his own part Hatton is confident that the world of politics mirrors his boyhood world of football: 'I went in fighting and won'; other councils fighting to protect their services 'just didn't have our bottle'.[93] A true man of action, he despises academics, 'who tend to see life from an armchair'. Politics is simple. Socialism is about fundamental truths, and they are not truths which can encompass sexism or racism (he sneers at those 'promoting black mayors and gay rights', 'with their obsession about anti-racist and anti-sexist politics'.[94] He joins Militant because, playing to win, he knows that, at least in Liverpool, they have 'political muscle' and operate with the kind of undemocratic, absolute certainty which leads him to boast that 'they are the only men in the Labour Party'.[95] Continually scornful of the leader of his Council, John Hamilton – 'a nowhere man' who 'has his uses', he simultaneously ridicules his gayness and demands for women's equal political representation by suggesting at one point "'Hey, John, if you put a skirt on that should solve the problem!'"[96]

Again flaunting the traditional masculinity of the old school, we find no new fatherhood here: 'I was never at home', he announces, of the period after his children were born – 'there were meetings most nights.'[97] But his disturbingly self-effacing wife who, in her own words 'knows when to step out of the limelight', creates the fantasy that he is 'the perfect father'.[98] We learn little of 'Degsy's' vulnerabilities amidst this apparently flawless acquisition of a type of ideal working-class masculinity, except that his interminable boasting would seem to hint at underlying insecurity. He does need props for his masculinity. We are told, for example, not once, but five times, that his son is becoming a very good footballer – which is just as well for the son: 'Like every father I desperately wanted a son – and (on the day of his birth) Shirley had her work cut out to stop me going out and buying his first pair of football boots there and then!' It is also clear that this man is not only a braggart but a bully, readily admitting his 'outbursts of temper': 'if someone gets in my way without good reason I'm likely to react violently without even thinking'; 'often I lose my temper with the people I like and respect most'.[99] It is likely that Hatton (a true authoritarian character) experiences a peculiarly strong need to avoid self-reflection and doubt – just as well for him, then, that his masculinity found a most agreeable home in the Liverpool left for many years. The 'burdens' of masculinity may be real, but they do not necessarily bear too heavily upon the man who can remain in a position from which to exert control over others, and – Hatton's fondest wish – 'keep hogging the limelight'. Margaret Thatcher's obvious grandiosity, her use of the royal plural and reputed delight in her title as the 'Iron Maiden', not to mention Kinnock's not infrequent resort to macho rhetoric, make it clear that it is not an exclusive prerogative of the hard left, nor of the working class, nor even of men, to use political forums for consolidating a sense of personal power.

One writer who has attempted in his fiction to dissect the way in which masculinity is essentially a structure of power, and therefore for many as much a source of anxiety as security, is John Fowles. As head boy at a British public school and later during military service, he received, he believes, an especially rigid training in masculinity. It gave him 'a violent hatred' of those who enjoy wielding such power over others as he had himself at public school: 'I used to beat on average three or four boys a day . . . Very evil, I think. Terrible system.'[100] True to his training, nevertheless, he confesses that he has 'always found it difficult to get on with men unless one's in a power situation'.[101]

Depicting 'men in crisis, analysed as case-studies of contemporary masculinity'[102] Fowles's novels mostly describe men who conform to masculine patterns of achievement: gaining power, success and access to the casually enjoyed and lightly discarded love of beautiful women – at least until some woman manages to teach these heroes the nature of a less self-serving, more committed form of loving.[103] Men use women, he tells us, to confirm their masculine identity. In one of his works Fowles interrupts his narrative to reflect upon the casual promiscuity and 'quite literal cocksureness' of his literary creation, the eponymous hero, *Daniel Martin*: 'He was arguably not even looking for women in all this, but collecting mirrors still; surfaces before which he could make himself naked – or at any rate more naked than he could before other men – and see himself reflected.'[104] Power, accumulated through his career (as a scriptwriter in the competitive world of the media) and through his relationships, have come easily to Daniel Martin, who, 'like every other middle-class child, (was) educated to see life in terms of success in examinations and games'.[105] But for Daniel Martin (as for Fowles), men, unlike women, are always something of a threat to any secure sense of masculinity:

> He had very rarely sought male company for pleasure, perhaps because it threatened his always precarious sense of uniqueness. He saw himself too easily in other masculine faces, mannerisms, machismos, ambitions, failings; his own sex always seemed to lack the variety and unpredictability of women (sic).[106]

Men remind other men, Fowles's fiction suggests, that successfully acquired masculinity has a hollow interior, for the structures which support it are those of a commercial world of manipulation and shallowness, compromise and betrayal. Such masculinity also carries with it a burden of guilt over the unjust power men exercise, as though of their birthright. Fowles bemoans the fact to feminist journalist Sarah Benton: 'Guilt. Men have been carrying this terrible load for thousands of years, this great superstructure.'[107] Yet at the same time, men who fail to acquire the requisite trappings of masculinity – power in the world, and power over women – can become quite literally deadly, as portrayed in Fowles's first published novel, *The Collector*. Here, based upon a real-life incident in the 1950s, Fowles creates a 'hero', Clegg, who exemplifies not the habitual egoism of men spoilt by the routines and assumptions of masculine power, but the terrifying reality of those who act out the masculine fantasy of asserting control over women, when the mundane means of such control elude them – in this case, through a kidnap which results in death.[108] Clegg, characterised as 'monstrous and pitiable', is a literally impotent male with no emotional attachments to others, whose insecurities as a man create the 'sourness' and 'beastliness' conducive to murder.[109]

Masculinity is described by Fowles (who believes himself to possess 'a feminine mind')[110] as an 'appálling crust' which, whether successfully acquired or not, creates 'the crude things in men'.[111] Yet, while criticising 'the selfish tyranny of the male'[112] for its contribution to the wrongs of the world, and although displaying some awareness of the structures which create masculinity as enactments of power – over women, men and things – he nevertheless endorses many of the dominant myths of masculinity. Fowles, for example, echoes rather than challenges the idealisation of women – or at least those women (like Allison in *The Magus*) who 'never, like so many English girls, betrayed their gender'[113] to become masculine women, but rather retain their femininity and hence embody the more creative, loving, sensitive and progressive 'feminine principle'. The redemption of men, Fowles believes, can come only via the salvation offered by women. Through their 'intrinsic oppositeness' to men, women can educate and liberate them from the shackles and guilt of their own power and egotism. Thus in exposing how the vulnerabilities of masculinity are bound up with its use and abuse of power, Fowles nevertheless remains trapped within the limits of the masculine mythology he seeks to confront – the intrinsic virtue of women and vice of men. Moreover, as Bruce Woodcock indicates, his writing offers us a moral rather than a political argument: 'It does nothing to tackle the problem of male power as a political reality, because it locates any process of change in men at the level of the individual being educated into a new awareness.'[114] And it places the burden of change on women, rather than on men themselves.

What Fowles does not see is that the masculinity he claims to abhor is far more complex than his own conceptual framework of opposed principles or essences (which he sees as Jungian) will allow. It is not a question of male urges propelling men either towards assertiveness or towards anxiety over impotence, but rather of how different groups of men occupy and maintain the particular positions of dominance they are awarded, or taught to expect – sometimes over other men, and always over at least some women. Yet, as we shall see in later chapters, not all men have found it possible, and not all men have found it desirable, to participate in the social relations which generate dominance.

Rites of Passage: The Men from the Boys

Most contemporary champions of the importance of the masculine ideal in the West are troubled by the alleged difficulties of young males achieving proper 'manhood' in the modern world. Even the critics of the virtues of masculinity seem to agree that men today are generally nervous and insecure about their own masculinity. 'The macho man and the wimp', observer of the male psyche Ray Raphael representatively comments, 'we seem to be shifting help-lessly back and forth between these twin manifestations of male insecurity':[115]

> Macho, we now know, is just one more indication of insecurity. Many of us really *believed* in John Wayne, but most of us probably suspect that Sylvester Stallone is little more than a joke. We quietly chuckle when we hear that Rocky . . . is scared, in real life, to travel to Western Europe.[116]

Raphael, like many another man worried about the hazards of contemporary masculinity, points out that in an urban, industrial society the traditional pursuit of manhood via displays of physical prowess and courage seem increasingly obsolete. Mind rather than muscle, manipulation rather than endurance, are the more likely attributes of men with power today. This cushioning of modern life, as writers like Robert Ardrey and George Gilder have already informed their millions of readers, inevitably frustrates the naturally aggressive and territorial instincts of man.[117] Though sympathetic to this conception of the human male's 'primordial urges' and 'archaic memories' of the need to assert dominance over women and rival groups of males, Raphael attempts a somewhat more sophisticated analysis of the malaise of modern man – or modern North American man, at any rate.

The problem, as he sees it, is the lack of social confirmation or proof of genuine 'masculine' identity. Consequently, North America is now apparently populated by confused, insecure, anxious, 'makeshift males'. Raphael laments the absence of the social institutions which have served in the past as initiations into manhood. The sudden and dramatic separation of young males from the childhood home and family meant that military conscription, for example, could serve to separate the 'men' from the 'boys'. Given suitable rites of passage, which must involve *separation* from the dependency and weaknesses of childhood and a new sense of *belonging* to a distinctive world of adult males, men can collectively acquire a confidence in their masculinity. Examples of successful initiation into manhood are the tasks of endurance, infliction of pain and suffering – if not permanent scarring and genital mutilation – in what he calls 'primitive society'. Such initiations always 'work', since, if they make the grade, men invariably know they are real men. All males thereby secure an enhanced sense of self-worth in traditional initiations.

In contrast, today in the West, we have no such collective initiation rites. As Raphael confirms in his interviews with a hundred different men, they are therefore forced to seek proof of manhood individually and competitively – through sporting achievement, sexual exploits, climbing mountains, or by other selected but isolated attainments, which often do not receive any widespread public acclaim. Now that the strength of anti-militarism has undermined people's acceptance of its unavoidability, even war can no longer successfully initiate men into manhood. As a result, Raphael and others complain, many or most men quietly but acutely suffer the private tragedy of seeing themselves as 'unmanly'. Denial, over-reaction and guilt are the defensive responses to the desperation men feel when their male identity has not been adequately affirmed: 'our competitive initiations tend to exaggerate rather than alleviate male insecurity, and the greater our insecurity, the more prone we are to overcompensating for our weakness by excessive and aggressive male posturing.'[118]

Significantly, though not surprisingly, Raphael fails to analyse what he means by 'manhood', except to say that we cannot dispense with the concept because the basic tasks of male development themselves cannot be abandoned: 'we must move from weakness to strength, from helplessness to responsibility, from dependence to independence.'[119] We need, he feels, more inclusive definitions of the achievement of manhood – giving as an example the attitudes of those engaged in sport for the disabled, where it is important only that everybody should finish the race: 'Manhood, too, is naturally inclusive. We all want to get there somehow; we all want to cross that line.'[120] Yet whilst the 'we' here must of course include anyone who seriously aspires to the status of autonomous human adulthood, women are definitively excluded.

The point is that it is insufficient for the 'men' to be distinguished from the 'boys'; the 'men' must be distinguished from the 'women'. Without the return of full-blooded patriarchy, many men are today condemned to live with ever increasing levels of insecurity over the distinctiveness of their 'manliness'. For it is no longer so easy to imagine that there are many significant activities or areas of life which, by definition, forever exclude women. Just as it is not so easy to imagine that there are many activities or areas of life which, by definition, can never include men. And this becomes ever more apparent, however much the reality of men's dominance continues to reproduce significant areas of actual exclusion for women, and opting out by men.

That the success of men's acquisition of 'manliness' involves a complex process of dominance and exclusion, inevitably shot through with contradiction, emerges from the reports we possess of what is universally agreed in Britain to have been the last rite of passage into manhood designed to include all young men – obligatory National Service.[121] 'Did it', the sociologist David Morgan asks, '"make a man of you" and what could this claim possibly mean?'[122] Drawing upon his own two-year stretch in the RAF, he reflects upon several perplexing anomalies of military life. Firstly, despite the pervasive masculine culture it shared with most other all-male institutions – the obligatory smoking, swearing and boozing, the obsession with football and women – the connections between military values and masculinity, apparently so strong ideologically, were in fact ambiguous. Too marked an enthusiasm for military ideals of combat, national security and discipline would arouse contempt and sarcasm: 'Only sprogs took such things seriously.'[123] Secondly, although violence was sometimes referred to with approval, and violent films or thrillers enjoyed, Morgan saw little overt violence throughout his time of service. Violence was celebrated, to the extent that it was, largely in its absence: 'Perhaps, more often than not, it was a matter of style, the tone of voice used in conducting arguments, of body language, of an overt disdain for anything that might appear soft or wet.'[124] Thirdly, as I will discuss more fully in the next chapter, the rampant homophobia of military life accompanied a paradoxical tolerance for blatant homosexual behaviour. Morgan concludes that National Service did indeed have something to do with the process of 'making men', but in more complicated ways than is often supposed:

> If it did make a man of you, National Service achieved these ends, largely
> indirectly and in a round-about manner. It did so through encouraging some
> distinctly unheroic, and presumably unmasculine traits to do with skiving and
> avoiding responsibility . . . National Service provided an arena in which young
> men might deploy various masculine attributes.[125]

It did encourage public accounts of human relationships which left little room for tenderness: 'It was not, then, so much a matter of actual conformity to a code but, more subtly, to present oneself as if one were conforming to a code or at the very least not making a virtue of not conforming to that code.'[126] It was more a matter of learning the gestures and display of masculinity, than of being 'injected' with actual masculine traits, desires and attributes. Men 'learned to talk about masculinity in a certain way, a way that was pervasive and dominant'.[127]

It is not surprising, then, that when the scenery changes the confident assurance of the masculine performance, the cosy assumptions of superiority, may also begin to falter. It is in this sense, and because social reality always does change, that masculine identity is never fixed. And some men never did acquire the appropriate gestures and display in the first place.

6. Competing Masculinities (II): Traitors to the Cause

There wasn't an age at which I didn't prefer playing with dolls or dressing up to playing football or playing with toy cars and tractors. Gifts of toy guns were left unused. This was punished by ridicule and being called jessie and cissie and so I would only do these things in secret . . . The attempt to mould me to what was expected of a boy growing to be a man were as persistent in school . . . games in particular became something which I dreaded.Football was compulsory and for boys such as me who were not good at it, we were made to feel not only that we were personally worthless but aberrant and morally wanting . . . Growing up was painful.

Angus Suttie[1]

For Angus Suttie desiring men rather than women was at first even more painful than growing up in a working-class family in Scotland in the fifties and sixties: 'Society told me . . . I was despicable, and so I thought everyone like me was despicable . . . I despised them as I despised myself.'[2] Most men may never be quite free of anxiety over whether they are man enough. But only some men are systematically oppressed by the dominant conceptions of masculinity, affirmed as they are in social institutions and practices, as well as ideologies, which routinely privilege men.

'Not being a gay', not wishing to be the object of other men's desire, is, as we have seen, perhaps the most immediate, concrete and consistent proof many men feel they have of their own masculinity: 'I'm a man, I must be a man, look I've got a prick and it works because I can tell you about the six women I've had.'[3] (This is how one contemporary gay man mocks the conversations he regularly overhears between his heterosexual peers.) The most persistent myths surrounding contemporary conceptions of homosexuality are bound up with men's need for the gender reassurance they obtain from the assertion of heterosexual interests and behaviour.

For over a hundred years now scientific and popular belief has held that male homosexuality derives from and expresses something 'feminine' in men – the absence of appropriate levels of masculinity. (In the same way, female homosexuality was seen as the expression of something 'masculine' in women – an absence of appropriate levels of femininity.) A medicalised conception of the homosexual as a congenitally maladjusted or 'perverse' type of person, with an inverted or mixed-up gender make-up, has dominated modern Western thinking on sexuality. Against this conception, sociological studies of gay and lesbian sexuality have been arguing for nearly two decades now that it was the institutionalised medical 'discourses' themselves which served to produce the very type of homosexual identity they described – along with homosexual sub-cultures for support, survival and, at times, resistance. On this view, a type of socially constructed, collectively expressed, subordinated masculinity came to exist in self-identifying homosexual men.

Fixing the Borders: The Emergence of the Modern Homosexual

The 'constructivist' sociological account, as it came to be called, draws most heavily upon the historical research of Michel Foucault in the mid-1970s, and the subsequent work of Jeffrey Weeks and others, who have suggested that 'the homosexual' as a type of *person* was literally invented in Western thought only in the late nineteenth century. First used by the Hungarian writer and translator Karoly Maria Benkert (whose real name was Kertbeny) in 1869, the term entered English currency in the 1890s when it was taken up by the sexologist Havelock Ellis in his pioneering studies and classification of varieties of human sexual experience.[4] Before that, attention focused simply on 'same-sex' *behaviour*, sex between men being considered similar to many other types of 'sinful' and 'depraved' sexual practices, like masturbation ('onanism') and even nocturnal emission – all of which were condemned as 'crimes against nature' because they involved non-procreative sex. In the late seventeenth century, for example, US historian Randolph Trumbach has argued that the sodomite was seen as an outrageous type of manly rake, who had sex with both women and boys.[5] (And in Britain up until 1885 the death penalty for sodomy applied equally to acts of anal intercourse with men, women, or animals.[6] In Foucault's famous epigram: 'The sodomite had been a temporary aberration; the homosexual was now a species.'[7] In Weeks's more cautious version: 'We have to distinguish between homosexual behaviour, which is universal, and a homosexual identity which is historically specific – and a comparatively recent phenomenon in Britain.'[8]

Some gay writers today suggest that there is a problem with the constructivist approach to understanding homosexuality. It correctly stresses the significance and power of the intervention of medical science in labelling and pathologising homosexual behaviour from the late nineteenth century onwards, but it ignores the agency of the people who have openly expressed homosexual interests and behaviour. Frederic Silverstolpe, for example, like Trumbach, argues that medical discourses of gender inversion in the late nineteenth century were themselves influenced by men and women who engaged in cross-dressing and homosexual practices as part of an oppositional cultural practice.[9] Silverstolpe argues that when Karl Ulrichs and Karoly Benkert, respectively, introduced the terms 'Uranians' and 'homosexualists' in the 1860s, to describe people with 'inborn' tendencies to love members of their own sex, they were not so much influenced by medical discourses as tactically stressing the 'natural' condition of their own homosexual desires. Their writings were part of an emancipatory struggle, which itself influenced doctors and sexologists who in turn added their own notions of degeneracy:

> When medical science intervened against the 'socio-political' claims of Ulrichs, Benkert and others with their pathology-approach, it can in fact be seen as a reaction *against* the invention of the homosexual category, with all its controversial social implications, as well as an effort to *control* and redefine this new category when it was already there.[10]

Nearly all researchers of the history of modern homosexuality agree, however, that it was only in the second half of the nineteenth century that the notion of 'homosexuality' as a matter of identity enters into scientific discourse and, through systematic medical and legal interference with homosexual activity, becomes associated with 'disease' and 'psychopathy'.[11] The modern homosexual, whether studied as a socially constructed identity or, as Silverstolpe prefers, more of an 'unholy alliance between science and homosexual emancipationists', throws a revealing light upon the nature of modern masculinity.[12] It does so because, as Jonathan Dollimore argues: 'the negation of homosexuality has been in direct proportion to its actual centrality, its cultural marginality in direct proportion to its cultural significance.'[13] The maintenance and stability of contemporary heterosexual masculinity is deeply dependent upon its distance from, and obsessive denunciation of, an opposing category – that of the homosexual. This, at all events, has been the revolutionary significance of the deviance and discourse theorists who have studied 'the making of the modern homosexual'.[14]

In her classic article, 'The Homosexual Role' (1968), Mary McIntosh wrote of the function of the creation of the homosexual – a distinct, despised and punished category of person – as a mechanism for controlling and policing the rest of society.[15] Pointing to the historical and cultural specificity of the 'homosexual' (it refers to a figure absent in many societies where homosexual behaviour is nevertheless prevalent), she argued that we should recognise that we are dealing with a social rather than what came to be seen as a fixed medical or psychiatric category. It is a category defined not in terms of actual behaviour, but in terms of the social ideas and expectations surrounding any manifestation of same-sex erotic desire. For male homosexual behaviour, these expectations involve an anticipated general effeminacy, sexual desire exclusively for men, and sexual desire aroused in all encounters with any men – but particularly boys and young men.[16] And yet it is easy to point to times and places, ancient and modern, where homosexual desire accompanies conventional manliness, heterosexual desire, and very specific relations restricted to particular men. Developing these themes more fully from within a symbolic interactionist perspective, Kenneth Plummer in *Sexual Stigma* describes how such sexual ideas and meanings are picked up from social interaction with others and then shape people's self-perception and developing identities.[17]

Jeffrey Weeks asks why this particular type of regulation of sexual behaviour, with its opposition between the heterosexual and the homosexual person, should have emerged so strongly during the latter part of the nineteenth century – helping to spread and promote (if it did not entirely create, as the deviance and discourse theorists assume) the emergence of a distinctive male homosexual sub-culture associating homosexuality and effeminacy.[18] He points to the restructuring of familial and sexual relations which occurred, as we saw in the last chapter, with the consolidation of the English middle-class culture throughout the nineteenth century. He traces the links made with increasing frequency between the 'feminine' and physical weakness, emotionality, and economic dependence, and the contrasting binding of the 'masculine' to physical strength, emotional self-reliance and economic independence.[19] Whole new categories of social problems were invented and treated by the social, legal and medical authorities of the day: 'the masturbating child, the hysterical woman, the perverse adult, the congenital prostitute, the degenerate and the homosexual'.[20] Indeed, the moral onslaught against childhood masturbation and adult sexual indulgence became ubiquitous. Masturbation – to be restrained by whatever means necessary – was thought to result in failure to develop proper manliness, as well as the particular 'vice' of homosexuality.[21]

Echoing some of this analysis, John Marshall notes that the most striking characteristic of the period was its consolidation of new ideals of domesticity, femininity, marriage and the family.[22] Central to this consolidation was the firm binding of sexuality to marriage – so firm, indeed, that the widespread social purity campaigns sought even to eliminate the double standard permitting greater sexual license to men. Moral purity was seen as important for both sexes. The elevation of marriage, the family, and the control of male lust, all rendered homosexuality a central target for moral campaigners. The connection made between gender inversion and homosexuality served not only to control and punish homosexual behaviour, but also to define and maintain appropriate definitions of masculine and feminine behaviour.[23] Studying male bonding in nineteenth-century British fiction, Eve Kosofsky Sedgwick suggests that homophobia served as an instrument for regulating the whole spectrum of male relations, rather than simply those of men engaged in homosexual relations.[24] The possible imputation of homosexual interest to any bonds between men ensured that men had constantly to be aware of and assert their difference from both women and homosexuals. In his last interview Foucault somewhat analogously, though as usual more sweepingly, argued that the emergence of homosexuality as a distinct category is historically linked to the disappearance of male friendship. Intense male friendships were perceived as inimical to the smooth functioning of modern institutions like the army, the bureaucracy, educational and administrative bodies.[25] Homophobia was the chief weapon against too great an intimacy in male friendships.

The new emphasis on physically fit and wholesome manliness thus went along with the increasing social stigma attaching to homosexual behaviour, and a growing fear of its contaminating influence, in the late nineteenth and early twentieth century: 'lusts written on his face . . . pale, languid, scented, effeminate, oblique in expression', was how the homosexual poet John Addington Symonds summed up the homosexual stereotype of the day.[26] It would last a very long time; indeed, it persists. Many have pointed to the decisive role of a series of public scandals in the 1880s – most notoriously, the three trials and subsequent imprisonment of Oscar Wilde – in dramatically associating and reinforcing public condemnation of sexual decadence and male homosexuality. To this day, the martyrdom of Wilde remains a historic landmark, signalling the dangers of deviant behaviour: a labelling process, in Weeks's words, 'of the most explicit kind, drawing an impassable border between acceptable and abhorrent behaviour'.[27]

The male homosexual stereotype of effeminacy and transvestism has had a profound yet complex impact on men who see themselves as homosexual. No automatic relationship exists between social categories and people's sense of self and identity but, as Weeks again comments, the most significant feature of the last hundred years of homosexual history has been that 'the oppressive definition and defensive identities and structures have marched together.'[28] Defined as effeminate, the largely secretive male homosexual sub-cultures that were able to develop in some of the major cities displayed cross-gender behaviour and transvestism. The self-mockery of men celebrating effeminacy became a way of homosexual men presenting themselves before a mocking public. Creating a style, language and meeting places of their own made life a little easier for men in search of homosexual contacts. Operating within, yet at odds with, mainstream conceptions of gender, Weeks stresses, allowed for some form of consistent, if dangerous and devalued, identity: 'The keynote of the homosexual world was ambivalence and ambiguity.'[29] By the First World War some prominent homosexual men, like Laurence Houseman, and their supporters (including the respectable voice of some of the sexologists engaged in studying and labelling the homosexual 'condition'), had begun to campaign for changes in social and legal attitudes towards homosexuality.[30]

Most male homosexuals reaching adulthood in the first half of the twentieth century in Britain would nevertheless continue to endure constant fear and anxiety, often, when they could, choosing to live abroad or else to remain sexually celibate.[31] Homosexual consciousness remained inevitably guilt-ridden and fragmentary. Indeed, since homosexuality was publicly so associated with gender ambiguity, many men who were attracted to their own sex but did not fit the public stereotypes, were unable to recognise themselves as 'homosexual'. As one elderly man interviewed by Marshall in the late seventies commented, echoing the sentiments of many of his peers:

> When I was a young man I got married because it seemed the natural thing to do. I had friendships, close friendships with other men, but nothing ever came of it. Loving other men and especially having sex relations with them was almost unthinkable. I realize now that I had deep desires in that direction but it was always something I fought. I didn't have the words to think it out, much less the courage to act upon it.[32]

By the same token, the prevalent opposition between 'homosexuals' and 'men' allowed others, by strictly adopting only an active role in sex with male partners, to reject the idea that they were 'really' homosexual. Marshall's elderly interviewees suggested that a man could thereby avoid seeing himself as 'queer'. In general, the taboo on even discussing homosexuality was so strong up to the

1950s that many of Marshall's older informants confided that until about twenty years ago they had little or no idea of what homosexuality actually was (D.J. West suggests that it could only be discussed hitherto 'in muted terms appropriate to a dreaded and scarcely mentionable disease').[33]

Ironically, the 1950s, which followed the publication of the Kinsey Report on male sexuality and a huge opening up of discussion on sex in general and homosexuality in particular, was also a time of renewed moral panic over homosexual behaviour. Nothing in the Kinsey Report offended public morality so much as its findings on homosexuality. Kinsey reported that over 'one in three' (37 per cent) of North American males had had at least one homosexual experience to orgasm, that 50 per cent of them had experienced some sexual response to other men, and that homosexual behaviour was widespread across all classes, ages and regions.[34] Far from increasing public tolerance of such behaviour, as Kinsey himself hoped, these findings were to fuel public outcries against it. As was noted in chapter one, in Britain there was a dramatic increase – a hundred-fold increase – in the arrest rate of homosexual men, including public scandals over the arrest of prominent public figures.[35] Homosexuals were once again scapegoated as moral decadents, and now – with a new twist – as traitors to their country. Male homosexuality was the main focus of attack, women, as usual, not being considered important enough to constitute a serious threat.[36] Caught up in the Cold War political context of McCarthyism, the fear and persecution of homosexuality in the United States was even greater. It reached hysterical heights in some towns, as in Boise, Idaho in 1955, where the arrest of three male homosexuals led to a curfew being imposed on the entire young population until an expert investigator could be hired to root out any remaining homosexuals.[37]

By this time, however, homosexual groups campaigning for legal reform were exerting more pressure on professional bodies and pioneering new forms of self-affirmation. But they still had only minimal influence on most practicing homosexuals, for whom there were few resources available to encourage any type of self-regard or more confident self-assertion. Once again the upsurge in homophobia at this time may be seen less as a way of persecuting homosexual men (though it certainly did that), than of regulating the behaviour and aspirations of men in general – in particular re-establishing the heterosexual bond torn apart through war. As Barbara Ehrenreich has argued:

> Fear of homosexuality kept heterosexual men in line as husbands and breadwinners; and, at the same time, the association with failure and immaturity made it impossible for homosexual men to assert a positive image of themselves . . . The ultimate reason why a man would not just 'walk out the door' was the taint of homosexuality which was likely to follow him.[38]

The association between soldiers' experiences and some form of homo-eroticism in the unusually womanless world of war was real enough. It reached its unselfconscious apotheosis in the poetry of the First World War when, as Martin Taylor's collection of love poetry from the trenches reveals, the emotions expressed, directly or indirectly, challenge the primacy of heterosexual love:

> Aye, the love of women draws ye, lad,
>   It's the oldest, sweetest spell,
> But your comrade Love is stronger love,
>   'Cause it draws ye back to 'ell.[39]

Despite the obligatory heterosexual boasting, the encouragement of pin-ups, pornography and even female prostitution characteristic of army life, the intimacy, unlikely friendships and extreme male bonding of men on the battlefield can, ironically, evoke the intense emotional compassion, self-sacrifice, love and devotion associated more with 'femininity'. These emotions have no parallel in the restrained, self-sufficient 'masculinity' thought appropriate for men in civilian life. The intensity of feeling of the male comradeship of wartime was thus dangerously at odds with the more prosaic male contacts and even heterosexual bonding of peacetime. These contrasts may help explain the fears which feed upsurges of post-war homophobia.

Institutions as sexually segregated as the army regularly display an apparently chronic homophobia (backed in the military services, by legal sanction), even as the intimacy, pleasures and paradoxical freedom from the responsibilities of civilian life in such all-male worlds create the space for homosexual contacts. As Sedgwick comments: 'For a man to be a man's man is separated only by an invisible, carefully blurred, always-already-crossed line from being "interested in men".'[40] Analysing the links encouraged in army life between virility, sexuality and bellicosity, Trevor Royle points out that 'effeminacy' is 'the ultimate soldier's crime'.[41] Yet David Morgan, in his reflections upon the 'masculine display' of National Service, recalls, as I have mentioned, how one army regular who chose to display a stereotyped 'camp' effeminacy (improvising his own version of popular songs like 'wish you were queer') was never treated with hostility, mock or otherwise: 'In a culture which officially and informally condemned homosexuals, he was not only tolerated, but liked.'[42] Other men 'of vaguely "feminine" appearance or artistic interests', however, were openly mocked: 'Watch him when you bend over.'[43] Both Royle and B.S. Johnson in their books on army life also report an apparently paradoxical tolerance for actual homosexual relations, despite the taboos on tenderness and rampantly homophobic ideology:

> Buggery was a constant theme of jest but honoured entirely in the breach. And yet the regiment, a small one, included a long established male marriage, apparently connived at and condoned by all, from the colonel down.[44]

In institutions committed to 'making a man' out of young men, those who suffer most from the homophobic, routine bullying and not infrequent sadism endemic to the initiation and training in such institutions, are, it seems, as likely to be heterosexually as homosexually inclined. 'Woman' and 'pansy' being synonymous with anything regarded as proof of physical or emotional 'inadequacy', all men are vulnerable to the supposed 'unmanliness' of failure in such cultures of misogyny.[45] In a terrifying tale of North American army life included in *You Can't Hack It Little Girl*, Eisenhart describes the savage treatment meted out by one sadistic drill instructor (DI) to a recruit who could not complete a seven-mile run. Not only was the recruit kicked and beaten as he fell from exhaustion, eyes glazed and mouth foaming, but he was forced into the role of scapegoat as his failure was used as a reason for further cruelty towards the rest of his regiment. The following incident ensued:

> The DI looked at Green (the recruit) and said, 'You're a no-good-for-nothing queer', then turning to the glowering platoon, 'As long as there are faggots in this outfit who can't hack it, you're all going to suffer.' As he turned to go into the duty hut he sneered, 'Unless you women get with the program, straighten out the queers, and grow some balls of your own, you best give your souls to God because your ass is mine and so is your mother's on visiting day.' With a roar 60–70 enraged men engulfed Green, knocking him to the ground and kicking and beating him. He was picked up and passed over the heads of the roaring, densely-packed mob. His eyes were wide with terror; the mob beyond reason. Green was tossed and beaten in the air for about five minutes and then literally hurled onto a concrete wash rack where he sprawled dazed and bleeding.[46]

It seems superfluous to add, as Eisenhart informs us, that this recruit – though slender, intelligent and unaggressive – was 'not effeminate' by civilian standards.[47] Barbarism such as this is not reserved for men who are homosexual. Society, at least such an internally regulated society as the military, needs its symbolic deviants; actual deviants may be beside the point.

The Male Homosexual Challenge: From 'Camp' to 'Gay' to 'Super-Macho'

Homosexual sub-cultures, we have seen, developed as a type of oppositional lifestyle which was itself greatly influenced by the characterisation of homosexual behaviour as congenital gender inversion.[48] Dominant definitions, Foucault argued (though perhaps in too linear a way), serve both to regulate and control the behaviour of all men and women, while nevertheless encouraging a type of complementary 'reverse discourse':

> Homosexuality began to speak on its own behalf, to demand that its legitimacy or 'naturality' be acknowledged, often in the same vocabulary, using the same categories by which it was medically disqualified.[49]

That reverse discourse, some would now suggest, was perhaps partially – if in a fragmentary and volatile way – to predate and interact with, rather than simply stem from, medical and legal regulation. But, however assertively or defensively seeking a space inside the dominant culture, homosexual sub-cultures have a tantalising relationship with the masculine ideal – part-challenge, part-endorsement.

Traditionally, men's behaviour within such sub-cultures has

assumed the form of 'camp' – the suppression of 'masculine' behaviour for a type of parody of 'femininity'. But 'camp' was about more than men pretending to be women. It was seen as involving a positive aesthetic sensibility: a sense of beauty, and a sense of pain. 'Do you know what "camp" is?' high camp evangelist Christopher Isherwood asks in one of his novels, written in the early fifties:

> You thought it meant a swishy little boy with peroxided hair . . . pretending to be Marlene Dietrich . . . What I mean by camp is something much more fundamental . . . You can't camp about something you don't take seriously. You're not making fun of it; you're making fun out of it. You're expressing what's basically serious to you in terms of fun and artifice and elegance. Baroque art is largely camp about religion. The ballet is camp about love . . . I admit it's terribly hard to define.[50]

A generation later Jack Babuscio writes similarly of camp as 'a creative energy reflecting a consciousness that is different from the mainstream; a heightened awareness of certain human complications of feeling that spring from the fact of social oppression'.[51] Traditional homosexual culture thus embraces a positive interest in forms of high culture – art, theatre, ballet, music, literature and, especially, opera. Indeed, as Richard Dyer indicates, such cultural interests in themselves might suggest to a man, or be used to suggest, that you were homosexual; cultural sensitivity in itself somehow seeming 'feminine'.

> For me, growing up gay and getting into this sort of culture felt like the same process, namely the process of establishing an identity. It was summed up for me in the word 'queer'. Being queer meant being homosexual, but also being different. It is easy to see how easily I formed an equation between this and being interested in culture. In an all-boys school in the late fifties and early sixties, culture was as peculiar, as 'other', as being queer.[52]

Up to a point, camp enabled men to be different and proud of it. But only up to a point, Dyer suggests, because the associations between artistic sensitivity, 'queerness', and femininity were – prior to the moment of gay liberation in the early seventies – still seen as somehow less serious and important than the masculine world of work and reason. ('The frivolity of camp,' David Fernbach suggests, 'hid the meaninglessness we could feel inside.')[53] Though traditional camp culture did not see itself as political, both Babuscio and Dyer insist that it did and still does possess political significance. It lays bare the superficial and constructed nature of gender identities and thereby discovers 'A way of poking fun at the whole cosmology of restrictive sex roles and sexual identifications which our society uses to oppress its women and repress its men.'[54] Babuscio sees irony – 'any highly incongruous contrast between an individual or thing and its context or association' – as the essence of camp.[55] As some radical gay men came to see it, camp was a way men could become more woman-identified and declare the conventions of masculinity oppressive.

Other gay writers, however, disagree over the extent to which camp culture, in mocking gender identities, thereby challenges and helps undermine them. Andrew Britton, for example, rejects Dyer and Babuscio's positions, arguing that although it ostensibly rejects the conventions of 'masculinity' and 'femininity', in reality it relies upon, and thus reinforces them.[56] Whichever position seems most plausible, and I myself see it in terms of creative contradiction, the issue of contention only arises with the new radical gay politics and culture which emerged in the seventies. It was a politics which provided the first exhaustive critique, and assertively self-conscious rejection, of dominant forms of masculinity by men themselves. It was a culture which experimented with gender identities and lifestyles, in an effort to transform existing power relations between women and men, and between men and men.[57]

Gay liberation took the reverse affirmation of homosexuality to its logical conclusion – turning the stigmatisation of the homosexual on its head.[58] In conjunction with the emerging women's liberation movement, it contested the prevailing definitions of gender so firmly bonded with heterosexual practices. Summing up the ideology of the Gay Liberation Front (GLF), Simon Watney has pointed out that it not only provided a positive self-identification in terms counter to the dominant heterosexual culture, but it undertook the more ambitious task of questioning all 'the most basic assumptions about what it means to be a man or a woman in this society, socially, economically and sexually'.[59] As the London GLF Manifesto of 1971 declared: 'The long-term goal ... is to rid society of the gender-role system which is at the root of our oppression.'[60] Towards this end, some gay men were to propose the most profoundly provocative tactics:

We are fighting an entire culture . . . If we are to gain our freedom we must focus people's attention on their frustration and their resentment on the source of it . . . We must be 'rotten queers' to the straight world, and for them we must use camp, drag, etc., in the most 'offensive' manner possible. And we must be 'freaks' to the gay ghetto world. Our existence must provoke a questioning of society.[61]

More succinctly, another gay man declared, 'By wearing drag, I feel that I am helping to destroy the male myth.'[62] (Unfortunately, in its relationship with a bewildered public the individual voluntarism of the 'gender-fuck', as it was known, did not manage even to convey its message, let alone accomplish its goal.)

The energy and collective endeavour of gay liberation were, however, to prove enduring, rapidly transforming the lives of gay men and gradually impinging on the consciousness of other men. Gay liberation grew with great speed in the United States and much of Europe in the early years of the 1970s, within and outside the homosexual sub-cultures which had expanded throughout the 1950s and 1960s as the taboos on any public mention of homo-sexuality weakened – despite persisting police harassment.[63] Challenging existing configurations of sexuality and gender, activist gay men, who in Britain were also often explicitly socialist and pro-feminist, insisted that homosexuality – far from being abnormal – was a natural capacity in everyone, suppressed by society and the family. Both men and women could be sensitive, sensual, gentle and caring, emotionally independent, strong and technically skilled.[64] Gay men saw themselves as united with feminists in a common struggle against the gender system – a struggle which would transform the whole of society. Gay writing on masculinity criticised its complicity with violence and warfare, its suppression of female sexuality, and the organisation of heterosexuality around the needs of men. 'Gay men,' David Fernbach felt it important to affirm against an emergent liberal tolerance, 'really are effeminate . . . we have failed to repress the maternal culture within ourselves and to develop the masculine culture of violence.'[65] (Fernbach proceeded to concede that gay men were not the only category of effeminates, they were simply more visible.) For Fernbach, gayness was 'the wedge that splits open the gender system',[66] and gay men 'a type of fifth column within the masculine camp'.[67] 'Gay shows the way,' as the GLF Manifesto declared: 'We have already, in part at least, rejected the "masculine" or "feminine" roles society has designed for us.'[68]

Gay liberation activists thus formed an important part of the optimistic left politics and climate of the early seventies. They operated as an autonomous group working primarily in the non-aligned libertarian left, committed to building an alternative co-operative culture, free of sexism and racism, with its own community-based newspapers, resource centres, and self-help groups.[69] Gay men offered a creative alternative to traditional homosexual lives, and sought to find new ways of being men, emphasising 'community instead of alienation, comradeship instead of isolation, love instead of competition, the struggle against sexism and ageism instead of enslavement to commercialism and the latest fashion'.[70] Of course, as Jeffrey Weeks pointed out ten years on, the reality proved a little more mundane:

> What I eventually had to face was the contradictions between the new possibilities and the old, resistant realities . . . But the struggle goes on because of those millenarian, wildly optimistic and utopian, but inspiring early days.[71]

Some of the contradictions which popped up were, not so surprisingly, the contradictions of masculinity itself. There were problems early on, particularly for women in GLF. In 1972 lesbians in London split from it to work exclusively in the women's movement, and lesbians from elsewhere soon followed. The pull of that movement was obviously strong for many lesbians. But women in GLF were also critical of gay men's failure adequately to confront their own sexism. Discussions on the issue were mainly led and held together by women, and seen as a concession to them.[72] In particular, women felt gay men were reluctant to discuss problems of relationships, like combatting jealousy and possessiveness, properly. They also felt that the connections between homosexual oppression and women's oppression were not being sufficiently emphasised. Whereas the early gay liberationists, like David Fernbach, had assumed that 'every step forward by the gay movement is a blow against the norm of masculinity,' that was not quite how things worked out.[73] Even within the newly visible gay communities, the huge growth in self-confidence and assertion did not seem to lead to the general blurring of sexual and gender boundaries, the transition to androgyny, or the triumph of more 'feminine' values and attributes desired by early liberationists.[74]

On the contrary, a new type of super-macho style developed in the gay milieu from the late seventies. As Dennis Altman documents, in the politically powerful, commercially successful, internationally trend-setting gay mecca of San Francisco, gay men could be distinguished from straight by their *more* 'masculine' appearance. Meanwhile many heterosexual men were displaying a perfumed, fashion-conscious, more narcissistic and androgynous masculinity.[75] This 'butch shift' – gay muscle men clad exclusively in leather and denim, or gay 'clones' with short hair, moustache, check shirt, blue jeans and bovver boots – would appear to be a celebration of conventional masculinity, just as the reality of much of the sexuality of gay men seems to be an exaggeration of the more promiscuous, emotionally detached, entirely phallocentric encounters characteristic of male heterosexuality. It is now a commonplace perception that gay men have more in common with straight men than with gay women, and vice versa.

Gay machismo is, however, defended by many gay men as a new form of camp – the super-macho style exposing the absurdity of masculinity more effectively than effeminacy. (Uniforms, worn by soldiers or policemen, for example, have been designed as a type of stiff, protective armour to assert status and function, whilst deflecting eroticism; worn by gay men to enhance eroticism, they subvert the more 'serious' intent.) Gay macho eroticism, Martin Humphries argues, also redirects gay men's desires away from unobtainable straight men back to gay men themselves as objects of desire.[76] As another gay man put it, 'I had gone after those straight boys because they were straight and because I had eroticised that difference. Now I began to see that gay men had their own differences.'[77] It is only with the changes in the self-image of homosexuals themselves over the last two decades that there has been any real challenge to the assumption that to be homosexual is to adopt some of the characteristics of the opposite sex.[78] The links between sexuality and gender have begun to fray, and many men, who were always 'macho' rather than 'sissy', have come out and become gay.[79] The fine line between a 'true' masculinity (which is heterosexual) and its opposite (which is not) has been increasingly transgressed. And yet the valuation of masculinity as the positive and powerful identity is, one might feel, hardly thereby subverted. Or is it? Yes, and no. Gay machismo does, albeit ambivalently, undermine the security of masculine identities: identities, we now know, often none too secure in the first place. Dyer captures precisely this ambivalence of contemporary gay style:

> Gender roles are crucially defined in terms of heterosexuality – 'men' as a social category are people who screw 'women'. By taking the signs of masculinity and eroticising them in a blatantly homosexual context, much mischief is done to the security with which 'men' are defined in society, and by which their power is secured. If that bearded, muscular beer-drinker turns out to be a pansy, how ever are you going to know the 'real' men anymore?[80]

Power and the Erotic: Dominance, Submission and Masculine Convention

Scott McIntosh, a macho gay interviewed by Yvonne Roberts, has a predilection for leather and sado-masochism. His butch regalia accompanies his complete enjoyment of what is seen as the 'passive' and 'feminine' side of sexuality (as well as the 'active'):

> It is an invasion but there is something else which women must feel as well, the physically pleasant thing about it . . . At the same time, when it's [the anus] filled with penis there is a feeling of fullness, of satisfaction which is totally different from the feeling a man gets when he penetrates.[81]

McIntosh suggests that 'macho' means something different in the gay world from the heterosexual world: 'Macho among straight men tends to mean they watch *Match of the Day*, drink beer, spill pizza on the carpet, treat their wives like ratbags. Now that doesn't interest me at all . . . Macho to me, I suppose, means a certain self-assurance . . . I like coolness and strength.'[82] But macho is compatible with crying and being open about one's feelings. Moreover, he believes that gay men into sado-masochism (S and M) have one thing in common: 'we're not as competitive. It's almost like a sisterly relationship that women have, you can talk about everything and you'll always be friends.'[83] I don't doubt a certain level of gay chauvinism in these remarks, but they do suggest some greater perceptiveness about masculinity, sexuality, and the use of power in erotic fantasy than one usually finds in most men, or women.

Because they have needed completely to rethink the meaning and politics of their sexuality for themselves, gay writers have tackled some of the most difficult issues around masculinity and sexuality – issues other men have preferred to avoid. In particular, they have repeatedly addressed the problem of the place of power, pornography, fantasy and ritual in sexual life. It seems correct to assume that male sexuality, gay and straight, shares certain common features, deriving from the pervasive identifications of 'masculinity' with power and with genital performance. Neither squarely within, nor fully without, the structures of male dominance, gay sexuality can, however, perhaps more easily highlight its contradictions. First and most obviously, gay sexuality offers further confirmation of the ambiguity, even ultimately, the unintelligibility, of the mapping of active/passive onto masculine/feminine. As George Stambolian comments on his interviews with ten very different gay men, 'As gay men we should know better than anyone else that many rather effeminate men are ferocious fuckers, and many who are super-butch love to get fucked.'[84] Men who act out their apparently passive and masochistic fantasies in sexual engagements with other men often characterise it as a way of *proving* their 'masculinity' through enduring the challenge of pain: 'I've learned to take pain like a man,' Stambolian is told.[85] Such an attitude, which would, of course, appear totally appropriate on the sports-ground or battle-field, becomes totally inappropriate – in the conventions of masculinity – in the bedroom.

What so many of Stambolian's interviewees tell him is that they like to be totally passive one day – picked up and carried about like a baby and made love to, totally macho the next – active and aggressive; or whatever combination pleases them.[86] So, it would seem, do most heterosexual men. Any prostitute can testify to her clients' cravings for submissive and receptive sexual experiences, but the constraints against men indulging what are seen as passive and 'feminine' feelings in their ordinary encounters with women can be harder to transgress. Some politicised gay men, determined to explore and accept all aspects of their sexuality, have thus been able to reflect more fully upon questions of identity and power – the desire to be penetrated and filled, to be a sexual object, while at the same time retaining a sense of male identity. One man tried to explain to Stambolian how he saw himself as made up of many different beings, 'the man who waits as well as the man who pursues':

> Well, since people are afraid of being vulnerable, they often transform their desire into aggression or hide it behind attitude . . . The trick is to create a situation where each person is given enough power so that he can have the opportunity and the pleasure of relinquishing at least part of it . . . There have been times when I've wanted to dominate or be dominated as fully as possible. I've (been) burned up by hunger, and I've done my pleading . . . There are fantasies that trap us and fantasies that free us . . . It's a question of whether they control us or we control them. If they control us, or we try to impose them upon others, fantasies can be very dangerous . . . Sexual fantasies, when consciously employed, can create a counter-order, a kind of subversion, and a little space into which we can escape, especially when they scramble all those neat and oppressive distinctions between active and passive, masculine and feminine, dominant and submissive.[87]

There has been so much discussion of sado-masochistic sex in gay writing (primarily male but also lesbian), that it appears an almost exclusively gay concern, (although Jay and Young's *The Gay Report* finds that only a relatively small number of their sample had ever been engaged in it.[88]) Yet psychoanalytic theory and evidence indicates that dominance and submission, pleasure and pain, are involved in all sexuality, as we inevitably relive the treats and traumas of infantile desire. The nature of much pornography, in conjunction with the routine experiences of prostitutes and evidence from documentation of both male and female fantasy, all indicate that S and M is a staple component of nearly all sexual desire.[89] In heterosexual pornography and fantasy, however, it becomes particularly disturbing because of its links with the more general cultural climate of misogyny, denigration and degradation of women – a problem to which I shall be returning in later chapters. Yet the links between sexual fantasy and social relations are not necessarily as tight as the congruence between heterosexual pornography and female subordination might appear to suggest.

Discussing male gay S and M, Altman, for example, convincingly argues that behind 'the ritual of much of this sort of sex there is a return to the forbidden pleasures of childhood: not only the play with urine and faeces, but the fascination with beating and slapping (so much the staple of nineteenth-century upper-class British s-and-m'.[90] The most commonly reported motivation seems to be a quest for enhanced sensation and new experiences, rather than any straightforward desire for pain.[91] As we saw with Scott McIntosh, many gay men are convinced that the ability to express needs for power, punishment, and so on through sexual play actually limits any need to express it in other ways. This would explain, according to Altman, 'why most studies suggest that men involved in s-and-m are likely to be personally gentle, liberal, and have above-average education'.[92]

While there is no evidence that play-acting S and M fantasies leads to actual relations of dominance and submission in everyday life (as we shall see in chapter eight, both straight and gay men who seek out and enjoy masochistic sexual experiences are often those who elsewhere routinely exert authority and power over others), there is certainly evidence that sexual repression can fuel actual violence against those seen as arousing desire. Rape by self-defined homosexuals is very rare, while the rape of men by other men who deny that they are homosexual is very widespread.[93] It is, as we shall see in chapter nine, extraordinarily common in men's prisons, but it is common as well in many other all-male groups. If sado-masochistic fantasy is currently such a prevalent aspect of at least male desire (though some, like Pat Califia, would suggest that it is equally common in women), it seems hard to deny that it is better to enact it in playful and consensual sexual encounters, rather than through the authoritarian outlets of the state where in police cells or on army parade grounds it is so frequently encountered. As Dennis Altman concludes, in agreement with Pat Califia: 'The straight world has a great deal to learn from the leather bars of the gay.'[94]

It would be quite wrong to suggest that gay men have solved the problems of exploitation and oppression within sexual encounters and relationships. It is right, however, to believe that, amongst men, it is gay writers and activists who have devoted most effort to addressing them. In an interesting article entitled 'Coming to Terms', Richard Dyer analyses male gay porn in relation to the social construction of male sexuality in general and male gay sexuality in particular. Rejecting both the puritanical attack on *any* pornography as objectifying and exploitative, and a libertarian acceptance of *all* pornography as essentially harmless, he undertakes to examine pornography (as, in his view, one might any cultural production) for the moments of contradiction and instability in order to find at which points it is most possible to push for change. Dyer suggests that gay porn, like straight porn (defined as material explicitly designed for sexual arousal), reinforces some of the worst aspects of the social construction of masculinity as men have come to experience it in relation to their bodies. Yet it can also be used for 're-educating desire'.[95]

Gay porn movies, for example, are full of the myth of male potency, and male sexuality is always seen as goal-directed – the goal being orgasm. In this sense gay porn offers no break with the norms of ordinary male sexuality – ordinary 'masculinity'. But more self-consciously and critically, gay men could work within pornographic production attempting to change it. Dyer describes some of the narratives of male gay pornographic film which bring together the dominant patterns of male gay sex: a basic romanticism combined with an easy acceptance of promiscuity; 'a utopian reconciliation of the desire for romance *and* promiscuity, security *and* freedom, making love *and* having sex'.[96] So despite the emphasis on orgasm, the romance, an altogether different matter, is still there. We do find displays of tender emotional feeling and delicacy between men: 'If porn taught us *that* more often . . .', we could use it to our ends.[97] Pornography, he concludes, is too important to leave to the pornographers. Tenderness and delicacy between men do create new masculine images, while also subverting the inevitability of heterosexuality. These may be mere cracks on the surface of the multiple representations of masculinity and power. But surface cracks can be exposed and deepened, can make us more aware, as another gay writer, Martin Humphries, puts it, of 'an eroticised reality of men who are both gentle and strong, who give full expression to their feelings, listen to their hearts and allow their warmth to be taken, used and reciprocated.'[98]

It is hard to sum up the support and the challenge gay male

sexuality offers to conventions of masculinity: 'We have not moved mountains,' Nigel Young reflected in the summer of 1979, 'but we have become more aware of the dilemmas and contradictions.'[99] Gay activists, importantly for the rest of us, have also tried to make others more aware of them. Most homosexuals in the big cities of Europe or the United States, in touch with the gay community, no longer internalise the old social condemnation of themselves as lacking in masculinity, suffering in consequence from guilt and self-hatred. But the growing self-acceptance of male homosexuals, their often greater ability to see through the hollowness and pretence of the masculine ideal, do not in themselves destroy the underpinnings of male dominance and related myths of male potency. Gay men relinquish some, but by no means all, the privileges they share with other men.

Indeed, the growth and success of the commercial gay world in cities like San Francisco stem from many men's freedom to pursue the lifestyle of their choice – provided they have the capital, which, as single men, they can the more easily acquire and dispose of. 'A buck is a buck,' as Altman quotes from a Toronto paper in the mid-seventies, displaying the new commercial tolerance; 'who the hell cares', the report continues, revealing the old sexist stereotypes, 'if the wrist carrying it is limp?'[100] Gay minority markets have often paved the way for subsequent mass markets – from disco music (which began in gay clubs) to perfume and jewellery for men, singles' bars, and much more. As Edmund White boasted in *States of Desire*: 'New York gays are justifiably proud of their status as tastemakers for the rest of the country, at least the young and up-to-date segment of the population. Our clothes and haircuts and records and dance steps and decor . . . soon become theirs.'[101]

Gays can be less proud, however, of surveys which suggest that their communities tend to contain a strong middle-class to upper-class bias; working-class, Black and ethnic minority gay men being largely excluded from the 'gay community' ambience.[102] The most visible form of racism Black American gays report is in the white bars, from which Black men tend to be excluded: 'White patrons do not want to rub shoulders with Black customers . . . Just to walk across the floor of the bar can be an ordeal'[103], Joe DeMarco reports from the Philadelphia gay male community in 1983. It is now urgent, he adds, that Black and white gay men get together to begin to come to grips with the problem of racism in their midst and create a genuine brotherhood: 'Our common bonds as men as well as our strengths, weaknesses, and concerns are still to be explored and exploited.'[104]

Despite the ambiguous nature of the commercial success of the male gay scene, the place where male homosexuality is likely to have its most lasting effect on conventions of masculinity is in its unambiguous affirmation of sexuality – of the pleasures of the body, every aspect of it, as a realm of the senses to be enjoyed. (Even Masters and Johnson, from their more limited quantitative surveys of male and female homosexuals, concluded that both men and women in their sample displayed more sexual engagement, more exchange of pleasure at all levels of sexual excitation, and more communication than heterosexual men and women.)[105] Such positive affirmation of sexuality is important when, as Ellen Willis argues, a 'distorted negative view of sex is basic to patriarchal psychology'.[106] The particular link made between masculinity and heterosexual performance within a culture which – despite its superficial permissiveness – is deeply anti-sexual in its fears of any signs of sexual pleasure outside marriage, is a dangerous one for women. Fear of sex, in male-dominated culture, has always meant fear of women as the instigators of sexual arousal. The historic harnessing of sexuality to the social creation of gender, along the lines of active male predator and passive female prey, is challenged, as it needs to be, by the visibility of both lesbian and gay sexuality.

Because the affirmation of homosexuality is the affirmation of sexual desire, it inevitably symbolises opposition to repressive sexual norms. Because the affirmation of homosexuality is outside the institution of the monogamous heterosexual family, it inevitably symbolises the possibility of real alternatives to that institution – the possibility of new types of community and morality which challenge patriarchal familial ideology. The gay challenge, in conjunction with the impact of feminism and other factors enabling women to live and love outside marriage, if they choose, means that the sexual liberalism growing – with hiccups – throughout the twentieth

century, can no longer be confined to marital, or *de facto* marital ,
partnerships. In the United States between 1970 and 1980 over 50
per cent of new households were of the non nuclear-family
variety:[107] more women and men were choosing not to marry, more
women and men were choosing a homosexual way of life, more
marriages were ending in divorce – usually precipitated by women,
particularly 'working' women. As Andrew Hacker concluded his
survey of the state of family life in the United States in the early
eighties: '"the family" as an institution is eroding.'[108]

Some politicians and policy makers in both Britain and North
America seemed prepared to offer some recognition to the new
plurality of family form.[109] The result, however, has not been any
straightforward acceptance of different lifestyles and sexualities.
Instead, there has been a complete breakdown of any general social
consensus around sexuality, creating ever sharper polarisations
between liberal and conservative positions.

Homophobia: The Enemy Within

The liberal view on sexuality popular in academic and medical
circles from the 1970s redefined homosexuality as 'a variant of
sexual expression', seeing homosexuals as a type of minority group
penalised by their social status as 'deviants'.[110] (The American
Psychiatric Association and the American Psychological Association
removed homosexuality from the category of illness in 1973.)
Expert opinion thus endorsed the status of homosexuality as an
alternative lifestyle and thereby contributed to its visibility –
alongside, and interacting with, the growth of a more confident gay
politics.

Neither, however, automatically increased its overall social
acceptability. On the contrary, greater visibility has produced a
greater degree of hostility towards homosexuals from many quarters
– official and unofficial. (Such hostility, as we shall soon see, was to
be dramatically fanned by the fear of AIDS.) In Britain we have
seen Clause 28 of the 1988 Local Government Bill become law,
with its vague and confusing wording declaring it illegal for local
councils or education authorities to be involved in the 'promotion of
homosexuality' or to teach 'the acceptability of homosexuality as a

pretended family relationship'. In the United States sections of the Republican Party have affiliated to the crusade of the moral majority, campaigning to strengthen paternal rights, oppose equal opportunities for women and remove abortion rights, at the same time as attacking all forms of sexual permissiveness and supporting the recriminalisation of gay sexuality.[111] There is nothing at all surprising about homophobia and the reassertion of men's rights and traditional masculinity operating in tandem. They are, in fact, the same thing. Both are a defence of the dominant form of masculinity enshrined in marriage, a 'masculinity' which is – despite its rhetoric – less a state of mind or body, than the various institutionalised routines for preserving men's power over women and over men who deviate from masculine ideals.

Homophobia, as we have seen, not only keeps all men in line while oppressing gay men; in its contempt for the 'feminine' in men it simultaneously expresses contempt for women. As Gayle Rubin observes, 'The suppression of the homosexual component of human sexuality, and by corollary the oppression of homosexuals is . . . a product of the same system whose rules and relations oppress women'.[112] Indeed, the fierce, irrational passion of homophobia in many men, as we saw in psychoanalytic thinking in chapter three, can be understood only in terms of men's fear of what they see as the 'feminine' in themselves – the enemy within. It also relates to fear, envy and anxiety about sex – an activity which seems so blatantly flaunted in male gay culture. George Weinberg, who invented the term 'homophobia' and defined it as 'the dread of being in close quarters with homosexuals', attributed it to five factors. The first, generally agreed upon nowadays, connected homophobia with the secret fear of one's own homosexual wishes (the psychoanalytically-minded would emphasise the significance of infantile anality, and its taboos; fear of castration and loss of manhood). The other four concerned the influence of religion, repressed envy, homosexuality's threat to established values, and in particular its threat to ideologies confining sexuality to procreation and the family.[113] As has been noted many times, the frequency with which men seek out homosexuals and engage with them sexually, before murderously turning against them, makes it appear incontestable that these are men not just attacking other homosexuals – but the homosexual in themselves. In the United States, for example, the six most active and horrific mass murderers in recent times (166 victims between them) have attacked homosexuals – though the media shows little interest in the issues this raises.[114]

Freud argued that the successful repression and sublimation of homosexual desire in men, attached initially to the father, formed the basis for the male bonding upon which human culture (and, he might have added, male dominance) is built.[115] If, as has often been suggested, homosexual repression is central to male bonding, and homosexual expression disruptive of the orderliness and discipline of classically all-male institutions like the army, police force, men's prison, football team or fire brigade, we can better understand the homophobic ideologies of such institutions.[116] Paul Hoch comments: 'The more one retreats to an all-male environment, presumably the greater the homosexual temptation and hence the continued need to "up the ante" in the way of violence to prove one's manhood.'[117] This strikes me as over-simplified, as David Morgan's army recollections of the low level of actual violence between conscripts would suggest. However, a volatile tension between homoeroticism and homophobia would appear inevitable when strong and exclusive bonds between men are being encouraged alongside a compulsory heterosexual masculinity.[118] It has also frequently been noted that openly gay men have little interest in many of the male bonding institutions which arouse such passion in other men – like competitive sport.[119]

Identified so closely with their sexuality, and so often the target of moral panics, gay men have been forced to grapple with almost every variety of contemporary sexual dilemma. From at least the nineteenth century there has existed a public terror of homosexual men corrupting minors. Outbursts of moral outrage over any signs of homosexual paedophilia have occurred throughout this century: 'The Vilest Men in Britain', was how the *Sunday People* referred to the members of the Paedophile Information Exchange engaged only in *discussing* the issue.[120] It is an outrage which exists in stark contrast with the near total *lack* of public outrage over the sexual abuse of girls – until very recently, and still controversially. Yet the overwhelming majority of cases of child abuse (90 per cent, according to one study) involve heterosexual men and very young girls – around 80 per cent taking place within the family.[121] The most common form of pederasty, in contrast, involves adult men and sexually experienced teenage boys.[122] Nevertheless, as *Gay Left* affirmed in a collective editorial: 'Paedophile relationships raise the question of power too sharply for us to treat them glibly.'[123] Equalilty in relationships between men and boys, they add, rests not simply on consent, but on whether the meanings attached to sexuality are also equivalent. In our society, with its continuing denial of childhood sexuality and its lack of adequate sex education for children, young people are unlikely to be able to form equal sexual relations with adults. What we need, the editors of *Gay Left* conclude, is to discuss how 'we ensure that (any) young person is allowed to grow at his or her own pace, untrammelled by over-rigid categorisation of childhood [the age of consent for young men in homosexual relations is currently still 21 in Britain], protected from abuses of power, and yet able to grow in caring relationships with other (perhaps older) people'.[124]

A Common Struggle: Homophobia and Misogyny in the Era of AIDS

Two things, at least, are clear today. Sexuality is a battleground within mainstream politics as never before in the twentieth century; and attitudes towards homosexuality are in the front-line. The wider implications of this struggle, however, concern whether sexuality can be returned to its reproductive marital context, and whether the differences between masculinity and femininity can be maintained with their traditional meanings intact.

Just when attitudes to sexuality in Britain and North America were at their most polarised – moral conservatives becoming ever more vociferous, yet people in general adopting more tolerant views on sexual matters than they ever had even at the height of the sixties – along came a brand-new sexually-linked disease, AIDS (anti-immune deficiency syndrome)[125]. As some saw it, like a thunderbolt from on high, it would galvanise the moral right and wipe out the new 'permissiveness', which many found so unsettling: 'If AIDS is not an Act of God with consequences just as frightful as fire and brimstone, then just what the hell is it?' demanded the editor of the *Sunday Express* in 1987.[126] For some time the agenda of the moral right in Britain, as elsewhere, had been to strengthen traditional family values (especially parental rights over young people and paternal rights over reluctant wives) and to associate all non-marital sex with sin and disease. The virus herpes, given sudden short-lived prominence as a sex-linked disease in the late seventies, was never sufficiently deadly to serve as a symbol which could renew the ties of sex with disease, and hence with sin. AIDS, it seemed, was tailor-made for the job. New York journalist Richard Goldstein has commented:

> AIDS knocks even liberals off their feet, not so much because of what it says about homosexuals as what it says about sex. AIDS puts us all up against the guilt we thought we'd left in the confessional and the rage that comes from having to curtail a vital source of gratification.[127]

AIDS is, it seems, the ideal providential symbol for a conservative sexual politics of the eighties: a politics of fear, rage and prejudice around sexuality. Nowhere is this stronger or more frightening than in the United States, where religious fundamentalism has combined with television evangelism and sections of big business – plus elements of the Republican Party – to form the powerful 'moral majority' ('Neither moral nor a majority', as other Americans point out).[128] Yet, ironically, AIDS has also become the symbol for a renewed educative and progressive sexual politics. Led by gay men, initially in North America, it has produced massive public information campaigns, self-help, and mutual aid to combat ignorance, prejudice and scapegoating. It is the cutting edge of sexual politics today. In Britain, as Elizabeth Wilson has commented, despite and because of AIDS and Clause 28, 'sex is fighting back'.[129] Lesbian and gay politics seem to have enjoyed a new lease of life as thousands have taken to the streets against Clause 28 and in memory of those who have died from AIDS – demanding better treatment for those with AIDS or who are HIV positive.

The problem for the right is that it is obvious to anybody who thinks seriously about the subject that the AIDS hysteria (based on misinformation and ignorance), itself spreads the dangers of AIDS. On its first appearance in the West (1980–1), in the US (where it remains most prevalent), AIDS initially spread among male homosexuals, Haitians and then other Black groups, as well as among intravenous (IV) drug takers. As a result government agencies for a long time believed they could, and would, ignore it. Indeed, in the grip of homophobia and racism, some Americans rejoiced over this new and deadly disease (perhaps shedding a tear for the haemophiliac with AIDS). As often happens in response to social problems, the fear and panic which the potential spread of the disease induced provoked only the naming of scapegoats and the blaming of victims. However, by the mid-eighties gay men themselves, at first entirely alone, but as an often already politicised community, were beginning to face up to the nightmare of AIDS: a brand new virus which, without any warning, had brought death and dying into their midst – particularly before 1983, when its method of transmission was unknown. (It is not casually infectious, transmission requiring the exchange of bodily fluids – primarily blood, semen and, to a lesser degree, vaginal secretion.[130]

Since then, extraordinary effort has been put into public information campaigns in the North American gay communities, promoting, not guilt and dread of sex, but individual and collective responsibility for sex and the importance of 'safe-sex' practices. The rate of new infection amongst openly gay men has reduced rapidly. In San Francisco, for example, it is estimated that 95 per cent of gay men now follow safe-sex practices, and fewer gay men than heterosexual men are currently contracting sexually transmitted diseases.[131] Recent studies from the United States show that in all the large urban areas, about 75 per cent of gay men always use safe-sex practices, which, it has been noted, is a remarkable achievement when a 10 per cent change in response to public pressure over other health issues is normally thought extremely good.[132] Men who don't identify as gay, though furtively engaged in homosexual practices, have proved harder to influence. But the gay community itself has been dramatically re-politicised, as well as pushed into even greater visibility.[133] Despite the upsurge of homophobia accompanying the public panic over AIDS, despite the personal terror and unspeakable tragedy so many gay men have had to endure seeing their friends and lovers – sometimes *all* of them – sick and dying, AIDS has demonstrated to the world the strength and resilience of the friendships and support networks of the lesbian and gay community.[134]

Meanwhile, by 1985 fears were growing in both the United States and Britain that the disease would soon be increasingly attacking 'innocent' people – that is, white, heterosexual, non-drug users. In Africa (where the virus appeared at the same time as in the West), it was mainly transmitted heterosexually, or via the contaminated blood used in the hospitals of countries too poor to screen it for the virus. It was becoming increasingly clear that promotion of a generalised fear of sex, and linking the disease to particular types of 'deviant' people, could not contain the spread of AIDS any more than such approaches had ever contained the spread of any previous sexually transmitted disease – as the history of syphilis reveals. Most governments in Europe, and many states in North America, were belatedly compelled by all relevant expert advice to confront the need to promote open discussion about sexual practices, together with the idea of 'safe sex', if they were to prevent medical catastrophe. Yet government AIDS campaigns in Britain have carried an ambivalent message. On television, for example, the images employed have been notoriously anti-sex, straightforwardly linking sex and death.[135] In leaflets, however, they have more explicitly detailed safe-sex practices, encouraging the use of condoms, mentioning anal intercourse, and using the morally neutral rhetoric, once confined to radicals, of 'straight or gay'.

Speculating on the impact of AIDS on anti-gay feeling in Britain, Bill Thorneycroft (now in his sixties and able to remember when being gay was only ever something 'to be sorry for, to apologise for') has commented that while AIDS has undoubtedly entrenched the homophobia of some and allowed papers like the *Sun* to incite an ever more blatant 'poofter bashing', it has led others to talk to him more openly about being gay:

> They never would have initiated it before, although they knew I was gay. One of them, the landlord of the pub, got pissed and kissed me on the mouth and talked about the problems of these demarcations – and this in spite of the AIDS hysteria.[136]

The point is that any open discussion always threatens the mainten-ance of barriers between the 'normal' and the 'deviant'. Jeffrey Weeks draws a rather similar conclusion from the overall social impact of AIDS on the gay world and beyond:

> The message I draw from this is that the gay movement is not ultimately about the liberation of any particular sexuality but actually about the liberation of a whole set of relationships; an affirmation of relationships which are sexual or non-sexual, relationships through which sexuality can be realized or transformed or denied or changed or just lived. The really important thing is that a public context for this has now developed and I don't think that this can be publically changed despite the impact of AIDS and the revival of the moral right . . . We are on the map for keeps.[137]

From the point of view of understanding and changing masculinity, however, the really important thing is that gay men have once again had to pioneer new attitudes amongst men – this time, the idea of more open, imaginative and responsible attitudes to sex, and of men nursing and caring for each other. Following the success of gay advice work in the United States, the Terrence Higgins Trust (the first and largest gay self-help AIDS organisation in the UK) has always advocated a positive and open attitude towards sex:

> *SEX IS GOOD, IT'S FUN. IT'S UP TO ALL OF US NOT TO SPOIL IT . . . be inventive sexually . . . get into wanking, massage and fantasies. There's more to sex than just fucking . . . make sure your partner wears a condom (if) you want to fuck.*[138]

It is clear that gay men in Britain have been responsive to this approach. David Rampton, for example, wrote a short account in the often notoriously anti-gay *Mail on Sunday* in 1986, describing how as a happily single gay man he had learnt to 'become comfortable with safe sex and enjoyed the positive, imaginative side of it, rather than just being stuck with the negative, difficult side of it all'.[139]

Meanwhile, we read that health authorities in the United States are concerned about how heterosexual men (who have never been politicised as a sexual community, or developed the networks of friendship and communication of many gay men) can be educated to take responsibility for women, let alone to begin caring for other men and women who have contracted AIDS.[140] Heterosexual encounters are so troubling because men's power over women is symbolised precisely in the most dangerous form of genital sex. Lesbian feminist and sexual radical Cindy Patton, working with women most at risk from AIDS in the US, has indicated how difficult and depressing the work can be, compared with promoting safe sex amongst gay communities.[141] Women, as we know, rarely exist as equal partners in their sexual encounters or relationships with men, in the way gay men mostly do. It is harder for women to feel the self-confidence required to make demands in situations of dependence, where they may be trading sex for security or money, or simply be subject to sexual coercion by men. Patton found that the women from the urban slums closest to the IV drugs scene and most at risk from AIDS – often poor, Black and ethnically oppressed women – complained that their male partners threatened them or beat them up at the mention of using a condom: 'Men seem to perceive the request to use condoms as an accusation that they are gay or hire prostitutes or are "cheating".'[142] Even more privileged women often had little experience making such demands on men around sex.[143]

Many heterosexual men, even – indeed often – those most at risk, like IV drug users, not only refuse to wear condoms but find talking about sexuality, feelings and relationships in any intimate context totally unfamiliar. Open discussion can arouse fear and anxiety, because it is regarded as essentially 'feminine' behaviour, at odds with heterosexual norms – at least for some groups of men. The overwhelming problem in meeting the challenge of AIDS in this respect, whatever the protestations of the moral right, is the continuing significance, not the decline, of men's power over women (particularly within the ideal model of the nuclear family), and the continuing fear and secrecy about sex. Men's need to prove their masculinity – their difference from women and from 'poofters' – through a compulsive heterosexuality (rarely free from anxiety about failure) is, in the context of AIDS, even more dangerous for women than it ever was before. (As well as more dangerous for gay men – with discrimination against homosexuals officially endorsed.) Today, it is clearer than ever that combating women's inequality, combating misogyny, and combating homophobia, are all part of the same struggle against the oppressive gender definitions sustaining an oppressive gender system.

Gay men are not, of course, the only 'traitors to the masculine cause'. There have always been men who supported the idea of female equality and attacked the idea of male dominance – like the men who argued and fought for women's suffrage over a hundred years ago.[144] They have often been men who have tried to become the type of people they believed free and independent women wanted them to be. I shall be looking in some detail at the predominantly heterosexual men who formed the 'men against sexism' groups of the 1970s and 1980s in the last chapter. But there is little doubt that it is homosexual men who have most threatened and angered those of their sex committed to affirming traditional manhood, and who have suffered most because of it.

Ninety years ago, in *Love's Coming of Age*, the British socialist and sexual radical, Edward Carpenter, expressed his passionate support for women's demands for economic and social independence and workers' struggles for a better life and recognition of the value of manual labour, along with the need to end the 'impure hush' shrouding sexuality in guilt and shame while denying the needs and pleasures of the body.[145] The link between the three, as he saw it, was the commercialisation of society, which prevented men and women alike from living together in loving communities based upon mutual support and true friendship, rather than rigid divisions and exploitation. Openly living as a homosexual at a time when such a practice was almost unthinkable, Carpenter believed homosexual men – 'Uranian' men he called them – were naturally closer and more sympathetic to women. Together with women and 'artisans', they would play a crucial role in creating a new and better world.[146] Carpenter thus anticipated the sentiments of many gay liberationists almost a century later – except that in accordance with the thought of his time he saw biological rather than social forces, intractable urges rather than personal choices, constructing such softened manhood. 'Uranians' were an 'intermediate', more androgynous sex, valuable because they could more easily bridge the gulf between women and men, communicate across the sexual divide and bring reconciliation.[147] Subsequently, he would describe them as a 'forward force in human evolution'[148] – a counterbalance to existing 'civilisation', which had unnecessarily exaggerated sex differences and made women, like his mother and sisters, prisoners in their own homes.[149]

Carpenter's ethical, utopian socialism, his exemplary practice of a homosexuality and a way of life geared towards the building of a new moral, spiritual and caring community within the 'philistine' body of the old, were short on practical strategy and tactics. And yet his rebellion against contemporary notions of manliness, still so familiar, to assert the reality of tenderness, vulnerability and passivity in men, and to demand the liberation of sex and love from darkness and shame, encapsulate for me what has been significant in the homosexual challenge to the masculine ideal. It is as relevant today as yesterday.

7. Competing Masculinities (III): Black Masculinity and the White Man's Black Man

If you're a Negro . . . you're the target for everybody's fantasies. If . . . you're a *black* woman . . . you know how to do *dirty things!* . . . And if you're a *black boy* you wouldn't be-*lieve* the holocaust that opens over your head – with all these despicable – *males* – looking for somebody to act out their fantasies on. And it happens in this case – if you're sixteen years old – to be *you*!

James Baldwin[1]

We were wanderers on a prehistoric earth, on an earth that wore the aspect of an unknown planet. We could have fancied ourselves the first of men taking possession of an accursed inheritance, to be subdued at the cost of a profound anguish and of excessive toil. But suddenly we struggled round a bend, there would be a glimpse of rush walls, of peaked grass-roofs, a burst of yells, a whirl of black limbs, a mass of hands clapping, of feet stamping, of bodies swaying, of eyes rolling, under the droop of heavy and motionless foliage . . . We were cut off from the comprehension of our surroundings; we glided past like phantoms, wondering and secretly appalled, as sane men would be before an enthusiastic outbreak in a madhouse . . . It was unearthly, and the men were – No, they were not inhuman. Well, you know, that was the worst of it – this suspicion of their not being inhuman. It would come slowly to one. They howled and leaped, and spun, and made horrid faces; but, what thrilled you was just the thought of their humanity – like yours – the thought of your remote kinship with this wild and passionate uproar. Ugly.

Joseph Conrad[2]

'Ugly', indeed, unbelievably ugly, were all the fruits of white men's four centuries of contact with Africa. Marlow's depiction of the people of Africa in Conrad's *Heart of Darkness* was, in many ways, more sophisticated than that of his contemporaries and predecessors. He thought he could detect a kinship with the 'black beast' of Africa created by the European imagination; others could not. One way of delving deeper into the fractured features of modern masculinity in the West is to explore the social construction of another subordinated masculinity – Black masculinity. What we will find is more evidence of the conflict and chaos at the heart of the dominant ideal of masculinity: heterosexual, white and – to the Victorian mind – English. The first 'fact' about the 'black man' which the white man knew was that he was not really a man at all – a child rather than an adult, a body not a mind. White men created the image of Black men as yet another contrast necessary for their own self-image. 'Travellers with closed minds', African writer and literary scholar Chinua Achebe comments on white men's and women's reportage of Africa, 'can tell us little except about themselves.'[3] What they reveal of themselves, however, is well worth pondering.

'Devils in Waiting': White Images of Africa

The beginnings of the European slave trade in Africa in the 1560s, which continued in British territories up until abolition in 1833, produced an accompanying literature of devaluation of the African man or woman as the 'beastly savage' – ugly, violent, lascivious. Ruling ideas never more lethally expressed the material interests of ruling groups. The barbarism and atrocities of slavery were rationalised as beneficial to its victims. As the slave trade came under increasing attack in the eighteenth century, standard descriptions of the people of Africa by pro-slavers grew ever more derogatory: 'Whatever evils the slave trade may be attended with . . . it is mercy . . . to poor wretches, who . . . would otherwise suffer from the butcher's knife.'[4] The growing anti-slavery movement countered the 'beastly savage' of the pro-slavers with its own invention, the 'noble savage' – innocent, sweet and simple – as in William Blake's memorable lines on the 'Little Black Boy' of 1789: 'My mother bore me in the southern wild / And I am black, but O! my soul is white'.[5] Aphra Behn's much earlier play *Oroonoko* had depicted another type of beautiful, brave and noble African Prince, and was so popular with its audience in England that some version of it was staged annually for over a century after its first performance in 1696.[6]

Yet, as Patrick Brantlinger and others have pointed out, the humanitarianism of the anti-slavery movement itself 'contained the seeds of empire'.[7] Genuinely humanitarian though the motives of the abolitionists were, their aims were nonetheless congruent with Britain's changing economic interests.[8] The leading industrial nation by the beginning of the nineteenth century, Britain became less dependent upon the use of slave labour earlier – when it was still crucial to the economy of her rivals.[9] Once slavery was abolished in British territory, while persisting elsewhere, British philanthropists came to see themselves as the saviours of the African people. Although Britain had been the leading Western slave-trader for nearly two centuries, her prior abolition of slavery served to establish the unquestioned moral superiority of the British, in their own eyes, over all other people's – white or Black.[10] And it was their historic mission, they now believed, to 'civilise' the world: 'Take up the White Man's burden / Ye dare not stoop to less', Kipling, their favourite poet, admonished them.[11] The possession of the largest empire the world has ever known – covering one fifth of the globe at the close of the nineteenth century – was regarded as the consequence and confirmation of the pre-eminence of the men of Britain and, in particular, the men of England. As the historian James Walvin reports on British thinking in the nineteenth century: 'Britain's unique role in the world – her apparently irresistable rise to global pre-eminence – was shaped by the distinctive qualities of her menfolk.'[12]

Attacking slavery at its roots, mid-nineteenth-century missionaries and explorers began to argue, meant converting Africa to Christian civilisation. And whereas the early abolitionists had correctly held Europe primarily responsible for the slave trade, their successors began transferring the blame onto African people. Thomas Fowell Buxton, who followed Wilberforce as head of the British anti-slavery movement, called in 1840 for increasing intervention in Africa to rescue its population from their own callous barbarity and lead them out of the 'kingdom of darkness'.[13] The crusade against slavery thus served to justify the British penetration into Africa: in the footsteps of Stanley Livingstone, intrepid explorers combined their voyages of discovery of the African continent with the missionary work of Christian salvation. (The use of quinine to prevent death from malaria rendered the journeys somewhat less hazardous than before.) As Nancy Stepan was later to conclude, 'Just as the battle against slavery was being won by abolitionists, the war against racism was being lost.'[14]

The idea of the English man as superior being, obliged reluctantly but inevitably to bring 'civilisation' to the inferior races of the world, was the unquestioned, unquestionable self-image of the Victorian gentleman. Livingstone, of all the mid-nineteenth-century British missionaries and explorers, probably the most humanitarian and respectful of African people, gives us a glimpse of the Victorian mind at its most benevolent:

> Let us hope that the Anglo-Saxon race will allow no other nation to outstrip it in the efforts to rescue thousands of fellow-creatures from the misery and degradation which must otherwise infallibly fall to their lot.[15]

Some of his contemporaries, less 'Christian' in outlook, believed that 'civilisation' would, either inevitably or from 'imperious necessity', wipe out the inferior breeds of man.[16] Sir William Harris, for example, argued that it was necessary to exterminate 'from off the face of the earth, a race of monsters'.[17] Thomas Carlyle, who also wrote of Blacks as of a different species, full of 'evil passions' and 'little removed in many respects from absolute savages' had declared in defence of Governor Eyre's murderous brutality in suppressing a riot in Jamaica in 1865: 'If Eyre had shot the whole Nigger population and flung them into the sea, would it probably have been much harm to them, not to speak of us.'[18] The savage racism of Carlyle was opposed at that time by the more liberal voices of men like James Stuart Mill, who did believe in the possibility of the white man educating the 'uncivilised' people of the world.[19] But the second half of the nineteenth century was a time when Carlyle's 'species racism' was to be strengthened by the spread of social Darwinism, which was used to reinforce the description of African people as an immutably different and inferior 'species' of human being. In Thomas Huxley's *Man's Place in Nature* (1863), as in Darwin's exposition of his theory of evolution, there is repeated reference to the Black man's greater proximity to the anthropoid ape precursors of humanity. Similarly, towards the close of the century, the female explorer Mary Kingsley argued that 'The difference between the African and the [European] is a difference not of degree but of kind . . . I feel the Black man is no more an undeveloped white man than a rabbit is an undeveloped hare.'[20] Africans themselves, all English men and women agreed, conceded the superiority of the white race: 'He is too low down, too completely severed from the white, to feel indignant.'[21]

In mid-nineteenth-century Britain the African explorers' tales of their journeys were to become extraordinarily popular, confirming the Victorian self-image. 'The public', as Alan Moorehead commented, 'could not have enough.'[22] But it was not until the 1880s, when the exploration and missionary work of the 1850s had turned into militaristic imperialist expansion in Africa, that fictional representations of the British encounter with Africa emerged to become the bestsellers of their day, and to consolidate the imperialist vision of the polarity of Black and white. The late-Victorian colonisation of Africa was the beginning of the end of 'the golden age' of British imperialism[23] – a reality which was not, however, reflected in its literature. English upper- and middle-class men departed for Africa to prove their 'manhood'. They read avidly about white men's adventures in the 'Dark Continent': the Black man serving as the necessary foil, the essential opposition, giving substance to the superiority of the white man.

The most successful of the white novelists on Africa, H. Ryder Haggard, began his literary career in the 1880s, capturing the British imagination at the peak of its interest in the subject. His books, be boasted, were written strictly for men to depict the superior physical, moral and mental attributes of white men: strength, stoicism, endurance, emotional restraint. (He dedicated his first African novel, *King Solomon's Mines* (1885), to 'all the big and little boys who read it'.[24] Immediate bestsellers, a new genre of imperialist fiction sought to portray an exclusively male world: 'I can safely say,' says the white hunter hero of *Allan Quatermain*, 'there is not a petticoat in the whole history.'[25] Of course, there were women in it. Women – Black women – existed at the very centre of these novels. Just as Africa itself is persistently depicted as 'female' (passive and inviting, wild, dangerous and deadly), so the language of the colonial narrative is one of sexual conquest. Like Africa itself, however, Black women are but the backdrop for the white man's testing of himself. The metaphor of the female object, to be opened up, penetrated, conquered, serves to underline the masculine features of the white man's testing of his 'virility'. 'There [in Africa],' as Somerset Maugham wrote, 'a man is really a man.'[26]

Unless he is Black, that is. Haggard often preferred the image of the 'noble savage' to that of the 'black beast' when portraying his Black men and women, but he never violated the rigid hierarchical division between civilised white heroes and primitive Black savages.[27] Though his books derived much of their romantic power and appeal from the desire of the white man for the Black woman, this was a forbidden fantasy never to be indulged – except metaphorically: 'Can the sun mate with the darkness, or the white with the black?' Haggard's Black female character asks.[28]. In its least malign forms, the colonial image of the Black man (and woman), portrayed him (or her) as child-like, emotional, servile, hyper-sexual: the exact antithesis of white manhood. Obviously and relentlessly, though presumably 'innocently', Victorians projected the full regressive force of their own repressed feelings onto African people, making manifest the nature of their own inner terrors. 'The radical psychoanalysis of racism,' as Joel Kovel argues in his compelling psychohistory of white racism, 'reveals the white ego in flight from the black, sensuous body':

> It is a quintessential fantasy of Otherness – for the black body from which the white ego flees is his own body, lost in the Cartesian split of the *cogito*, and projected into the Otherness of the black.[29]

'Western psychology', as Achebe says, has always needed 'to set Africa up as a foil to Europe, as a place of negations at once remote and vaguely familiar, in comparison with which Europeans' own state of spiritual grace will be manifest.'[30]

Joseph Conrad's fiction about Africa, apart from being of more enduring literary interest, was also, as I have suggested, more sophisticated; more sophisticated because it anticipated some of the twentieth-century psychoanalytically informed reflections on Africa. It was less innocent of the exploitative brutality of imperial rule ('robbery with violence, aggravated murder on a grand scale');[31] and it was less innocent of psychic ambivalence and denial ('But the wilderness had found him out early . . . whispered to him things about himself which he did not know . . . It echoed loudly within him because he was hollow at the core.'[32] Yet it was no less derogatory about the 'hand-clapping, eyes-rolling', pitiable 'nigger'. And it was no less certain that Africa and its people represented darkness and evil.

The image of Africa as dark and malevolent, primitive and unchanging, is with us still. But increasingly in the twentieth century, with British colonial imperialism contested and collapsing, the idea grew that Africa was not simply unchanged, but unchange-able. Attempts to 'civilise' the 'dark continent' and its 'alien people' were futile. Indeed, Westernised Black people evoked the fiercest scorn and contempt. 'The more they copied the white man the more funny it was', Graham Greene wrote in the 1950s.[33]

But Greene, following the path which Conrad had trod into twentieth-century thinking on Africa, no longer saw its native population as a different species. Reflecting the Freudian impact on Western thought, he saw Africans more as symbolising the id, the inner brute, the psychic centre of all humanity:

> What has astonished me about Africa was that it had never really been strange . . . The 'heart of darkness' was common to us both. Freud has made us conscious as we have never been before of those ancestral threads which still exist in our unconscious minds to lead us back . . . one is not certain how far the explorers knew the nature of the fascination which worked on them in the dirt, the disease, the barbarity and the familiarity of Africa.[34]

In *Journey Without Maps*, Graham Greene tells us that Africa is not so much a place as a shape, 'And the shape, of course, is roughly that of the human heart.'[35] It is this heart which Western civilisation has attempted to crush, suppressing our sexuality, along with all our other instincts. Here the Black man and woman are to be envied for their sexual being, their rhythm, their instinctual life. As Jablow and Hammond conclude in their survey of four centuries of British writing about Africa:

> The liquidation of empire by no means bankrupted the traditional images. On the contrary, the new situation has been as much a stimulus for proliferation of the tradition as had been the growth of empire.[36]

The legacy of colonialism still dominates Western thinking on all non-Western people. It is important, as some writers are now doing, to examine the diversity and specificity of its effects on the construction of, and interaction between, different kinds of ethnic masculinities in various parts of the world. The permutations are endless, whether looking at the effects of white colonialism in Africa, Australia, Asia and Latin America, or, from the other side, the situation of the Algerian confronting the European in France, the Irish, West Indian or Asian confronting one another and also the English in Britain or the American Indian confronting the European American in North America, and so on. The feminist historian Mrinalini Sinha, for example, has recently explored the connections between Victorian ideals of masculinity and the maintenance of British rule in India.[37] She argues that the ubiquitous attribution of 'effeminacy' to Bengali men, in particular, in colonial discourses on India in the late-nineteenth century was central to the rationalisation of colonial oppression there. A pervasive emphasis on the 'puny' and 'diminutive' size of Bengali men and on the practice of marrying 'child' brides was the 'evidence' of lack of sexual restraint and control.[38] Such denunciation of effeminacy in Bengali men also, Sinha suggests, reflected late-Victorian fears of homosexuality.

Though consistent in their attribution of inferiority and forms of sexual decadence, colonial stereotypes of Asians and 'Orientals' have always been distinct from the stereotypes of Africans. Rudie Bleys has suggested that whereas nineteenth-century literature equated 'black' with an undifferentiated sexual energy 'black = animal = lascivious' it equated 'eastern' or 'oriental' with hyperdifferentiated eroticism 'eastern = decadent = hypersensitive: satyriasis, nymphomania, androgyny, pederasty'.[39] It is impossible even to begin to encompass the complexity of the representations of ethnicity in colonial discourses and the differing forms of racism they articulate and reproduce in the space of this chapter. Instead, I shall focus upon Western images of the African (and Afro-Caribbean) which remain, overall, the most pernicious, destructive and tenacious.

Sex and Racism: The Black Male as Phallic Symbol

White men, as James Baldwin anticipated Kovel and Achebe in

portraying, have always needed someone on whom to act out their fantasies. In all his essays and fiction Baldwin passionately pursues this theme: 'The white man's unadmitted – and apparently, to him, unspeakable – private fears and longings are projected onto the Negro.'[40] 'You'd be surprised,' echoes Charles Wright's messenger boy and prostitute in *The Messenger*, 'how my colour helps business. Though I've missed out several times because, of course, I wasn't dark enough.'[41] Frantz Fanon, whose fierce evocative polemic on the white man's preoccupation with the Black man as beast and penis symbol was written in the 1950s, on one occasion used a word association test to measure the fears of his white psychiatric patients. He established (for those who prefer a quantifiable 'scientific' methodology to his more characteristically powerful literary analysis) that in almost 60 per cent of replies the word 'Negro' elicited the associations 'biology, penis, strong, athletic, potent . . . savage, animal, evil, sin'.[42] His conclusions were in turn echoed by the sociological enquiries of Roger Bastide working in Paris and Brazil in the early sixties: 'In the course of a great number of interviews the question "race" always provoked the answer "sex".'[43]

Hell, death, darkness, and the fearsome but enticing route to damnation, have always been entangled – in Western consciousness – with sex. For four centuries the relations between Black and white, Othello and Desdemona, have been overlaid by Black sexual imagery. Black is the colour of the 'dirty' secrets of sex – relentlessly represented in the image of Black 'boy' as stud, and Black woman as whore. In Britain the apotheosis of racialist thought and literature associating Black people with sex and bestiality was reached in the days of its imperialist 'glory' in the nineteenth century. In the US, at much the same time, it served to justify the gruesome practice of white lynchings of Black men well into the twentieth century. By now Western thought is long familiar with the theory equating Black men and sex: Freud, as Greene says, and Fanon analysed, having 'made us conscious' of the projection of one's own punished and therefore threatening, repressed impulses onto others who can be seen as inferior. Nonetheless its continuing and pernicious reality remains startling. If you want to know about the unhealthy psyche of the white man, ask a Black man, Baldwin declares over and over again:

> I have spent most of my life, after all, watching white people and outwitting them, so that I might survive. I think I know something about the American masculinity which most men of my generation do not know because they have not been menaced by it in the way that I have been. It is still true, alas, that to be an American negro is to be a kind of walking phallic symbol: which means that one pays in one's own personality, for the sexual insecurity of others.[44]

The price Baldwin paid, doubly negating, yet successfully surviving, the ideals of white masculinity (proud as he was to be Black *and* homosexual), is what indeed made him one of the most powerful and persuasive male commentators on white American masculinity over the past three decades – right up until his death in 1987. Baldwin describes the 'unbelieving shock' during his first visit to the Southern states, on being suddenly groped by some of the most' powerful, most 'nigger'-hating, white men of America: 'it is absolutely certain that white men, who invented the nigger's big black prick, are still at the mercy of this nightmare, are still, for the most part, doomed in one way or another, to attempt to make this prick their own'.[45] There are few things harder to understand, Baldwin asserts, or (as he says he felt when he was younger) to forgive, than the American idea of masculinity, which in his view is identical with the American idea of sexuality:

> On every street corner, I was called a faggot. This meant I was despised, and, however horrible that is, it is clear. What was *not* clear at that time of my life was what motivated the men and boys who mocked me and chased me; for, if they found me when they were alone, they spoke very gently and wanted me to take them home and make love . . . The bafflement and pain this caused in me remain beyond description.[46]

Black people suffer, but white people remain pitiful:

> If Americans were not so terrified of their private selves, they would never have needed to invent and could never have become so dependent on what they still call 'the Negro problem'. This problem, which they invented in order to safeguard their purity, has made them criminals and monsters, and it is destroying them.[47]

White people suffer, but Black men were literally destroyed: destroyed by the lethal combination of white sexual insecurity and racism. It was Black men and women who lived and died with the daily nightmare of the white lynch mob. Between 1925 and 1950 around two and a half thousand Black men in the United States were lynched.[48] Such lynching – often public spectacles staged before the fascinated gaze of white men, women and children – were routinely concluded with a final act of literal castration. The emancipation of Black slaves in the Southern states of America had been followed by the immediate violent upsurge of lynching of Black men, at least one every three days between 1885 and 1900.[49] In *Southern Horrors*, written during this period, the Black writer Ida B. Wells noted that the *accusation* of rape had been made in only a third of the lynchings in the years she analysed, but that the *justification* given for lynching always referred to the protection of white womanhood from the bestial Black man.[50] In fact, it was Black womanhood which was being systematically violated by white men. These were the men, in the words of Pauline Hopkins, another contemporary Black novelist, 'who created the mulatto race, who recruit its ranks year after year by the very means which they invoked lynch law to suppress, *bewailing the sorrows of violated womanhood!*'[51] The reality, however, was repressed and displaced on to the virginal white woman.[52] Lynch mobs could thus operate as a form of political terror, ensuring the social and economic subordination of Black men, but be excused and condoned by manipulation of the sexual fears and repressed longings of white men and women. The ideological fictions involved are perfectly captured in *Gone With the Wind*, written in 1936 and one of the bestselling books of all time (as well as the most popular film ever made.) The narrative is a vindication of the Confederate cause in the American Civil War and a celebration of the growth of the Ku-Klux-Klan as necessary for the preservation of the Old South and its belles from the negro menace. Its hero, Rhett Butler, goes to jail for killing a Black man who was rude to a white lady and, as Helen Taylor notes, the book contains long passages of vitriolic description of the ingratitude and insolence of the 'black apes out the jungle', with their 'huge black paws'.[53] To this day, although 50 per cent of men convicted for rape in the Southern states are white, over 90 per cent of men executed for rape are Black (mostly accused of raping white women). No white man has ever been executed for raping a Black woman.[54]

The image of the Black person as mere body – primitive, sexual and violent – is, however, not only a staple component of the bigoted thinking of the traditional racist. Carried in all the race symbolism of Western culture, it has been equally important to white people who support Black rights and equality. The Beat rebels of the fifties, like Jack Kerouac, wrote wistfully of Black sensuality: 'I walked with every muscle aching . . . in the Denver colored section, wishing I were a Negro, feeling that the best the white world has offered was not enough ecstacy for me, not enough life, joy, kicks, darkness, music, not enough night.'[55] More elaborately, Norman Mailer has passionately promoted Black equality, 'for the Negro's equality would tear a profound shift into the psychology, the sexuality, and the imagination of every White alive'[56]:

> Knowing in the cells of his existence that life was war, nothing but war, the Negro (all exceptions admitted) could rarely afford the sophisticated inhibitions of civilization, and so he kept for his survival the art of the primitive, he lived in the enormous present, he subsisted for the Saturday night kicks, relinquishing the pleasures of the mind for the more obligatory pleasures of the body, and in his music he gave voice to the character and quality of his existence, to his rage and the infinite variations of joy, lust, languor, growl, cramp, pinch, scream and despair of his orgasm.[57]

Inevitably, in a white dominated culture, the same racist images are internalised by Black people themselves. This was the bitter message of Fanon's *Black Skin, White Masks*.[58] In the type of complementary 'reverse discourse' we have already encountered, Black men and women take on board the attributes of the sensuous, sexual creatures of white imagining. 'There is a further contradiction, another turn of the screw of oppression', as Kobena Mercer wrote recently in Britain, 'which occurs when Black men subjectively internalise and incorporate aspects of the dominant definitions of masculinity in order to contest the definitions of dependency and powerlessness which racism and racial oppression enforce.'[59] All the standard sociological enquirers confirm this. In *Dusky Venus, Black Apollo* Roger Bastide asserts that in Brazil the Black males questioned 'were certain of their superiority over the white', while throughout the French West Indies 'all the Negroes we questioned affirmed their superior masculinity, claiming that white women preferred them to whites.'[60] More literary proof exists everywhere. The Black writers and scholars who set out to celebrate a genuinely African personality, like Aimé Césaire, Leopold Sedar Senghor and Leon Dumas re-used but revalued the old racist stereotypes. They built a new literary movement, known as Negritude, around the journal *L'Etudiant Noir* between 1934 and 1948, which echoed some of the earlier themes of the North American Black writers of the Harlem Renaissance in the 1920s. Black people, they argued, reasoned through touch rather than sight, were more intuitive than analytic and had, as their most distinctive feature, a sensual feeling for rhythm: 'Emotion,' Senghor declared, 'was Negroid.'[61] By this, as the contemporary North American Black writer and critic Charles Johnson indicates, Senghor meant that Black people had a sympathetic, poetic, spiritual, even magical grasp of the world, adding, 'What we have in Negritude, I suspect, is an inversion of black typifications derived from earlier white stereotypes.'[62]

The Black man yet again represents the body; the white man, the mind. What we have here, it might be added (as Johnson does not), is in most respects the very same polarity usually drawn between the 'feminine' and the 'masculine' in white discourse and consciousness. And thus, consistently enough, the language of Negritude is today reflected in the inverted patriarchal discourse characteristic of many of the most popular feminist texts. They contrast the *essentially* 'feminine' with the *essentially* 'masculine', by reaffirming the links between women and 'nature', women and feeling.[63] Black writers have also emphasised the greater commitment to communalism, rather than individualism, on the part of Black people in both Africa and the US,[64] alongside the idea of the negro as the 'natural nonconformist', the necessary re-humaniser of white people. Analogous themes also reappear in contemporary feminist writing: 'Women,' Petra Kelly argues, must lead the way to a better world, for only she 'can go back to her womb, her roots, her natural rhythms, her inner search for harmony and peace.'[65]

The homology of the 'black' and the 'feminine' here is hardly surprising. Both groups share the experience of social subordination and cultural devaluation (each constructing the more familiar 'consolations of the powerless' to achieve some sense of dignity and self-worth)[66] and, as we have seen, the colonial stereotype of the stereotype of the Black man existed precisely to provide the essential contrast with white 'manliness', 'true' manliness. The Black man was to be divested of his masculinity, save that which he shared with the sub-human male animal. Addressing the stereotype of Black physicality in *Soul on Ice*, Eldridge Cleaver, one of the leaders of the Black Panther movement of the 1960s, maintained that the gulf between mind and body did indeed coincide with the gulf between Black and white. Stripped of a mental life Black people lived out the superior bodily existence of the 'Supermanual Menial', or the 'Supermasculine Menial' with the attributes of 'strength, brute power, force, virility'. He contrasted this with the white man as the Omnipotent Administrator', associated, among other things, with 'weakness, frailty, cowardice and effeminacy'.[67]

The issue of 'manliness' was thus crucial to the confrontation between white men and Black. It reveals once again the inner contradictions of 'masculinity': on the one hand its symbol, the phallus, stands for adult *human* power and worth, on the other hand it is physically tangible only as a piece of biological equipment men share with rats, bats and every other higher vertebrate male. The contradiction lived by the white man consisted in the fact that assertion of what he saw as the inferior, 'bestial' side of manliness – the physical proof of his own biological 'potency' – was also necessary for the confirmation of his own superior male status and identity. Hence his simultaneous fear and idealisation of the Black man: the power of the Black man's penis. The doubling of fear and desire detected in men's contradictory relations to 'the feminine', and projected outwards to construct the Madonna/Whore dichotomy, reappears in the white man's image of the Black man, projected outwards, this time in the noble savage/black beast dichotomy. Cleaver's homophobic, super-macho bravado notwithstanding, however, the problem for the Black man compelled to conform to racist stereotypes, deprived of all but a biological maleness, was of another, altogether more painful, order.

Black Male Rage: The 'Emasculation' of Black Men?

Call Me Not a Man is the title of the collected fiction of Mtutuzeli Matshoba, who was born in Soweto in 1950: 'For neither am I a man in the eyes of the law / Nor am I a man in the eyes of my fellow man.'[68] His stories describe the current routine brutalisation and humiliation of Black men in his country:

> By dodging, lying, resisting where it is possible, bolting when I'm already cornered, parting with invaluable money, sometimes calling my sisters into the game to get amorous with my captors, allowing myself to be slapped on the mouth in front of my womenfolk and getting sworn at with my mother's private parts, the component of me which is man has died countless times in one lifetime. Only a shell of me remains to tell you of the other man's plight, which is in fact my own.[69]

It is not the plight of the Black man in South Africa, however, but that of his brothers in the US which currently constitutes most of what literature there is on Black masculinity available in Britain. Notwithstanding its cultural specificity, it is relevant to any analysis of 'masculinity', and to the problematic intersection of race and sexual politics in Britain, as well as in the US. (As we shall see Black people, having been in Britain in large numbers only since the late 1940s and 50s, have been excluded from writing and publishing until very recently.) As in South Africa today, North American Black literature, at least that written before 1970, has been one of pain and despair. The North American critic David Littlejohn wrote of Afro-American novels in 1966: 'A white reader is saddened, then burdened, then numbed by the deadly sameness, the bleak wooden round of ugly emotions and ugly situations: the same frustrated dreams.'[70] Alas for the poor white reader! The desperate struggle of Black people simply to survive, and then to assert the most minimum of human rights, created a tradition of Black protest literature representing extremes of human suffering. Richard Wright's *Native Son*, which became an overnight bestseller when published in 1940, is the outstanding classic of this genre of Black protest fiction. Bigger Thomas, its hero, is a man so mutilated by fear and self-hatred that murder becomes the sole act through which he can assert his own power, his manhood.

In *Black Boy* Richard Wright provided an autobiographical sketch of how it felt to be forced into the 'role of a non man' – the powerlessness of knowing that white people could violate your life at will: 'Each of us [Black male workers] hated and feared the whites, yet had a white man put in a sudden appearance we would have assumed silent, obedient smiles . . . Each of us felt the same shame, felt how foolish and weak we were in the face of the domination of the whites.'[71] Before escaping the South, Wright realised that only three options were open to him. He could accept inferiority with resigned subservience, like his workmate Shorty, who would quite literally present his arse to be kicked. He could turn his rage and hatred against fellow Blacks, as had happened when he reluctantly allowed whites to arrange a fight between him and another Black worker. Or he could find 'release from anxiety and longing in sex and alcohol'.[72] He could accept none of them. Through the exceptional combination of good fortune and literary talent, Wright himself escaped the degradation he feared and described so well, the degradation which destroys his fictional heroes. Many Black men could not. Chester Himes, writing five years later, describes the same hopeless options facing his hero in *If He Hollers Let Him Go*: 'I felt small and humiliated and desperate, looking at the two big white men laughing at me . . . Living every day scared, walled in, locked up.'[73] Murder, to these men, seemed the only act of self-assertion possible, the only route out of a lifetime of enforced, child-like submission and powerlessness.

> I wanted to kill him so he'd know I was killing him and in such a way that he'd know he didn't have a chance. I wanted him to feel as scared and powerless and unprotected as I felt every goddamned morning I woke up.[74]

Black people's rage at racial segregation and discrimination in the United States burst out of resignation and peaceful protest into the race riots of the 1960s – whereupon the study of the Black psyche became the object of new forms of scientific scrutiny and social concern. The 'problem', it was discovered, was Black masculinity. Protest and violence were being fuelled by the injury which injustice and brutality had inflicted on the Black personality, new voices proclaimed throughout the 1960s. Black psychiatrists, psychologists and sociologists began to be heard alongside white professionals describing the psychology of the American Negro – always focusing on the 'damaged' Black man. 'I'm not a man, none of us are men,' was the cry the Black psychologist Kenneth Clark repeatedly heard and subsequently reported in *Dark Ghetto*. Black men and women, denied social respect and dignity, had low self-esteem: 'These doubts become the seeds of a pernicious self- and group-hatred, the Negro's complex and debilitating prejudice against himself.'[75] In 1968, the two Black psychiatrists, William Grier and Price Cobbs, published their case studies in *Black Rage*, concluding that:

> Every black man in America has suffered such injury as to be realistically sad about the hurt done him . . . He develops a sadness and intimacy with misery which has become a characteristic of black Americans. It is a *cultural depression* and a *cultural masochism*.[76]

The Black Muslim leader and radical Malcolm X was passionately preaching the same message: 'The worst crime the white man has committed has been to teach us to hate ourselves.'[77]

Meanwhile, white sociological writing like that of Charles Silberman in *Crisis in Black and White* was also describing the Negroes' 'crisis of identity': 'What Negroes need is to be treated like men . . . to believe in their heart that they *are* men.'[78] Negro children, he argued, have a negative picture of themselves by first grade, or earlier. Their sense of powerlessness is particularly destructive to Negro men, who cannot enact 'the usual male role', with consequent feelings of shame and failure: 'To avoid hating himself still more, he turns his hatred against his family, or simply cuts off any feelings for them at all.'[79] The literature on the American Negro, from the mainstream conventional analysis of the Moynihan Report on the Black family in 1965 to the fiery polemic of Malcolm X, also concurred that a 'matriarchal family system' was at the heart of 'the Negro problem'. Unemployment, and the requirements of welfare benefits (paid only in the absence of a male breadwinner) meant that many Black men, unable to find adequate or decent employment, could not provide for their families – who could often survive better without them. Black families were therefore frequently held together by women (a tradition dating back to the times of slavery), with fathers either absent or exerting only a weakened paternal influence.[80] Once again 'the Negro problem' was seen in terms of Black men.

What constitutes this specifically masculine problem, however, has become an even more complex issue over the last few decades. Anxiety about the 'emasculation' of the Black man co-exists with anxiety over the super-sexual, super-macho nature of the Black man. Is he not-man-enough, or is he too-masculine-by-half? The contradiction, of course, lies in Western notions of masculinity itself. Baldwin had perceived it back in 1951:

> In the truly awesome attempt of the American to at once preserve his innocence and arrive at man's estate, that mindless monster, the tough guy, has been created and perfected, whose masculinity is found in the most infantile and elementary externals and whose attitude to women is the wedding of the most abysmal romanticism and the most implacable distrust.'[81]

His countrymen, nearly four decades later, Black and white alike, remain confused as they face the puzzle of 'black masculinity'.

The contradiction is repeatedly and explicitly revealed in the first, single-authored North American text which addresses itself exclusively to the task of exploring Black masculinity. In his book *Black Masculinity*, written in the early 1980s, Robert Staples emphasises that it is the intersection of the 'masculine mystique' with institutional racism which lies at the heart of Black men's problem. But he cannot make the next move to question 'masculinity' itself. He complains, for example, that after placing obstacles to self-realisation in the way of the Black man, 'America then has its bearers of ideology, the social scientists, falsely indict his lack of manhood.'[82] But that is not the problem, he argues; indeed, Black men learn to be men all too well: 'Not only do their mothers train them for a masculine ideal but they provide them with a deference which they come to expect in later life.'[83] Yet, contradicting himself, Staples takes as his own starting point the argument that the Black male is in conflict with the normative definition of masculinity: 'This is a status which few, if any, black males have been able to achieve.'[84] Exactly like the texts he criticises, Staples stresses that Black men are 'insecure in their male identity, and lacking in a positive self-concept.'[85] Surveying Black male youth, he instances the extraordinary high rates of homicide (the number one cause of death among Black males 15–34), of suicide (higher than that of the total population of all ages), of imprisonment (five and a half times their representation in the society at large), of drug-taking (an estimated one third of Black men in the inner city have a drug problem) and of educational failure (Black male children perform below grade level at twice the rate of Black females, who have a higher level of educational success at every level below doctorate.) 'It is patently clear,' he concludes, 'that the central concerns of Black men are *not* about relinquishing male privilege or forging new concepts of androgyny or sex-role egalitarianism.'[86] They are about giving men 'the minimal prerequisites of manhood – life-sustaining employment and the ability to support a family'.[87]

But are things quite so patently clear? Staples also emphasises the 'unmitigated male chauvinism' of Black youth, the 'virility cult' of 'lower-income Black males' who, denied other forms of masculine fulfilment, prove their manhood through sexual 'conquest' and domestic dominance. Fifty per cent of all reported rapes in the US involve Black men (who constitute around 11.5 per cent of the population) and wife abuse is reported as 400 per cent higher in low-income Black families,[88] where child abuse is also reported at over three times the rate for white children.[89] There is no doubt, as Staples and many others have observed, that racism enters into these official statistics – the violence of 'respectable' men being so much more easily concealed. There is equally little doubt that they reveal very real Black male exploitativeness and violence against women and children – however much this is conditioned by Black men's specific experience of the brutalisation of white racism, merely at its most blatant in the everyday violence of racist policing. 'The strongarming of black women into sexual submission is pervasive in the sexual histories collected by this writer,' Staples admits, 'and is not a practise confined to working-class blacks but equally represented among the bourgeoisie.'[90]

While pointing to these realities, Staples himself remains principally concerned with how Black *men*, rather than women, have been 'victimized the most' by what he calls the 'masculine mystique'. He observes that with homicide, suicide and accidents being the main cause of death among Black youth, 'proving one's manhood can be deadly as well as costly'.[91] True; but it does not, as Staples seems to suggest, exonerate Black men. Ignoring men and women's moral agency, however appalling the social conditions, Staples blames the media for the 'carefree hustling superstud caricature' of Black men it has been presenting to them since the seventies. The old image Black men had of themselves, particularly in the South, as stable husbands and fathers, has been undermined by the new images which mesh with the reality of Black urban youth today – 50 per cent of whom are unemployed (four times higher than twenty years ago.)[92] Staples is clearly right to stress the impact of social conditions and media messages on what young Black men feel and do, but disappointing insofar as he sees the solution to the tough, narcissistic images of Black masculinity today in what he regards as the better, more responsible images of yesterday. Black men's sexism and exploitation of women, it seems, is to be tackled by restoring old masculine privileges, and not by listening seriously to the critiques of Black feminists who, he argues, blame the victim – men being the main victims of their own machismo. It is the acceptance of this excuse which, as bell hooks observes, prevents Black men from seeing that Black male domination has never enhanced or enriched Black family life: 'The seemingly positive aspects of the patriarchy (caretaker and provider) have been the most difficult for masses of black men to realise, and the negative aspects (maintaining control through psychological or physical violence) are practiced daily.'[93] The struggle of Black people, she adds, should not, as it so often has, be made synonymous 'with the efforts of black males to have patriarchal power and privilege'.[94]

Part of the confusion and ambivalence in Staples' writing derives, I am suggesting, from his failure to appreciate the contradictions in 'masculinity' itself. Masculinity, he is well aware, involves a certain level of personal autonomy and control over people and things. It is not some type of internal essence, which Black men have or lack, but the assumption and possession of an array of privileges many of which are denied most Black men. For the Black male underclass, like other men denied the usual confirmations of gender superiority, the only mechanisms of dominance available are frequently the mechanisms of self-destruction – internecine violence, sexual coercion and self-hatred. For Black men, however, there is the added poison of a cultural climate of devaluation, its literal racist contours now inscribed in language – uniquely summed up in the word *de-nigration*. Instead of exploring this further, however, Staples adopts more essentialist categories of masculinity which lead him to defend the intrinsic masculinity of Black men, rather than to criticise the mechanisms of dominance necessary to establish it in the first place, or, when such mechanisms of dominance cannot be taken for granted, the resort to the destructive use of violence to shore up a personal sense of masculinity. This is well illustrated when he examines the 'empirical' data on Black masculinity obtained from those bizarre psychological 'measures' of masculinity/femininity discussed in chapter three. Staples objects to psychologists concluding that Black men are more 'feminine' than white men (agreeing with questions like 'I think I feel more intensely than most people do') on the grounds that white standards cannot always be used in evaluating Black behaviour.[95] Of course, psychologists do operate with ethnocentric measures of 'masculinity', 'femininity', and all other personality variables. Yet Staples is here failing to identify the deeper problem – namely, that there is something wrong with the concept of 'masculinity' itself when it is defined through some fixed set of traits, attitudes or stereotyped behaviour.

It is certainly of interest that the stereotypes of white masculinity – the typical silence on feelings and inability to express emotions, for example – are so much at odds with the Black jazz, blues, soul and reggae tradition, so expressive of Black men's (and women's) feelings and emotions. But it reveals no essential truths about masculinity. It reveals, rather, the types of resistance, strength and creativity, alongside pain and brutalisation, which characterise the subordinated existence of many Black men today. Despite their grim picture of contemporary Black manhood, the 1960s books on the psychology of Black people had nevertheless all concluded by detecting optimistic signs of change. In concert with the emergence of Black Power, Black rebellion and Black consciousness of oppression, they had argued, was the growth of new confidence and self-esteem in Black men and women. The times, according to Clark, Grier, Cobb and Silberman alike, were changing: 'No matter what repressive measures are invoked against blacks, they will never swallow their rage and go back to blind hopelessness.'[96]

The times were indeed changing. But by the close of the 1970s, with growing economic crisis in North America, they were about to become a lot worse for many Black people and other ethnic minorities. What we have witnessed in both North America and Britain since the mid-seventies is a resurgence of white racism, which, in the context of a 70 per cent unemployment rate for Black teenagers in many North American cities, takes the form of the increasing criminalisation of the image of the Black male.[97]

It is now clear, as many have noted, that white racism was a significant factor behind George Bush's election as President of the United States, most blatant in the Republican flier used in Maryland featuring Michael Dukakis beside released Black rapist Willie Horton: 'You, your spouse, your children, your parents, and your friends can have opportunity to receive a visit from someone like Willie Horton if Mike Dukakis becomes president.'[98] The Ku-Klux-Klan has reappeared as a political force in the Southern States of America and, more disturbingly, been assimilated into certain sections of the Republican Party. Some members have even been elected to local office in some states of the South, like David Duke in the 8th Congressional District of Louisiana. The strength of this new racism was hideously evident in the stunning support offered the white gunman Bernhard Goetz who, in December 1984, shot four unarmed youths – two in the back – in a New York subway train. He became an overnight celebrity and hero for millions of Americans. Throughout the media, people vented their rage against Goetz's victims – one of whom had asked him for five dollars – mourning the fact that these 'Wounded Muggers', as they were instantly labelled, were still alive – though one, Darrell Cabey, would be brain damaged and paralysed for life. At first refusing even to indict Goetz for assault or attempted murder, the New York courts eventually cleared him of all charges other than unlicenced possession of a gun – even though Goetz had coldly confessed, 'My intention was to murder them, to hurt them, to make them suffer as much as possible.'[99] In the courtroom, his victims were repeatedly referred to as 'savages' and 'vicious predators'.[100] Invisible and silenced, neither visited nor interviewed, the Black youths were remorselessly pilloried as arrogant, intimidating, violent. Only Les Payne, the Black editor of *Newsday*, pointed out the racist nature of the celebration. Had the gunman been Black, his victims white (or Black), there would have been outrage not celebration: '[But] the world knows that black teenagers are subway muggers. In picking up the gun, Goetz, the blonde hero, struck a blow for white manhood.'[101] The message was written on the subway walls 'GOETZ RULES NIGGERS'.

In the face of such hatred, Black manhood in the United States – since the politicisation of the sixties – remains conscious of its rage against white power and privilege. Black Panther leaders, like Eldridge Cleaver, Bobby Seale and Huey Newton, had hoped to build a confident, combative, Black identity through collective self-help, which would enable Black people to organise and control their own communities, as well as to resist white policing and repression by armed self-defence.[102] But the 'armed struggle' destroyed, imprisoned or eventually silenced nearly all its leaders. The hopes of more moderate Blacks for better times for working-class Black people were snuffed out by the economic recession of the late seventies. And there followed a decade of Reaganism, pursuing warfare politics to the virtual exclusion – indeed, elimination – of welfare policies. Black manhood remains, at its broad and harshest edge, still in the grip of what Kovel describes as 'the usual mechanisms of submission' – self-hatred and the compensation or relief offered through drugs, alcohol and violence.[103] (He fails to add, or analyse, the fact that these mechanisms primarily attach to men.) Today's North American drug gangs are but another crushing reiteration of the same regression. And yet, while the Black man's search for a confident, or even liveable, identity in North America today remains for many as perilous as ever, there is another side to Black identity, which, though constructed out of subordination and racism itself, has always served to challenge and threaten white masculinity.

'The Negro, as he exists in America now,' LeRoi Jones (now Amiri Baraka) wrote in 1963, 'is a natural nonconformist. Being black in a society where such a state is an extreme liability is the most extreme form of nonconformity available.'[104] Despite the romanticism here, self-identified 'outsiders' do have a special and troubling presence in their own societies, which gives them a certain power – at times, a certain glory. 'I don't want to be fitted into this society,' Baldwin said, 'I would rather be dead. In fact, there's no difference between being fitted into this society and dying.'[105] For all that Cleaver, LeRoi Jones and other Black radicals might deride Baldwin's homosexuality, and reject his more nuanced and doubtless more accurate perception of the 'disquieting complexities' of Black ambivalence – hating white people but despising themselves as well – they nevertheless shared the belief that Black people, precisely because of their oppression, had much to teach the white world.

What they had to teach was not only the dignity and courage of survival, but something extra which derived from reappropriating and reversing the negative meanings attached to the Black body as bestial, unclean, menacing and criminal. It related to the areas of life white men could not handle – their fear of the body, fear of sex, fear above all, as Baldwin saw, of men touching men. Through dancing, athletic and erotic performance, but most powerfully through music, Black men could express something about the body and its physicality, about emotions and their cosmic reach, rarely found in white culture – least of all in white male culture. As Jones rightly boasts:

> In the evolution of form in Negro music it is possible to see not only the evolution of the Negro as a cultural and social element of American culture, but also the evolution of culture itself. The 'Coon Shout' proposed one version of the American Negro – and of America; Ornette Coleman proposes another.[106]

Few could deny the compelling role of Black music throughout Western culture; 'life-affirming in its expression of deep emotion, of hope, of 'community' and of belonging. The expressive power of Black culture is also evident in Black literature. Discussing North American Black literature since the 1970s, Charles Johnson portrays a fiction still 'desperately searching for strong models of black manhood', still struggling to see beyond the despair of Black life destroyed by racism, and yet now offering an affirmative and celebratory vision of Black wisdom and community.[107] From its vantage-point inside and outside mainstream society, Black culture continues to assess and criticise white culture and consciousness. And ironically, for Black radicals, it serves also as a means to taunt notions of white masculinity. It is difficult becoming a man if you are Black, LeRoi Jones tells us, but much harder if you are white: 'In fact you will find very few white Americans with much knowledge of what manhood involves. They are too busy running the world or running from it.'[108] Or as Baldwin similarly suggests: 'The only thing worse than being a black man in America is being a white man in America.'[109] Black and white men continue to fight over the badges of 'masculinity'.

The many parallels between the troubled relations of race and masculinity in the United States and Britain are not accidental. As Stuart Hall *et al.*, convincingly demonstrate in *Policing the Crisis*, the term 'Mugger', with its American connotations of social chaos, urban violence and, above all, race conflict, crossed the Atlantic ocean to Britain by the mid-1970s.[110] The image of the 'new' criminal, with his new label, was Black: youth crime and Black youth were becoming synonymous (characteristically, Black women remained invisible – 'Black youth' was male.) Polarisation between the police and Black communities, between white working-class and Black youth, steadily increased in Britain throughout the seventies, especially after the disproportionate rise in Black unemployment with the onset of economic recession in 1974. The low pay, poor housing and whole paraphernalia of white racism which the Black British had endured in the fifties and sixties, believing things would improve for their children, were now revealed as not merely chronic, but worsening. Yet amidst the increased impoverishment, police brutality, rising racist assaults and entrenchment of state racism through discriminatory immigration controls, Black youth had grown more confident and less deferential to white authority:

> Between the late 1960s and the 1970s, the seeds of cultural resistance have not only sprouted in Britain's 'Harlems' up and down the country, they have blossomed – but now in a distinctly Afro-Caribbean form . . . In and through the revivalist imagery of the 'dreadlocks', the music of the dispossessed (dispossessed . . . in Kingston as much as it was in Brixton or Handsworth) and the insistent, driving beat of the reggae sound systems came the hope of deliverence from 'Babylon'. The 'culture' of the back-to-Africa sect, the Ras Tafari, is crucial here; both in Brixton and Kingston in recent years it is the dress, beliefs, philosophy and language of this once marginal and despised group which has provided the generalisation and radicalisation of black consciousness amongst sectors of black youth in the cities: the source of an intense black cultural nationalism. It is this 'religion of the oppressed' which has swept the minds as well as swayed the bodies of young black men and women.[111]

Black wageless youth, drifting between the search for jobs, and surviving through petty crime and 'hustling' (earning a living outside of wage labour, usually through dope dealing, pimping or gambling), have a culture which can taunt and terrify, even as it influences, the white mainstream culture from which it is marginalised. As Dick Hebdige has written, the Rastafarian movement has turned 'negritude into a positive sign, a loaded essence, a weapon at once deadly and divinely licensed.'[112] And once again it is through music, largely absent from the licenced airwaves, that this celebration of Black identity is maintained. Reggae provided the focus, the new values, the definitions, the 'streetwise' style, the movement, the walk, of Black youth: 'It's a Black Man Time' as I-Roy sang out. In his recent survey of racial politics, Paul Gilroy offers a rich account of Black expressive cultures of affirmation and protest in Britain. He writes of the importance of the sound system, and the performances of the Black DJ and the MC (or toaster) in promoting active and celebratory musical consumption: 'It is above all in these performances that black Britain has expressed the improvisation, spontaneity and intimacy which are key characteristics of all new world black musics, providing a living bridge between them and African traditions of music-making which dissolve the distinctions between art and life, artefact and expression which typify the contrasting traditions of Europe.'[113] With the hugely successful commercial marketing of Bob Marley's amalgam of pop and reggae in the late 1970s, Gilroy notes, many young whites as well as Blacks jubilantly identified with his blend of anti-racism, egalitarianism, Ethiopianism, anti-imperialism, and rejection of demeaning labour.[114]

Noting its potential for promoting a sense of community and collective identity amongst Black British, Gilroy has little to say, however, on the links between Black expressive culture and masculinity. 'Rastafarians', where they have become visible as a 'social problem' have, he writes, been 'overwhelmingly constructed as male'.[115] Here Gilroy is content to comment that, identifying with Rastafari ideology, women too have become popular reggae performers, just as Black women have participated actively in riotous protest.[116] But the dilemmas and contradictions for Black male youth, and the appeal of 'anti-woman jive talk', seem to require deeper probing. In *Heart of the Race* Beverley Bryan *et al.* suggest that male contempt for women, 'which defines us as sexual prey, is reflected particularly in the DJ style of reggae music, which perpetuates the notion that Black people are defined and obsessed by our own sexuality'.[117] Part of the appeal of the hustler role amongst many Black male youth is, according to other Black commentators, the attraction of being a stud – in a context where job prospects are bleak. Such is the view of Ken Pryce, who studied the men and women from the St Paul's district or 'Shanty Town' of Bristol in the early 1970s. He investigated the lives of young Blacks forced to live on the margins of society, yet who were, as Gilroy suggests, often assertively Black British. He describes men who, like the then relatively prosperous and leading 'cocksman' Bang Belly, were able to exploit white women as a source of income, rather than having to accept menial work which threatened their pride and dignity as a man. Almost all the men, Pryce reported, shared the desire and, temporarily at least, often the opportunity, to use white women in this way: 'It's a white chick, right? She don't mean anything to me, and a white woman shouldn't mean anything to you.'[118] Pryce has been criticised, I think rightly, for identifying the disorganised, impoverished, female-headed household as a major factor behind what he saw as young men's 'damaged self-image as a man' and their consequent exploitative attitude towards women.[119] He failed to stress the strength and resilience of many Black families (by assuming families need fathers at their head), and the realistic protest involved in rejection of the racist context of demeaning labour. But it is not so easy to dismiss his observations on the exploitativeness, irresponsibility and, at times, destructiveness of many young Black men's relations with women – Black and white.

Interestingly, the assertion of Black manhood is both macho and largely homophobic, and yet at the same time, as we saw with earlier assertions of Negritude, more in tune with Western notions of the 'feminine' in its claims to physicality, bodily awareness, emotional expressiveness, and a greater sense of communality. With the important exception of Black gay men, however, it is a challenge which has yet to be issued. Indeed, it is Black feminists, rather than Black men, who have tried to grapple with the potential significance of Black men's challenge to dominant forms of white masculinity.

Black Feminism and Black Masculinity

In 1969, with Black Power still flourishing, Toni Cade was busy writing and speaking in New York of 'a dangerous trend observable in some quarters of the Movement to program Sapphire out of her "evil" ways into a cover-up, shut-up, lay-back-and-be-cool obedience role'.[120] She warned of the problem of the Black man attempting to 'reclaim his manhood' at the expense of Sapphire, that is, at the expense of Black women. 'Perhaps we need,' she argued, 'to let go of all notions of manhood and femininity and concentrate on Blackhood.'[121] She wrote, in sorrow, of suspicion and fear between men and women as one of the most characteristic features of contemporary Black communities in the United States, of antagonism between 'hardheaded bitches' struggling to feed and clothe their children, and 'jive-ass niggers' in the bars and pool halls: 'Our blues singers have chronicled that madness for generations.'[122] Since then Toni Cade Bambara, as she became known, has continued, with hilarious humour and joyful affection, to satirise the shortcomings of Black masculinity.[123] Always celebrating the nurturing and solidarity prevalent among Black women, while describing the joys and pains of loving Black men (you can tell when they've been 'sleeping white', their rhythm is off), she urges rejection of any man not 'ready to deal with no woman full grown', not able to reject macho posturing for tenderness, commitment and responsibility.[124]

Even earlier, a decade before the second wave of North American feminism, Paule Marshall had written eloquently of sexual inequality within the Black community. In *Brown Girl, Brownstones*, published in 1959, she vividly describes the distortions of character that racism produced in her own American Barbadan community. Her heroine is torn between ambivalent feelings towards her parents: her hard and forceful mother, adopting the harsh, materialist values necessary for upward mobility out of immiseration; her soft and gentle, dreamy father, who, endlessly frustrated and physically damaged by the viciousness of North American racism, has long ago given up on any responsibility for rescuing his family from poverty.[125] Some years later Marshall again comments on Black women's resentment that their men reject them as threatening, castrating, independent and ambitious, when, for the sake of their families, they have *had* to become 'almost frighteningly strong'.[126] She remains, nevertheless, in sympathy with the men, as she explores their painful history, and their troubled search for dignity as Black and male, in the US.

By contrast, bitterness and anger intensified in the new wave of Black women's writing in the United States which began during the 1970s. Blamed alike by a white male establishment and Black male insurgents for the crisis in relations between men and women in the Black community, accused of 'emasculating' their men, told that they had enjoyed all the privileges in the Black world, Black women were at last beginning to make their own assessments. Having nothing to fall back on – 'not maleness, not ladyhood, not anything', as Toni Morrison observed in 1971 – they must finally speak for themselves.[127] (They sought out, as well, the long forgotten words and wisdom of so many Black women before them: 'De nigger woman is de mule uh de world so fur as Ah can see', Zora Neal Hurston had written back in 1937; 'I ain't good lookin' but I'm somebody's angel child', Bessie Smith had sung out her sense of freedom and defiance a decade earlier.[128] By the late 1970s, with half of all Black children born, officially, to single parents (twice as many as in the sixties)[129], with death, drugs, imprisonment and military life creating a situation in which there was a great shortage of available Black men for Black women seeking male partners, with lightness of colour continuing to define beauty in women for white men and Black, the prospects for relationships between Black women and men were looking increasingly desolate and desperate. Gloria Naylor captures the mood: 'All the good men are either dead or waiting to be born.'[130]

Alice Walker, soon to become the best-known of all Black writers, internationally, has repeatedly exposed the bleakness of Black women's lives, battling against a reality in which men are brutal and their wives, daughters and lovers are their main victims. Walker's fiction depicts the escalating cruelty in Black women's lives if, accepting guilt for their men's failure in the face of North American racism, they meekly accept their men's rage. In *The Third Life of Grange Copeland*, for example, Brownfield abuses, beats and torments all the women and children in his life – 'Only way to treat a nigger woman!' he tells his male friends – until eventually he shoots his submissive wife. Only once has she tried in vain to rebel, recalling all the pain she has accepted: 'And just to think of how many times I done got my head beat by you so you could feel a little bit like a man.'[131] In *The Color Purple*, the men are sadistic and brutal, but the women, supporting each other, are fighting back against such manifestations of manhood. The beaten down and battered wife Celie is transformed under the impact of the healing intervention of Shug, and, in turn, forces her husband to confront and change himself. It is Walker's utopian portrayal of a non-sexist Black community.[132]

The fiercest polemic against Black masculinity, however, is the long essay by Michele Wallace, *Black Macho*, published in 1978.[133] She begins, as have so many others, pointing to the extensive damage attending Daniel Moynihan's report on the Black family in 1965, in which he argued that the main problem in Black communities stemmed not so much from white racism, as from an 'abnormal family structure'. The complex pathology surrounding the 'matriarchal' nature of the Black family and the relative advantages of Black women educationally and in employment, he argued, 'impose a crushing burden on the Negro male'.[134] The report was immediately criticised by Black men and women, who pointed out the absurdity of portraying the desperate struggle of women on their own attempting to clothe and feed their families as a situation of 'power', and the fact that Black women's wages remained the lowest of all groups in America. Nevertheless, it remains to this day influential in both media and academic circles in the US, Britain, and beyond: the standard discourse on the Black community and its problems. It serves to bolster the general belief in the priority of the problems of the Black male and to endorse Black men's own prejudices that Black women are domineering and 'castrating'. These prejudices, according to Wallace, 'dissipated and distorted' the Black movement of the sixties. They turned the Black movement into Black Macho: 'nothing more nor less than the black man's struggle to attain his presumably lost "manhood" ... One could say, in fact, that the black man risked everything – all the traditional goals of revolution: money, security, the overthrow of the government – in the pursuit of an immediate sense of his own power.'[135] Cleaver's words ring out today, seeming to confirm her case: 'We shall have our manhood. We shall have it or the earth will be levelled by our attempts to gain it.'[136] The words of LeRoi Jones – 'the white woman understands that only in the rape sequence [with a Black male] is she likely to get cleanly, viciously popped'[137] – equally corroborate Wallace's claim that it was the Black man's assertion of a manhood in terms of his physical sexuality which inspired much of the rhetoric of Black Power, eventually negating its revolutionary potential for the Black community as a whole.

Wallace's evocation of the 'profound distrust, if not hatred', between Black men and women is remorseless and, though she sees it as 'nursed along largely by white racism', her book offers little hope of change.[138] Other writers, though similarly prepared to hold Black men themselves, not just white racism, responsible for some of the abuses of Black women, remain very cautiously hopeful of change. Audre Lorde, Maya Angelou, Toni Morrison, and even the fiercest critics like Alice Walker and Ntozake Shange, seek some reconciliation with Black men. 'As a people,' writes Audre Lorde, 'we should most certainly work together to end our common oppression ... the Black male consciousness must be raised so that he realizes that sexism and woman-hating are critically dysfunctional to his liberation as a Black man because they arise out of the same constellation that engenders racism and homophobia, a constellation of intolerance for difference.'[139] Or, as the Combahee River Collective announce, 'We struggle together with black men against racism, while we also struggle with black men about sexism.'[140] In 'comin to terms', Shange has her female protagonist battling with her male lover's self-centredness, sulks and physical coercion, and, through learning to assert and enjoy her own independence, achieving a new type of equality with him.[141]

The writing of Black women on men in Britain, Lauretta Ngcobo suggests, has been even more 'conciliatory' and 'lenient' than the North American literature. It contrasts with women's daily criticism of their men's assertive sexism and failure to share domestic responsibilities.[142] She regards this as 'conscious self-censoring', protective for the whole community, when it is the pain of racism which is the ultimate cause of domestic troubles.[143] Rhonda Cobham, introducing another collection of Black women's writing in Britain, similarly comments that 'Black women do not spend their lives putting down men.'[144] Joan Riley, on the other hand, has harrowingly depicted the fate of a young West Indian girl arriving in Britain, in *The Unbelonging*, to be incestuously abused by the cowed, self-hating father whose household she joins.[145] Beverley Bryan, Stella Dadzie and Suzanne Scafe, writing of Black women's lives in Britain, are also more outspokenly critical of Black men as 'sexual predators' and, at times, violent abusers of women. But they too stress that Black women have their own ways of challenging and redefining their relations with men in the context of racism, where 'Black men's oppression of us is merely a facade of power ... The domestic arena has become the only area in which men are able to conform to the dominant male role.'[146] And many other stories and poems draw a fuller picture: sometimes of pain, sometimes of joy, but always of women's struggle, with, and without, men. Here are the words of Grace Nichols:

Man I love
but won't let you devour
Even tho
I'm all watermelon
and star-apple and plum
when you touch me
even tho
I'm all sea moss
and jelly fish
and tongue
Come
leh we go to de Carnival
You be banana

I be avocado . . . But then
Let we break free
yes leh we break free
an keep to de motion
of we own personality.[147]

Black women may be making common cause with Black men against racism, and some of them celebrating the sensuality, humour and resilience of Black men while also condemning the destructiveness of a masculinity defined in terms of sexual conquest and power over women. But relations between Black men and women remain fraught and tension-laden, particularly in the US. They remain fraught because, despite two decades of Black feminist criticism, it is unclear whether Black men have been listening: is there a new sexual politics emerging amongst Black men, has Black male consciousness been raised? Or, as Mary Helen Washington wondered, have 'The old male rituals – the slick rap, the assertion of physical power, the sense of women as a man's property – hardened into immutable patterns?'[148]

Pessimism may seem appropriate when so many Black men continue to focus so fixedly on the problems of their own sex, even when, like Staples, they have some insight into the problems of Black machismo. It is not enough simply to keep insisting that it is men who are the 'victims', and that as such care must be taken not to blame them: 'Black men are not such privileged creatures as many women seem to think, for there is a high price to pay for being male in this society.'[149] Black women have been hearing this theme for decades. Excusing men for their abuse of power, in the only sphere in which they possess any, is not the way to lead them to question it. And pessimism may be unavoidable on hearing the popular voice of Black male literary celebrities in the US, like that of Ishmael Reed who, the day *The Color Purple* received its Academy Award nominations, went on national television to 'expose' its artistic and moral flaws. His own novel, *Reckless Eyeballing*, is a complicated and bitter satire in which he accuses white feminists and Black women of a co-conspiracy to silence Black male writers and scapegoat Black men generally.[150] Yet, certain signs suggest that there are Black men who have been listening to the voices of

Black women, accepting, if like Charles Johnson, rather halfheartedly, 'the darkness of Black male attitudes towards Black women . . . the tincture of exploitation that resides in some cases of heterosexual relations'.[151]

Most clearly and passionately, however, it is Black gay men, in the tradition of Langston Hughes and James Baldwin, (who knew that 'most women are not gentle, nor are most men strong'),[152] who are today thinking and talking about the combination of racial and sexual politics. Just two years before his tragically early death in 1988 – a fate he shares with so many Black gay Americans – Joseph Beam wrote of his new dreams in 'Words from the Heart':

> I dare myself to dream of us moving from survival to potential, from merely getting by to a positive getting over. I dream of Black men loving and supporting other Black men, and relieving Black women from the role of primary nurturers in our community. I dream, too, that as we receive more of what we want from each other that our special anger reserved for Black women will disappear.[153]

For the Gay Black Group which formed in London in 1981, as Kobena Mercer and Isaac Julien explain, 'A critical conversation on sex and race has already begun – and there's no turning back.'[154] It has entailed addressing the silence of the gay community on racism, confronting the resistance of the Black community to talking about sex and, more generally, examining the underlying issue of the cultural construction of masculinity: 'the racial dialectic of projection and internalisation through which white and black men have shaped their masks of masculinity'.[155]

Drawing on the work of Ernesto Laclau and Chantal Mouffe, Mercer and Julien pose as the central problem of difference – in this case, 'racial' difference – the question of whether identity can be reconstructed without the need for binary oppositions, 'in which some of us, or maybe all of us, are burdened with the role of representing somebody else's Other'.[156] A vision of radical equality, without hierarchical ordering, they maintain, must always be the basis of any progressive restructuring of diversity and difference. But how you get there, they concede, is a complex affair. One starting point, as Mercer argues, is to realise that the prevailing Western conception of sexuality 'already contains racism'. As we have seen, and as Frantz Fanon portrayed so forcefully in *Black*

Skin, White Masks, the whole mystique surrounding Black sexuality arises from white colonialism, as both an outlet for the white man's fears and fantasies, and a justification for his brutality.

The dilemmas this creates for Black men and women around sexuality can assume, and have taken, forms other than the mirror-image of white racism to be found in Black macho – as promoted in the writing of Cleaver, or Stokely Carmichael's notorious statement that the only place for women in radical Black politics was 'prone'. Once again, Mercer directs us to the medium of music, with its erotic potentialities, where Black men and women have always articulated a more complex sexual politics: 'Male-female antagonisms are openly acknowledged in soul; sex is celebrated in the blues, but it is also problematised; some of Billie Holliday's songs offer succinct critiques of Black men's manipulative attitudes, but they also address the ambivalent "messiness" of longing for their intimate embrace.'[157] Black male musicians have, Mercer suggests, struggled with the contrasting meanings of 'masculinity', and above all they have been capable of an emotional expressiveness which contrasts vividly with the 'emotional illiteracy' of white men. Herein, he suggests, lies the challenge of Black masculinity. The most famous of the Black pop singers, like Michael Jackson and Prince, quite blatantly set out to disrupt the codes and conventions of white masculinity in ways which 'send-up the whole masquerade of masculinity itself'. In Mercer's view, 'By destabilising signs of race, gender and sexuality these artists draw critical attention to the cultural *constructedness*, the artifice, of the sexual roles and identities we inhabit.'[158]

Outside the world of music, we also witness growing complexity and change in Black people's own constructions of masculinity. Watching a Richard Pryor concert from 1971 is a chilling affair. The humour is relentlessly misogynist: women are referred to exclusively as bitches; white women, not Black, are the obsessive object of an aggressive desire: 'I like white bitches, that's my disease. Such big tits, so noisy when they come [blah-de-blah].'[159] Today, however, Pryor devotes much of his act to sending up such macho posturing, once apparently so deadly serious in his act.[160] In Britain, constantly and effectively, the immensely popular comedian

Lenny Henry satires Black machismo (as in his hilarious portrayal of soul singer Theophilus P. Wildebeeste), while also offering us an alternative image of masculinity in the self-mocking, gentle and compassionate humour of pirate radio DJ, Delbert Wilkins. Meanwhile the people's hero, Black boxer Frank Bruno, publicly embraces fatherhood as his most meaningful commitment.

Black culture in both the United States and Britain is rediscovering and celebrating the work of earlier generations of Black writers, like the poet Langston Hughes, who always sought to convey the caring and gentle folk wisdom and pervasive humour of Southern Black culture and 'the beauty of the people with freakish ways'.[161] He wrote of the easy friendship of the dispossessed, so at odds with any form of macho virility: 'whenever a fight broke out I made an especial point of heading for the *tobac* so that I would not be called upon to stop it', he tells us cheerfully of his hard times struggling to survive as a doorman in Paris in the 1930s.[162] Black culture today is also questioning the very notion of the 'Black' subject. Black identities, it is clear, are cut across not only by gender, class and sexuality, but also by the most complex multiplicity of ethnicities, which vary according to the particular histories that have constructed them. In looking at the oppositional meanings inherent in Black masculinity today, the stress is on diversity.[163]

Some Black men have seen only too clearly that fighting racism is also about fighting dominant images of masculinity, about rejecting racist fantasies of Black sexuality – oppressive to men and women, Black and white alike. As the North American poet Essex Hemphill laments:

> But we so called men,
> we so called brothers
> wonder why it's so hard
> to love *our* women
> when we're about loving them
> the way america
> loves us.[164]

Or as Isaac Julien affirms in *Gary's Tale*:

the last fight, the last battle, territory, will be with one self,
the important terrain, the psyche.
The mind will be the last neo-colonialised space to be decolonialised, this I know
because I have been there, backwards and forwards.[165]

In decolonising the image of 'the Black male', while reconstructing themselves, Black people have, of course, exposed its pernicious origins in the preoccupations and desires of white men. But white men cannot take back the desire they have projected onto Black men, and also maintain their traditional image of themselves. In challenging the images of Black masculinity, Black men threaten the centrality of white masculinity. As Black people, like women and gay men, dissect and reject the conceptual hierarchies which construct them as subordinate, and struggle to transform the power relations they express and maintain, the mantle of white manhood, its preeminence once so seemingly obvious, looks increasingly frayed and threadbare.

8. The Belly of the Beast (1): Sex as Male Domination?

I suppose I do genuinely believe that any movement that liberates women will liberate men too . . . It's a difficult time to be a man: it's a difficult and fascinating time to be a woman. Right now we are the active ones and men are on the receiving end. I wish men would be more active in terms of initiating change and trying out different ways to be opposite women. I'm sure this will come and I'm very optimistic about the outcome of the present 'sexual crisis'.

Nancy Friday[1]

So we agonise over what to do with the men. If we engage in relationships with them it is almost inevitable that we will be exploited . . . If we support them we help to perpetuate patriarchy; if we fight them we run the risk of repeating the error of their ways . . . What we are beginning to appreciate is that NO MATTER WHAT WOMEN DO it can be arranged to suit patriarchy.

Dale Spender[2]

'Man is complicated', Catherine Stimpson announces, introducing one of the recent North American texts in 'Men's Studies'.[3] The more we explore the social and historical dimensions of masculinity, the more it is revealed as heterogeneous and contradictory, defined through a series of hierarchical relations: rejection and suppression of femininity and homosexual desire, command and control over (often seen as 'protection of') the 'weak' and 'inferior'. But while the notion of masculinity becomes ever more complex, the 'problem of men' becomes ever more pressing. We may come to understand sexual difference in terms of a shifting reality – a multiplicity of meanings rather than simple opposition – but the cultural, social and political domination of men over women persists. The vexing paradox for feminists has been the need to criticise and challenge the social construction of 'woman' as definitively less-than, subordinate to or complemented by, 'man', while at the same time retaining for ourselves those aspects of womanhood which we value but which are disparaged in dominant male-centred discourses and realities. In consequence we may end up defending notions of feminine experience which we need to demolish as *exclusively* 'feminine'. A similar paradox in relation to men lies in the importance of challenging the existence of any fixed essence of 'man', while at the same time insisting upon the continuing practical problem of men. The danger here is that we may end up dismissing the diversity and changing meanings of 'masculinity', some of which we might need to help strengthen as a challenge to the more traditional ones.

In the early 1970s, when the women's liberation movements of the West emerged from the radical movements of the sixties, men were not identified as the central problem. Feminists, with the excitement and confidence of what they saw as the 'boundless possibilities' of a brand new beginning, were busy taking control of their own lives.[4] They were challenging women's subordinate place within radical politics and radical perspectives, while attacking the language and iconography of a form of 'sexual liberation' in which women as 'chicks' remained the passive objects of men's desires, instead of the self-affirming subjects of their own. Above all, they were busy enjoying the pleasures and excitement of their own company. They were, for the first time in their lives, meeting together in small groups simply as women, talking about sex and relationships, organising for nurseries, playgrounds, better jobs and training, and demanding control over their own fertility.[5]

Men were an issue in these early days insofar as feminists knew they must exclude them from the women's liberation movement – in the face of fierce hostility in Britain from a small group of Maoist women who consistently opposed the idea of an autonomous organisation of women.[6] Men, as women then knew from working with them in radical groups, would otherwise dominate and silence women, insisting upon their own political agendas. Only once the women's movement grew stronger and more powerful, drawing in women with different histories, did some women begin to speak about the previously unspeakable, to discuss men's violence and their fears of men. The problem of men intruded itself, often uninvited, upon these passionate feminist beginners, as the prevalence of rape and men's domestic violence against women and children began to enter feminist consciousness. It emerged as women began paying more attention to the pains and burdens of the women around them, and voicing their own inner fears. Contemplating the extent of men's violence against women, their sexual coerciveness, and what, once sensitised to it, soon appeared as a seemingly boundless landscape of cultural misogyny, feminist anger against men rose throughout the seventies.

The universality and tenacity of men's dominance over women began to undermine the earlier optimism that women's conscious rejection of ideologies of female subordination could eventually create a future of gender equality – at least, once it joined up with struggles against social policies, workplace practices, and domestic arrangements which were exploitative of women. The decline of all progressive radical movements and socialist groups and parties from the late seventies, with the successful rise of the political right internationally, also played a large part in this process. More feminists were drawn to a type of feminist analysis which blames individual men for women's oppression, and stresses men's transhistorical primordial drive for power, rather than one which explores how changing social arrangements and their ideological articulations institutionalise men's power.[7]

The Sexuality of Men

In seeking a single transhistorical basis for male dominance, the most popular and accessible feminist writing from the late 1970s, most of it coming from North America, was focusing on male sexuality. In the early 1980s the US feminist attorney Catherine MacKinnon summarised this new type of radical feminist orthodoxy: 'I think that feminism fundamentally identifies sexuality as the primary social sphere of male power.'[8] Sexuality in and of itself, it was suggested, is at the heart of male dominance. In addition, MacKinnon, Andrea Dworkin, Robin Morgan, Susan Griffin and others were now arguing, male sexual dominance is at the heart of all other power relations in society. As MacKinnon expresses it: 'That male sexual dominance, a social construct, may be centrally involved in the nuclear arms race, imperialism, colonisation, psychoanalysis [!], class exploitation, political torture, fascism, and racism may have been obscured and underestimated, including by women.'9

Ironically, the origins of this new radical feminist analysis of the phallic imperative as the literal motor of human history is, we should be clear, neither radical, nor feminist. It is the old conservative common sense we were raised on, associated, most prominently, up to and including the present, with the thinking of the right rather than the left; with arguments against sexual equality, and against feminism (and, especially with that bastion of male evil – psychoanalysis!). Right-wing ideologues like Roger Scruton have always warned us that women's primary task is to work tirelessly to 'quieten' and 'constrain' the 'unbridled ambition of the phallus'.10 He claims to see feminist ideology as a perfidious plot hatched by men, in the hope that they could thereby 'rid the sexual impulse [which he sees here as exclusively male] of its debilitating commitment . . . and so allow no claims of allegiance to extinguish the claims of power.'11

There is no doubt that Dworkin and MacKinnon, on the one hand, and Scruton on the other, are repeating the dominant contemporary cultural discourses and iconographies surrounding sexuality. The new 'scientific' study of sex, with the birth of sexology in the mid-nineteenth century, depicted male sexuality as an overpowering instinct which, as Richard von Krafft-Ebing wrote at the time, 'with all-conquering force and might demands fulfilment'.12 Today, popular magazines, advertising, hard- and soft-core pornography, are all saturated with the same image of 'masculinity' as some type of insatiable sexual appetite. The Western literary canon has its own dramas and metaphors of phallic power. 'Down, Wanton, Down', Robert Graves expresses men's boastful narcissism, here thinly disguised as self-mockery, when lovingly addressing his penis, and conferring upon it a life of its own.13 'He never understands when certain things can be done and when they can't', the fictional hero, Rico, similarly addresses his genital organ, in Alberto Moravia's short story, *The Two of Us*.[14] The standard discourses of the natural sciences contain elements of the same ideology, as they have for the last hundred years and more: 'Males will always strive to control female reproductive behaviour', biologists Randy Thornhill *et al.* deduce from their study of the behaviour of scorpion flies of the genus, *Panorpa*, in 1986; 'this may result in a conflict of male and female reproductive interests.'[15] More popularly, as Rosalind Coward has pointed out, we are daily bombarded in our living rooms with the folk wisdom of a Desmond Morris or a Richard Dawkin in nature programmes which illustrate for us the inevitability of male sexual dominance: the male instinct in every living creature propelling its tireless pursuit of the female to disseminate anywhere and everywhere conception may ensue.[16]

The ubiquity of the discourses and imagery of 'conquest/ submission', 'activity/passivity', 'masculinity/femininity' constructing heterosexual intercourse as *the* spectacular moment of male domination and female submission, is inescapable: 'The man "mounts" and penetrates; the woman spreads her legs and "submits"; and these postures seem to ratify, again and again, the ancient authority of men over women.'[17] But we must be cautious in assuming an equation between such sado-masochistic discourse and people's lived experience of sexuality. Internal and external meanings are not always identical. Our experiences do not simply mirror social meanings; though they are inevitably filtered through them. We must tread very carefully if we wish to tease out the connections between the nature and significance of many layers of sexual and bodily experience for both women and men. These include the subjective of psychic experience of sex from infancy onwards; the cultural ideas and values surrounding sex; the social contexts allowing or forbidding sexual expression; the medical and other social practices applied to the body – particularly women's bodies – all of them taking place within the wider context of gender hierarchy. The place to begin, I believe, is where in chapter four we came to an end: recognition of the cultural force of the equation of 'the phallus' with power – solid and unlimited.

It is the phallus which creates the seemingly ineluctable bond between 'male sexuality' and power. Yet this symbol of the phallus as power, grasped by boy and girl child alike, cannot be equated with the lived experience of male sexual domination. Childhood sexuality, those who acknowledge its existence would agree, takes both active and passive forms, with multiple outlets and objects, most of them not congruent with the meanings attached to adult heterosexuality. (I shall be looking separately at the important exception of cases of child sexual abuse). Psychoanalytic accounts have been used to argue that it is the physical visibility of men's genitals which creates men's swaggering commitment to putting them to use, from boyhood onwards, while women's apparently invisible equipment creates their greater sexual reticence. But, while the anthropological debate over cultural relativism is an intricate and vexed one, the literature overwhelmingly suggests that the meanings attached to anatomical difference are neither fixed nor universal.[18] Even within Western culture, the meanings and significance given to male and female anatomy have shifted over the last hundred years. It seems more plausible to assume that the phallus as symbol condenses the multiple significances of the whole configuration of male dominance, with its diverse social practices at once conferring power and authority on 'men', and giving most actual men some real power over the lives of others – at the very least within domestic life. The whole configuration, I have suggested, includes divisions of labour (with their differing connections to technological expertise and financial reward), institutions of authority (political, juridical, educational, medical) and, finally, family arrangements, tied in with patterns of desire and the expression and control of sexuality. All of these structures and practices work in concert with ideologies of 'femininity' and 'masculinity' to construct women as dependent on men; dependent, at least, on men within their own class and group.

Bolstered by the multifaceted reality of men's power, the phallus, as a symbol, is not, however, available for individual men to possess. It is that which they attempt to possess, or perhaps to reject; or maybe that which they approach with uncertainty and disquiet. We still need to explain how it is – if it is – that men's sexual performance, or their psychic and physical experience of sexuality, becomes a (and on the new radical feminist/old conservative analysis, *the*) source of male dominance. So the question remains: to what extent does the actual reality of men's sexual lives, the deployment of the penis, give men power and control over women? Can we assume that there is something about men's shared experience of the physical presence of the penis which underlies the way men in general relate to their bodies, and gain a sense of 'masculinity' and power? Or are we to assume that there is something else common to men's experience of sexuality which constructs a shared masculinity, and hence 'male dominance'?

There are, of course, the all too familiar rituals of male bonding produced through derisive sexist sniggering, the inexhaustible joking, the suggestive gestures, around 'cunts', 'pricks', 'queers', 'studs', 'shafting' and 'wanking'. Men's workplace culture, particularly it seems in manual jobs, is built around this form of sexual signalling: 'In the machine noise, a gesture suggestive of masturbation, intercourse or homosexuality was enough to raise a conventional smile and re-establish a bond over distances too great for talking.'[19] Collectively, it is clear, calling up images of male sexual performance serves to consolidate and confirm masculinity, and to exclude and belittle women. Sociologists like Gagnon and Simon, or therapists like Ethel Spector Person, convincingly argue that the need to reassert and confirm masculine gender identity lies behind the obsessive force propelling men into sexual engagement, or at the least, into pornographic thoughts of sexual engagement:

> An impotent man always feels that his masculinity, and not just his sexuality, is threatened. In men, gender appears to 'lean' on sexuality . . . In women, gender identity and self-worth can be consolidated by other means.[20]

Heterosexual performance may be viewed as the mainstay of masculine identity, but its enactment does not in itself give men power over women. (Even in violent situations, it is the use of muscular force or weapons which gives men the power to sexually abuse other men, women or children.) Most of the men who can talk honestly about their heterosexual experiences, admit to considerable confusion, often feeling it is the woman who has all the power.[21] The tub-thumping white cocksman Norman Mailer, for example, quite rightly describes himself as a 'Prisoner of Sex', a 'Prisoner of Wedlock', for 'he had never been able to live without a woman'. Like many an egotist, Mailer prefers to contemplate the fascinating phenomenon which is himself in the third person: 'Four times beaten at wedlock, his respect for the power of women was so large that the way they would tear through him (in his mind's eye) would be reminiscent of old newsreels of German tanks.'[22] Women lost their respect for men, he concludes, when pregnancy lost its danger. Once, he mourns, a woman had known that her lovers might be the agency of her death: 'Conceive then the lost gravity of the act, and the diminishment of man from a creature equally mysterious to woman (since he could introduce a creation to her that could yet be her doom) down to the fellow who took lessons on how to satisfy his wife from Masters and Johnson and bowed out to the vibrations of his superior, a vibrator.'[23] In Mailer's view, technology, 'by extending man's power over nature, reduced him before women'.[24] Such paranoid bleating, from the brave bull contemplating his own lost power, contains, to my mind, a certain truth. Whatever the meanings attached to 'the act' of sexual intercourse, for many men it confirms a sense of ineptness and failure: the failure to satisfy women. Images of a sexually satisfied woman are culturally relative, and our culture has increasingly impressed upon men the importance of the female orgasm – a man must, as it were, stand firm as the instrument of repeated female orgasm. Yet we also know, from myths and narratives of popular culture, if not from clinical evidence of the castration complex, the force of psychoanalytic observations on men's sheer terror of female genitals and female sexuality.[25]

Unsurprisingly then, for many men it is precisely through sex that they experience their greatest uncertainties, dependence and deference in relation to women – in stark contrast, quite often, with their experience of authority and independence in the public world. And certainly for many men it is precisely through experiencing themselves as powerless and submissive that they experience the greatest sexual pleasure. Ian McEwan vividly depicts men's ambiguous sexual awakenings in his collection *In Between the Sheets*:

> O'Byrne lay on his back on the clean white sheets, and Lucy eased herself on to his belly like a vast nesting bird . . . from the beginning she had said, 'I'm in charge'. O'Byrne had replied, 'We'll see about that.' He was horrified, sickened, that he could enjoy being overwhelmed like one of those cripples in his brother's

magazines . . . Finally she spoke, more to herself than to him. 'Worm . . .' O'Byrne moaned. Lucy's legs and thighs tightened and trembled. 'Worm . . . worm . . . you little worm. I'm going to tread on you dirty little worm.' . . . His eyes were sunk deep, and his words travelled a long way before it left his lips. 'Yes', he whispered.[26]

As Nancy Friday discovered in her survey of three thousand sexual fantasies sent in to her by men, overpowering women against their will seem to be the exception, rather than the rule, of men's fantasy. By a ratio of four to one, men's fantasies were masochistic.[27] (She received only three fantasies of enacting rape from men, whereas being raped or forced were the most popular themes among women respondents). Her findings accord with the evidence we have from sex workers, who reveal that more of their clients pay to play the victim than the aggressor in sexual encounters. Men are almost as likely as women to select a masochistic role in fantasy, seeing pain as the symbolic price for pleasure, feeling guilty about wanting something they see as 'dirty'.

Eileen McLeod interviewed thirty prostitutes and twenty male clients (all 'normal' and married men, and thus representative of the men who go to prostitutes) for her book on prostitution, and concluded that a 'common feature of men's sexual activity with prostitutes is the opportunity it provides to escape conventional male heterosexual roles with their heavy emphasis on masculine prowess and dominance'.[28] As one prostitute comments of her clients, 'I think they must all have it in their minds somewhere they'd like a woman to take advantage of them'; or another, 'It makes them feel relaxed, they haven't got to put on a performance . . . be a big stud or produce multiple orgasms or anything like that.'[29] The clients spoke of liking what they experienced as the 'role shift': 'Here is the woman doing to the man'; 'I go there because I know I can lie down and just leave it to the girls.'[30] The desire for the passive experience of 'domination' and the feminine experience of dressing as women were also identified by both prostitutes and clients as the most consistent of men's desires after straight sex, oral sex or masturbation. (About a quarter of the prostitutes' customers expressed such desires.) North American studies of thousands of prostitutes and their clients have revealed similar findings, with 48 per cent of men classified as desiring to be 'sexually passive' in one study, 74 per cent in another.[31]

Men's fantasies, desires, and experience of sex in actual relationships with women are not, it seems, so very different from women's in terms of images of submission – presumably recalling pre-pubescent fantasies in both sexes. Here is Dave Feintwick's story of his sexual awakening. If we did not know his sex, we might have assumed it was female. Certainly, his memories are little different from my own erotic history when, as a young girl, my fantasies always focused upon some older woman:

> Going back to when I was five or six, my earliest sexual fantasies included the (conventionally) attractive mother of one of my class-mates. I imagined myself sitting on the wooden swing . . . and her coming up to me . . . arms outstretched like a biblical figure, and kissing and stroking me . . . Later I fantasised about my women teachers both chastising me and being kind to me . . . [Later again] My fantasies became more complex. They involved most of the females I knew from everyday life and saw in the media. Age and conventional good looks were largely irrelevant as in my mind I dreamt of women who would be nice to me, make love to me and who would enjoy acting out sadomasochistic scenes. To an extent these fantasies still attract me, but have diminished power and impact as I have found completely different involvement and satisfaction in a good physical sexual relationship, something which I thought would never happen . . . I cannot banish them [the fantasies], but they are slowly being disarmed as I begin to actually like rather than feel neutral, or even arrogantly disdain, other people with whom I have begun to feel myself luxuriously close.[32]

Neither men's masturbatory fantasies, nor men's experience of sex in relationships with women, reduce to the conventional rituals of sex as male dominance. As Nancy Friday's survey shows, men strongly desire to be caregivers just as much as women, though their need to give love can conflict with their rage at past rejections and at being made to feel dirty and guilty.[33] Men dream about intimacy with women, at the same time as they fear it. Similarly in Britain, Wendy Hollway's interviews of men and women's hetero-sexual experience describes the complex negotiation of power which occurs.[34] Women often fail to perceive men's dependence on them ('That guy – I didn't even know he was so *dependent* on me – I had no *idea*'), while men, in line with Freud's thoughts on castration anxiety, often perceive women as all-powerful ('She was very strong and very emotional . . . I didn't feel safe I wasn't going to be knocked out and sucked in by her.'[35]) The dominant 'male sexual drive' discourse encourages these misrecognitions – men's denial of need and vulnerability, women's denial of their own power in sexual relationships. Hollway criticises a feminism which reproduces the assumption of men's power through sex as monolithic:

> Heterosexual sex is the site of politics because it is so contradictory; because it is a primary site of women's power and of men's resistance. A part of that politics is the production of alternative – feminist – accounts of men's sexuality which do not corroborate in sexist assumptions that the power of the penis is incontestable. It is not. The power of the penis is a 'knowledge' produced by sexist discourses; a knowledge which is motivated and thus reproduced by men's vulnerability to women because of the desire for the Other/mother.[36]

The point is that it seems wilfully blind for feminists to buy into the bravado behind many men's repression of their sexual anxieties and insecurities, by endorsing myths of the inevitable link between sexuality and male dominance. It becomes a way of women colluding in men's defensive denial of their own confusion and doubts about sexuality, concealing that which we most need to reveal and understand. Male sexuality is most certainly not any single shared experience for men. It is not any single or simple thing at all – but the site of any number of emotions of weakness and strength, pleasure and pain, anxiety, conflict, tension and struggle, none of them mapped out in such a way as to make the obliteration of the agency of women in heterosexual engagements inevitable. Male sexuality cannot be reduced to the most popular meanings of sex acts, let alone to sex acts themselves. It becomes intelligible only if placed within actual histories of men's intimate relationships with others – or the lack of them.

Carole Vance and Ann Snitow, two North American feminists who have written extensively on the debates on sexuality within feminism, and who reject the new feminist 'common sense' of the eighties which equates sex and male dominance, consistently highlight the complexity of sexuality – male and female – and criticise the radical feminist reduction which takes ideology to be lived behaviour:

> If patriarchy fuses gender and sexuality, the analytic task of feminism is to take them apart. The political task of feminism is to work for concrete material changes

that enable women and men to experience sexuality less attached to and formed by gender. These changes include social and economic equality; the end of compulsory heterosexuality; access to birth control, abortion, and sex education; recognition of children as sexual; a reconsideration of public/private distinctions; and the protection of mothers and children outside of marriage.[37]

What power male sexuality does have in perpetuating male domination does not simply obtain at the level of symbolism. While certainly facilitating male bonding and mediating some of the most oppressive ways both men and women relate to men's bodies, men's talk of sex has an ambiguous relationship to their experiences of sexual pleasure; male sexual dominance derives from the way in which the general social power of men sustains the symbolism of phallic power through encouraging or controlling how women and men may relate to their bodies. It is not, for instance, that male sexuality is irredeemably violent, coercive or connected with emotions of domination – often it is not – but, as we shall see in the next chapter, that the possibility of men's sexual coerciveness towards women has been socially tolerated, often, indeed, both expected and encouraged. It is not that women's experience of sex is irredeemably linked with danger and sentiments of submission – often it is not – but that men, through such institutions as marriage, medicine and law have managed to exert extraordinary levels of control over it. The level of symbolic does not operate autonomously. It is sustained or diminished by the impact of social practices upon it. Change in the dominant gendered meanings surrounding sexuality is possible.

Indeed, transforming the meanings attaching to sexuality is a political task which men and women can share. But the recognition of its necessity is still fragile; and the task itself fraught with difficulties. Reflecting on male sexuality in 1979, the editors of the British anti-sexist magazine, *Achilles Heel*, concluded: 'There's a lot wrong with current patterns of heterosexuality – one of the main things that's wrong is that there just aren't very many really positive images of heterosexual relationships.'[38] Why should this be? We all know that many women are not gentle, many men not violent. These universal constructions of sexual difference are challenged in our fantasies, and, at times, in our experiences, of sexual engagement. Yet despite two decades of fierce feminist criticism, ridicule and the use of every available weapon to undermine and transform sexist ideology and practice in the West, male sexuality is still constantly presented to us as predatory and overpowering. Indeed, in these same decades, we have seen the pornography business become the fastest growing industry in most Western countries, and the number of reported sexual attacks and violence against women continue to increase. If pessimism and despair now pervade so much feminist reflection on sex, its focus on rape, pornography and violence against women is hardly surprising. Before we can rest upon those joyful shores where more positive meanings connect to sexuality, we have to wade through the swamp in which men's pornographic fantasy and actual sexual violence suffuse our consciousness of sex.

Should we even embark upon such a journey? We have been warned that it may be pointless. If 'the sexual dynamic of history', as a group of British feminist historians has written, reveals that one of 'the deep structures that serve male domination is heterosexuality',[39] who dares defend sex? If Peter Sutcliffe, the murderer and mutilator of 13 women was, as feminist graffiti in Britain explained in the 1980s, 'Not Mad, Not Bad, But MALE', then maleness is nothing more nor less than murderous insanity. This graffiti encapsulates the conviction of the impossibility of a sexual politics *vis-à-vis* heterosexuality. The thinking behind it has helped reverse the promise of sexual liberation of the sixties, and weakened the more confident feminist sexual politics of the early seventies. The journey, it is clear, will be a rough one.

The Appeal and Function of Pornography

Let us embark by considering the persistence and power of pornography. Its place at the pinnacle of the sexist iconography of insatiable male sexual activity and ubiquitous female sexual availability is obvious in most of its manifestations. Pictures, movies, texts, all deliver up 'his' tirelessly active, rock-solid penis, 'her' slavishly desiring, wide-open cunt. It is rather less obvious just who is being controlled and exploited in the penis-worship of pornography, and why. As both the main producers and consumers of pornography, the answer, it might immediately appear, is men: men in their most solitary relationship with themselves. Describing the man attempting to lose himself in his pornographic book, Angela Carter comments: 'The text constantly reminds the reader of his own troubling self, his own reality – and the limitations of that reality since, however much he wants to fuck the willing women or men in his story, he cannot do so but must be content with some form of substitute activity.'[40] Studying the pornographic magazines *Mayfair* and *Knave*, Andy Moye describes the gruelling phallic regime they institute for men, and the punishments they threaten for failure. Proper equipment and proper technique are necessary for pornography's fictions of manliness: sprays, creams, ointments, tablets, gadgets – sexual aids of endless variety – are the accompanying commodities promising the realisation of these fictions. The fictions of manliness are those of *penis size* – the bigger the better; of *erection on demand* – as often as possible; of *skilled performance* – producing female orgasm, preferably multiple. The alienation from sexual desire and sexual pleasure which these texts articulate, Moye suggests, 'represents a depth of sexual bewilderment that can be described as an autism – a self enclosed fantasy world of sexual mystification conducted to the rhythm of the phallic regime'.[41] The man who fails to match up, the pornographic narrative threatens, will soon lose his woman to the man who is 'always ready with a stiff prick'.[42]

The psychic casualties produced by phallic failure create a booming trade for another fast expanding industry, that of sex therapy. Pioneered in the United States, particularly in the wake of Masters and Johnson's work, the most common sexual complaints of men seeking therapy are *erectile dysfunction, inhibited sexual desire* and *premature ejaculation*[43] – the exact inversions of the fictions of pornography. These anxieties are fed by pornography, even as pornography, like a dangerous drug, provides an addictive but insufficient outlet for the very anxieties and needs it helps to generate. In pornographic fantasy women are available, and women are satisfied. Men can passively consume them, hallucinating their own active engagement. Men terrified of possible failure to please women sexually, and therefore of failing to prove themselves 'real men', often experience a lack of sexual interest in wives or lovers, so the sex therapists report, or avoid relations with women altogether, while being strongly drawn to the sexual substitutes of pornography and masturbation.[44] '"Performance anxiety"', in actual sexual encounters, Jeffrey Fracher and Michael Kimmel inform us from the United States, 'is a normative experience for male behaviour.'[45] This in turn threatens whatever relationships men do have or yearn to have, with women.

Doctors and sex therapists are now stressing the pernicious role of pornography in feeding the anxieties which drive ever increasing numbers of men to seek help for sexual problems. They are men having trouble with their self-image as men, because the social ties which bind masculinity with sexual adequacy, and sexual adequacy with penile potency, are drawn so tight as to allow little real room for manoeuvre, and even less room for any comfortable, pleasurable way of experiencing their own bodies.[46] Seeking help of any sort is difficult for most men, at odds with prevailing ideas of masculine self-reliance and avoidance of feelings, or any form of self-exposure. But men's sense of shame and embarrassment at sexual incompetence, their terror of unmanliness, has meant increasing numbers of sexually unhappy men consulting physicians, seeing sex therapists or, more damagingly, approaching surgeons in search of penile implants. Hundreds of thousands of men, it is estimated, received penile implants over recent decades – a type of surgery which is likely to disrupt or even eliminate naturally-occurring erection, and remove physical sensation.[47]

There has been a new type of medicalisation of male sexuality, analogous to the nineteenth-century medicalisation of female sexuality. Reflecting men's increased sexual anxieties, a survey of psychological literature in the mid-eighties revealed that articles on 'impotence' had risen dramatically since 1970 while, significantly, reference to 'frigidity', so frequently focused on before 1970, had almost totally disappeared.[48] This is no small change, when we reflect that in the late 1920s sex advice experts like Wilhelm Stekel were writing that 40–50 per cent of women were 'frigid', particularly women of 'the higher cultural levels', and warning that this was 'a social disease that can take on the proportions of an epidemic'[49]; while Van de Velde was estimating that all women suffered some form of 'temporary anaesthesia' during marriage, and promoting an equally stern view of the need to 'cure' reluctant wives: 'The wife must be taught, not only how to behave in coitus, but, above all, how and what to feel in this unique act.'[50] There has thus been a dramatic shift in the professional identification of which sex is to be blamed for heterosexual failure.

Visiting the porn emporiums of Times Square, the North American feminist Deirdre English describes being totally overwhelmed by the tragic, joyless sense of sexual failure and inadequacy she perceived on the faces of the men around her:

> I felt overwhelmed by the presence of so many layers upon layers of exploitation . . . The men are here to exploit the women; the women are here to exploit the men . . . the overwhelming feeling is one of the exploitation of male sexual desire. There it is, embarrassingly desperate, tormented, demeaning itself, begging for relief, taking any substitute and *paying* for it. Men who live for this are suckers, and their uncomfortable demeanor shows they know it.[51]

Fellow American journalist, Henry Schipper, writing on the dazzling profits being made from the seven billion dollar pornography business, submits the same report. Porn may be the last frontier allowing newcomers to thrive in business on relatively small capital. In these times, it may be almost unique as an industry whose entrepreneurs can boast: 'It's a very, very hard business to lose money in.'[52] There may be three to four times as many adult bookstores in the United States as there are McDonald's restaurants, but their clients appear uniquely miserable: 'As they open the door [of the "adult entertainments" centre] their faces twist into expressions at once helpless and bitter.'[53] There seems little doubt that men's sexual frustration and men's sexual fears and anxieties *are* exploited by the pornography industry.

Make no mistake about it, though, the industry is now targeting women as its new growth area. Currently a secondary spender, consuming the occasional X-rated movie or at times visiting an adult bookstore (one telephone survey of women in Washington D.C. found 68 per cent had been to a porn movie and 38 per cent a porn bookshop), the porn bosses are confident that 'women are the fastest growing market in the business'.[53] They may be right. In Britain, women are now buying 10–20 per cent of porn videos, Ann

Summers sex shops are organising 'parties' for women to buy their products in their own homes, and video-makers like Mike Freeman are shifting from 'hard core' to 'romantic focus' pornography for women.[54] Most of the widely available pornography is non-violent images of naked women or sexual activity designed for heterosexual men, but there is also a fast growing industry aimed at gay men, lesbians, transvestites, submissive male partners, dominant female partners, sado-masochists, and so on.

All this might be thought to have little bearing on the feminist argument against pornography. From the outset women's liberationists attacked pornography as degrading and demeaning in its reduction of women to flesh, and bits of flesh, commodities for male titillation. But this was one aspect of a generalised attack on the sexist stereotyping in all forms of commercial and cultural representations of women. ('Miss America and Playboy's centerfold are sisters over the skin. To win approval, we must be both sexy and wholesome ... demure yet titillatingly bitchy', a leaflet at the first feminist demonstration against the Miss America contest declared in New York in 1968.[55]) Only subsequently was pornography singled out by many feminists as uniquely demeaning of women – the principal cause of women's oppression and violence against women, and itself an act of violence against them. Whatever the markets for pornography, it is still predominantly men who consume it. And it is still overwhelmingly men who rape, men who batter and men who kill; while women are raped, battered and made to fear the streets as enemy territory. It is easy to see in pornography a celebration of, and incitement to, these crimes against women, when it so blatantly depicts women as sexual objects (around 25 per cent of it, in Andrea Dworkin's survey of her local sex shops, depicting some form of violence).[56]

Many people, both men and women, have come to regard pornography as a type of rapist's charter, teaching men to hate and abuse women. Andrea Dworkin's writing from the late seventies remains the bedrock of this analysis. Describing the penis as a 'symbol of terror', a weapon 'even more significant than the gun, the knife, the bomb, the fist',[57] Dworkin concludes that the function of pornography is to assure men of their eternal right to abuse women:

> No act of hers can overturn the way she is consistently perceived: as some sort of thing. No sense of her own purpose can supersede, finally, the male's sense of purpose: to be the thing that enables him to experience raw phallic power. In pornography, his sense of purpose is fully realized . . . She is the thing she is supposed to be, the thing that makes him erect.[58]

The problem is that the reason Dworkin's prolific writing is so powerful, so shocking and, it would appear, so popular, is that it is not an *analysis* of the most violent pornographic texts, but a *reproduction* of them. They speak for themselves, or Dworkin speaks for them: look at that, that is what men really want to do to women – feed them into meat grinders! (The majority of women still have only limited experience of pornography – the range and variety of sexually explicit material produced simply for sexual arousal – making it all the more strange and alien when we do encounter it.) In her presentation of pornography Dworkin refuses to analyse fantasy as fantasy, and so can shed no light on its often troubling nature. She fails to trace it back to its origins in infantile desire for/rage against the all-powerful mother. She fails to connect it up more generally with the longing, fear and guilt which surround most aspects of contemporary sexuality, as they are differently experienced in the lives of women and men. And she fails to acknowledge, let alone probe, the insecurities of contemporary masculinity. Dworkin, in fact, will not concede that fantasy life operates with a degree of autonomy, preferring to see it as composed of straightforwardly conscious wishes and intentions. That our fantasy life usually has little or no connection with what we would enjoy in reality is ignored or denied, along with Freud's claim that '*psychical* reality is a particular form of existence not to be confused with [what he called] *material* reality'.[59] (Hence the failure to analyse female fantasy, and the denial by Dworkin and her followers that many or most women enjoy rape *fantasies*.)[60] Above all, in her many books, Dworkin refuses to analyse *how* pornography succeeds in creating men's dominance over women, or to reply to the arguments of her critics in the debate over pornography within feminism. Yet this is a debate which has aroused the fiercest disagreements and the most passionate antagonisms within contemporary feminism, helping to destroy Western feminist movements as coherent movements at the close of the 1970s.[61]

The evidence of possible causal connections between pornography and violence remains complex and contradictory. It is weakest if we attempt to correlate actual sex crime with the use of pornography. There is evidence that sex criminals have been *less* exposed to pornography than men in general throughout their lives, including before arrest and conviction.[62] A typical North American study by Michael Goldstein and Harold Kant, published in 1973 and apparently in agreement with forty previous studies, found that convicted rapists had less than the usual experience of pornography in adolescence and adulthood, displayed less enjoyment on exposure to it, and were generally more guilt-ridden and less sexually permissive – opposing premarital sex, for example.[63] If porn is alleged to lead to male sexual aggression, Black sociologist Robert Staples asks, 'why are the lowest consumers of porn (Blacks) so over-represented among those arrested for and convicted of rape?'[64] Or again, countries which have removed restrictions on pornography show either no increase in the rape rate, or a decrease.[65] We also know that countries where there is no pornography, like Saudi Arabia and Iran, are far from free of rape and violence against women – the fate of women prisoners in Iran being only the most horrific example.

On the other hand, some laboratory experiments – for example, those of the American psychologists Neil Malamuth and Edward Donnerstein – have found that exposing male college students to sexually violent films in which a woman is raped and 'enjoys' it, causes these subjects, who have also been provoked by insults from female experimenters, to score higher on a Rape Myth Acceptance Scale. (Exposure to sexually explicit, non-violent pornography, on the other hand, did not correlate with greater tolerance of sexual violence.) Malamuth and Donnerstein conclude that such forms of violent pornography will make men more disposed to accept the current mythology that women enjoy being raped.[66] Donnerstein further suggests that after exposure to pornography depicting women sexually aroused by rape, 57 per cent of men agreed they might commit rape if guaranteed they would not be caught (25 to 30 per cent of 'normal, healthy' college student males, he adds, indicate some willingness to commit rape in such circumstances).[67]

Exposure to violent pornography, he concludes, both desensitises men to violence against women and increases its likelihood.

Critics of Donnerstein have questioned his experimental procedure, suggesting, like Augustine Brannigan, that the results may be an artefact of the experimental situation (the procedure of female 'testers' angering and insulting subjects at the outset, for example).[68] However, even if we accept that the research indicates that exposure to certain forms of violent pornography increases sexist attitudes in some subjects, we should also note that these same researchers found that 'debriefing' sessions after the experiments, in which subjects were informed of the falsity of rape myths, meant that they subsequently held fewer sexist attitudes towards rape than control subjects not exposed to any pornography, even when tested months later. The context of exposure and discussion is important and, in this case, effective in countering the sexist messages carried by pornography.[69] Other psychologists, like Donald Mosher in his laboratory experiments, have produced results contradicting the findings of Malamuth and Donnerstein.[70]

Donnerstein and Malamuth's work, together with the fact that in the US rape rates are highest in states where pornography consumption is highest, was used by the American Meese Commission of 1986 to conclude that pornography is harmful, and to urge legal action against the production and sale of 'obscene materials'. The Commission, reflecting the growth of the moral right in Reaganite America, was controlled by moral conservatives and deluged with witnesses from the religious right and vice squads, as well as supported by anti-pornography feminists like Dworkin and MacKinnon. As anticipated, it reversed all the decisions of the previous official US report on pornography in 1970, which had recommended the repeal of all laws against sexually explicit materials involving consenting adults, and the need for a massive sex education programme.[71] Interestingly, however, Larry Baron, the sociologist presenting the correlation between pornography consumption and rape rate to the Commission, had himself pointed out at the time that it could be spurious 'and due to some common underlying factor'. Later, with Murray Straus, he was to do an analysis which led him to reject the correlation altogether.[72] More surprisingly perhaps, even Donnerstein has since objected that his studies are being misused in anti-pornography campaigns.[73] It is also of interest that two of only four women on the eleven-person Commission dissented from the Commission's report:

> To say that exposure to pornography in and of itself causes an individual to commit a sexual crime is simplistic, not supported by the social science data, and overlooks many of the other variables that may be contributing causes . . . We cannot tolerate messages of sexual humiliation directed to any group. But to make all pornography the scapegoat is not constructive. In the absence of significant social sanctions against pornography, the possibility of halting its use seems as slim as was the chance of halting the sales of liquor during Prohibition.[74]

It does seem ironic that this Commission should win the approval of feminists against pornography when its chairman, Attorney General Ed Meese, had been responsible for cutting funds to refuges for battered women. And so the battle continues. The anti-pornography feminists have been increasingly used by, and prepared to work in ever closer alliance with, the most blatantly conservative, most explicitly anti-feminist, anti-gay and pro-patriarchal family groupings in the United States. These are groups who oppose pornography only as part of their opposition to *all* non-marital and non-reproductive sex, in support of their moral crusade against the forces which threaten traditional gender roles and men's authority in the family. Strange bedfellows for a feminist, with or without a shared interest in sex. Catherine MacKinnon, for example, as Lisa Duggan's investigations have revealed, was called in by the Republican Mayor and Presbyterian minister William Hudnut (III) to draft anti-porn legislation in Indianapolis. There she worked successfully with another far right Republican, Beulagh Coughenour, a leading activist in the Stop ERA (Equal Rights Amendment) movement, and also with the Reverend Greg Dixon, a leading member of the moral majority, who not only declares contraception, abortion, and homosexuality crimes against society (opposing equal rights legislation and promoting criminalisation of all gay sex), but sees them as part of a global terrorist conspiracy to bring moral destruction to America.[75]

Feminists cannot afford to ignore the links between anti-pornography feminists and the programme of the moral right. The anti-pornography Civil Ordinance which Dworkin and MacKinnon successfully pioneered and had adopted in Minneapolis in late 1983, and which was later passed in Indianapolis and considered by dozens of other states in the US (although, pending appeal, it has since been declared unconstitutional), is currently being promoted in Britain by some feminists, like the writer Cathy Itzin. It is constructed around the belief that pornography is central in creating and maintaining the inequality of the sexes.[76] And it is seen by its supporters (which include the notorious leader of the moral right, Phyllis Schaffly) as progressive because it allows individuals to claim damages against the makers, sellers and distributors of any pornography (publically or privately available except in libraries), defined as 'the sexually explicit subordination of women, graphically depicted, whether in pictures or words', rather than requiring resort to the old criminal obscenity laws.

Its potential scope, however, is even more frightening than those laws, and certainly, in its vague and obviously ambiguous wording, would encompass material far beyond the violent pornography it claims to target. Any material can be deemed pornographic according to nine different criteria. For example, if women are shown in 'postures of sexual submission or sexual servility, including by inviting penetration'; or 'presented as dehumanised sexual objects, things, or commodities'; or as 'body parts . . . such that women are reduced to those parts'; or seen as 'whores by nature'.[77] It is clear that on these descriptions anyone could bring a complaint against any sexually explicit representation, since to some men and women, as Dworkin herself explicitly affirms, all representations of sex are 'degrading' and 'subordinating', and *any* penetrative sexual act violates women. If women don't feel subordinated, they have simply been 'brainwashed' by men. Men may also file suits under these ordinances against gay male porn on the grounds that it depicts men with other men in 'degrading' or 'submissive' or 'objectified' positions, men being treated like women! Since it is for judges to decide whether complaints are upheld, the idea that these laws circumvent the state and its existing heterosexist, male-dominated powers and prejudices is manifestly absurd. How far would I get seeking damages against Dworkin's *Right Wing Women*, objecting to her degrading portrayal of my own and all women's relations with men as no different from that of cows to be milked or meat to be bought?[78] Will I receive compensation for her demeaning accusation that women who enjoy heterosexual genital sex, or consensual lesbian sado-masochism, are the victims and dupes of men?

In the United States the Feminist Anti-Censorship Task Force (FACT) was formed in 1984 to oppose the anti-pornography ordinances drawn up by Dworkin and MacKinnon. There is no doubt that many women, whether describing themselves as feminist or not, dislike forms of pornography which they see as reflecting the prevailing culture of sexism and misogyny. But many women, feminists or not, are equally aware that men's contempt for women, associated with women's inferior status to men, does not hinge on the sexually explicit images of pornography. It may be comforting to believe that banning pornography would eliminate men's fear and hatred of women, wipe out men's violence and women's vulnerability; but we simply have no reason to think that it would. Violence against women long predates the explosion of commercial pornography, and historically and geographically exhibits little or no relation with its incidence and consumption. Indeed, contrary to Dworkin's picture, in which pornography silences women and teaches us that we must tolerate sexual assault and physical violation, it is precisely since the 1970s, and the explosion of pornography in the West, that women have been most vociferously – and successfully – *objecting* to men's violence against them.

Before pornography, in the staid and censorious fifties where there was little explicit pornography openly available, there was no public outcry against wife-beating, marital rape, child abuse; indeed, little fuss was made over any type of rape or violence against women. It simply went unnoticed. Unlike Dworkin, we need not rush to simplistic causal connections and opine that the availability of pornography in itself raised public awareness and consciousness of these issues. The rebirth of feminist movements did that. But it does seem likely that it is when sexual expression is most contained within a sanctified private sphere that least public awareness of, and discussion about, women's vulnerability to abuse exists. If we attach sexual exploitation to pornography, rather than to wider systems of inequality and powerlessness, we fail to see across time and place who is most vulnerable to exploitation and why. Looked at globally, for example, it is manifestly the case that it is not the availability of pornography, say in rural Thailand, but vulnerability according to class, race, and national patterns of dominance, as well as the power relation of age and gender, which determine who is most likely to be the victim of rape and violence, and which young girls and boys will be forced into prostitution.[79] One of the aspects of pornography that some women (and some men) have always objected to is the actual use of women and their bodies in the pornography industry. Certainly, what we are dealing with here is not just symbolic exploitation of women. But sex workers themselves have almost always objected to others' attempts to save them from such forms of 'exploitation', knowing full well that the economic alternatives open to them are likely to be no less, indeed perhaps a very great deal more, exploitative.[80]

It may be far easier, as Snitow, Stansell and Thompson remark, in a period of political retreat and discouragement, for feminists 'to attack the picture of what oppresses us than the mysterious, elusive yet powerful thing itself'. [81] But it is far from useful. Far from useful if, by divorcing pornography from other systems of exploitation and the wider political context, we blind ourselves to the roots of women's oppression in conventional family life, religion, science, technology, the law, national and international state policy – in short, all the most respectable institutions of contemporary society. Far from useful if, as the conservative pessimism of the eighties wipes out the liberal optimism of the sixties, today's feminist anti-pornography movement discounts the gains women have made in the struggle to establish their social, sexual and economic independence, by suggesting that pornography is a portrayal of women's transhistorical defeat. Ann Snitow suggests, correctly I think, that the movement against pornography began to flourish as feminists began to lose heart about women's ability to challenge men's power directly.[82] (Oddly, of course, this mirrors the solace men seek from pornography – the sense that they remain in the world they have lost: the world where woman, her person and property, belonged totally to them.) The sense of female defeat, so pervasive in the writing of Dworkin and MacKinnon, reflects the pessimism of a decade in which victories for some women in some places can be dispelled in the surrounding gloom of other women's further entrenchment in poverty, and the misery of living in cities marked by violence and squalor. But it also reflects women's own anxieties and fears about surrendering the old-time certainties of gender identity. As women we may be less powerful than men, but we could claim a monopoly on virtue. Such compensations of the powerless, I have often suggested, are not easy to relinquish – least of all in the embarrassing and risky negotiations of sexual desire.

All feminists can agree on the need to attack the phallic myths endorsed in most sexual imagery. But we cannot all assent to its reduction to the rallying cry against pornography without trampling upon many women's struggles over the pursuit of pleasure, love and friendship with, and without, men. (The fact that in North America the feminist anti-pornography movement is the most visible, and one of the best-funded and best-organised campaigns in feminist history, only strengthens the conflict.) We could argue that since pornography *symbolises* men's power over women (hence its compensatory popularity in these times of intensified struggle around gender and increasing insecurity about masculinity and male sexuality), women's attacks on it *symbolise* women's resistance to men's power over them. Perhaps. But this does not align us with the combined feminist/conservative anti-pornography crusade, for the logic of this crusade is the demand for state control over all representations of sexuality, or civil ordinances which, in the end, amount to the same thing.

At a time of sexual panic over the AIDS epidemic, and when moral crusades with official backing are being mounted against all the sexual freedoms so recently attained by women, gays, and other sexual minorities (including against sex education in schools), it is frightening that any progressive thinking could pursue this path. Can feminists really have forgotten so soon that censorship has always served to defend established power relationships, above all, to 'legitimate' male control over female sexuality in marriage? Do we not remember how feminist texts were but lately banned in so many parts of the world? It was not so long ago, indeed, that birth control information, or any reference to abortion, were defined as pornography in Britain and the United States. (And they still are in Ireland, today.) If feminists have forgotten, the moral right remembers – remembers that golden age of sexual silence, ignorance and taboo. Is it not obvious that there can be no absolute definition of 'pornography', of what is 'offensive' or 'harmful' (however we try to delimit it), on which we, as women acting in women's interests, could all agree? For the very same material will appear markedly different depending on its context, who is presenting it to us, and who is consuming it. The use of images of sexual titillation in encounters based on love or trust bear no relation to the use of such material by – as some battered wives report – abusive husbands in situations of compulsion and violence. The problem here, however, is surely the situation of compulsion, rather than the availability of pornography. We cannot legislate against images themselves without reference to context.

At a direct interpersonal and collective level objecting to sexist and violent pornography, and demanding that men reflect upon their attachment to it, can be of use in revealing the extent of cultural misogyny, male self-affirmation and woman-baiting. It is particularly worth attacking when it is displayed in workplaces or other public sites, serving not only to promote male camaraderie, but to exclude women or create spaces where they, and no doubt some men, feel uncomfortable. And there have been many examples of women and men, individually or collectively, taking such action.[83] This opens up the possibility of reflecting on why standard pornographic imagery, though varied, is limited and impoverished in its phallocentrism and reduction of women to 'cunts'. Women could suggest, for example, that we want different, non-sexist, non-violent pornography. Perhaps, as Deirdre English has suggested, we need more women pornographers to confront misogyny with new images, less divorced from social context and featuring different types of emotional relationships. She adds 'I can imagine some pretty intriguing scenes of older women with younger men, images of different body types, images of non-phallocentric lovemaking.'[84] While there is an ever proliferating variety of pornography today, there are still few women creating their own pornography – or erotica, if we prefer that term for the sexually arousing material we happen to like.

Women would need, however, to be far more honest than the anti-pornography feminists have thus far been. 'I have always been titillated by sexy images and stories,' writes Pat Califia, who does produce lesbian sado-masochistic erotica:

> The images of capture, helplessness, and torture (reassuringly followed by miraculous escape and revenge) were the most exciting: Superman being drained of his strength by Kryptonite, Aquaman dying slowly in a net hung over a swimming pool, Sheena hung upside down and threatened with a hot spearpoint. The fact that my mother strictly forbid us to own or read comics more risque than Donald Duck or Little Lulu only made my enjoyment more intense.[85]

She is not alone. As some feminists have noticed, the massive popularity of the paperback romance serves as pornography for women. Formula romance routinely conveys the eroticisation of male power. Every aspect of phallic power is celebrated here no less ardently, if less explicitly, than in any men's pornography. The older, richer, more sexually experienced, authoritative male hero may not drop his trousers (though increasingly today, he may), but our female heroine can never for one moment take her mind off the penetrating presence of the hard, resilient signs of his power: a power he regularly abuses, coldly, and sometimes violently, threatening danger to the heroine. His power and menace are also essential to his appeal:

> His lean, hard body held a menacing sexuality, an implicit threat of sexual violence which attracted women like iron filings to a magnet . . . He had hated her with a burning intensity only because he had loved her so deeply. His hatred was as strong as his love. And that was what made up her mind for her. When a man loves you as much as that, she reasoned happily, how can you turn him down?[86]

Romantic fiction, written by and for women, not only eroticises men's sexual power, but economic power in general, while glamorising women's social and sexual subordination to men.[87] Feminists need to admit, rather than deny, that at present many standard images of pornography do arouse women as well as men. Given the link between sex and the intensities of feeling about dependence and power which transport us back to those of childhood, perhaps we will always, at least in fantasy, tend to eroticise relations of power and hostility. Indeed, I believe that this is one very strong reason many women find the explicitness of most men's pornography so offensive. What arouses us sexually, at least in fantasy, is not quite what we feel it should be, leaving us ashamed of our fantasies and afraid to be honest about them. Better to reject sex completely, or at least to blame men for what goes on inside our own heads, seeing it as imposed from outside; better to project sexuality and its contradictions onto men, as Susan Brownmiller does with her claim: *'The rape fantasy exists in women as a man-made iceberg.'* [88] Here women's reactions resemble those of men, who likewise feel guilty about sex, blame women as the source of their own sexual fantasies, and see sexuality as imposed on them from without, therewith projecting sexuality and its contradictions onto women.

But once we can separate sex from guilt, and have the power to refuse others the right to exploit us, there is always scope for the playful enjoyment of the links between sex and power. So much remains unsaid about women's sexual fears and longings that the last thing we need, as Ellen Willis comments, 'is more sexual shame, guilt and hypocrisy – this time served up as feminism'.[89] Ironically, perhaps, it is also the last thing men need. What men need is to become more in touch with, more articulate about and more responsible towards, the varieties of their own sexual needs and desires. Identification of sex as the source of human, or at least women's, oppression, endows it with the kind of omnipotent power that can serve only to continue to bolster the most oppressive aspect of male mythology. It is itself the spinning flywheel of the existing pornographic imagination.

9. The Belly of the Beast (II): Explaining Male Violence

'I have never been free of the fear of rape,' Susan Griffin declared in a memorable article in the radical Californian magazine *Ramparts* back in 1971, adding: 'I never asked why men raped; I simply thought it one of the many mysteries of human nature.'[1] Nearly two decades later – decades in which feminists have repeatedly asked the question, devoting books and articles to finding the answer – the puzzle of men's cruelty to women remains only just a little less mysterious. Griffin herself had an answer. In patriarchal culture, she argued, the basic elements of rape are present in all hetero-sexual relationships: 'If the professional rapist is to be separated from the average dominant heterosexual, it may be mainly a quantitative difference.'[2] Men in our culture are taught and encouraged to rape women as the symbolic expression of male power. Rape serves as 'a kind of terrorism' enabling men to control women and make them dependent: 'Rape is the quintessential act of our civilization.'[3]

Other feminists in those early days of women's liberation, including Kate Millett and Shulamith Firestone in the US, did not share Griffin's analysis that rape and male violence play such a central role in establishing and perpetuating male power.[4] Germaine Greer's popular feminism, urging women to become tough, hedonistic and autonomous, dismissed outright the significance of men's use of violence against women.[5] And in Britain, the early feminist texts (the classic books of Juliet Mitchell and Sheila Rowbotham, for example) assigned male violence little weight in their analysis of the way in which the sexual division of

labour and its concordant ideologies produce men's power and
women's subordination.[6] It was the publication of Susan Brownmiller's international bestseller *Against Our Will* in 1975 which was
to prove a landmark in feminist thinking, in providing an analysis of
male power which placed rape and male violence at the centre of
the feminist problematic.[7]

Retrospectively, it is startling to realise that rape and men's
violence towards women became a serious social and political issue
only through feminist attention to them. There is no woman over
forty who cannot recall men's jokes trivialising rape as a violation
which women secretly desire. This was true whatever the grouping
of men, and however terrifying and violent the sexual assaults in the
headline a mere twenty or so years ago. There was much merri-
ment, at that time, among male staff in the psychology department
of Sydney University when I was a student over a rapist known as
'The Slasher', who climbed into women's bedrooms at dead of
night raping and knifing women. The day the joking died was the
day the headlines replaced 'the Slasher' stories with accounts of 'the
Mutilator' – the deadly deeds of a man attacking *men's* genitals late
at night in the Sydney parks.

There are still men today, pronouncing legal judgements, treating wounded women, writing psychological tracts, laughing with
their peers, who downgrade women's suffering at the hands of men.
The same cultural misogyny fuels their sentiments, but not the
same casual ignorance, the same 'innocent' complicity with men's
expressions of hatred and contempt for women. Today, they know
they are doing it despite, and perhaps because of, the passionate
protests and organised resistance of so many women against the
many acts of male violence towards their sex. The first job of
feminist analysis – and one which was performed with considerable
success – was to expose the myths surrounding rape and male
violence.

Myths of Rape: Sexist and Anti-Sexist

The first rape myth, swiftly exposed in feminist writing, was the idea
that rape was a rare event in modern society, the product of some
pathological sex-crazed maniac. Rape is a common event, often

planned by the rapist, who usually has a wife or girlfriend, and attacks a woman he knows. The second rape myth concerns the assumption of men's desire to protect women from violence. Police, hospital and judicial treatment of rape victims were rapidly revealed to be frequently hostile to the assaulted woman, more protective of the 'rights' of the rapist (of his self-proclaimed 'misreading' of a woman's rejection as assent) than the rights of a woman – at any time, in any place – to say 'no' to sex. To take just one example from what is now a multitude of studies, Elizabeth Stanko's *Intimate Intrusions* (1985), based upon her research in Britain and the United States, describes the police and the courts as 'the second assailant' insofar as they have in practice so often made it hard for women to press charges against attackers or get convictions: 'Above all, the process of inquiry – from police to prosecutors to judges – is assaultive to women.'[8] Feminists emphasised that the prevalence of rape as a social practice exists precisely because of the myths surrounding it: because of the belief that women 'invite' or provoke attack, that men can be 'victims' of their own overpowering sex drive. Rape is a product, they argued, not of male libido, but rather of a culture which encourages men to see sexual activity as a way of 'conquering' women, and of a society which allows men to indulge in the sexual exploitation and physical abuse of women without, in many cases, fear of punishment.[9]

There are other rape myths, however, which dominant strands of feminist thinking have not demolished. Indeed, they have underwritten them. Susan Griffin, for example, states bluntly (and falsely): 'Men are not raped.'[10] And Brownmiller's popular elaboration of Griffin's analysis begins from certain basic definitions and premises about 'rape' which endorse at least some of the prevailing beliefs and myths surrounding it. She sees it as an 'accident of biology' that men can rape, and women cannot:

> When men discovered that they could rape, they proceeded to do it . . . Indeed one of the earliest forms of male bonding must have been the gang rape of one woman by a band of marauding men. This accomplished, rape became not only a male prerogative, but man's basic weapon of force against woman, the principal agent of his will and her fear.[11]

But what, apart from lack of inclination and possibly access to weapons, is to prevent a woman (or marauding gang of women) from buggering a man with bottle, fist or tongue, or from demanding orgasm through oral sex? These are, after all, among the most common forms of male sexual assault on women, and well within women's capacities should we so choose. (Feminists long ago rejected the misleading definition of 'rape' exclusively as forced penile penetration of the vagina.) I have little doubt that just a few women have precisely so chosen, as I seem to remember one or two men have alleged in courts in the US. After all – any woman could argue in her own defence should prosecution attend such rape – do men not fantasise about sexual assault by women? Against Brownmiller it seems clear to me that men's capacity to rape has very little to do with some men's *proclivity* to rape, and other men's tendency to condone it – any more than women's capacity to cook can explain why a few wives drop poison in their husband's supper, and other women have celebrated such deeds in song.[12] So why do men rape?

To men's biological capacity to rape, Brownmiller adds her conviction that men rape women as part of a conscious and collective, transhistorical and transcultural, political strategy to ensure women's subjection to them. Rapists are the 'shock troops' of patriarchy, necessary for male domination.[13] Some men may not rape, but only because their power over women is already secured by the rapists who have done their work for them: rape 'is nothing more or less than a conscious process of intimidation by which *all men* keep *all women* in a state of fear'.[14]

The force of Brownmiller's argument derives from her exposure of men's long-standing silence about violence against women, which in itself enables her to clarify many aspects of the history of rape. Although this very silence means we have little evidence of the historical incidence of rape, it seems unlikely that it was unknown in, say, late nineteenth-century Vienna. Yet Sigmund Freud, who not only developed the most complex and sophisticated psychology of human behaviour we possess, but based his life's work on theories of human sexuality and human aggression, failed to give even passing mention to rape – except in a philosophical aside illustrating differences between conscious and unconscious motivation.[15] Alfred Kinsey and the sex researchers at the Kinsey Institute, although interviewing tens of thousands of men and women in the late 1940s and early 1950s, dismissed the significance and horror of rape in women's lives, suggesting most 'rape' cases, as they referred to them, were the result of women attempting to conceal their sexual activity. They further claimed that only a small proportion of sexual advances made to young girls involved physical assault, and that when they did any consequent psychological damage could be attributed to 'cultural conditioning' rather than to anything intrinsic to the experience itself.[16] Like so many feminists in the years just before and since the publication of her book, Brownmiller exposed the routine and chilling under-reporting of rape, its extremely high incidence, the tendency of authorities and professionals (mostly male) to blame women who are raped for 'victim-precipitation' – that is, causing men's violence against them. The explanation of rape, Brownmiller – and all feminists – would now agree, cannot be sought in terms of isolated acts by individual rapists. It can only be seriously approached in terms of the wider social context of the power of men, and a general cultural contempt for women.

The weakness of Brownmiller's argument, however, is its sweeping generalisation in the face of evidence that the prevalence of rape in modern Western societies is neither historically nor cross-culturally universal. Peggy Reeves Sanday in her oft-cited anthropological work shows that the extent of rape in different societies varies considerably. She contrasts societies which are relatively 'rape-free', like West Sumatra, with those which are most 'rape-prone', like the United States. The former, in her description, are societies in which women are respected and influential members of their community, participating in public decision making, and where 'the relationship between the sexes tends to be symmetrical and equal'.[17] They are also societies with far lower levels of overall violence. Other anthropological studies of pre-industrial societies have reported little or no sexual violence. Margaret Mead's well-known study of the Arapesh American Indians, although now surrounded by controversy, reported a gentle, non-aggressive society and culture, free from sexual violence.[18] The accounts we possess of some African hunter-gatherer societies, like that of the Mbuti, report the same low incidence of violence, and no evidence of rape or sexual violence. Notwithstanding the methodological problems associated with such studies, they do seem to indicate that sexual violence against women (or men) corresponds closely to the general level of violence in a society.[19]

Somewhat less controversially, historical studies of Western societies also suggest wide variation in the incidence of rape. Roy Porter has carefully sifted historical data on British society. The writings of women in diaries and elsewhere provide no evidence of female fears of the menace of rape in pre-industrial England – despite the expression of a multitude of other fears.[20] Early feminists – from Mary Astell to Mary Wollstonecraft – decried the wrongs of women, yet did not mention rape. Those nineteenth-century feminists who wrote and campaigned against sexual abuses (child prostitution and the forcible medical examination of prostitutes) likewise fail to mention anxiety about rape. Porter concludes that rape, and women's fears of it, probably did not loom so large then as they do today. Contrary to Brownmiller's history of rape, it does not seem that rape was the principal agent used to subordinate women in this period. The historical reality of men's oppression and exploitation of women in British society is not in doubt. But what Porter suggests is that men had little need to employ the threat of rape to maintain their dominance: 'Men no more cherished the threat of the rapist in the wings to maintain their authority over women than property owners encouraged thieves to justify the apparatus of law and order.'[21]

A study of eighteenth-century Massachusetts by Barbara Lindemann comes to similar conclusions.[22] Only one rape per decade reached the high court before 1729, and the *recorded* rape level remained consistently low throughout the century, averaging one every two years. Neither wars, the presence of high concentrations of bored and lonely American and British troops, nor economic crises and rootless destitution affected recorded rape levels. Lindemann considers, more fully than Porter, the possibilities of unreported rape and, more significantly still, the narrow definition of rape – defined by law and custom to refer exclusively to a woman who resisted a man who had no rights of sexual access to her. One reason so few rape cases occurred, she suggests, was because sexual assaults committed by upper- and middle-class men on servants would not be perceived as rapes, even by the women victims. They were a form of men's sexual assertion of authority for which neither wives nor servants would have legal redress. Notwithstanding these factors, however, Lindemann nevertheless argues that 'The conclusion is inescapable that the number of rape prosecutions was so much smaller in eighteenth-century Massachusetts than it is today because many fewer rapes were committed in proportion to the population.'[23] She attributes this to the cultural condemnation and frequent punishment of extra-marital sexual activity by men and women alike, and to the belief that women were as interested in sex as men: 'The rape prototype of female enticement, coy female resistance, and ultimate male conquest was not built into the pattern of normal sexual relations.'[24] This was a culture which, while securely patriarchal, discouraged rape, and a community which offered fewer opportunities for its perpetration.

Other studies highlight historical contrasts in men's expression of sexual violence. Writing of the high incidence of husband-wife violence in working-class lives in London between 1870 and 1940, when many wives 'did not hesitate to beat up their husbands' (though it was the former who would more likely be injured in violent rows), Ellen Ross links such violence to the upheavals of domestic life and men's power in the home caused, in particular, by male unemployment and chronic family poverty.[25] This overt physical antagonism between men and women was usually over money; men's failure or inability to provide for wife and children inducing women to challenge their domestic authority. And yet despite this violence, and despite men's belief in the 'right' of husbands to beat up wives, Ross suggests that London's pub culture in the generations before the First World War was 'less poisonously misogynous' than it would later become: 'Sexuality was not yet the domestic and social battleground it had become by the mid-twentieth century or the locus of the belligerent assertion of male power.'[26]

Even in contemporary Western societies the prevalence of rape, and its threat, seem to vary greatly: the United States, for example, has not twice, but over seventeen times the rate of reported rapes as

Britain, (34.5 forcible rapes per 100,000 of population in 1979 compared to 2 per 100,000 in the United Kingdom in 1981).[27] Rather than being the indispensable weapon used by men to ensure the subordination of women, might not rape be the deformed behaviour of men accompanying the destabilisation of gender relations, and the consequent contradictions and insecurities of male gender identities, now at their peak in modern America? It may be, as Porter wryly observes, an anachronism 'to assume that all the world has been America'.[28] Although it may be a possibility, of course, and a disastrous one – not only for women – that all the world could become North America!

In terms of developing a sexual politics against rape and male violence, it hardly seems helpful to refuse to distinguish, in the manner of Brownmiller and so many subsequent Western feminists, between men who rape and men who don't. Although not without its justifications, it is a politics of the profoundest pessimism. Feminists' increasing despair at the ever-mounting evidence of men's sexual violence against women is captured by Brownmiller when she says: 'Never one to acknowledge my vulnerability, I found myself forced by my sisters in feminism to look it squarely in the eye.'[29] It was the new visibility of the extent and the horror of rape, especially for feminists engaged in aiding its victims to cope with the trauma, which created the rising levels of feminist fear and anger. 'All men are potential rapists', became the disturbing slogan of many a feminist activist in the late 1970s and 1980s. The rapist is 'the man next door', whoever he might be; he is the man in our beds, the father of our children, the man who 'pays the rent'.[30] 'It was almost as if,' Ann Snitow comments, 'by naming the sexual crimes, by ending female denial, we frightened ourselves more than anyone else.'[31]

Is any man a potential rapist? The simple answer, I believe, is 'no' – insofar as the word 'potential' has any practical significance. Is any woman a potential victim? In theory, yes; in practice, the risk we face is far greater for some women than for others. Both these statements, however, are not just controversial but explosive in feminist discourse. They need the most careful study.

They are explosive because what feminist analysis has so far been unwilling to explore is why *some* men become rapists and use violence against women, and *some* men do not. The reasons feminists have been unwilling to make such distinctions are important. First, it is seen as a reversion to an individual, rather than a social, treatment of the problem of rape. (Although it seems to me that no human problems, however apparently 'individual', from cancer to catatonic schizophrenia, can ever be adequately understood isolated from their social context.) Secondly, it is seen as facilitating victim-blaming – if we can differentiate between men, then it can be suggested that some women are more likely to choose violent rather than non-violent men – a form of explanation insidiously popular amongst male (and a few female) professionals and social scientists. Finally, it is seen as letting men off the hook, for all men are certainly a part of the climate and culture of misogyny which permits violence against women to occur with so very little protest or protection from men, (though a handful of men, now growing in number, have always protested – from John Stuart Mill to pro-feminist men today).

Continuities and Discontinuities in Men's Use of Sexual Violence

One body of work which Brownmiller and many other feminists have drawn on in support of the claim that *all* men are potential rapists is the research of Menachim Amir in *Patterns of Forcible Rape*. (Although they quickly rejected his concept of 'victim precipitation' in the explanation of a significant minority of rapes.) Amir studied 1,292 men arrested for rape in Philadelphia between 1958 and 1960, concluding, as had other studies before him, that rapists tend to be seen as 'psychiatrically normal', usually men with girlfriends ('not deprived of sexual outlets'), different from other men primarily in terms of their proximity to delinquent sub-cultures.[32] Ninety per cent of his sample of rapists, and their victims, came from 'the lower classes or low status groups' with, proportionately, four times as many Black rapists and Black victims. Rapists in this prison population were mostly between the ages of 15 and 19 and drawn from 'a "parent" subculture of violence'.[33] Interestingly, while Amir's work has been used by feminists to suggest the rape proclivities of all men, Amir himself drew a different conclusion: 'Of course, it is always people who commit rape, but the rate of rape is conditioned by the cultural norms and social organization or disorganization of the groups to which they belong.'[34] In stressing predominantly social factors rather than individual psychopathology in his description of the typical rapist, Amir was not failing to distinguish between rapists and non-rapists – quite the contrary. From his research, all men are no more potential rapists than they are potential house-breakers, potential drug takers, and so on.

However, there are problems with Amir's account. In emphasising the overwhelming predominance of Black and working-class rapists, Amir, and Brownmiller after him, was accused of racism and classism. Other feminists pointed out the massive under-reporting of rape, suggesting that Black and working-class men were simply more likely to be among the tiny percentage of rapists arrested and punished. Even the official North American National Crime Survey of 1979 estimated that only 50 per cent of forcible rapes were reported to the police, while feminist surveys indicate that the percentage of unreported rapes is far higher. Diana Russell, for example, who interviewed a random sample of 930 women in San Francisco in 1978, reported that 41 per cent claimed at least one attempted or actual rape (excluding the 3 per cent who reported marital rape). But only one in ten of these incidents had been reported to the police.[35] In England 75 per cent of women reporting sexual assault to the London Rape Crisis Centre between 1976–80 did not go on to alert the police.[36] In *Ask Any Woman: A London Inquiry into Rape and Sexual Assault*, a survey conducted by Ruth Hall for Women Against Rape in 1982, one in six women reported having been raped (over one third by their husbands), and a further one in five reported incidents of attempted rape. Only 8 per cent of raped women, however, had reported the assault to the police.[37]

Hall's survey has been criticised as highly self-selective, insofar as only 1,236 of the 2,000 questionnaires she distributed were completed. And contrary to Hall's claim that her sample was 'fairly' representative of the population as a whole, its respondents were apparently considerably younger than the general population, as well as geographically localised in the inner city of London.[38] These factors, in conjunction with one-fifth of Hall's sample having experienced the sexual assaults they reported as children, account for at least a part of the contrast between her findings and the official statistics. (The British Crime Survey of 1983 found only 10 cases of assault out of a sample of 11,000 men and women, but this was based on interviews with people of all ages, and asked only about experiences in the previous year.)[39] Whatever the difficulties with these empirical surveys, however, there is no escaping the evidence of high rates of sexual assault on women, and low rates of police reporting. Women failing to report assault to the police usually give as their reason the belief that police would be unsympathetic and unhelpful.[40] It is a belief for which there is ample corroboration, not least from 'reformed' policemen themselves.[41]

The high incidence of sexual assault – so much of it unreported – together with the well-established tendency to victim-blaming reflected in criminal law and the justice system,[42] have led many feminists to conclude that the 'police-blotter rapist', described by Brownmiller as 'the boy next door', can be extended to men of all classes, races, and ages. Indeed, the introduction to a recent feminist collection exploring the dynamics of sexual violence states:

> In understanding violence against women the concept 'class' is simply not a significant factor in identifying either victim or offender. Nor is it relevant in explaining why this violence occurs. To put it bluntly, the realities of male violence and the sociological language of class seem entirely divergent.[43]

Its authors, however, reject the need for evidence to establish their claim – which is just as well for them, given that, to put it bluntly, every conceivable source of evidence we possess on the realities of male violence suggests the opposite.

There is a second development in feminist thinking on sexual assault which also directs us towards seeing all men as perpetrators of violence, and all women as its victims. This is the feminist extension of the definition of 'male violence', whereby it is seen as not only general and pervasive, but occurring along a 'continuum of sexual violence'. The continuum ranges from the everyday abuse of women in pornographic images, sexist jokes, sexual harassment and women's engagement in compliant but unwanted marital sex, through to the 'non-routine' episodes of rape, incest, battery and sex murder. Elizabeth Stanko, for example, groups together a wide selection of such behaviour from men towards women as threatening or violent, arguing that they all serve to remind women of their vulnerability to men: 'Try as they might women are unable to predict when a threatening or intimidating form of male behaviour will escalate to violence.'[44] In her recent, clear and comprehensive overview of work on male sexual violence, Liz Kelly adopts a similar position. She makes three key points which she presents as the background to her own research: most women have experienced sexual violence; the different forms of violence are connected along a continuum of abuse; sexual violence occurs in the context of men's power and women's resistance.[45] This means, she argues, that rape is but one of the ways men maintain power through sexual violence. It is men's 'taken for granted' use of aggression – for example, in sexual harassment in workplaces – which enables men's gender power to override other power relations like that between teacher and pupil.[46] And it is the limited definitions of sexual violence, she adds, which have enabled men individually and collectively to benefit from distinctions between a so-called 'deviant' minority of men and the 'normal' majority.[47]

Such feminist extensions of notions of sexual violence have real advantages. There is no doubt that men's intrusive staring, touching, sexist joking and worse is not only often extremely discomforting for women, but also consolidates sexual hierarchy, affirming in men a shared sense of themselves as the dominant, assertive, active sex. Similarly, the so-called 'harmless' acts of flashing, grabbing of breasts or obscene phone calls are not only frightening in their sudden violation of women's immediate personal space, but can induce a more chronic sense of fear in women – turning public places into hostile environments. Furthermore, there is truth in the feminist reflection that what gross and petty acts of sexual intrusion have in common is the sexist myths to which they give rise, and which seek either to render them harmless or, when regarded as more serious, to blame women for not preventing their occurrence.

Nevertheless, there are problems both with the idea that the high incidence of unreported rape suggests all men are guilty, and with the notion of a continuum of men's sexual violence, from hetero-sexual acts initiated by them (rather than women) through to acts of rape and sex murder. At least, there are problems if we are seeking to understand the causes, and prevent the occurrence, of men's use of violence. Although absent from most feminist writing on men's violence, there is evidence that there are significant differences not only between men who commit sexual assault on women and other men, but between different types of violent men – and between different types of violent acts – and their meanings. Rather than ignoring these differences, the endeavour to understand them seems to me crucial to tackling the problems of violence and to finding the appropriate variety of solutions to prevent men from resorting to them.

Rapists are most certainly not all poor or Black or from specific ethnic minorities. However, these are the men most likely to commit the most common form of non-marital rape. They are young men from inner cities, like those who constitute Amir's sample and every other North American study of convicted rapists.[48] They are part of the sub-cultures of violence which form around urban unemployment and poverty. Ever-increasing in num-ber, Black and white, but in the US predominantly Black, it is they who, as Robert Staples and others have indicated, are most removed from the confirmations of manliness derived from wealth or position; most removed, indeed, from any type of 'respectable' status or identity.[49] The portrait of the typical English rapist, whose actions are reported to the police, is almost identical to his North American counterpart. In Richard Wright's study of 292 rape cases in six south eastern counties (excluding London) during the years 1972–6, for example, the suspects were mostly young (in group assaults rarely over 20), almost all unskilled working class, fre-quently unemployed, 70 per cent of whom had already been convicted for some other non-sexual crime of violence.[50] Wright notes, in his view significantly, that there were few non-white suspects – although, disappointingly, he provides no relevant demographic data on the non-white population.

These are also, of course, the men most targeted for police

surveillance and arrest. But the statistical evidence that there are higher levels of sexual assault and battery from such men seems to me a reality which cannot be evaded by invoking the perennial debate about the bias of criminal statistics – significant as it is; or by pointing to police and judicial racism – vicious as these are. For, since most rapes and domestic violence are intra-class and intra-racial, it is poor and Black women who are unquestionably the main victims of this type of violence from men. These are not the women the police and courts are most concerned to protect. Quite the contrary; they are the ones least likely to trust the police, and hence least likely to initiate complaints. In addition, Robert Staples is, I believe, correct in arguing that, 'When other expressions of man-hood such as gainful employment and economic success are blocked, those men will express their frustration and masculinity against women.'[51] Such men are the ones most likely to commit gang-rape – in which victims can suffer the most brutal forms of physical violence – as they compete for status with one another.[52] And it must be added, they are the men most likely to express their frustration and masculinity in violence against themselves and against other men, as their now soaring rates of drug addiction, suicide and homicide demonstrate. As Roy Porter suggests: 'Rapists are . . . the waste of patriarchy, but they are its wayward sons not its shock troops; not its life-blood but a diseased excrescence.'[53]

This type of analysis helps to explain the ever-increasing rates of rape in post-Reagan America, which has seen the solidification of an urban 'under-class' with no realistic prospects of progressing beyond their dependent status into jobs of any kind. In suggesting that the extremely high proportion of Black men in this group means that a larger number of men who resort to violence, including sexual violence, will be Black, it is not being suggested that such violence occurs because they are Black. The higher probability of violence here, on the contrary, exists because of the specific structuring of exploitation and oppression, which we looked at in chapter seven, in a white-dominated, racist society. While the possibility for racist misinterpretation is obviously deeply worrying, it would seem equally racist to avoid confronting the problem.

That the type of rape which we have been looking at involves men attempting to establish their power and masculinity in situations where they have been deprived of more conventional means to them is also supported by studies of male rape in prisons. Men raping men, according to Ken Plummer, 'rarely, if ever, involves men who are "gay" in the modern sense of the term'.[54] Donald West similarly reports from crime figures that homosexual offences 'almost invariably' involved men over 16 (98 per cent) and were 'virtually always' consensual (99 per cent). [55] Homosexual rape, however, has been found to be well-nigh universal in North American male prisons and juvenile institutions, and most often involves Black men raping white men.[56] Such rape occurs, various studies conclude, as a way of asserting power and masculinity: 'A male who fucks another male is a double male,' Scacco quotes from the men in his survey.[57] Plummer concludes that studies of both prison rape and the rape of women suggest that many men feel vulnerable about their masculinity. But some men are more vulnerable than others: 'For the working class and racial minorities this crisis may be at its greatest: at the bottom of the heap, their sense of masculinity is absolutely pivotal.'[58] Plummer is quick to add a point which should be obvious, but which many feminists writing in this area reject, namely that to say that men are insecure is in no way to condone their coercive conduct, but part of the attempt to understand it.

Any serious attempt to tackle the prevalence of rape committed by the typical convicted rapist involves more than an ideological assault on prevailing cultural sexism and misogyny. It involves, as well, social policies that are quite the opposite of the Reagan and Thatcher legacies, which have attacked all community spending, undermined welfare provision and dramatically increased the poverty and disorganisation associated with escalating street-crime, pimping, hustling, and violence.

A different type of rape – one which usually goes unreported – is assaults by relatives or acquaintances, whether violent or not. Paul Wilson's study of unreported rape incidents in Australia found that these were more often committed by relatives or acquaintances.[59] His study further suggested that the typical middle-class rapist, less often caught or punished, is more likely to be involved in family or situational rape – coercing women through power and trickery – although this form of rape also has its working-class parallels.[60] Several studies of American college student dating experiences show that at least 50 per cent of women report incidents of sexual aggression from men, while around 20–25 per cent of men admit to using sexually aggressive behaviour. These incidents are rarely reported to the police.[61] In her study of nearly 2,000 male college students in the United States, Mary Koss found that around 22 per cent used verbal coercion to obtain sex, and around 5 per cent some form of physical force.[62] According to Donald West, it is unusual for this form of sexual assault, even when physically coercive, to be the sort of brutal and injurious kind more common when the attacker and victim are not known to each other, or in group rape.[63]

West himself, while insisting on his belief in the woman's absolute 'right to refuse', downplays the significance of such assaults – referring to them as 'annoying behaviour by boy-friends'.[64] Indeed, he seems more to echo than to condemn the ideology of men's entitlement to women's bodies which he sees as underlying these incidents: 'They reflect the continuing divergent attitudes of men and women, the former often believing that a woman's seductive manners, acceptance of treats and willingness to accompany a partner to his room amount to sexual teasing which invites and deserves an aggressive response.'[65] West thus reduces such assault to little more than a problem of communication, rather than to men's frequent use of force to obliterate women's sexual autonomy.

Nevertheless, I think he is correct to distinguish this form of rape from other types of more violent rape, to the extent that it is not the kind which connects so closely with women's everyday fears of rape. But West is right, it seems to me, mainly because the strategies needed to prevent rape in a context where people have chosen to be together (although *not* agreed to have sex) are, at least in part, different from those needed to prevent the types of sexual assault which women most fear, which come out of the blue. Rape occurring on dates, or in similar situations, connects most directly with the dominant masculine rituals and iconography of 'girlie' calendars, sexist joking, sexual harassment: the ordinary, daily encounters of women with men in contexts which demean women and ostentatiously celebrate 'manhood' and its presumed hetero-sexual imperative and prerogatives.

One way of attacking men's sense of entitlement, and affirming women's rights of sexual refusal, in 'dating' situations would seem to be intensive anti-sexist consciousness-raising for boys and for girls, for men and for women, in schools, colleges, workplaces, unions and all social and political groupings. This could be backed up by fines, expulsions and sackings where there is evidence of men's sexual harassment of women (as happens, for example, in Australia, where employers can be fined heavily for making sexist remarks.[66]) In Britian initiatives are already underway in some schools and in many unions, with the goal of eliminating all forms of men's sexual coerciveness.[67] They should also be part of a deter-mined ideological assault on beliefs supportive of the idea of the predatory male and his female prey, combined with relentless contempt and derision for the suggestion that 'the man can't help it', and the woman has to 'take it'. It is harder, however, except on conviction in association with counselling, to see any immediate structures for implementing this kind of strategy in relation to the type of more random, violent rape discussed above. For it is precisely the position of such men outside the normal institutions conferring status and reward which energises their abuse of women in the first place. This is not to deny that such men, whatever the impact of social conditions, are responsible for their own immoral acts. But prevention here, as distinct from condemnation, will need to include interventions of a more general economic and political nature.

The most unusual and abnormal of sex criminals – whose crimes are closest to women's deepest fears of rape – constitute a third and smaller group of rapists. They have been studied by West, Roy and Nichols, and Levine and Koenig, both studies in Canada.[68] These rapist are the men who make headline news, who act alone, commit repeated assaults over many years, and use extreme violence and sadism; the men who murder, or try to murder, their victims. The victims are mostly complete strangers to these rapists. The men of this type, in the Canadian studies, are mostly described as coming from disturbed and sometimes brutal upbringings, combining extreme ignorance and guilt about sex, and anger against women, with a personal sense of failure and inadequacy. Both West *et al.*, and Koenig and Levine, emphasise these men's sense of crippling doubt over masculinity, fears of homosexuality and the use of sex to establish masculinity: 'They think that to be a "real man", they must perform the sexual act – whether they have any interest in it or not – because it enhances their standing amongst their peers and adds to their self-image.'[69] Both studies describe men who were teased for their lack of manliness, who feel weak, inadequate and dependent. Typical statements from such rapists recall continual ribbing and bullying from other males, producing feelings of guilt, rage and inadequacy: 'This left me with the feeling of being a sissy, or at least, not much of a man';[70] 'I wondered, "Am I homosexual?" Maybe I care for guys . . . I tested that out and I felt more repulsion from that than I did from getting to the point of raping a girl';[71] 'I think that I was feeling so rotten, so low, and such a creep and I had so many secrets from everybody about myself'.[72]

These Canadian case studies seem to correspond to Robert Brittain's account of the typical 'sadistic murderer' from twenty years clinical observation of such men in Britain. He describes men who are introspective, withdrawn, obsessional, mild and generally non-violent, prudish in sexual matters and perhaps appearing effeminate to others – men who differed markedly from the more typical rapist highlighted by Amir.[73] Brittain's description also corresponds quite precisely with the accounts we have of England's most recent, most prolonged terror-inducing sex killer, Peter Sutcliffe, who hunted and haunted women in the North of England for six long years, murdering and mutilating thirteen of them, seriously wounding seven others. The different biographies of Sutcliffe all describe him as a man who was from an early age small, weak, shy and gentle, the son of a violent and bullying father, John Sutcliffe, and a very unhappy mother. He was teased and persecuted at school, reluctant to fight, quite at odds with the tough, aggressively masculine Northern working-class world around him: 'He was a right mother's boy from the word go,' his father told Gordon Burn.[74] He was a man who remained a gentle husband until the end – according to his brother, at least, who described Peter Sutcliffe's relations with his wife, Sonya: 'He wouldn't say owt to her . . . I just said, "Well that's up to you, but I'm going to tell her what I think, and you should do bloody same" . . . If owt wanted doin', he'd do it for 'er.'[75]

Sutcliffe, it seems, was a man who failed to conform to the aggressively masculine values of his social milieu. (Although he did, upon leaving school, belatedly seek to acquire 'real' manhood through the solitary pursuit of body-building and an obsession with motorbikes – he is said to have kept the engine of his favourite motorbike under his bed.)[76] His feminist biographer, Nicole Ward Jouve, detects clear indications of homosexual tendencies, repressed and despised, in Sutcliffe's lack of interest in girls, in his own girlish temperament and his passionate friendship with other more gentle men.[77] Sutcliffe's father was certainly over-anxious to establish that his son had 'no affectations whatsoever', giving Ward Jouve the impression that he would rather have a multiple murderer than a homosexual for a son. She comments:

> That the taboo should be so great on feminine tendencies, so little on violence, gives a terrifying measure of the scale of the values present. Femininity is bottom – and meant to stay bottom wherever it may be traced. That is what killed, more than anything else.[78]

Sutcliffe was, up to a point, at odds with the masculine values around him. But he also imbibed them. They helped destroy his women victims, and they destroyed him, bringing a terror which lives on into the lives of tens of thousands of women in Britain.

A Roman Catholic, and an altar boy for several years, Sutcliffe *believed* in the links between sex and sin. He *believed* it was Eve who brought sin into this world and that female sexuality was both fascinating and 'loathsome'. He observed it time and again, we are told by Burn, on his regular visits to the Morecambe wax museum to gaze upon the life-size opened bellies, foetuses, scabs and sores of pregnant and diseased female bodies.[79] Sex as Sin, Sin as Monstrous, was the warning spelled out in these Victorian antiques. And Peter Sutcliffe was also, whatever the charade of his trial, suffering the symptoms of psychosis. He was deluded. He heard voices. But his delusions were constructed out of the most familiar fantasies around him: some women are good (pure and asexual), some women are bad (sinful and sexual). Women's sexuality menaces men and threatens society. It is responsible for all the temptations and miseries men suffer. And the voices from God were but echoes of the voices of the most prominent mortal men around Sutcliffe – of the press, the police and later the prosecution. They were all voices which, like Sutcliffe himself, could understand why any man might *want* to murder prostitutes. The voice of God which told Sutcliffe, in his own words, 'to kill people called scum who cannot justify themselves to society', found its weaker echo in the voice of Sir Michael Havers commenting on Sutcliffe's victims, 'Some were prostitutes, but perhaps the saddest part of this case is that some were not'.[80] God, Peter Sutcliffe and the Assistant Chief Constable of Yorkshire could all speak with one voice when the latter announced: 'It would seem as if in this case, as with Miss McDonald, he [Sutcliffe] made a mistake ... [in murdering] a perfectly respectable girl.'[81]

It is for this reason that feminists are right to proclaim that the cause of violent crimes against women cannot be located *simply* in pathological individuals, brutal families, or the stresses and humiliations of poverty and racism (alongside the violent sub-cultures) of many rapists, batterers and murderers. But, contrary to many feminist claims currently being made, these factors are also crucial in understanding *which* men are most likely to resort to sexual violence or violence against women and children, what *type* of violence they are most likely to display, and which women are most likely to be its targets. The wider causes of men's violence must be located in societies which construct 'masculinity' in terms of the assertion of heterosexual power (in its polarised difference from 'femininity'), and which continue to see sex as sinful, while locating the object of sexuality in women, and the subject of sexual desire in men. But this does not mean that any man could be Peter Sutcliffe, even when, like his younger peers on the Leeds football grounds, they may delight in taunting police with chants of 'You'll never catch the Ripper' and '11–0' (referring to what was then the number of Sutcliffe's victims).[82]

Peter Sutcliffe was nicknamed 'the Yorkshire Ripper'. In her analysis of the hundred years of 'Ripper' stories and iconography since the original Jack the Ripper murdered and mutilated five prostitute women in London in 1898, Judith Walkowitz points to the crucial role of the popular press in establishing the Ripper as a media hero, and amplifying the threat of male violence to women. The message of the Ripper mythology, as Walkowitz sees it, was to establish the cities as a dangerous place for women, and to sanction the covert expression of male antagonism towards women, as well as to buttress male authority over them. But feminists, Walkowitz argues, need to probe behind Ripper mythology to uncover the complex reality it masks:

> By flattening history into myth, the Ripper story has rendered all men suspect, vastly increasing female anxieties, and obscuring the distinct material conditions that generate sexual antagonism and male violence . . . In the 'real' world, neither male violence nor female victimization has single-root causes or effects. Only our cultural nightmares and media fantasies construct life this way.[83]

Women are right to see our society as riddled with the cultural expression of contempt for them as the subordinate sex – a contempt by no means confined to pornography. The continuum of men's violence is real in the very particular sense that it is experienced by women as such, in a world where we are everywhere threatened by petty acts of violence or at least of sexual intrusiveness. Overall, women are less at risk from men's violence in public than are other men. But women feel more vulnerable. They feel more vulnerable because, as Elizabeth Stanko illustrates from her research, and women know from everyday experience, if we include all the forms of intimidation women suffer at men's hands – the smacking of lips, muttering of obscenities, kerb crawling, grabbing of breasts and so on – women are subject to a kind of constant intimidation.[84] When a flasher jumps out at a woman, or a voyeur lurks at our window, he is usually not a rapist or killer. But he just might be. His actions certainly serve to make the world feel unsafe for women, particularly when we are likely to have read fairly recently of some serious sex attack – always given greater media prominence than men's attacks on men.

There is a continuum of men's violence insofar as the effects of the variety of men's intrusive acts all contribute to women's experience of lack of safety. What is not convincing, however, is some feminists' insistence that all men really are similar in terms of the individual threat they pose for women. We need to get to grips with the paradox that while women are mainly afraid of men whom they do not know, those women who are physically attacked are generally assaulted by men they do know.

As feminists, however, we can agree that a society which equates masculinity with assertiveness, sexual and otherwise, is one which encourages and condones men's violence against women. People with power have usually been allowed to express anger at, and often use force against, the less powerful with relative impunity. It is surely true that a central aspect of men's use of violence against women lies in social assumptions of men's right to dominate women and expect servicing from them. This has allowed men to express anger and use physical force to get what they want, and get away with it – at least in the domestic sphere. Looking in more detail at the history and politics of family violence will help to illuminate the different levels of social, cultural and personal factors which combine to cause male violence and, at times, violence from women. They are factors which intersect with, rather than diverge from, inequalities of class, ethnicity, race and age.

Behind Closed Doors: Violence in the Family

Irene Hanson Frieze, examining the causes of marital rape in the United States, found that in nearly all cases it was associated with other types of physical violence in the relationship, and rare in cases where husbands were not otherwise violent. The most extensive studies of family violence have been conducted in North America. From her own and other surveys Frieze estimates that marital violence is experienced by around 10 per cent of married women.[85] In Britain Jan Pahl reports that one study which collates the available research estimates that serious violence occurs in up to 5 per cent of marriages, and milder forms of violence in another 1 per cent.[86]

There is less agreement on its causes. In his book on family violence, a leading American researcher, Richard Gelles, isolates childhood exposure to violence as a major factor determining adult use of violence – whether by women or men. He suggests that a person who has been the victim of parental violence is 'as much as 1,000 times more likely than a child raised in a nonviolent home' subsequently to use violence against a spouse or child.[87] Straus, Goode and others have also pointed to greater risks of domestic violence when the wife has a higher status than her husband.[88] Along with their emphasis on the disastrous effects of male unemployment and poverty on family violence, they attribute this to men responding violently to threatened loss of dominance, status and privileges. Gelles' research, however, like that of Straus, Steinmetz and others, also points to high levels of women's violence against children, indeed higher than men's, and also to women's violence against husbands – though the latter is more often in self-defence and less likely to be as physically damaging as men's violence.[89] In general both Gelles and Straus, like other researchers in this area, refer to the interaction of social class and social stress – in the form of unemployment, underemployment, number of children, and social isolation – as significantly contributing to violence between spouses and against children, from women, but, far more significantly in terms of its physical destructiveness, from men.[90]

We need to be clear as to the implications of this. It is not being suggested that middle-class men do not use violence against women and children, when we know that their social status will serve to protect them from the surveillence of agencies of social control. And it is not being suggested that middle-class men do not possess a variety of means, often contingent upon their economic and social resources, of organising their domestic lives, selfishly and insensitively, in ways which bring sorrow or despair into the lives of their wives or children. There are other ways, perhaps even more effective ways, through which people exert control over others – without the use of violence. Jean Thompson, for example, in 'The People of Color' describes a woman, as she listens to the physical violence which takes place in the next apartment, beginning to question the nature of her own non-violent marriage, realising that it 'works' only because she indulges her husband's infantile needs for domination and ego support.[91] In a culture which constructs masculinity around ideas of dominance, social power and control over others, but then denies to some men any access to such prerogatives, it is not surprising that subordinated men may be more likely to resort to violence as the only form of power they can assert over others. Both contemporary and historical studies indicate that family violence is affected by material deprivation, interacting with women's dependence and powerlessness and men's assumptions of their right to control women.

Jan Pahl, for example, sees domestic violence as occurring in all social classes and groupings, and links it first of all with men's assumptions that they should be dominant in the home. But she points as well to the role of women's economic dependence, bad housing and male unemployment in causing men's violence towards women, making wife-battering 'somewhat more common among lower socio-economic groups'.[92] Even more importantly, she identifies women's financial dependence and lack of adequate accommodation as the main factors preventing women from leaving violent marriages.[93] From her own survey of women in the Women's Aid refuge in Kent, she found that middle-class women were less likely to need the refuge for support and, if they did, less likely to return to husbands upon leaving the refuge.[94] Removing the structural roots of violence against wives, Pahl concludes, involves changing the rhetoric and reality of 'traditional family life'. It entails social change which reduces the financial and legal dependence of married women. It means attacking the assumptions of male dominance within marriage and the reluctance of police and public agencies to intervene in the 'private' sphere of the family: a privacy which protects men's rights at the expense of those of women and children.

Along these lines, Black American feminist bell hooks has pointed to the need for feminist strategies against physical violence to focus on how people react to and prevent isolated acts of physical abuse, not just the most extreme and chronic forms of men's violence against women.[95] 'Increasingly', she reports, 'in discussion with women about physical abuse in relationships, irrespective of sexual preference, I find that most of us have had the experience of being violently hit at least once.'[96] Feminist arguments need to address the problem of such occasional hitting, and why it is that women so often feel such physical abuse is justified. It is here that the importance of people's experience of physical abuse as children, whether from men or women, is crucial. In case after case, hooks suggests, women who have experienced physical punishment as children from those they love find that they end up as adults accepting as inevitable the abusive behaviour of lovers (who are sometimes women).[97]

The fullest historical study available of family violence, Linda Gordon's excellent research based on the case records of social work agencies in Boston between 1880–1960, identifies poverty as the single most pronounced characteristic of clients who were victims of violence.[98] Gordon is well aware that these clients, usually poor and uneducated, often immigrant and non-white, were the people most likely to be reported to social work agencies for neglect and violence. But they were also those, mostly women (and some men), who actively sought help and protection. The most isolated and the most powerless, these women were also the most angry. Studying case after case, Gordon suggests that underlying family violence is not so much men's 'need' to demonstrate 'masculinity', as power struggles in which family members were 'contesting for material, and often scarce, benefit'; women's resistance, as well as men's accustomed dominance, was the trigger.[99] Unemployment, for example, intensified violence, as women were angered not so much by men's lack of financial support for themselves, but for their children. It was frequently women's refusal of deference and servicing when men failed to provide economically that initiated men's violence:

> Accustomed to supremacy, acculturated to expect service and deference from women, and integrating these expectations into the ego itself, men were understandably disoriented to encounter resistance and unskilled at negotiating compromise . . . Wife-beaters are by no means commonly crazy or even temporarily disoriented, but they may indeed have more self-destructive behaviours than less violent men.[100]

Gordon's research also indicates that wife-beating is quite often associated with incest, child abuse and neglect. Although it is also true, she notes, that there can be differences between men who sexually abuse children and men who engage in other forms of family violence and neglect. Wife-beating and physical abuse are more closely connected with the stresses and frustrations of poverty than is sexual abuse. Incest perpetrators have also been less likely to express shame, claiming a sense of entitlement or placing the blame on the abused child. Gordon strongly emphasises that despite its sudden emergence as a leading social problem in Britain and the United States in the 1980s (as in the public explosion in Britain over the vast number of cases diagnosed in Cleveland in 1987), child sexual abuse is not a new issue. She notes that charity and social workers were dealing with incest cases daily a century ago, when there was great public outrage over the notion of 'the helpless young female victim'.[101] In the 1920s and 1930s, however, although incest cases were still prevalent, a remarkable reinterpretation occurred whereby the culprit was thought to be a perverted stranger, rather than father or other male authority, and the victim was portrayed as no longer innocent, but a complicit sex delinquent. By the 1950s and 60s childcare experts were dismissing incest as a very rare, one-in-a-million occurrence, and psychiatrists and other professionals alike were viewing children's allegations of incestuous abuse or sexual mistreatment with scepticism or disbelief.[102] The rediscovery of child sexual abuse from the late 1970s was unquestionably a product of feminist thinking and campaigning.

As with rape, there is great controversy over the incidence of such abuse, but few professional agencies today doubt that it is very common. In the United States, 4.5 per cent of Diana Russell's sample reported incestuous assaults and 8.4 per cent of Finkelhor's sample had been sexually abused by a member of their family.[103] Some social services departments in the UK use figures which suggest that as many as 20 per cent of girls and 10 per cent of boys will have been abused as children.[104] In all of these studies the perpetrators are almost always men, the vast majority of them fathers or (more commonly) step-fathers. And yet, while the professional literature now stresses the extent and problem of child sexual abuse, it predominantly adopts a theoretical approach which fails to view men as responsible for its occurrence.[105] 'Family dysfunction theory' – the prevailing orthodoxy – describes the whole family as complicit in the abuse, ultimately pointing the finger of blame at the mother, who fails to meet her man's sexual and emotional needs. As two leading authorities in this field, Kempe and Kempe explain, 'Incest . . . is not initiated by the child but by the adult male, with the mother's complicity . . . we have simply not seen an innocent mother, although the mother escapes the punishment that her husband is likely to suffer.'[106] The problem of men's customary power over women and children, and the agonising dilemma faced by financially dependent women – even accepting that at some level some mothers may suspect, or at least try to avoid, facing up to the truth of the abuse of their children – is grotesquely ignored in much of the professional literature on child sexual abuse.

Although men's domestic violence might temporarily succeed in getting them what they want, Gordon, Pahl and others suggest, this would usually only be the case while women lacked the resources to escape. In particular, wife-beating, even more than non-family violence against women, Gordon believes, was usually 'dysfunctional' for the assaulters: 'Men benefitted more from camaraderie, mutual respect, and friendship.'[107] Gordon does not spell out what she means here, but others have. I am reminded of Martin Scorcese's film *Raging Bull*, which exactly captures the futility of a man clinging to a form of aggressive masculinity, even as it destroys him. Based on the life of middleweight champion Jake La Motta, we see a portrait of a man whose infantile emotions, inability to communicate, competitiveness with other men, and above all possessive aggressiveness towards his wife, gradually destroy his friendships, his career and his marriage. Throughout the film La Motta's acts of violence are inseparable from his pent-up frustration and his actual powerlessness to express how he feels and to get what he wants.[108]

There is no doubt that the idea that men have a right to servicing, combined with the social reality of women's economic dependence and the lack of adequate deterrence for violent men, all play a crucial role in men's violence. But Gordon is also convinced from her research that women, although extremely rarely directly implicated in sexual abuse of husbands or children, have been 'as aggressive, irrational and destructive' as men in marital conflict: 'Many who were victims were also aggressors.'[109] However, women have usually been the ones who have lost out in violent relationships. Even so, Gordon ventures that the decline in women's violence which occurred in the late nineteenth century in Britain and North America was not a clear gain for women and their families.[110] She argues that the growing idealisation of female passivity and condemnation of female violence increased women's shame and silence over wife-beating. Indeed, she maintains that feminists themselves helped construct a femininity oppressive to battered women at the turn of the century: 'By emphasising the superiority of women's peacefulness, feminist influence made women loathe and attempt to suppress their own aggressiveness and anger.'[111] History is apt to repeat itself. When feminists today, like Sara Maguire, suggest that explanations of marital violence which point to the contributing effect of 'deprivation, poverty, overcrowding, the stress of unemployment and even racism' are presenting 'excuses' and aligning themselves 'with men beating up their wives', I feel troubled.[112] When they conclude that the sole acceptable 'feminist' explanation of marital violence is all men's potential to abuse power, I see nineteenth-century biologism back in the saddle, cloaked in a spurious sociological rhetoric:

> An analysis of violence against women based on power structures explains the potential for all men in emotional/sexual relationships with women to exert control over them using violence . . . Interestingly, when discussing the issue with women whose male partners do not beat them up I have frequently heard them say 'I keep my man under control' . . . These women know that violence is a possibility in their relationship and 'their' man is as likely as the man next door to be violent towards them.[113]

And women's potential for anger and violence? It once again disappears from history. In defending women from men's violence in the home, we cannot resort to the very alibis of biological difference which have sustained men in their beliefs in its inevitability. What we can do is fight for the social policies and wider social and economic change which, by enabling women to leave violent marriages, puts an end to them. Terminating, along with them, the 'sanctity' of marriage as men and women once knew it. As Linda

Gordon concludes her massive text: 'Even women who have never been struck have benefited from the "disestablishment" of marriage that is now taking place, the process of transforming it from a coercive institution, inescapable and necessary for survival, to a relationship that is chosen.'[114]

Is Violence Masculine?

One reason it has been so easy to ignore women's relationship to violence is that terms like 'power', 'force', 'aggression' – so seemingly direct and obvious – are not the simplest to define. Feminism begins from an awareness that relations between men and women have, in all known places and times, occurred in a context in which there has been an apparently inextricable connection between gender and power – though it has assumed different forms and obtained to differing degrees. Feminists writing on men and violence have always tended to see this power as an exclusively uni-directional, top-down, process. Viewed in this way, women's participation in maintaining or undermining men's ability to control them according to their own needs, is obscured. But this is not how power has been theorized in more traditional sociological literature or, indeed, more sophisticated feminist analysis. Power relations imply a process whereby those with power can organise those who are less powerful according to their own ends. Yet this, according to sociologists like Anthony Giddens, does not necessarily – indeed, does not 'normally' – take the form of any straightforward process of control through threat, force or violence. Rather, the exercise of power involves the deployment of resources and skills to which some people have easier access, the use of force being exceptional.[115] And despite this differential access to resources, power relations, as Kathy Davis argues, are always reciprocal, involving some degree of autonomy and dependence in each direction:

> Power is never a simple matter of 'have's' and 'have-not's.'
> Such a conception can only lead to an over-estimation of the power of the powerful, closing our eyes to the chinks in the armour of the powerful as well as the myriad ways that the less powerful have to exercise control over their lives, even in situations where stable, institutionalised power relations are in operation.[116]

As we saw with domestic violence, in the area of personal life it has been women's traditional lack of any access to independent economic resources within the institution of marriage which has been pivotal to the normal functioning of domestic arrangments to suit men's needs. That institution is now changing, and the most significant common characteristic of women who are battered today is not their gender as such, but their lack of resources to escape marriages which are violent.[117] That domestic violence is not some fatality inscribed in male-female relationship is apparent if we look at the different types of family forms which have generated violence. In *Naming the Violence: Speaking Out About Lesbian Battery*, various women in the United States write of their experience of violence from other women. 'We were so clear about violence as a feature of heterosexual relationships,' Barbara Hart announces with dismay, that it was hard to accept that 'women were beating and terrorizing other women.'[118] These women report daily episodes of violence which had become almost a ritual in some lesbian bars in the US. Moreover, as with heterosexual violence, other lesbians 'shunned the victim', and the battered lesbian tended to blame herself.[119] In addition to psychological and emotional abuse, these battered lesbians reported physical assault with guns, knives and other weapons, experiences of rape, sex on demand, forced sex with others and involuntary prostitution – as well as economic dependence through their partners' control over income and assets.

Most of the dynamics of lesbian battering seem similar to heterosexual abuse – in particular, the tendency of women to remain in an abusive relationship because they feel sorry for the abuser: 'I still feel sorry for her . . . She came from a home situation where she was the victim of what ranged from severe neglect to severe violence,' writes Donna Cecere of her experience of lesbian battering;[120] 'I had returned once again because . . . she said she had changed . . . when she held me I felt loved . . . In those years love was a scarcity and myself hardly lovable,' explains Cedar Gentlewind;[121] 'On a subconscious level I felt I got what I deserved . . . Our social life was limited to gay bars where physical violence was also the norm,' writes Breeze.[122] The majority of the lesbian abusers and victims in these accounts are working-class lesbians, many from ethnic minorities, often already victims of family violence, as well as of the violence and racism which surrounded them.

That women, like men, are affected by the general levels of violence in their immediate social world is illustrated by the dramatic increase in young women's involvement in crimes of violence over the last fifteen years – an increase which, comparatively, exceeds that of men. As Anne Campbell argues in criticism of much feminist rhetoric, virtually all our ideas of 'femininity' are derived from the middle-class 'lady': 'To be pampered, egotistical, passive, nurturant, care-taking requires a certain level of economic security.'[124] Surveying a sample of 251 sixteen-year-old schoolgirls from working-class areas of London, Liverpool and Oxford, Campbell found that 89 per cent of them had engaged in at least one physical fight. These girls were mostly negative in their attitudes towards fighting, but did not see it as 'unfeminine'. The Borstal girls whom Campbell interviewed, on the other hand, mostly felt positive about fighting, regarding it as a good way of releasing anger and perhaps settling disputes.[125] As with young male delinquents, most of them had been systematically encouraged to fight by their parents: 'In the subcultures from which these girls come . . . interpersonal violence emerges as the vicious expression of hatred and resentment and is bound up more with establishing and maintaining a tough reputation than with settling disputes.'[126] Campbell is critical of a feminism which can see women only as the victims of men, rather than of a whole economic system: 'Without more radical change in the *status quo*, we shall succeed only in liberating women into poverty, alienation, despair and crime – along with the men who are there already.'[127]

Somewhat analogously, in his study of soccer hooliganism David Robins asks, 'What were the girls doing while the boys were putting the boot in on the terraces?' Many, he says, were up there with them. There are more boys than girls, but the girls do join in the fighting and encourage the boys to fight. Where girls' gangs do exist, they not only emulate but may try to outdo the boys: 'We go to fight,' the 'Leeds Angels' told Robins. 'At Norwich and Ipswich, there's sometimes more lasses than boys . . . When Man. United played Norwich . . . there were forty arrests and must have been thirty lasses got arrested.'[128] It is obvious that in our society physical violence and aggression are still predominantly seen as masculine, and acted out by men. Working-class images of masculinity in terms of physical hardness have been analysed, by Tolson and others, as bound up with the requirements of manual labour and earning a wage.[129] This image persists. But with nearly 50 per cent of young people in Britain leaving school for the dole, enjoying little hope and not much self-esteem, Robins argues, 'working-class youth is being forced into a position of wildness and irresponsibility'.[130] And while they may lack the symbolic trappings of power which unite the boys in their sexist jibes, and rarely be afforded the same freedom of action and choice as men, young women, Robins believes, are learning that they can give as good as they get.[131]

Nevertheless, even if aggressiveness is not exclusively masculine, there is no doubt that the media and the public at large display their greatest anxiety in connection with violence from men – mostly from young, working-class men in the form of vandalism, gang fighting and football hooliganism. Football hooliganism is now a prominent cause of social concern, feeding the appeal of the law-and-order politics of the right. Some researchers, like Peter Marsh, Elizabeth Rosser and Rom Harre, have stressed that the degree of serious violence, as distinct from ritual violence, on and around the football terraces is exaggerated by the media.[132] But the extent of young men's violence is not merely a media creation; nor is its association with lower working-class men merely middle-class phobia. Sociological studies of football hooliganism like that of Eric Dunning and his co-workers conclusively demonstrate men in football gangs are overwhelmingly from the lower levels of the working class.[133]

We need to ask why a type of working-class aggressive masculinity seems such a perennial feature of the social environment, a feature which feeds today's feminist imagination in its equation of violence as male. Dunning stresses the inevitable homogeneity, circumscribed horizons and narrow neighbourhood loyalty of men who, at best, will find work in low-paid, insecure and monotonous jobs at the bottom of all authority and status hierarchies. Moreover, in jobs sex-typed as male, and with home lives which remain strongly male-dominated (the equivalent jobs for women of this class, if any, being even less well-paid, lower in status and more insecure) the lower working-class tends to produce sharper sex-role distinctions than other classes. Just as there is a Black underclass, so too a white underclass exists, in which the men are the most likely of all men to adopt aggressive masculine styles and values whereby status is imparted to males who display loyalty and bravery in confrontation with 'outsiders':

> Apart from the 'street smartness' and the ability and willingness to fight of [these] adolescent and adult males, they have few power resources. This combination of narrowness of experience and relative lack of power tends to lead them to experience unfamiliar territories and people as potentially threatening. Usually it is only in the company of people with whom they are familiar and who are like themselves that it is possible for them to feel a relatively high degree of social assurance . . . Being part of a group augments their sense of power. It also provides an opportunity to hit back at the established order and a context in which they can 'get their own back' by taking the lid off . . . For a short illusory moment, the outsiders are the masters; the downtrodden come out on top.[134]

The aggressive masculine style which lower working-class men are more likely to value and adopt is not exclusive to them, of course. It is part of the fantasy life, if not the lived reality, of the majority of men enthralled by images of masculinity which equate it with power and violence, (where would Clint Eastwood be without his gun?). However, as I have suggested before, there is no simple, direct transmission from men's shared collective fantasies to individual action. Many social mediators – from school, jobs, friends, family, religion and politics – effect the way fantasies may, or may not, be channelled into any active expression, and determine what form, if any, they take. It is the sharp and frustrating conflict between the lives of lower working-class men and the image of masculinity as power, which informs the adoption and, for some, the enactment, of a more aggressive masculinity. There was a time, it seems to me, when feminists would not so readily have lost sight of the signifi-cance of class oppression for the sake of identifying a universal male beastliness. But that was in the early seventies, when they were more actively a part of a left politics and culture which was itself more aware than it has since become of the alienation and exploitation of class relations.

It is true that women can be, and some women are, as aggressive and violent in their behaviour as men. It is equally true, however, that from an early age most women are made aware of obstacles to, and restrictions upon, the expression of their own desires – if only in terms of the expectations of those around them. More importantly, they are sensitised to greater social condemnation of female aggressiveness – shouting, fighting, swearing, and so on. Men, by contrast, in sport and elsewhere, are more likely to engage in at least the rituals of aggressive display, and to enjoy greater social tolerance for many forms of aggressiveness.[135] But I think we should be aware that women's greater suppression of their own aggressiveness is not necessarily healthy. Women's attempts to disown and repress their feelings of frustration and aggression almost certainly result in them turning such aggressive feelings against themselves, or their children. This would account for women's greater vulnerability to depression (twice as high as that for men), or expression of their own pain in emotional abuse of children.[136] It can also lead, as Janet Sayers, Jean Temperley and other clinicians have commented, to women projecting their aggressiveness and violence onto others, or onto the world in general, as in paranoia and agoraphobia.[137] As we saw in chapter three, Jane Temperley suggests from her work with women patients that we need to consider whether women's perception of, preoccupation with, and (as she sees it), attempts to provoke, men's violence towards them may not be overlaid by women's projection onto men of their own frustration and aggression; thereby permitting women to retain for themselves a monopoly of moral righteousness and virtue.[138]

Some feminists, as well as therapists like Temperley, have seen in women's image of the all-pervasive, all-threatening nature of male sexuality a projection of women's own aggression and frustrated power. The political journalist and feminist Sarah Benton, for example, suggests that because it is less legitimate for women to be aggressive and powerful, and because women are so much less accustomed to taking responsibility for the state of the world, 'We project all power, all aggression onto men.'[139] Moreover, she detects in this projection, women's denial of sexuality itself. It is a denial bound up with women's difficulties, in sexist culture, in accepting and expressing their own sexuality; in particular, acknowledging that female sexuality can be violent, cruel and 'perverse', as well as masochistic, yielding and submissive. 'The barrier to that acceptance and expression,' she concludes, 'is more to do with our difficulty in getting, exercising and accepting power in the world at large than any specific sexual threat from men.'[140] The fact that women are the main readers of true-crime magazines, which provide salacious case histories of the most violent, often sexual, murders,[141] and that it is women who appear in large numbers at the trials of sex-murderers, where they feel entitled to display extremes of punitive moral aggression, verbal and even physical violence, would seem to lend credence to such interpretations.

However, the extent of some men's violence (and many men's viciousness) towards women, the tendency of those with power either to ignore, or to blame women for, its occurrence, and the general context of men's greater power and control over women, all dictate that we must proceed very carefully – more carefully, at any rate, than Temperley and most psychoanalytic commentators have done – in assigning weight to arguments which suggest that women may have an investment in feeling victimised. There is no doubt that many women's entrapment in dependency and powerlessness makes it hard for them to envisage any positive alternative to suppressing their own anger and aggression, while suffering, however resentfully, aggression from men. At the same time, it is equally necessary for us to be aware of the need to understand what happens to women's aggression, and for us to abandon the dominant conservative and, more recently, popular feminist attachment to idealised views of women as inherently less aggressive than men, (the former regarding the connection as biological, the latter, more often as cultural).

Some of our perception of the social and cultural linkages between 'masculinity' and violence derives from the fact that most of the socially approved uses of force and violence are the jobs of men – the police, army, prison officers, and other agencies of 'defence' or correction. It is men, rarely women, who are officially trained to use violence in our society. Yet, as David Morgan has suggested, it is possible in this context to reverse the assumed causal links between 'masculinity' and 'violence'. It could be that it is men's socially determined, systematic involvement in various forms of violence which constructs our notions of 'masculinity' as indissolubly linked with 'violence'.[142] The idea that what is at stake here is state violence in the hands of men (rather than, as many feminists believe, male violence in the hands of the state) is supported by reports of women's use of force and violence when they are placed in jobs analogous to men's. For example, women prison officers were found in the late nineteenth century to enforce especially severe physical and corporal punishments on their female charges for any infraction of rules, by comparison with those meted out to male prisoners and, to this day, women prisoners are more consistently punished and put on report by their female warders than are men.[143] Similar tales of women's zealous use of force, including conventionally defined acts of violence, appear in many accounts of women's behaviour when in positions of power. I have written elsewhere of the importance, often repressed or denied, of women's relationship to war and military enterprises – both as passionate supporters of war or in active military engagement themselves.[144] Nevertheless, it is apparent that some men's far more formal training in the use of violence is something which can, and from the evidence of women who are battered, frequently does, spill over into these men's greater resort to violence in their personal relations with women. It also provides opportunities for men to be particularly vicious to women (and men) in the performance of their public 'duties'.

Black feminists have been especially clear on the importance of distinguishing state violence from male violence. Kum-Kum Bhavnani, for example, rejects the idea that violence is 'essentially masculine'.[145] Such a belief denies Black people's knowledge of white women's past-and-present involvement in violence against them – both directly and indirectly, in the support and maintenance of racism. And it denies the reality of the violent resistance from women and men which state violence brings forth, not only in the streets of South Africa, but in the street-uprisings in Britain. The idea prevalent in white feminism that women 'have a peaceful past', Bhavnani argues, is offensive to Black women. (It is also, she points out, offensive to white working-class women, who have resisted, sometimes violently, attacks on their class; and to the many other women who have fought against violent and oppressive conditions; not to mention its erasure from the history of the British Suffragettes.) 'Non-violence' and 'peace', she suggests, 'end up being meaningless terms unless given tactical accuracy and political definition.'[46] Bell Hooks also writes of learning to oppose war from the persistent anti-war stance of her grandfather, and of so many other southern Black males who despised militarism: 'Their attitudes showed us that all men do not glory in war, that all men who fight in wars do not necessarily believe that wars are just, that men are not inherently capable of killing.'[47] The sex-role division of labour, she adds, does not necessarily mean that women think differently from men about violence and about war, or, if empowered to do so, would behave differently from men.

'Violence', it seems clear, cannot simply be equated with 'masculinity'. Neither are unitary phenomena.[48] There are many different types of violence, some legitimated (from sport and beating children to policing and warfare), and some not (from corporal punishment in state schools to rape and murder). It is easier to understand and attempt to change men's engagement in these practices if we see them as operating relatively autonomously from each other. Fear of violent attack from men is the number one fear of women in both the United States and Britain today. But if we want to get to the heart of this fear, and the escalating rates of violence in modern society, we shall have to include, but also progress beyond, an analysis simply in terms of gender.

There are links between the prevalence of violence in our society and men's endeavours to affirm 'masculinity'. And these links may even be reinforced, as the assumption of men's dominance over women – part of the traditional definition of 'masculinity' – continues to crumble. Some men, increasingly less sure of such dominance, may resort more to violence in their attempt to shore up a sense of masculine identity. Others, however, may not. Some, indeed, may turn towards new ways of being men, even to support for the struggle to put an end to men's use of violence against women. For it should be remembered that some men have always worked in organisations committed to non-violence – even when this has provoked the harshest ridicule and punishment, including loss of life. At the same time, there are links between the prevalence of violence in our society and forces which are not those of gender: forces, indeed, which have impacted as strongly on certain groups of men as on certain groups of women. There are close and frightening links between sexual assaults on women and the steep rise in crimes of violence generally – the primary targets of which remain other men.

These links derive from the creation of a permanent under-class in many Western societies – an under-class built around dependency, self-destruction, crimes against property and crimes against people. Twenty years ago Martin Luther King was shot dead for his vision of a more equal society in the United States. Today, that society is less equal than it was then: the number of Black men leaving college is dropping, the life expectancy of Black men is decreasing, and economic segregation of Blacks and other ethnic minorities into the worst schools, worst neighbourhoods, worst housing (if they are lucky), is increasing.[149] Drugs, crime and violence are the desperate and bitter legacy of the withdrawal of federal funds for welfare provision at local and national levels throughout the United States, in combination with the smashing of the trade union movement and the restructuring of labour which has destroyed many traditional working-class jobs and communities. With welfare all but eliminated, homelessness, joblessness, and hopelessness are now escalating in the US. Comparing the contrasting appeals of Martin Luther King for peaceful Black protest thirty years ago, with Malcolm X's justification of violent protest a decade later, Black film-maker Spike Lee announces today:

> Things are leaning more towards Malcolm than King. I think black people are getting tired of being on the receiving end of police shotguns and nightsticks.[150]

Who or what, then, do we identify as the epitome of 'violence', 'abuse' and 'aggression' in that society? Those who are brutalised within an underworld of fear and exploitation? Or those who may never directly engage in acts of violence or physical force, but orchestrate the degradation and brutalisation of others? The entrenchment of poverty and inequality in the world's richest nation has occurred precisely to enable the US to spend ever-greater sums on 'defence', and to conduct aggressive interventions in Central America, the Caribbean and the Middle East.

The USA shows the way, and through the International Monetary Fund (IMF) and other such agencies attempts to force the American Way on the rest of the world. If feminists are seriously to confront the problem of sexual violence, we shall have to realise that what we are up against is something far worse, something far more destructive, than the power of any man, or group of men – something worse even than the mythic qualities of Dworkin's atomic phallus. However old-fashioned it may sound in these 'post-political' days, what we are confronting here is the barbarism of private life reflecting back the increased barbarism of public life, as contemporary capitalism continues to chisel out its hierarchies along the familiar grooves of class, race and gender.

10. Beyond Gender Hierarchy: Can Men Change?

Approaching her 70th year in 1982, the US novelist and critic Elizabeth Janeway wrote of the revolution she had witnessed in her own lifetime – a revolution centred on gender: 'We were part of a reversal of history, an absolute shift in the quality of reality'.[1] Born in 1913, the first half of her life had been a time when 'hopes existed only in the masculine mode': 'We copied men in our dreams because there was no one else to copy.'[2] What is most interesting about Janeway's reflections on women's transition from fantasy and tokenism into a reality where some women at least are visible as free agents – men's equals in the public world – is her suggestion that within feminist writing at least, *nobody says so*.[3]

We may admit to some shifts in the lives of women over the last hundred years, but there is an assumption that when it comes to the lives of men, *plus ça change, plus c'est la même chose*. And if men do not change, nothing really changes, since women still live in a world dominated by men. At least as often as we hear the assertion of change, we hear its denial. 'Women; what revolution?' the British feminist Ann Oakley demands in her autobiographical reflections, *Taking it Like a Woman*.[4] Yet, when 'manhood' is defined relationally, in terms of dominance over and difference from 'womanhood', it is difficult to see how women's lives could shift fundamentally without some corresponding impact on the lives of men. That it is hard to acknowledge change, however, is less than surprising, when change is never smooth, uniform, or free from contradiction and backlash.

Oakley's autobiographical writing is a tantalising condensation of the contradictions many feminists seem to feel after two decades of feminism. 'The women's liberation movement', she tells us, 'changed my life'.[5] A mere two pages later, however, she asks, 'Has any progress been made at all?'[6] 'I strongly believe,' she adds, 'that men are enemies of women . . . Without men the world would be a better place: softer, kinder, more loving; calmer, quieter, more humane.'[7] Or again, we are told: 'Women can't find in men whole human beings, and the whole human beings women are are not what men have been led to believe they want.'[8] Yet she also tells us of her strongest recollections of her own parents, 'My mother angry and reluctant to comfort, my father with open arms and a gentle patience.'[9] Her autobiography describes her relationship with her young husband as changing from one 'which started out on such a traditional footing' around housework and childcare, and became 'the unrecognisable egalitarian affair it is today'.[10] This is a husband who defines the 'good life' as one 'in which people are closely in touch with other people and with their children, and do work which is intrinsically satisfying to them'.[11] In the space of a generation, Oakley's life seems a complete reversal of that of her mother:

> I have achieved all of what I dreamed about, twenty years ago. Successful work – even a degree of international repute; love, friendship, marriage, motherhood. And yet, and still, I am not satisfied.[12]

Oakley is not satisfied, she feels, because: 'Sex doesn't have the same meaning for men that it does for women . . . personal relations don't have the same value for the two sexes.'[13] The difference in her view (like that of Nancy Chodorow and so many other feminists) proceeds from the fact that women's mothering produces contrasting gender identities. But has she correctly identified the cause of women's disappointment in loving men? Oakley's own engagement with romantic fantasy in this book, and her subsequent venture into fiction, suggest to me a different problem. In writing of men's perfidy, for example, she laments: 'Promising sublime intimacy, unequalled passion, amazing security and grace, they nevertheless exploit and injure in a myriad subtle ways.'[14] For sure, sublime intimacy, unequalled passion, amazing grace are not what men can deliver. Nor women either. And yet, they remain what most women (and, in fact, large numbers of men) weave their obsessive and foredoomed dreams around: the promise is no more than the projection of our own desire onto the loved one. As Ann Snitow has argued, 'romance is a primary category of the female imagination[15]', containing within it an idealisation of the helplessness and purity of women, the power and danger of men, every bit as objectifying as typical men's pornography. Moreover, it is constructed around infantile pleasures of power and submission. Might not feminist disappointment in loving men stem partly from the incompatability of their own romantic longings with women's conscious pursuit of equality? The object of romantic desire is, by definition, he (or she) who dominates and disappoints.

When the majority of those people in the West (particularly in the US) who are currently organising against equal rights for women, sexual liberation, abortion rights and divorce, are women, and when some of those organising for paternal rights, access to children, paternity leave and the discussion of domestic responsibilities in workplaces and trade unions, are men – then we see the contradictory effects of some type of fundamental gender change. We see also the emergence of new fears and tensions alongside old dreams and hopes.

Problem Partners: Sexual Liberation, Women's Liberation and the Crisis of Personal Life

Something happened during the sexual revolution of the 1960s, not just in men's more public celebration of the joys of sex outside marriage, but in young women's attempts to join them. The tangled sense of sexual freedom, inferiority and confusion women felt then – suddenly freer than ever before to engage in sexual encounters with less fear of pregnancy, moral condemnation and guilt, increasingly questioning the hypocrisy and double standards of all bourgeois values, yet still, and ever more blatantly, surrounded by media messages of themselves as little more than the belittled playthings of men – pushed them ineluctably towards finding each other and finding a voice.[16] The permissive moment of the sixties slowly prepared the stage for its major event, its last and lasting climax: the eruption and consolidation of the women's liberation movements of the West. With their new collective voice, feminists at the close of the sixties both affirmed and attacked the new permissiveness. They demanded not merely women's rights to sexual pleasure and reproductive control over their own bodies, but a thorough re-thinking of all aspects of sexuality and relationships away from the male-centred, male dominated acts and relationships of life as they had mostly known it – away, perhaps, from relationships with men at all, in love affairs with each other, or enjoying more solipsistic pleasures with themselves. Much of the confidence and asser-tiveness of women's liberation in those early days derived, however, from the idea that sexual liberation for women was, in itself, enpowering – the route out of passivity and subordination to men.[17]

Such inflated belief in the positive power of sexual pleasure (for some the buried truth of the female orgasm) was to fuel later disap-pointment with talk of sexual revolution and, worse, lead some femi-nists, along with anti-feminists, to undervalue or even dismiss the significance for women of the permissive reforms and attitudes of the 1960s. In Sara Maitland's collection of pieces by women (mostly femi-nists) looking back, two decades on, at their lives in the sixties, some writers express not ambivalence but near total denunciation of that time: 'Now it seemed no more than a greedy male fantasy of omni-potence,' Sheila Macleod reflects, adding that once she had been 'well disposed towards the so-called sexual revolution in that it substituted openness for hypocrisy'. She feels it was a revolution only 'for men, who could thereby indulge their preferences for irresponsibility and lack of emotional commitment'.[18] Angela Carter, in contrast, finds it very odd that women's new possibilities to engage in sex with men should be dismissed as simply pleasure for men, rather than a time when women were better able to avoid 'all the foul traps men lay'[19] to force women into some permanent relationship with them:

> I can date to that time and to that sense of heightened awareness of the society around me in the summer of 1968 my own questioning of the nature of my reality as a woman. How that social fiction of my 'femininity' was created and palmed off on me as the real thing.[20]

Maitland herself, rightly in my view, sees it as a 'pre-feminist' time, with women as well as men greedy for personal adventure and, though still standing behind their menfolk, eager to change the whole world into a more co-operative, less selfish place.[21] 'It was, ' Marsha Rowe declares, recalling memories I too recollect, 'an experience of metaphysical joy and utopian sharing.'[22] That is how it was, at least for some women, at least some of the time.

Not content with dismissing the real gains for women made in the 1960s, there are women today who suggest (significantly once again in economically less settled times) that the assertion of sexual liberation has never served the interests of women, even when articulated by women themselves. Women are more sexually assertive today and, so they claim, more sexually satisfied.[23] Yet, reporting from New York in 1980, Alix Shulman informs us of a meeting where several feminists who had been active in the earliest, most confident and sexually assertive days of women's liberation, were discussing their sex lives. For all of them sex had changed, but few felt it had really improved. Though several were now, unlike former times, regularly physically satisfied by sex, they nevertheless remained unhappy in love.[24] *The Hite Report on Male Sexuality* (1982) also describes men's continuing uncertainties and conflicts around sexuality.[25] As the opportunities for greater sexual experience inside and outside marriage have increased, so too has the awareness of its limitations ... its pain, conflict and ambivalence, in the minds of women and men alike. It is this contradiction which feeds women's vocal dissatisfaction. And they hold men responsible. If the rapist is not, as some feminists believe, the archetypal human male, the latter creature is nevertheless thought to be a far from pleasing person. 'There are so many kinds of awful men – One can't avoid them all,' the English poet, Wendy Cope, bemoans.[26]

The US feminist Shere Hite echoes the thought. She offers the additional support of what she sees as her empirical proof of the existence of change in women's lives, and its absence in men's. She herself has eluded the fate of other women, having acquired a husband who is 'brilliant and inspiring', 'understanding and supportive', who fills her life with 'music and poetry'.[27] Not so fortunate, in her view, are the four and a half thousand women she spent seven years interviewing for her massive 900-page survey *Women and Love*, 98 per cent of whom desire fundamental change in relationships with men.[28] 'The biggest problem', Hite reports, is not women's lack of financial independence or men's absence from domestic work, but men's 'reluctance to talk about personal thoughts and feelings'.[29] Only 17 per cent of women said the communication in their relationship was good. Eighty-four per cent of women said that love relationships should come first in life, but only 19 per cent of women said that it actually did.[30] Seventy-four per cent of women complain that men don't put love relationships first in their lives.[31] 'Strangely, hauntingly,' Hite writes, 'most women in this study . . . say they have not yet found the love they are looking for' – the love they hope is yet to come.[32]

'America,' Sara Maitland wryly comments on Hite's interpretation of this research, 'seems to be full of women whose dream is to be a fully autonomous, self-expressing individual who will then spend her entire energies engaged in mutual self-analysis with the beloved other.'[33] What women perhaps need, Maitland suggests, is less of the romantic individualism of the bourgeois dream, and more emphasis 'on the political, public and communal structures of life (just as feminism originally proposed)'.[34] As others have pointed out, Hite's survey is methodological mayhem. She picks and chooses from the millions of words she collects in her survey to draw the conclusions she seeks; and there is little internal consistency even in the statistical observations she chooses to draw. For example, '96 per cent of women say they are giving more emotional support than they are getting from men',[35] '19 per cent describe real and equal relationships with the men they love'.[36]

Nor does Hite offer a single observation on the influence of class or race on women's relationships with men, a fact which the psychologist Naomi Weisstein explains for us in the introduction to the survey: 'Class analysis has never struck me as appropriate in an understanding of women's oppression.'[37] That is a pity, since what struck me, reading Hite's latest report, was women's continual insistence – almost despite the orientation of her questions – on their desire for financial independence and for satisfaction in those parts of their lives which were quite separate from their dreams of love. Hite herself comments, in sections which have been disregarded in the fanfare around her text: 'Over and over, women say they love their freedom; it could almost be a theme song for this book.'[38] By 'freedom', Hite is referring to women's social and financial independence from men: 'women here say they work because they like to have a life of their own';[39] '87 per cent of women who are or have been financially dependent feel uncomfortable and unhappy in this situation'; 'many women (even those with very low salaries, even women with children) are now choosing to leave unsatisfying marriages.'[40] Women today, her book suggests, are in a better position to make choices about the lives they wish to lead. The choices they make, however, allow some women to lead rich and fulfilling lives, with or without men, and condemn others, and their children, to lives of desperate poverty.

Were Hite in the least sensitive to issues of class and race, she could have made a stronger, but different, case for seeing how the goals of equality for which many women have fought have often been frustrated by their entry into the sexually segregated, super-exploitative labour market which has always treated men (or at least most groups of men) better than women. (Of course, some men, as well as many women, are worse off today than they were twenty years ago.) Hite, like other cultural feminists, blames all problems of the human condition on the 'male' ideology of hierarchy and aggression. But now that patriarchy has been named as *the* belief system underlying all others, 'It is possible for new beliefs and reflections of reality to spring forth': 'Our [women's] knowledge of how to give, how to love, is a richness we can diffuse throughout the whole culture.'[41] Love will conquer all. Have we not heard this before? Was it not once what we heard from Our Father who art in Heaven?

Hite's faith in the power of love – women's love – to transform the world brings to mind Richard Sennett's argument in *The Fall of Public Man*. Here he expressed concern that fundamentally social problems were being seen as essentially private or personal problems, and suggested that the new 'tyranny of intimacy' threatened not so much to change the world as to produce political immobility:

> The reigning belief today is that closeness between persons is a moral good. The reigning aspiration today is to develop individual personality through experiences

of closeness and warmth with others. The reigning myth today is that the evils of society can all be understood as evils of impersonality, alienation and coldness.[42]

Much of the revolutionary thrust of second-wave feminism lay in the rejection of women's traditional and exclusive preoccupations with personal life for an emphasis on the importance of the public world, and women's subordinate place within it, in shaping women's self-image and self-identity. Now, reversing this wisdom, feminists like Hite suggest that women's traditional preoccupation with love and personal relationships will somehow change the public world – a type of gradual diffusion of the idealised and subordinated 'female' essence from the confines of personal life into the world beyond.

It is not that feminists ever rejected the idea of close and loving intimacy in their personal lives. On the contrary, as I have suggested, feminists fought for women's rights to sexual pleasure and personal happiness, insisting, above all, on the need to change dominant conceptions of 'the sex act'. But in its heyday the women's movement was very aware that the search for personal happiness and fulfilment involved change not only in relations between individuals but in society as a whole. As Sheila Rowbotham comments, 'The women's movement did not approach public institutions like the health service or the lived environment of houses, nurseries, streets and shops as "things" but as contexts for human encounters.'[43] Seeking to promote a new vision of democratic communities, with real resources for sharing the caring usually confined to women on their own, feminists dreamt of a world where relationships beyond the couple would be invested with some of the meaning, commitment and passion never for long fully nourished by the search for love alone. Some men shared this dream.

Dismantling 'Masculinity': Some Men's Attempts to Change Themselves

'If I come back, I want to come back as a woman . . . I spend more time with women,' Ken Livingstone confided to his interviewer and an audience of millions on prime time TV in Britain in 1988.[44] Men are not so popular today as they once were. There can be few times in history when being female has been quite so fashionable a preference for men. A minority of men have always hated the 'masculinity' they felt they were not born with, could never acquire, but which fate remorselessly tried to thrust upon them. Some, far outnumbering women so drastically at odds with their gender identity, now find their way to transsexual clinics in search of savage surgery to rid themselves of the burden of masculinity. Others, consciously influenced by feminism rather than deep psychic torment, have sought less painful methods of attempting to re-gender themselves – methods which leave their biological sex intact. Their efforts have often received faint praise from feminists, sceptical of the potential for individual men to overturn a gender identity so bound up with the customary assertion of power and privilege.

I have suggested that since 'man' and 'woman' are conceptually polarised and complementary, and men and women responsive to and dependent upon each other, it is hard to see how women's lives could change substantially without affecting men's. One way of looking at men and women in relationship to each other is to consider some of the responses of men to feminism. When feminism first emerged in radical circles at the close of the 1960s, most men reacted with disbelief, often turning swiftly to ridicule and anger.[45] Within a few short years, however, as women's liberation went from strength to strength, a very different reaction emerged. The experience of being left out, on the sidelines, was the new and threatening reality for many a young male radical, no longer feeling as certain as he had in the 1960s of his own participation in the making of history.

'We felt guilty being men, frightened at what was opening up underneath our feet . . . We became very envious of the togetherness of women,' a group of men from the inner north London borough of Islington explained in 1975.[46] 'We as men . . . seemed to be lacking the sense of community and understanding that many women seemed to have in the Women's Movement,'[47] a similar group in the neighbouring borough of Hackney was to write. 'We men must learn from women', their brothers across the Thames in south London declared.[48] What these pro-feminist men, who were to form the 'men's groups' in Britain from around

1972, hoped to learn were new, non-oppressive, life-affirming ways of being men. In consciously pursuing this goal they stirred up many of the contradictions surrounding the nature of 'masculinity' itself, which have been explored throughout this book.

Men in men's groups were quite often men in a muddle. From the beginning, there was debate over whether they should be called Men Against Sexism, and see themselves as primarily a support group for women's liberation, or whether they should be called Men's Liberation, a movement for exploring and transforming male consciousness.[49] They wanted to listen to and learn from women: they adopted both the ideas and the practices of women's liberation. But (a fact their critics rarely acknowledged) many of these men were also aware that in meeting together to change themselves, they could be accused of collectively seeking new ways to preserve old privileges: 'I'm in a men's group and I'm O.K., I don't compete, but I win any way.'[50] Such was the self-parody of some of the men I was closest to – friends, comrades and lovers – who for a decade and more from late 1973 formed part of the Islington men's group. It was a defensive reaction to the mockery they always faced from their closest women friends and lovers.

Most socialist feminists working with men in diverse political struggles throughout the 1970s did in fact also support men, as well as mock them, in both their individual and collective attempts to change themselves. Indeed, we often attacked men who were not self-consciously trying to change. ('All my women friends were very critical of us men,' one man recalls, 'for not doing something about our lives, for not trying to approach politics from the position of being men . . . seeing ourselves as streetfighters, and not thinking about children.'[51]) Other feminists saw little hope that men would change themselves: 'Men in men's groups, are men in bad company', some women said. Others, with less wit and more earnestness, condemned anti-sexist men as 'worse than the old breed'.[52] The dilemma facing anti-sexist men was an old one, with a new, more immediate edge: was 'the enemy' aspects of men themselves, their psychology, their acquired roles – 'we have met the enemy, and he is us'?[53] Or was it something much bigger than that, of which they partook whatever their personal attributes and behaviour?

Learning from women's liberation that 'the personal is political', men against sexism spent much of their time in small and stable 'consciousness-raising' groups addressing the former problem – attempting to change themselves entirely, nearer to what they felt women desired. They sought a transformation which would enable genuine relationships of love and trust between women and men: 'The groups which were formed worked in widely different ways . . . but the shared basis was a desire and intention to dissolve the oppressive character of our relations with women, children, and each other . . . to learn gentleness and collectiveness.'[54] They argued that men must change because men oppress women: 'All our identity, position, self-confidence . . . rests on centuries of our exploitation of women.' However, they also affirmed their own sense of oppression:

> It's not all roses being dominant, taking the initiative, being the breadwinner, having to be a wage slave for forty years . . . [And] it's lonely because the other half of the conditioning is to separate us not only from women but also from men . . . As men in the 'Men's Movement' we recognise that we have to retrace our steps and rediscover in ourselves those traits which have been called 'feminine' . . . passivity, warmth, intuition, tenderness, love, EMOTION. We have to discover in ourselves that which has lain dormant for hundreds of years, that society has obscured and hidden until we act as robots – stiffly, automatically, coldly.[55]

Anti-sexist men by and large agreed that their main enemy was conventional 'masculinity', seen as a social role into which men were forced. As Nigel Armistead argued:

> Masculinity . . . is power-seeking, it is being closed-up, competitive, drab, insensitive, interested in things and goals rather than people and processes . . . Men *are forced* into this role . . . We can join encounter groups with women and gays, we can go on demonstrations, pickets, etc., but the most important thing we can do about it is change ourselves. And that involves consciousness-raising – especially for men, who tend to resist sensitive exploration of each other's experience and feelings.[56]

Men in men's groups wrote frequently of their joyous feelings as they learned to be more open to, and expressive about, their emotions, closer to children and closer to women as they sought and found new ways of loving, caring and sharing. But above all they celebrated being more in touch with and supportive of each other: 'I can remember there being a whole period when there was a big high getting to know one another, sharing all these things.' Exactly like many women describing their experiences of the early days of women's liberation, this man from East London recalled: 'It was a bit like falling in love.'[57] From trying to 'feminise' themselves, express feelings, and become more open and loving, many men moved on into therapy groups and co-counselling, in the belief that they could only change themselves properly by confronting past hurts and their own unconscious feelings of anger, violence and misogyny, in order to understand and overcome them. An account of a London Men's Conference of two hundred men in 1978, reported that emotional and sexual relationships were the focus of attention at almost all of the eighteen workshops, with the workshop on male sexuality – devoted to the search for non-oppressive sexual relationships – attracting the largest numbers of men.[58] John Rowan, now a therapist busy exploring the spiritual world of the Goddess and the Horned God, has written of what he saw as the breakthrough in men's politics around 1974, when some men in men's groups began entering therapy groups to explore their unconscious feelings about their mothers, their fathers and their own internal female nature.[59] Like many feminists, these men stressed that personal life is an important part of political life – especially in prefiguring and building hope and confidence in the possibility of a better, more co-operative, egalitarian world. But, again like some feminists, they were travelling along a road which would finally reduce politics in its entirety to the individual struggles of personal life. Cocooned in relative comfort, as most of these men were, it was easier for them to assert, in their own words, 'the *primacy* of sexual politics in the struggle for socialism'.[60]

The point is these men *liked* displaying and developing what they experienced as 'the gentler parts of ourselves, our spiritual and nurturing capacities, our ability to love', the 'feminine' side of themselves. Indeed, so similar to the preoccupations of many women did those of anti-sexist men become that one of the main complaints of feminists was that they seemed 'a peculiar kind of inward looking mimicry of the WLM [women's liberation movement]'.[61] This should hardly surprise us. If, in fact, 'masculinity' is not some internal psychological property or learned role, but rather something which, as we saw in chapter three, is constructed at a psychological level out of complex and contradictory layerings of different emotions and fragmented identities, we might expect many men to enjoy expressing 'feminine' emotions. With its inter-personal and therapeutic outlook, however, the men's movement was less able to reflect upon the public side of 'masculinity'. As I suggested in chapter four, 'masculinity' gains its meanings, its force and appeal, not just from internalised psychological components or roles, but from all the wider social relations in which men and women participate which simply take for granted men's authority and privileges in relation to women. Men inevitably see themselves and are seen in the light of this seemingly 'natural' authority, in ways which for some groups of men at least, particularly a radical intelligentsia (who are not usually at the most gruelling, exploited, and least esteemed end of the workforce) might be easily compatible with the expression of soft and tender emotions. Such a view of masculinity helps us to understand the limits of psychic change in men, however important and useful it may be for those around them – especially women and children. But it was not the theoretical construction prevalent at that time.

Anti-sexist men were, by and large, men whose personal and often public lives within a radical middle-class culture permitted, if not encouraged, them to behave in less traditional ways. They were the men who could more easily choose, like Nigel Armistead, 'to live more collectively, to share in childcare, to work part-time, to appear more "feminine"', and thereby, 'be more sensitive to the experience and needs of women and gays ... less interested in domination'.[62] By 1975 there were between twenty and thirty groups of such like-minded men around Britain, who were predominantly heterosexual and involved in relationships with feminists.[63] A decade later, as Jeff Hearn suggests, almost all towns in Britain, and even rural areas, had some men's group, with larger towns like Bradford and Leeds boasting three or four such groups.[64] The problem for anti-sexist men, however – which caused at least some of them considerable anxiety – was the worry as to whether changing themselves did actually help destroy male domination more generally.

These men shared in domestic work and childcare, and the main public presence of men against sexism in Britain was probably their involvement in childcare, providing crèches, for example, for women's events.[65] They often helped to set up playgroups or community nurseries, as well as other locally based welfare, tenants and community groups incorporating feminist ideas and ways of working. In the US and, based upon that experience, more recently in Britain, there has also been a significant and important involvement of anti-sexist men's groups working alongside feminist Rape Crisis Centres and Battered Women's Refuges to counsel and change the behaviour of violent men.[66] (In Bristol, Birmingham and elsewhere, men's groups working against violence have begun counselling men who are violent or potentially violent.)[67] Anti-sexist men everywhere actively supported women's demands for abortion rights and improved maternity services. They did attempt (many feminists felt with less success) to listen to, and behave less selfishly with, women friends and lovers, becoming less demanding and admitting rather than hiding their own dependencies.

These are all activities which, in my view, were often important in providing personal support for individual women. They were also important in sustaining a wider radical milieu which helped women's liberation to flourish throughout the 1970s, challenging, as it did, the economistic priorities and authoritarian practices of other left groupings. Though it is now often hidden from feminist history, many women who helped build women's liberation in its earliest days were mothers, seeking escape from the loneliness and uncertainties, the feelings of guilt and inadequacy, accompanying isolated mothering. Often, they were able to put their energies into women's liberation from its earliest days only because the men in their lives accepted new responsibilities of sharing childcare, helping to run playgroups and community nurseries, and supporting them more generally. One such woman – and there were many (myself included) – was Sue O'Sullivan. She has described how her political activity was made possible by her husband (a husband, incidentally, who never did join a men's group, though working in tenants organisations, on a local socialist paper and in other community campaigns):

His political and personal integrity, and a kind of stoic attitude to life, meant that he had the ability to empathise with my changes while expressing his sorrow. He chose to be the mainstay in the children's lives. He scrubbed and cooked and cleaned and took them to the One O'Clock Club, the zoo, cinema and plays; he liased with the schools, spoke to the teachers, took them juice in the night . . . He isn't a saint, but if he hadn't been who he is, could I have left my young children, with pain but little guilt?[68]

The problem was, as Andrew Tolson comments of his own men's group in Birmingham, 'These all remained personal, or at least local, solutions to general questions . . . always, as "straight men" we were wary and peripheral in relation to their outcome.'[69] Predominantly heterosexual, these anti-sexist men were also confronted at their national Men Against Sexism conferences by gay men accusing them of doing nothing to undermine gay oppression. Indeed, with the special variety of political moralism and cavalier voluntarism which often bedevils 'sexual politics', they were faced with the demand by some gay men that they should 'become gay or shut up', as the only way to experience gay oppression and stop oppressing women.[70] The language and behaviour of the self-righteous and hectoring sectarian dogmatist can be all too evident in sexual politics, as in any other form of politics, and it caused chaos and confusion within the fledgling men's movement as they read: 'The only way forward is to *really* open yourself up to the mirror image of yourself and experience through another, *yourself as a man* (you are a male remember) – and build something from the ruins of your male ego that will result.'[71] At a London-wide men's conference in 1975 the destructiveness of such recriminatory rhetoric from some gay men halted further conferences for another three years.[72]

In both Britain and the US doubt and frustration accompanied the activities of many anti-sexist men, creating deeper splits between those who stressed the need for 'men's liberation', as a kind of parallel to women's liberation, those who stressed men's supportive role to women and gays as 'men against sexism', and those, like the editorial collective of the anti-sexist men's magazine, *Achilles Heel*[73] who wavered about between the two positions. One prominent anti-sexist men's activist, Keith Motherson (formerly

Keith Paton), was writing in 1979 of his fears that his men's group was 'too much of a men's club', and not doing enough to 'hassle [other] men to change'.[74] Another had written earlier of his fears of the dangers of more male bonding, questioning the taken-for-granted premise of men against sexism that men needed to create more warm and loving relations with each other:

> I see no evidence that men have ever had much difficulty relating to each other intellectually or emotionally . . .they all too readily form warm and comradely groups to the exclusion of women – sports clubs, monasteries, expeditions, scientific collaboration, trade unions; activities in which men are bonded together in intimate interdependence which can only be called loving.[75]

Most anti-sexist men, however, remained convinced that, as an editorial in *Achilles Heel* expressed it: 'Our power in society as men not only oppresses women but also imprisons us in a deadening masculinity which cripples all our relationships – with each other, with women, with ourselves.'[76] Their views seemed widely shared, and this men's anti-sexist, socialist magazine, which had begun publishing in 1978, received large quantities of letters and support from all parts of Britain and beyond for the next five years.[77] By 1980, this particular collective of pro-feminist, anti-sexist men was acknowledging the justice of feminist criticisms of their politics for being confined to the personal, rather than seeking public ways to struggle against male dominance at work, in trade unions and left groups.[78] Nevertheless, they reaffirmed 'the importance and the necessity . . . for consciousness raising, therapy, involvement in childcare, developing relationships with other men', without which, they believed, 'men's support for feminism will tend to remain abstract'.[79] This, oddly, would seem to suggest that men's engagement in trade union struggles around equal pay for work of equal value, in mainstream political struggles over social policies for increased care allowances and welfare provision, or for more women in positions of political power in trade unions and government are 'abstract' issues rather than central to undermining men's power and our images of 'masculinity'.

The confusions of this perspective return us to the problem of seeing 'masculinity' in terms of personal attributes or individually acquired social roles. This makes it simply a personality issue rather than, underlying the personal, an ideological and social issue. 'Masculinity', I have suggested throughout this book, is best understood as transcending the personal, as a heterogeneous set of ideas, constructed around assumptions of social *power*, which are lived out and reinforced, or perhaps denied and challenged, in multiple and diverse ways within a whole social system in which relations of authority, work, and domestic life are organised, in the main, along hierarchical gender lines. As Tolson concluded in his book over a decade ago: 'To simply deny, or vaguely wish to "relinquish", the reality of this power is to fall victim to a liberal myopia.'[80]

Interestingly, the last issue of *Achilles Heel* which was still produced by most of its original collective, in 1982, unselfconsciously reflected one aspect of the problem in an account of a miner's life. Writing of his experiences as an underground miner, following in the footsteps of his father, Kevin Devaney describes the humour, aggression, comradeship and physicality of one type of working-class masculinity, presenting an utterly different picture to the lonesome, 'deadening', rationalistic masculinity, cut off from body and feelings, which most of the middle-class members of *Achilles Heel* had written of as their own particular masculine heritage. At the end of each day the miners would wash together in the open:

> You would talk to the man in the next shower and another would come up and start washing your back without a word. You would start washing someone else's back and soon there is a chain of men talking and washing backs . . . It gives you a good attitude to your own body, that of not being conscious of it as something special.[81]

After leaving the mines for Ruskin College, Devaney missed the comradeship, solidarity and humour which the miners always displayed to relieve the tensions and boredom of work. Describing the aggressiveness of the humour, which served as signs of affection in a culture with few words for tenderness or affection, Devaney reflects that he nevertheless saw almost no actual physical aggression between the men at work: 'I saw more in college and university.'[82] Parochial, limited and sexist, the miners' life – perhaps precisely because of this – involved deep friendships between men and was, as Devaney recalls, good for building confidence in general and 'confidence and awareness of my essential masculinity'.[83] In contrast, in the previous issue of *Achilles Heel*, Vic Seidler had asserted that 'Masculinity is never something we can feel at ease with,' suggesting moreover that because of the fear of physical violence men have very little relationship with their bodies, 'We don't see them as a source of contact and satisfaction.'[84] Diverse testimony like this reinforces the need to think in terms of 'masculinities', rather than any single masculinity, and even then to be wary of attempts to impart to them any fixed psychological dimensions.

In his recent work on gender and power, Bob Connell, while applauding the anti-sexist men's movement for its political project of attempting to root out their own sexism, almost completely dismisses the theorizing behind their therapeutic project of repairing the psychic damage of 'masculinity'.[85] According to Connell, it is wrong to assume that because there are difficulties and anxieties for boys in acquiring the aspects of dominant masculinity appropriate for their specific social and historical contexts, these will persist in the form of permanent insecurity. Most men, he argues, become secure in their physical masculinity. To be sure, there are real costs and tensions, as anti-sexist men suggest and, as we saw in previous chapters, quite enormous strain and tension for some men in maintaining a sense of their own masculinity. But surely many men, especially those who occupy positions of social power and privilege, display all too much self-confidence and complacency in their sexual identity? Connell's words ring true to me when he writes:

> I disagree profoundly with the idea that masculinity is an impoverished character structure. It is a richness, a plenitude. The trouble is that the specific richness of hegemonic masculinity is oppressive, being founded on, and enforcing, the subordination of women.[86]

When we know that from schooldays onwards boys collectively succeed in getting more attention, talking more, demanding more, showing off, occupying public spaces in more relaxed and confident ways than women, it seems hard to sustain the notion of 'masculinity' as inherently oppressive to men. It seems more plausible to conclude from what we know about the ambivalent construction of male sexual identity that men, although the favoured sex, with higher levels of self-confidence and self-esteem, may nevertheless experience a lack of certainty over their 'masculinity', rather than a lack of satisfaction with it. Psychological studies all seem to suggest that men are more preoccupied with masculinity, and more likely to be anxious over the lack of it.[87] (Women, in contrast, may demonstrate less satisfaction with 'femininity', but are less preoccupied with, or anxious about, their own 'femininity'.)[88] Interestingly, these same studies also found that those men who describe themselves as more 'androgynous', were not necessarily men who supported ideas of women's equality; nor were those who described themselves as more traditionally 'masculine' necessarily opposed to more liberal gender ideologies.[89]

The influence of feminism may of course make men less certain of the desirability of what they see as their masculinity. What the pro-feminist men's movement literature and practice make clear is that, once aware of it, at least some men are very unhappy with the idea that they are caught up in a system which is exploitative of and oppressive to women, gays, and certain other men. They do want change. They do have an absolute commitment to richer, more fulfilling and egalitarian relations with the women they are closest to, and they do wish to share what are usually women's more specific pleasures and pains in parenting and caring for others. This is very important in breaking down polarised gender images, and foreseeing the possibility of a future beyond them. It is important, most of all, simply in the evidence it provides that men *can* change. However, as I suggested when looking at the new images and practices of fatherhood in chapter two, change is itself contradictory. It may be seen as primarily a way of modernising certain types of contemporary masculinity, allowing men to experience some of the pleasures more traditionally connected to women's lives and 'feminine' pursuits, while nevertheless retaining privileges and power over women more generally, even if undesired.

The last national Men Against Sexism conference took place in 1980, although there have been some regional gatherings of men against sexism since that time. There has been only one issue of

Achilles Heel since 1983, though there have been a number of attempts to revive it. The national *Men's Antisexist Newsletter* has appeared ever more sporadically since the mid-1980s, and those anti-sexist men's networks which still exist are either locally based or organised around more specific issues.[90] In general, while some anti-sexist men's group pioneers have abandoned all political engagement (often for personal and professional commitment to full-time therapy), the 1980s has seen a far greater spread and diversity of men's involvement in anti-sexist activities – in schools, training centres, workplaces, media productions, and elsewhere. From pulling down pin-ups to more formal trade-union engagement in workplaces,[91] from producing a men's magazine to TV programmes on the changing lives and experiences of men,[92] from attempting to explore masculinity to men's studies courses in colleges and universities,[93] from discovering their own repressed violence to working with child abusers,[94] the seeds of men against sexism politics have begun to take root and spread beyond personal relationships and local political engagements. What is important, Jeff Hearn suggests, and I would agree, is men making the links between the public and private worlds as they attempt to build non-oppressive, loving relationships between all men and women, all men and men: 'This is just as possible between neighbours, friends, lovers, relatives, shoppers, workmates, pickets, and men on the street, as it is in more formally organised men's groups.'[95] In the process, however, anti-sexist men need to reflect on the changes which are occurring in the acceptable and commercial face of dominant masculinity, in which the 'new man' – a softer, more emotional, self-conscious sex object himself – may still retain, if less infallibly than ever before, his hegemony over women, and over other subordinated groups of men.

'Something is happening to young men,' dedicated followers of fashion like Frank Mort have been informing us for some time now.[96] They are being sold 'images which rupture traditional icons of masculinity', providing more fluid gender images for the 1980s.[97] Fashions, interests, pleasures, previously seen as quintessentially 'feminine', taboo for all but the most 'unmasculine' of men – the gay male – are today eagerly consumed by young men. The cold, drab, disembodied, insensitive masculinity the men's groups were fighting to destroy within themselves, their predominantly middle-class and Eurocentric fifties image of the man in the grey flannel suit, would already seem obsolete to many modern, sensuous, perfumed, mirror-hogging males, now swaying to the words of LoveSexy Prince – coyly laid back, pouting and stark naked on his album cover: 'Anna Stesia come 2 me, talk 2 me, ravish me, liberate my mind.'[98] Throughout the world of popular culture there has been a sexualisation of the male body: the sale of commodities designed for men now exploits many of the techniques and meanings attached to the more traditional fetishised display of the female body – designed to stimulate women's narcissism and appeal to men's voyeurism.

In the metropolitan regions of most Western cities signs of change are ubiquitous, in both private and public consumption – a change in many cases heralding decline in polarised images of gender, an opening up of previously sexually segregated spaces. Pubs, once the clearly demarcated, spartan, often seedy men's territory designed to contrast with the soft, carpeted, comfort of domestic territory, and to exclude women, are today refurbished as ersatz living rooms, with soft cushions and books on the wall, seemingly as welcoming to women as to men. In the home, the man about the house no longer sticks to his own sphere, but is appealed to as creative chef, childcarer, and expert carpet cleaner.[99] Recent psychological studies of men's self-perceptions in the United States and Britain, for example, all report men describing themselves in more 'androgynous' terms, as both 'feminine' (warm, sensitive, caring, gentle) and 'masculine' (strong, tough, competitive).[100] On the other hand, the signs and tokens of a slide towards greater gender similarity and more 'feminine' traits in men, are mocked by the continuing production and popularity of all the old hard, assertive, violent images of masculinity from *Rocky* to *Rambo*, from *Dirty Harry* to *Top Gun*, which continue to make box-office records. Throughout most of the eighties the world was bombarded by the militaristic rhetoric of Reagan, explicitly endorsing the 'Rambo' model of man-with-machine-gun in pursuit of his goals, justifying US aggression around the globe. (Although today it is Gorbachev as messenger of peace and *perestroika*, who has been capturing the hearts and minds of Europe, triumphing over the chauvinistic bellicosity of Britain's tough-minded, tough-maiden, Margaret Thatcher.) A diversity of 'masculinities' jostle to present themselves as the acceptable face of the new male order. They allow men to partake of the fantasy gratifications of phallic power and the compensatory pleasures of displaced aggression, while also perhaps sharing more ambiguous gratifications as passive objects of desire. Men today, insofar as they are more open to new experiences, may be the irresponsible and self-indulgent consumers of pleasure, or, perhaps, growing closer to women and children, enjoy their involvement in childrearing and domestic pursuits.

It is this new diversity in masculine styles and behaviour which has suggested to many feminists that men are simply superficially accommodating to new times in new ways. Despite great squabbles over whether or not men have changed in tandem with change in women, overall it is clear that men *are* now spending more time on housework and childcare, as women spend more time in paid work; some men have changed little, other groups of men have changed a great deal.[101] But is this, as we saw Yvonne Roberts conclude from her interviews reported in chapter two, men now having the best of all worlds? [102] Things are not quite so simple. The anti-sexist men's movement was right to suggest that at least some men do suffer as they try to live out more traditional masculine ideals. Men may be permitted greater flexibility today, but it may not be easy for all men to adopt such flexibility. American data reveal increasing rates of psychological distress in men, fast catching up with the relatively higher levels experienced by women. According to several studies, the growing levels of depression and low self-esteem in men are related to wives' employment, but not to wives' higher earning capacities, or men's increased participation in housework. Depression in men occurred when husbands of employed wives did *not* contribute to housework and childcare, when men's traditional role was not changing.[103] There have also been rising levels of 'breadwinner suicides' and despair in men with increasing male unemployment, suggesting that many men cannot abandon the 'breadwinner' role without serious damage to themselves.[104]

It may well be true that what men would like, and indeed what some men have found, is the possibility of adapting to the changes in women's lives, and to the intensified consumerisation aimed at men, by adjustments which allow for a new loosening up of masculinities while leaving older privileges and power relations intact. Women, however, may not be content with this. And some men, as well as many women, would like to see more fundamental change. The stronger and more confident the pressures from women for men to change, both at a personal level and through collective political struggle, the more men will be forced to question the unthinking presumptions and unexamined prerogatives of 'masculinity'.

Socialism, Feminism and the Problem of Men

Undermining the power relations between men and women, questioning existing images of 'masculinity' cannot, I am suggesting, simply be a process of men individually expressing their doubts and hesitations over, and their refusals to conform to, what they see as masculine ideals in favour of developing their 'feminine' side. Personal change is important. But beneath and beyond possibilities for personal change lies the whole web of interconnecting social, economic and political practices, public policies, welfare resources and understandings of sexuality which actually confer power upon men.

Dismantling gender hierarchies necessitates the pursuit of change in the economy, the labour market, social policy and the state, as well as the organisation of domestic life, the nature of sexual encounters and the rhetorics of sexual difference. Change here is partly a process of conscious collective action in pursuit of equality, and partly the unforeseen consequence of technological and economic mutations. Fortunately for those interested in sexual equality, the accidental effects of historical change as well as the conscious efforts of feminists and their allies, have been constantly destabilising former gender hierarchies, threatening the truths of 'masculine' transcendence. And yet, accustomed as we are to rhetorics of the individual, it is not so easy to get a grip on the social underpinnings of our perceptions of gender.

One thing is certain: although, individually, women and men can and do exhibit every combination of active and passive, gentle and aggressive, dependent and assertive thoughts and behaviour, our attachments to the ideas and discourses constructing polarised gender images live on. At the heart of the matter, the equations of the 'feminine' and 'love', the 'masculine' and 'power', endure, bound up with the institutionalised continuities of past and present – of women's central engagement with childrearing and personal life, men's with economic and social power. Our commitment to individualism is so pervasive, however, that it is difficult for us to grasp the institutional dimensions of 'masculinity' and 'femininity', to understand the assertion of men's power and the subordination of women embodied within the functioning of the state or the labour market, as much as in personal relationships and family life. We always tend to see individuals themselves as the basic unit of explanation.

'There is no such thing as society; there are individuals, and there are families,' Thatcher informed British society in 1988: a society ever more sharply divided by a decade of her economic and social policies into distinct social groupings, with huge and increasing inequalities of opportunities and life prospects. Neither Thatcher's individuals, nor the members of her families, are appealed to as a sex. But neither individuals nor families have an existence except as seen, by others and themselves, through sex and gender arrangements. As a sex, the problems women face today, according to many feminists, must be understood primarily in terms of masculinity and male power. The issue most central to women's prospects for happiness and equality is whether men can and will change. On this view, the fact that many women's standard of living relative to men's has declined over the last decade, suggests that male power has become more entrenched. This is, however, a serious and fundamental misreading of social trends. Men's unemployment rates have been rising faster than women's since the mid-1980s, as have men's rates of suicide, illness, psychological stress and earlier death. The suggestion is a misreading akin to Thatcher's refusal to acknowledge social forces beyond individuals, even if, for these feminists, individuals are sexed.

As I argued at the opening of this chapter, a funny thing happened in the late 1970s. Just as a new dawn of sexual equality seemed finally in sight in Britain, many feminists began to doubt its possibility. Women had won legal rights to equal pay and anti-sex-discrimination practices in employment, as well as maternity rights, new laws against domestic violence and trade union support for abortion rights, against sexual harassment, for equal pay for work of equal value. These gains could be added to the more liberal abortion law, and women's easier access to contraception achieved a decade earlier. It was precisely then, in the late seventies, as socialist feminist Cynthia Cockburn explains, that the 'foregoing history of the women's movement brought home to women that "equality" was an unachievable, indeed undesirable goal, that equality could not be achieved by women as we are, with men as they are, or in a world as it is – and that "difference" was the name of the game'.[105] What was it that fed the new political pessimism that began to pervade feminism and, it must straightaway be added, all progressive politics, from the close of the seventies?

One contradiction informing the new pessimism is immediately apparent: two decades of resurgent feminist thought and action has benefited some women and had little obvious impact on others. If we survey the decade from the mid-seventies to the mid-eighties, women's voices were heard as never before, and women remained at the forefront of many of the most important progressive struggles of the decade. Almost equal numbers of women as men are now being recruited into professions like law, medicine and accountancy (double the numbers a generation earlier), and the number of businesses owned by women has grown rapidly.[106] At the same time, however, if we ignore the increasing differences *within* sexual groupings, women's situation overall has worsened over the decade. Is it that women's voices, despite limited gains, are still largely ignored by men, and their struggles inevitably foredoomed? I don't think the evidence supports this view. It does support the conclusion that it is still true, as it always was true, that the peculiar vulnerability of women engaged in reproduction and childcare as their primary responsibility and work makes it particularly hard to protect them from the depredations of capital in search of cheap labour. But blaming an economic system which has always been built upon the greatest exploitation of its weakest members, whether female, immigrant or ethnic minority, can be seen as a way of condoning men as a sex for not fighting to remove – indeed, often organising to maintain – the vulnerabilities of women. Have men collectively done anything in the public world over the last two decades to remove women's greater vulnerability to exploitation? Have they acted at all to eradicate their own relative power and privileges over women?

It has become increasingly fashionable of late to suggest that, as far as women are concerned, there is little difference between left and right. Both 'the left' and 'the labour movement', for example – the organisations ideologically most committed to the pursuit of equality – have been described as 'almost exclusively male, [their] language, practice and institutions defined by masculine percep- tions of the world, and fashioned in men's interests'.[107] There is no doubting the deeply rooted 'masculine' character of the labour movement. It has always reflected, in a special way, the masculine character of all other cultural and political sites; the character, that is, of men's greater power to define and control. But it has also incorporated more of the contradictions and tensions of 'mascu- linity'.

'Make room for the men!', was how Mary Macarthur, one of the great feminist trade unionists, summed up the trade union attitude to women workers back in 1909.[108] Work, it has often been noted, is one of the main anchorages of male identity. Men's engagement in paid work, in 'skilled' work, is central to the social construction of masculinity, or, as the contrasts in men's working lives would suggest, of masculinities. Women's presence in the workforce has always been a threat to men's sense of their 'masculinity'. But it is a threat which has been systematically manipulated by employers to control men, as well as women, in the capitalist quest for cheap labour. 'Make room for the men' was a central tenant of trade unionism because the ideal of the 'family wage' – a wage sufficient for a man to support wife and children – was crucial to the birth of the labour movement.[109] In understanding the supports for and threats to male dominance and men's sense of masculinity, it is instructive to uncover some of the history of women's relationship to trade unionism. It is one of the areas where the combined effects of economic shifts and women's struggles for change are clearest, beginning, as they are, to undermine the traditional images and practices linking masculinity, work and male dominance.

In the early nineteenth century, before the notion of the male breadwinner was fought for and won by the combined struggles of social reformers and trade unionists, men, women and children worked in factory production. The most outrageous exploitation of women, working 78 hours a week for less than half the pay of men at sub-subsistence wages in noxious working conditions, was exceeded only by the even more scandalous exploitation of child labour.[110] There is no doubt, as male workers have always feared, that employers have consistently turned to female labour, or any other source of cheap labour, as a way of lowering the general value of labour. Sarah Boston argues that most married women, whose lives in the nineteenth century were already ones of relentless toil (with on average around six children surviving birth, supported men in their demands for a family wage.[111] The family-wage ideal was promoted by both men and women as necessary for the maintenance of the working-class family, and for the prevention of the undercutting or 'dilution' of men's wages by the super-exploitation of women and children. Similarly, Martha May has suggested from her historical research on women and trade unions in the United States, that the family wage initially emerged as a working-class demand of women and men alike, fiercely opposed by capital.[112] There is no doubt either, however, that this principle at the heart of trade unionism, while originally seen as a protection for all members of the working-class family, and upheld and policed by the state, served also, and increasingly, to consolidate men's power and privileges over women in the workforce. It led male trade unionists to perceive women as a threat, to drive women out of the skilled workforce, and to keep them out – with most male trade unionists completely unconcerned about the precarious plight and subordinate status held by women who remained in the workforce.[113]

Furthermore, as Anne Phillips and Barbara Taylor among others have argued, the very notion of 'skill' was from the outset 'saturated with sexual bias', and part and parcel of men's struggles to maintain their wage, status and identity within the workplace.[114] According to Phillips and Taylor, the work which women do tends to be low in status and reward simply because it is women and not men who do it. Ben Birnbaum has illustrated this from his study of the clothing industry: the same type of machine work was classified as skilled when performed by men, and semi-skilled when performed by women.[115] A lowering of status also occurred in certain jobs when women were taken on to replace men, for example as cashiers in banks. However, it was more often the case, as Paul Thompson argues, that it was only after employers had already deskilled and degraded jobs, in order to lower wages, that women would begin to take them over from men. Where women were not prepared to act as cheap and docile labour, Thompson continues, they might be replaced by other more vulnerable groups, as happened in the New England textile industries where Irish immigrants replaced local women.[116]

To explain rather than merely describe the sexual hierarchies of the workplace, we need to understand the interaction between the logic of capitalist accumulation and men's needs and desires to maintain their dominance in the workplace. Men's desire for dominance at work is connected with the preservation of their 'masculine' identity. This sexual hierarchy at work, although acquiring its own autonomy, keys in with all the other sites of sexual hierarchy outside the workplace. As numerous workplace studies show, employers and management use gender hierarchy as a way of organising and controlling workplaces, correctly assuming that women will generally be more likely to accept men's authority, and to diffuse conflict, being more used, as they are, to reacting in this fashion to male authority at home.[117] Women, as the studies of Anna Pollert and others illustrate, may also *experience* their jobs differently to men – at least, young women in factory jobs who are oriented primarily to future prospects of marriage: 'What was specifically female in the women's conception of their wage labour was the fact that they still considered themselves dependent on a man, and their pay as marginal to a man's – even if they were single.'[118]

Both the manipulations of capital in the interest of profit and external hierarchies of gender affect the sexual division of paid labour. However, there is no doubt that men, both individually, and collectively through trade unions, have acted to preserve their own power and interests at the expense of women. Worse than this, they have frequently displayed real hostility to women workers, including women trade unionists, seemingly incapable of extending the putative solidarity at the base of trade unionism to women. But relations between male trade unionists and women workers have been far from consistent or uniform. If we look at trade union history we find instances where men have defended and fought for women workers, and instances where they have fought against them. As Ruth Milkman comments for her study of the uneven support of men for women in certain industries in the United States:

> It would be far more fruitful to examine the conditions under which male workers' class interests have prevailed over their gender interests and the conditions under which the opposite has occurred, than to invoke the interests of 'men as men' to explain the dominant historical trend.[119]

In England the early textile unions, unlike other craft unions of the nineteenth century, not only accepted women members, but negotiated for equal pay for women and men.[120] Women were early on as active as men in the textile unions, and in the remarkable case of the Dundee Jute and Flax Workers Union they had won, by 1906, a constitution giving them representation on the executive committee according to their numbers.[121] But even in the textile industry, as Sarah Boston illustrates, conflict between women and men still arose in areas 'where organization was weakest and where employers tried to take advantage of that weakness by employing women to do "men's" jobs for less money'.[122] The National Union of Clerks also accepted women members from 1890 and campaigned for equal pay for women, rather than treating women as 'the enemy'.[123] In all other industries throughout the nineteenth century, however, rates were fixed according to sex, with women completely excluded from most of the craft unions, and 'the problem' of their cheap labour setting the stage for continuing conflict and division between women and men. In certain places, at certain times, exceptional support and solidarity would occur between male trade unionists and women workers – in Bristol, for example, between the Dockers Union and women factory workers throughout the 1890s. And a few individual trade union men (like Mark Wilks, Mr Tate and Mr Croft in the National Union of Teachers (NUT) at the beginning of this century) bravely and passionately supported women's struggles despite attack and abuse from their union brothers.[124] But, overall, men's attitude was more often openly hostile to women workers.

Despite the valiant efforts of a few men and many women (the women largely organising themselves separately through their own women's associations),[125] and despite a formal commitment to equal pay for women from 1880, the trade union movement as a whole remained opposed to giving women (especially married women) equality with men in the workplace throughout the early and middle years of this century. Furthermore, many women trade unionists (as well as women at home) supported their male colleagues, insisting that the primary function of a woman was in the home, and demanding, for example, after each World War, that skilled jobs must be returned to men. It was not until the close of the 1960s, with militancy in the air, feminism in the wings, and women accounting for 70 per cent of all those recently joining tade unions, that a new and sustained assault began to reverse the trade unions' historic failure to represent women's interests adequately.

Although the women's liberation movement was from the beginning suspicious of the bureaucratic and male-dominated trade union movement, there were very soon alliances between women in and outside each movement. At first more from the outside, feminists both supported and helped initiate campaigns to unionise the most exploited women workers in the early seventies – the night cleaners, nursery workers, home-workers and others. They actively supported women on strike, occupying their factory against redundancy at Fakenham, demanding equal pay at Trico and elsewhere, supporting Black women workers victimised by employers and white workers at Imperial Typewriters, demanding an end to agency nursing and better pay and conditions for nurses.[126] By the mid-seventies, feminists were becoming more active on the inside of their unions – mostly white-collar – and, inspired originally by some women in the Communist Party, had drawn up their own Working Women's Charter. This Charter expanded trade union issues to include childcare, maternity leave, contraception and abortion, alongside the more traditional union agenda of pay and training. The Trade Union Congress of 1975 rejected the Charter on the grounds, its General Council proclaimed, that a sizeable minority of its members would not consider contraception and abortion 'appropriate matters' for trade-union politics. But, at the very same Congress, such sentiments were soon in honourable retreat as a separate motion in support of women's rights to contraception and free abortion on request was passed.[127] It would culminate in the historic trade union march in support of abortion rights in 1979.

Henceforth, women within trade unions – often, whether describing themselves as feminist or not, organising separately in their own women's committees and holding women-only courses, only gradually officially recognised – were consistently to work at breaking down the boundaries between the private and the public, bringing women's situation at home into the workplace: boundaries central to the maintenance of men's relative strength in the workforce as well as to their control of the labour movement. Gradually, despite persistent opposition from many men, feminist demands were to become little short of the new common sense, at least of the white-collar unions. In a useful survey of a decade of women's activity in trade unions in 1984, Ruth Elliot concluded:

> There is no doubt that, particularly in the area of childcare and family responsibilities, we have managed to influence official union language and policy. It is 'working parents' now, and not 'working mothers'. 'Parental leave' or 'family responsibility' for men and women is endorsed as trade union demand by the TUC and a number of individual unions . . . There seems to be a growing sense of confidence and achievement . . . As women we are clearer about our demands. We are more confident in each other as women, less easily threatened by tactics of trying to divide off 'feminists' from 'non-feminists'. Unions have policies that ten years ago would have been undreamt of – on abortion, childcare, sexual harassment, positive action. There are new structures of women's committees within most major unions.[128]

Elliot, however, also discusses the painful contradictions and the costs involved, as women toughen themselves to work in bureaucracies dominated by men, and regulated by their standards. The policies have changed, but the culture and priorities are harder to shift:

> There are times I think when all women activists wonder if it's worth it. At times even the victories seem hollow. We win gains on paper but at a time when women are increasingly under attack, how much do these paper commitments inform every day trade union strategies?[129]

Other women (not only in Britain but, it would seem, almost everywhere) have written of the bitter struggle to feminise trade union hierarchies, practices and priorities (including the exhausting offensive merely to eliminate the most blatant forms of bottom-pinching sexist put-downs and harassment) in line with changed policies representing women's interests and expanding grass-roots membership and activity. As Inez McCormack from NUPE in Belfast reports: 'There's a coldness in me because it seems that the women's issue becomes a progressive issue when it is of use to the progressive forces, rather than when it is serving the needs of women.'[130] But then, I wonder, when have any group of people, including women, given up power without struggle, pain and conflict? Now that they are losing men through unemployment, trade unions need to recruit women workers, and to do so they have to change – and are changing.

Beyond the labour movement, when there was a Labour government in power after 1974, it seemed as if rapid progress was being made for women. Legislating for equal pay, against sexual discrimination, for paid maternity leave, and for improved childcare facilities – at least for women in greatest need – the Labour Government of the 1970s did, up to a point, prove responsive to many of women's demands for equality. By the second half of the 1970s the combination of goverment legislation and official trade union commitments appeared to have laid the groundwork for women's full equality in the workplace.

What went wrong? One thing which went wrong was that employers were given the time to deepen existing job segregation between women and men in order to avoid equal pay, confining large numbers of women to an even narrower range of jobs. Another problem was that paid maternity leave hardly dealt with the demands of women's domestic responsibilities. Women could not share equally with men at work until men shared equally with them in the home. And finally, as newly militant women often engaging in industrial action for the first time were to find, although men sometimes supported women's actions (and sometimes did not),[131] attempting to assume positions of power within the trade union movement was a more difficult matter. Being perhaps the only woman on an executive committee meant slotting into what is usually felt to be a very male type of behaviour, as well as shouldering often gruelling work-loads. As a woman on the National Union of Journalists'(NUJ) national executive commented of activities at the Trade Union Congress (TUC):

> It's all performance . . . Most women feel that speaking isn't something they're particularly good at. I spoke very little at meetings. I'd only intervene if I had a new, specific point to make, but I think that was probably interpreted as me not having much to say and being rather feeble.[132]

This same woman also observed, however, that she experienced some hostility from women seeing another woman 'at the top', although there was encouragement for women working within the union at its base. Overall, however, she feels that unions have changed considerably during her own years of involvement, with male trade unionists, if only out of expediency, no longer able to reject feminist ideas. While some women union officials speak warmly of their time as union officials ('The satisfaction you get from being able to do something for your members – I dunno, it is something money just can't buy,')[133] other active trade union women have reported even greater bitterness than the NUJ woman official over the difficulties of working with their male comrades.

Cynthia Cockburn's research into women's secondary role in the trade unions and the Labour Party led her to conclude that there is a 'tightly packaged association of working-class identity, union membership, Labour loyalty and masculinity', which exludes or undermines women. Used to seeing only themselves as central, men tend to ignore women or to regard their assertiveness as aggression: 'If a woman wants a place on the executive then she can't be a normal woman.'[134] Yet, however wearying the struggle to force men to listen to women may be, it is quite beyond doubt that the face of trade unionism has finally changd in the 1980s. Covering 45 major trade unions accounting for 92 per cent of all union members, a recent survey finds remarkable shifts in many of them. In around a quarter, in stark contrast with a decade earlier, women's presence at the TUC conference and on the executive closely mirrored their membership numbers, exceeding it in five unions. Thirty-one of these 45 unions now have women's committees, most now provide crèches at annual conferences, a few, like the NUJ, meet childcare expenses for all union meetings. Many unions now run special courses for women. All now accept sexual harassment as a serious problem – many campaigning around it. A few have secured entry to pension schemes for part-time workers, and at least a dozen unions have begun to fight seriously for upgrading women's skills on the principle of equal pay for work of equal value. The clearest trend to emerge from this survey was that a woman's status in her union was affected by her status in her job; low pay and low wages proving the greatest obstacle to women's status within the union.[135]

What these shifts suggest is that the particular image of 'masculinity', rooted, as Cockburn suggests, in the links between work (especially manual work), trade unionism and Labour Party support, is today in tatters. Men may still be dominant at all levels of influence in the trade union movement but, with industrial decline and restructuring, that movement now knows it can survive *only* by its initiatives to involve women members, which means expanding union concerns to encompass the links between the workplace and the home. What would the print unions of old make of the thoughts of their 'brother' today in his 'opinion' column in *British Printer*?:

> Get used to the idea. When the hard pressed printer gets home from an exhausting day a helping hand with the washing up won't be enough. She'll expect to find her dinner on the table and the kids bathed and ready for bed. And no gripes.[136]

Only very, very slowly, only with enormous pressure from, and corresponding bitterness for, feminists and others, have we seen change in the culture, priorities and practices of the left and the labour movement. Black and gay people, likewise, silenced within and excluded from trade union agendas and hierarchies, have faced similar difficulties and experienced similar bitterness. Today Jack Dromey, from the archetypally 'male' Transport and General Workers Union, tells us he can announce that he is leaving meetings early to mind his children. He can raise the issue of equal pay for work of equal value; activities and issues, most likely, he would no more have thought of, than raised, till recently.[137] It was never an easy battle. But we do need to celebrate the fact that some battles have been won. The obstacles to progress are no longer primarily men as such – at least, not men of the left – however irritating and offensive their ignorance of, or defensive reaction to, the economic shifts which are inexorably placing women more centrally within what was once a securely male-dominated movement, may be. As we saw in chapter one, only a little over two decades ago, there was neither hint nor whisper of the problem of men's power over women, either from women or from men. Left agendas really have changed. The issues of sexual politics – abortion, sexuality, single mothers, male violence, sexual harassment – were not even a part of the language, let alone the policies, of any section of the left in those days. Today there are few feminist issues which cannot, at the least, be raised in any left grouping.

As distinct from the situation of the minority of middle-class and professional women, the primary obstacles to the progress of the majority of women towards equality with men at present derives from the policies of the right in power: policies which systematically lower welfare spending and attack all collectivist ideologies to promote the return to an exclusively profit-based capitalism which allows massive unemployment and the growth of an increasingly impoverished underclass. The 'feminisation' of poverty which has accompanied the greater impoverishment of certain groups of men over the last few decades, partakes of the resurgence of this more naked form of capitalist restructuring, wherein a shrinking number of economically secure core workers – still primarily men – are surrounded by an ever-expanding part-time, peripheral or home-based supply of workers – still primarily women. Indeed the very notion of the feminisation of poverty is itself misleading. The trend towards poverty occurs only *within* the working class, and race and nationality remain far more important determinants of poverty then gender.[138] As Linda Burnham argues of the situation in the United States, the growing number of working class, Black and minority women and children sinking into poverty is the combined effect of discriminatory low wages in segregated female manual employment and the dramatic increase in female-headed households over the last decade. The latter, however, is itself related to the massive increase in male unemployment, with many of the men closest to impoverished women disappearing into jails, or unaccounted for in the chaos of the urban dispossessed [139] A government which pursues exclusively market strategies cannot but allow existing inequalities to be exploited in the pursuit of profit, which is why our current Tory government, by abolishing minimum wage councils, delaying the implementation of European Economic Community (EEC) regulations, and so on, has consistently attempted to undermine the long and hard fight of women in progressive movements seeking change.

It is not that men on the right are necessarily more opposed to ideas of women's equality than men on the left (some of them are and some of them are not). Our national leader, using her uniquely packaged 'feminine' image of the narrow-minded, hardworking, authoritarian, all-powerful 'good housekeeper', has battled hard against equality legislation in the EEC. Her motives, it seems clear, are not an attack on women as a sex. In a recent interview in *She* magazine, she urged women to challenge men for election to public office and promotion in business. [140] They are simply the profits-before-equality position of the class attack her government has waged to create cheap flexible labour and maintain profits by reducing taxation and public expenditure. This not only keeps women with dependent children in their position as the most vulnerable and over-burdened of citizens, but preserves our ideals of 'manhood' intact, seemingly without shadow of turning. The abolition of gender inequality requires, as well as individual efforts to attack men's prerogatives, a commitment to socialist policies for achieving democratic production and welfare systems which can remove, rather than entrench, existing inequalities.

The Road Ahead: A New Agenda for the 1990s

In spite of two decades of feminist struggle, in spite of some men trying hard to change, inequalities between the sexes everywhere persist. Their persistence daily nourishes, and in turn is nourished by, the grim authority of images of masculinity, the inviting cosiness of images of femininity. Yet neither our images of men and women nor sexual inequalities themselves persist everywhere equally and unbroken. In Britain we have seen the appearance of many new popular TV heroines, typified by the Black and white female duo operating as private eyes in *South of the Border* who, while articulating the personal complexities of their private lives, can stand up to any man and, when necessary, walk right over him. Not only has the visibility of alternative lifestyles, and the availability of psychodynamic writing, made many people increasingly aware of the instability and potential fragmentation of fixed gender identities but, more publicly, gender orderings are frequently overturned: women gain authority, men lose it. Images of the power of men and the servility of women are mocked and subverted in our daily lives, if not by some actual inversion of customary sexual hierarchies, then by the search for new ways of appealing to men as consumers, or to the women who shop for them. (The seriousness of men's sexual prowess, for example, is derided by the silliness of boxer shorts, or softened by the sensuousness of Niko's briefs.)[141]

The conscious subversion of men's power, on the other hand, is partly the work of those who travel the slow and grinding route taken by mainstream reformist political parties and organisations committed to sexual equality. It is also the work of those engaged in the more erratic, more radical, spurts and retreats along the volatile route of interpersonal sexual politics, as feminists, lesbians, gay and anti-sexist men refashion and live out their new visions of what it is to be 'woman' or 'man'. It is finally, as feminists have always preached and often practised, also a matter of cultural subversion – the creative work of revaluing the lives and experiences of women and de-centring the androcentric positioning of men in all existing discourses. Though it may be difficult to perceive, these routes do intersect. Interpersonal struggles to change men, attempts by men themselves to refashion their conceptions of what it is to be a man, always encounter and frequently collide with other power relations. Men are changed by greater involvement in childcare and domestic work and by being required to pay attention to the demands and interests of women. But not all men could assume more domestic responsibilities, even if they wished to. And not all women have the same power to demand, or the same interest in ensuring, change in men. State policy, and expansions and contractions of welfare, as well as patterns of paid employment for men and for women, affect the possibilities for change in men. The competitive, individualistic nature of modern life in the West exacerbates the gulf between what is seen as the feminine world of love and caring and the masculine world of the market-place – wherever women and men may individually find themselves. As some socialist feminists have always known, the difficulty of changing men is, in part, the difficulty of changing political and economic structures.[142]

Research like that of Pippa Norris on the comparative position of women and men in Western democracies makes it clear that state policies and political parties do matter. They have a major influence on women's pay and positions, with social-democratic governments substantially reducing pay differentials and occupational segregation (both vertical and horizontal) between women and men, and right-wing parties in power producing the opposite effect.[143] Social-democratic governments have also been more likely to grant women reproductive freedom (although the Catholicism of a country can be a constraining factor)[144], and they have tended to provide more opportunities for women in politics – except in Britain, Greece and Austria, where the difference is slight. (The 'first past the post' electoral system in Britain is one which has been shown to be less favourable to women compared with the strict porportionality in some electoral systems of Northern Europe.)[145]

In Sweden, where the Social Democratic Party has been in government since the 1920s and developed the most expansive social, health and educational welfare system, male domination, though still a reality, has been the most seriously challenged. Along with other Scandinavian states, it provides a model for considering the potential and limitations of state and labour movement commitment to equal opportunites. Women's economic dependence on men has been weakened by the expansion of welfare services, and their caring responsibilities for the young, the old and the sick have dramatically declined.[146] Organised labour, as many observers have noted, played a central role in initiating women's economic progress in Sweden. It could play this role because 90 per cent of all male and female workers in both public and private sectors in Sweden are trade union members and, as in Denmark, organised labour works closely with both state and capital in a governing tripartite coalition.[147] The importance of organised labour in achieving greater economic equality for women would also explain why it is that of all the major Western democracies excluding Japan, and despite the presence of a strong feminist movement, it is *only* in the United States that women overall have failed to improve their wages relative to men's – remaining at 59 per cent of men's hourly wage. (Only 17 per cent of all workers are unionised in North America.)[148]

By all standard indicators, the status of women in Swedish society is higher than in any other advanced industrial country – excluding Denmark.[149] On 1981 figures women earned on average 87 per cent of men's pay (compared to 69 per cent in Britain or 59 per cent in North America.)[150] Both childcare facilities and parental leave are the most generous anywhere.[151] And, as in other Scandinavian countries, women's representation in parliament is the highest in the world. Women occupy 28 per cent of parliamentary seats, compared to 4 per cent in Britain in the 1980s and 5 per cent in the United States.[152] Again, in common with its Scandinavian neighbours, abortion is available to women on request, and in Sweden maternal mortality rates are the lowest in the world – less than 1 per 100,000 live births compared to ten times that in Britain.[153] The Swedish Marriage Act of 1987 contains clauses specifying that housework and childcare must be shared equally by spouses.[154] Experiments in collectively shared municipal housing schemes have also proved popular, with long waiting lists for buildings which provide separate flats, but shared services, common rooms, day-care centres and restaurants.[155] That ideological change has accompanied material change would seem indicated by a United Nations survey of changing gender ideals which found both men and women in Sweden expressing the lowest support for traditional gender roles, 14 per cent, compared to 26 per cent in Britain and 33 per cent in North America.[156] Dissatisfied by the sexual inequalities which do persist – in particular, men's domination of the state and labour movement hierarchies – the Swedish government set up a Working Party on The Role of the Man to further explore the obstacles to change in 1985, urging more commitment from government agencies, employers and trade unions to programmes of training in equality of opportunity directed towards men.[157]

Such shifts as have occurred in gender roles in Sweden, however, remain severely limited by the continuing constraints of a capitalist economy and labour market which provide little scope for change in lifestyles, particularly for its sex-segregated manual workers. They remain limited, as well, by the individualistic culture of Western capitalism which, whatever the benefits of a progressive social policy, still puts great pressure on individuals to compete and succeed, which inevitably downgrades the work of care and nurturing, and creates little sense of community or commitment to others beyond individual families. And they remain limited, of course, by most men's continuing commitment to, and experience of, at least some of the dominant images and discourses of 'masculinity'. For men are still addressed as the central and superior sex: 'responsible' for the welfare of women and children, 'entitled' to sexual and emotional servicing from women. In Sweden, as elsewhere, there remains a neat fit between success in capitalist cultures and the type of single-mindedness, competitiveness and ambition which is still fostered and celebrated at the heart of dominant competitive masculinities in the West (or attacked and derided by feminists and anti-sexist men). The openness, sensitivity and capacity to give – and keep on giving – integral to successful caring in the home, remains completely at odds with the focused instrumentality required for most types of successful working lives. For women combining the two worlds of home and career, or for those men who do decide to join women in the balancing of the two, there inevitably remains tension and conflict. Yet we would be wrong to conclude that social reforms designed, as in Sweden, to promote women's interests, are futile.

In line with the pervading pessimism over sexual politics today, it is commonplace to read that men in Sweden have simply failed to make use of the paternity provisions available to them, that women continue to do the bulk of childcare and housework. The formal commitments of political parties and the labour movement are thus dismissed as useless.[158] Such dismissal, however, reflects more a commitment to cynicism than an interest in exploring where and in what circumstances change does occur. For the first six months after the birth of a child it is true that only 6 per cent of fathers in Sweden assume primary childcare, and only one in five assumes such responsibility in the first year of the child's life.[159] (For them to do so would mean adopting a strategy of role reversal, with the mother returning to work.) However, nearly half of all fathers do take time off work to look after a sick child in the 1–12 year old bracket. As Karin Sandqvist argues: 'Clearly, at workplaces all over Sweden, the idea of a father's responsibilities to his child taking precedence over his responsibilities at work is becoming commonplace.'[160] Commenting on these figures Sandqvist points out that there are clear differences in the *social* positions of fathers who assume childcare responsibilities and those who don't. The husbands of professional women are far more likely to take parental leave in the first year (in the highest income group of women, 50 per cent of fathers took such leave).[161] Men employed in the state sector, where more women work, were nearly twice as likely to take parental leave as men in the private sector, in more sexually segregated workplaces.[162] There were thus clear class and occupational differences in the likelihood of parental role reversal. Blue-collar workers, in less secure job situations to begin with, are far less likely, far less able, to use their entitlement to paternal leave.

What we are again witnessing here, as we saw in chapter two, is not some intractable aspect of male psychology at work, so much as its interaction with other social factors. Studies suggest that most men in Sweden are now sharing the tasks of caring for non-infant children about equally.[163] But while men are doing more housework, women still continue to assume overall responsibility for routine tasks. The influence of women around a man – wife, workmates, and even his mother – Sandqvist concludes, is also crucial to change in men. Men's commitment to equality, and their actual sharing of personal and public life with women is, whatever its limitations, affected by the possibilities afforded by a combination of welfare provision, trade union struggles, and educational and social strategies devoted to encouraging these goals, as well as the needs and demands issuing from women and men's own interest in change.

It is in North America, after a decade of new right Republicanism and half a century of crippled trade unionism, that we find the starkest contrast between what feminists have fought for – and what many women have come to expect – and the overall political and economic dominance of men over women. And it is in the dominant strand of North American feminism – in the voices of Andrea Dworkin, Mary Daly and others (successfully drowning out the voices of their protesting socialist feminist sisters – Barbara Ehrenreich, Linda Gordon and so many others – at home and abroad), that we hear the most consistently cynical attitudes towards the possibility of change in men.[164]

Fortunately, as I have remarked above, North America is not the world. Alarmingly, however, our own Conservative government has sought throughout the 1980s to reconstruct Britain in its image. Faced with the success of Thatcher, many feminists joined the Labour Party at a time when it seemed to become more open and democratic in the early 1980s. But, at its national level, the British Labour Party has proved more resistant to feminism (and socialism) than virtually any other European socialist party. As Sarah Perrigo has argued, apart from the acceptance of one woman on short lists of candidates at its 1988 Conference, there has been no institutional reform to increase the representation of women within the Labour Party at national level.[165] Nor, despite the commitment to what has proved a marginalised Ministry for Women, has there been any serious attempt to strengthen women's voice in policy debate. The dramatic shift to the right in British politics generally, a consequence of ten years of Thatcherism, has produced an increasingly conservative Labour leadership which suppresses, where it does not simply ignore, criticism from within.

Such influence as feminists have had within the British Labour Party, in undermining its rigidly male-dominated, male-centred character and perspectives, has been largely confined to local government, where women have always played a more active role. It was here, building on the pioneering work of the Greater London

Council (GLC) before its abolition, that some socialist feminists made a determined effort in the 1980s, in the words of Di Parkin and Irene Breugel, 'to make the local state work for women'.[166] Establishing Women's Committees to work out priorities for women, improving the pay and prospects of the lowest paid women council staff, vetting local firms used by the Council for equal opportunities practices ('contract compliance'), feminists in local government have challenged some of the practices, as well as the language and style, of bureaucratic rituals traditionally prioritising men's interests over women's – whether as council workers, or as users of council services. This has helped open up many traditionally male jobs to women – in plumbing, bus driving and even, in places, that bastion of male preserve, firefighting – and it has led to a regrading of many manual jobs stressing the skills involved in, for example, the work of home helps, with a concomitant increase in pay and status. (It has also meant some of the cushier 'male' manual jobs, like that of dustmen, becoming relatively less privileged.) Women in local government have tackled some of women's previously unacknowledged needs – whether for improved safety in the streets, training schemes with childcare available, or more sensitive services around child sexual abuse.[167]

Women's Committees, however, have also highlighted some of the contradictions involved in notions of 'women's issues' and 'women's demands'. There are no universal issues equally pressing for all women. Equal opportunities victories, as Ruth Elliot comments, can evaporate in the face of privatisation and cuts. The weakening of statutory employment rights, like the abolition of the Fair Wages Resolution (in 1983) and the abolition of extra payment for weekend-working and unsocial hours (in 1986), are the methods the Tory government has used to further the production of a new marginal and 'flexible' workforce, in which traditionally low-paid women (and some men) are experiencing further deterioration in their working lives.[168] Kathryn Harriss draws on her experience with local government to suggest that the process of addressing *sectional* interests, whether of gender or race, can obscure overriding class interests: 'This suggests to me,' she concludes, 'that if feminists are looking to engage in local government from the inside, the most fruitful areas for intervention will be those in which class issues *can* be confronted – for example, in planning units which assist unions to resist privatisation, or in contract compliance to influence employers' terms and conditions.'[169]

Whatever the increasing limitations and contradictions for feminists working in local government, there is no doubt that it did temporarily act as a beacon of hope for many feminists in Britain wishing to prioritise women's interests and introduce sexual politics into mainstream political agendas. However, the remorseless Tory attack which has systematically removed the sources of funding for local government – precisely because it was offering an alternative vision – has undermined not only the welfare services, childcare and other care schemes which councils have fought to provide, but much of the radical creativity and energy which had begun to flourish around local government in the mid-eighties. Meanwhile, the introduction of 'sexual politics' – by which I mean issues of sexual harassment, rape, male violence, lesbian and gay rights, and indeed all aspects of how we see ourselves and relate to each other as women and men – had frightened many Labour politicians, as well as their Tory opponents. It was precisely the emphasis on challenging traditional sex and race hierarchies and, in particular, addressing issues of personal life and sexuality, which provoked such widespread anger from the more traditional labour movement, dismissing these new perspectives as those of a London-led 'loony left'.

Sounding indistinguishable from old-style Labour rightists like Denis Healey, old-style Labour Militants like Derek Hatton jeered and scoffed at any whiff of the new feminist, anti-racist or gay politics in the Labour Party: 'Gay liberation, chairperson as opposed to chairmen, and token Black mayors won't be the things which win us support from workers be they Black or white.'[170] The Labour leadership is also manifestly frightened of any mention of sexual politics, any questioning of sexuality and 'the family', in the name of recognition of sexual diversity and choice – though it is more willing to discuss the problem of working mothers and the need for childcare and other caring services. The new sexual anxieties surrounding AIDS have also hardened old fears and taboos. Determinedly promoting the traditional 'family image' through the paternalistic stance of Neil Kinnock, the Labour leadership today is endorsing rather than challenging the anti-permissive, pro-family rhetoric of the right, especially in the run-up to elections: 'I am a father and no matter how far I try to convince myself toward the course of "enlightenment" I know damn well that, put to the test, I'm what people would call a reactionary,' Kinnock boasted in 1986 (admittedly, in the context of drug-taking).[171] The right has been able to exploit homophobia and traditional family sentiment to attack progressive Labour councils and savage Labour generally. Indeed, they have succeeded in frightening the more reflective Labour voice, as political journalists like John Lloyd pronounced feminism and sexual politics too hot to handle.[172]

It is true that campaigning against the ingrained sexual moralism of nuclear family sentiment cannot be undertaken without careful thought about its threatening potential for those with indentities invested in their bread-winning powers or mothering responsibilities. Whatever our recognition of the intolerant and prejudiced exclusion of so many who live beyond traditional family borders, or the suffering of battered women or abused children within them, we cannot speak of sexuality and family life without awareness of the anxieties we thereby unleash. But whether we like it or not, sexual politics is already at the centre of the political agenda. The right resorts to a traditional family rhetoric to justify its cutbacks in welfare – dishonestly pretending that the full-time housewife, adequately supported by her husband, is around to look after 'granny' or any other family dependents. (It thereby ensures, of course, enormous strain on most families which are attempting to look after elderly, disabled or other dependent relatives.) The right relies upon an authoritarian and repressive morality of guilt and blame to back the punitive individualism it supports, which would hold people responsible for their own ill fortune in a brave new world of private affluence and public squalor. It thereby ensures incessant competition, anxiety and fear of failure even in most of those who see themselves as 'winners'.

But there is reason to believe that even in this blighted political environment, as we witness the relentless rise of poverty, inequality, greed and fear, a new moral agenda *could* be proposed. It would be one which connects with peoples' deepest fears, anxieties and ambivalences, while also tackling questions of personal diversity, choice, freedom and desire. On the threshold of the twenty-first century, could we not be working to promote a thorough-going egalitarian vision of a world free from all fear? It is not so hard to imagine a world free from the fear of too little work for men, and all too much work for women. Nor is it hard to describe a world free from the racial violence and discrimination which today damages or quite literally destroys women and men. It is just as easy to envisage a world free from fears of the interpersonal violence, rape, and child sex abuse which, in their most dangerous and prevalent forms, are the violent acts of men who abuse what power they have over women and children. It would be a world where people were free to work and free to love and find pleasure with the maximum amount of choice and minimum amount of compulsion, constrained only by the growth of real responsibility and mutual co-operation and care.

Such a world comes into focus only once we can cast off the shackles of gender polarities. We will always live our lives as women and men with our distinctive sexual and reproductive capacities and differences. But as many feminists believe, these differences do not necessarily create the sexual contrasts we have come to expect, and many feel they must demand, in themselves and others (a situation where sexual pleasure can be tolerated only to the extent that it confirms such gendered oppositions). For it is only in a world free from gender hierarchy, where women and men alike participate routinely in the spheres of the home and 'work', that we will finally see an end to the oppressiveness of 'masculinities' as we have known them. For that oppressiveness is precisely men's wretched fear of not being male-enough, which is identical with their fear of 'femininity' – and hence of weakness, dependence, intimacy and closeness. At a personal level, most of the crimes of men against women – and other men – are an aspect of men's deep fear of, and hence hostility towards, femininity, in societies which tolerate or excuse many forms of male violence.

We already possess, it seems to me, an outline of the moral and political agenda which could take us nearer to a society free from fear. It can be found clearly stated in the goals of socialist feminism. What socialist feminists have repeatedly sought are ways of building a public world of employment and politics more closely connected with the world of caring, sharing and co-operation ideally characterising family life. Socialist feminists have always stressed that a society which could genuinely meet the needs of all, and in particular the needs of those it now serves so badly – of carers and their dependents – would be one where the barriers between the private and the public were more easily traversed than they are today. Towards this end they have emphasised the importance of shorter working hours, adequate incomes for all to provide economic independence for women as well as men, publically funded and democratically run welfare provision, men and women sharing active working lives with adequate time to meet whatever might be the differing demands of their personal lives. Such solutions, as Elizabeth Wilson comments, are utopian, because they are based on 'a vision of a cooperative and egalitarian order'.[173] And yet, she rightly adds, 'However utopian they now sound, these still seem to me the only solutions'.[174] I agree.

If we study the lives of those men who have changed (once we accept that, notwithstanding the weary feminist and triumphant anti-feminist chorus, some men have changed), or the lives of those women who now feel that they are closer to having 'the best of both worlds' (mothers with rewarding careers), we see people who have been able to obtain for themselves the conditions which socialist feminists sought for all. The men most likely to be happily parenting together with women (and who have a material interest in fighting for shorter working hours and improved state welfare provision) are professional men with professional wives – like those described in Diane Ehrensaft's study.[175] Here both the men and the women have genuine flexibility in their working lives, the support of additional privately funded childcare in the absence of public provision, as well as an ideological commitment to transcend existing gender divisions.[176] Such couples, where women and men share equally, though a minority, are not a utopian fantasy; they do exist. When it occurs the arrangement is very often taken for granted by both partners. Jennifer Uglow, a publisher with four children married to a law lecturer, for example, simply comments that their equal sharing of childcare is based upon what time each of them has rather than on any allotted tasks, adding that her husband is 'far more domesticated' than her, and 'I'm invariably in London when someone has to be rushed to hospital.'[77] However, men sharing caring and pursuing careers, and, even more, women in this situation, still describe the tensions of moving between what seem like two worlds. 'A working mother', Jean Radford, who lectures in literary studies, comments: 'I live not in the peaceful garden of my imaginings, but between two worlds, symbolically divided: the world of work which I experience as a man's world, where children are rarely mentioned: and the world of home, full of nappies, noise and perpetual mealtimes.'[78]

The best of both worlds is only rarely possible for women. Although some men have embraced such opportunities as they have for entering the traditional female domain, others remain as fearful and contemptuous of it as their fathers before them. Yet, with women today permanently entrenched in the Western workforce, the absurdity of the traditional gendered divide between public and private is daily more apparent. Men could continue to strive to maintain their privileges and dominance in both spheres. But it is likely they will increasingly be battling all the way. More justly and more creatively, they could join women in fighting for an end to the exploitation of women at work and at home. If they do, of course, it will spell the end of masculinity as we have known it.

Notes

Preface

1. Virginia Woolf, (1977), *A Room of One's Own*, p.28, London, Granada.
2. Peter Schwenger, (1989), 'The Masculine Mode', in Elaine Showalter (ed.), *Speaking of Gender*, p.110, London, Routledge.
3. Deirdre English, (1980), 'The Politics of Porn', *Mother Jones*, San Francisco, Mother Jones Reprint.

1. *Look Back in Anger: Men in the Fifties*

1. Fay Weldon, (1971), *Down Among the Women*, p.106, Harmondsworth, Penguin.
2. Walter Allen, (1960), Review of *Lucky Jim*, (first published 1954), reprinted in G. Feldman and M. Gartenberg (eds.), *Protest*, p.286, London, Panther.
3. Kenneth Allsop, (1964), *The Angry Decade*, p.203, London, Peter Owen.
4. Storm Jameson in Allsop, ibid, p.201.
5. Jean McCrindle, (1987), 'The Left as Social Movement' talk given at *Out of Apathy Conference*, on 30 years of the British New Left, organised by Oxford University Socialist Discussion Group. 14th November.
6. Quoted in Denise Riley, (1983), *War in the Nursery*, p.193, London, Virago.
7. Michael Young and Peter Willmott, (1962), *Family and Kinship in East London*, p.30, Harmondsworth, Penguin.
8. John and Elizabeth Newson, (1963), *Patterns of Infant Care in an Urban Community*, p.145, London, Allen & Unwin.
9. Anthony Sampson, (1962), *Anatomy of Britain*, p.73, London, Hodder & Stoughton.
10. Peter Biskind, (1983), *Seeing is Believing*, p.252, New York, Pantheon Books.
11. Elizabeth Wilson, (1980), *Only Halfway to Paradise: Women in Postwar Britain 1945–68*, p.69, London, Tavistock.
12. Colin Willock, (1958), *The Man's Book*, London, Edward Hulton.
13. Geoffrey Gorer, (1955), *Exploring English Character*, p.153, London, Nelson.
14. ibid, p.66.
15. Richard Hoggart, (1957), *The Uses of Literacy*, p.49, Harmondsworth, Penguin.
16. ibid, p.50.
17. Young and Willmott, op.cit., p.24.
18. ibid, p.27.
19. ibid, p.145.
20. ibid, p.150.

21. ibid.

22. ibid, p.132–3.

23. N. Dennis, F. Henriques and C. Slaughter, (1969), 'Introduction to the Second edition', in *Coal is Our Life*, p.8, London, Tavistock.

24. ibid, p.183.

25. ibid.

26. Elizabeth Bott, (1957), *Family and Social Network*, London, Tavistock.

27. Olivia Harris, (1984), 'Heavenly Father' in Ursula Owen (ed.) *Fathers*, p.61.

28. Sheila Rowbotham, 'Our Lance' in Owen, ibid, p.209.

29. Quoted in Jonathan Rutherford, (unpub.) 'Dads can do it'.

30. ibid.

31. ibid.

32. Sara Maitland, 'Two For the Price of One', in Owen op.cit., p.35.

33. Allsop, op.cit., p.204.

34. Judith Hubback, (1957), *Wives Who Went to College*, p.75, London, Heinemann.

35. Alva Myrdal and Viola Klein, (1956), *Women's Two Roles*, London, Routledge & Kegan Paul.

36. Denise Riley, (1983), *War in the Nursery*, London, Virago.

37. John Bowlby, (1953), *Childcare and the Growth of Love*, Harmondsworth, Penguin.

38. Peter Lewis, (1978), *The Fifties*, p.45, London, Heinemann.

39. in Riley, ibid., p.88.

40. Peter Rabe, (1955), *From Here to Maternity*, London, Frederick Muller.

41. Jane Hope, (1957), *Happy Event*, London, Frederick Muller.

42. Betty Thorne, (1987), 'Life in Our Street (1960)' in Mary Stott (ed.), *Women Talking – An Anthology from The Guardian's Women's Page*, p.85, London, Pandora.

43. 'J.B.H.' 'Bored Mum and "Talkback"', (1959) in Stott ibid., pp.240–1.

44. ibid.

45. J.D. Salinger, (1951), *The Catcher in the Rye*, Harmondsworth, Penguin.

46. Alan Sillitoe, (1961), 'What Comes on Monday' in *New Left Review*, 4, July/August, p.59.

47. Alan Sillitoe, (1960), *Saturday Night and Sunday Morning*, p.36, London, Pan.

48. ibid, p.65.

49. ibid, p.126.

50. Nigel Grey, (1974), *The Silent Majority – A Study of the Working Class in Post-War British Fiction*, p.129, London, Vision Critical Studies.

51. Alan Sinfield (ed.), (1983), *Society and Literature 1945–1970*, p.2.

52. Quoted in ibid, p.4.

53. David Lodge, (1982), Afterword to *Ginger You're Barmy*, pp.215–16, Harmondsworth, Penguin.

54. John Osborne, 'Sex and Failure', in G. Feldman and M. Gartenberg (eds.), op.cit.

55. Quoted in Sinfield, op.cit. p.27.

56. ibid.

57. Colin MacInnes, (1959), *Absolute Beginners*, London, MacGibbon & Kee.

58. Quoted in Sinfield, op.cit., p.177.

59. Hoggart, op.cit., p.246.

60. Geoffrey Gorer, 'The Perils of Hypergamy', in G. Feldman and M. Gartenberg, op.cit., p.315.

61. In Sinfield, op.cit., p.26.

62. Eve Kosofsky Sedgwick, (1985), *Between Men: English Literature and Male Homosexual Desire*, New York, Columbia University Press.

63. Craig Owens, (1987), 'Outlaws: Gay Men in Feminism' in A. Jardine and P. Smith (eds.), *Men in Feminism*, p.221, London, Methuen.

64. B. Seebohm Rowntree and G.R. Lavers, (1951), *English Life and Leisure*, p.212, London, Longmans.

65. ibid, p.215.

66. See Jonathan Dollimore, 'The Challenge of Sexuality', in Sinfield op.cit., p.52.

67. See Tony Gould, (1983), *Inside Outsider – The Life and Times of Colin MacInnes*, p.64, London, Chatto & Windus.

68. ibid, p.99.

69. Quentin Crisp, (1968), *The Naked Civil Servant*, London, Jonathan Cape.

70. Quoted in Dollimore, op.cit., p.74.

71. James Baldwin, (1963), *Another Country*, London, Michael Joseph; (1957) *Giovanni's Room*, London, Michael Joseph.

72. In Gould, op.cit., p.89.

73. Trevor Royle, (1986), *The Best Years of Their Lives*, p.XIII, London, Michael Joseph.

74. B.S. Johnson, (1973), *All Bull*, London, Quartet; see also Lodge, op.cit. and Sillitoe, (1960), op.cit.

75. Colin MacInnes, (1966), 'Pacific Warriors', in *New Society*, 30 June.

76. Royle, op.cit., p.116.

77. Ray Gosling, (1960), 'Dream Boy', *New Left Review*, May/June, 3, p.31.

78. David Morgan, (1987), 'It Will Make a Man of You: Notes on National Service, Masculinity and Autobiography', *Studies in Sexual Politics*, no. 17, University of Manchester, p.48.

79. ibid, p.82.

80. Ken Walpole, (1983), *Dockers and Detectives*, London, Verso.

81. ibid, p.62.

82. Helen Hacker, (1957), 'The New Burdens of Masculinity' in *Marriage and Family Living*, 19, p.229.

83. Willock, op.cit., p.viii.

84. ibid, pp.352–354.

85. In Lewis, op.cit., p.63.

86. Quoted in Jean McCrindle, (1982), 'Reading *The Golden Notebook* in 1962' in J. Taylor (ed.), *Notebooks/Memoirs/Archives: Reading and Rereading Doris Lessing*, p.49, London, Routledge & Kegan Paul.

87. Doris Lessing, (1972), *The Golden Notebook*, p.395, St Albans, Panther.

88. Quoted in Jean McCrindle, op.cit., p.53.

89. ibid, p.50.

90. ibid, p.51.

91. Margaret Drabble, (1963), *A Summer Bird-Cage*, p.29, Harmondsworth, Penguin.

92. David Cooper, (1964), 'Sartre on Genet', *New Left Review*, 25 May/June, p.71.

93. Stuart Hall, (1987), Introductory talk at *Out of Apathy Conference*, op.cit.

94. Raphael Samuel, (1987), 'Class and Classlessness' talk given at *Out of Apathy Conference*, op.cit.

95. Jean McCrindle, (1982), op.cit., p.55.

96. ibid.

97. ibid.

98. ibid, p.53.

2. *The Good Father: Reconstructing Fatherhood*

1. Angela Carter, (1983), 'Sugar Daddy', in Ursula Owen (ed.), *Fathers: Reflections by Daughters*, p.25, London, Virago.

2. Eileen Fairweather, (1983), 'The Man in the Orange Box', in Owen, ibid, p.194.

3. Simone de Beauvoir, Quoted in Owen, ibid, p.31.

4. Sheila Rowbotham, (1983), 'Our Lance' in Owen, ibid, p.212.

5. ibid, p.219.

6. Margot Farnham, (1986), 'In the Name of the Father – Fathers and Class', *Trouble and Strife*, no. 8, p.6.

7. ibid, p.9.

8. See, for example, Toni Morrison, (1979), *The Bluest Eye*, London, Grafton; Alice Walker, (1970), *The Third Life of Grange Copeland*, London, Women's Press, or *The Colour Purple*, (1982), London, Women's Press and Joan Riley, (1985), *The Unbelonging*, London, Women's Press.

9. Quoted in Elaine Showalter, (1987), 'Critical Cross-Dressing' in Alice Jardine and Paul Smith (eds.), *Men in Feminism*, p.122, London, Methuen.

10. ibid.

11. Judith Williamson, (1987), *New Statesman*, 3 October, p.12.

12. Reported in Brian Jackson, (1983), *Fatherhood*, p.9, London, Allen & Unwin.

13. ibid.

14. Ian McEwan, (1987), *The Child in Time*, p.216, London, Jonathan Cape.

15. Yvonne Roberts, (1984), *Man Enough: Men of 35 Speak Out*, p.111, London, Chatto & Windus.

16. ibid, pp.124–5.

17. Peter Moss and Julia Brannen, (1987), 'Fathers and Employment' in Charlie Lewis and Margaret O'Brien (eds.), *Reassessing Fatherhood*, p.87, London, Sage.

18. Madeleine Simms and Christopher Smith, (1982), 'Young Fathers: Attitudes to Marriage and Family Life', in Lorna McKee and Margaret O'Brien, *The Father Figure*, London, Tavistock.

19. McKee, (1982), 'Fathers' Participation in Infant Care: A Critique' in ibid.

20. Graeme Russell, (1987), 'Problems in Role-Reversed Families', in *Reassessing Fatherhood*, op.cit., p.176.

21. Melanie Henwood, Lesley Rimmer and Malcolm Wicks, (1987), *Inside the Family: Changing Roles of Men and Women*, p.7, London, Family Policy Studies Centre.

22. Fraser Harrison, (1985), *A Father's Diary*, London, Fontana.

23. Lou Becker, (1987), 'An Older Father's Letter to His Young Son' in Franklin Abbot (ed.), *New Men, New Minds*, pp.32–3, Canada, The Crossing Press/Freedom.

24. Quoted in Diane Ehrensaft, (1987), *Parenting Together: Men and Women Sharing the Parenting of Their Children*, p.252, New York, The Free Press.

25. Quoted in Henwood, Rimmer and Wicks, op.cit., p.20.

26. See, for example, Tony Eardley, Martin Humphries and Paul Morrison, (1983), *About Men*, London, Broadcasting Support Services.

27. in Yvonne Roberts, op.cit., p.266.

28. Tony Bradman, (1985), *The Essential Father*, London, Unwin Paperbacks and Peter Moss, (1981), Quoted in Anne Wiltsher, (1981), 'Fatherhood' *The Guardian*, March 6, p.21.

29. Bradman, ibid, pp.37–8.

30. ibid, p.261.

31. Quoted Ehrensaft, op.cit., p.251

32. See, for example, Sue Sharpe, (1985), *Double Identity*, Harmondsworth, Penguin, for the importance of paid work in the lives of women with children.

33. W. Miller, (1958), 'Lower-Class Culture as a Generating Milieu for Gang Delinquency' in *Journal of Social Issues*, vol. 14, pp.5–19; Thomas Pettigrew, (1964), *A Profile of the Negro American*, New Jersey: Van Notrand; J. Silverman and S. Dinitz, (1974), 'Compulsive Masculinity and Delinquency', in *Criminology*, pp.499–515.

34. H.R. Schaffer and P. Emerson, (1964), *The Development of Social Attachment in Infancy*, Monograph No.29. Society for Research in Child Development; Charlie Lewis, (1982), 'The Observation of Father-Infant Relationships: An "Attachment" to Outmoded Concepts' in *The Father Figure*, op.cit.

35. Lewis, ibid; Ross Parke, (1981), *Fathering*, London, Fontana Paperbacks.

36. Lewis, ibid.

37. Quoted in *Reassessing Fatherhood*, op.cit. p.3, and Polly Toynbee, (1987), 'The Incredible Shrinking New Man', *The Guardian*, April 6, p.10.

38. Charlie Lewis, (1986), *Becoming a Father*, Milton Keynes, Open University Press; Kathryn Backett, (1982), *Mothers and Fathers*, London, Macmillan.

39. In Bradman, op.cit., p.166.

40. In *Inside the Family*, op.cit., p.12.

41. ibid, p.25.

42. Bradman, op.cit., pp.223–4.

43. Lorna McKee and Colin Bell, (1986), 'His Unemployment, Her Problem', in Sheila Allen, et al., *The Experience of Unemployment*, London, Macmillan.

44. Lorna McKee, (1987), 'Fathers', *The Guardian*, 19 January, p.12.

45. Colin Bell, et al., (1983), *Fathers, Childbirth and Work*, Manchester, Equal Opportunities Commission.

46. Polly Toynbee, (1987), op.cit.

47. ibid.

48. ibid.

49. Peter Moss and Julia Brannen, in *Reassessing Fatherhood*, op.cit., p.40.

50. ibid.

51. Lorna McKee in *The Father Figure*, op.cit., p.124.

52. ibid.

53. ibid.

54. Rhona Rapoport and Robert Rapoport, (1971), *Dual-Career Families*, Harmondsworth, Penguin; Rhona Rapoport and Robert Rapoport (1976), *Dual-Career Families re-Examined*, New York, Harper & Row.

55. Caroline Bird, (1979), *The Two-Paycheck Marriage*, New York, Pocket Books; Rebecca Bryson et al., (1978), 'Family Size, Satisfaction and Productivity in Dual-Career Couples', in *Psychology of Women Quarterly*, 3: pp.167–77.

56. Rosanna Hertz, (1986), *More Equal Than Others: Women and Men in Dual-Career Marriages*, p.67, London, University of California Press.

57. ibid, p.198.

58. Bebe Moore Campbell, (1988), *Successful Women, Angry Men*, p.17, London, Arrow Books.

59. ibid.

60. Graeme Russell, (1983), *The Changing Role of Fathers*, London, University of Queensland Press.

61. 'Living Your Politics: a discussion on communal living ten years on' in *Revolutionary Socialism*, Big Flame Magazine, no.4, p.7, 1981.

62. McKee and Bell, op.cit., p.142.

63. Stephanie Dowrick and Sibyl Grundberg (eds.), (1980), *Why Children?*, London, Women's Press.

64. Peter Bradbury, (1985), 'Desire and Pregnancy', in Andy Metcalfe and Martin Humphries (eds.), *The Sexuality of Men*, London, Pluto Press.

65. Gavin Smith, (1987), 'The Crisis of Fatherhood', in *Free Associations*, no.9, p.73.

66. Jonathan Rutherford, (unpub.), 'Dads can do it'.

67. Fay Weldon, (1975), *Female Friends*, p.164, London, Pan.

68. In Graeme Russell, (1983), op.cit., p.8.

69. ibid, p.46.

70. Graeme Russell, (1987), p.120.

71. See Ehrensaft, op.cit., p.120.

72. ibid, p.126.

73. Quoted in Jonathan Trustram, (1985), 'A Co-Operative Creche', in Caroline New and Miriam David (eds.), *For the Children's Sake*, p.305, Harmondsworth, Penguin.

74. Tony Bradman, op.cit.

75. Trustram, op.cit., p.305.

76. ibid, p.289.

77. ibid, p.292.

78. Russell, (1987), op.cit., p.171.

79. ibid, p.167.

80. ibid, p.162.

81. Tony Hipgrave, (1982), 'Lone Fatherhood: A Problematic Status', in McKee and O'Brien, op.cit., p.179.

82. Russell, op.cit., p.69.

83. Quoted in *For the Children's Sake*, op.cit., p.225.

84. Russell, (1983), op.cit., p.114.

85. ibid.

86. See Ehrensaft, op.cit., pp.56–75.

87. Russell, (1987), op.cit., p.168.

88. Rochelle Wortis, (1972), 'Child-rearing and women's liberation' in Michelene Wandor (ed.), *The Body Politic: Women's Liberation in Britain 1969–1972*, pp.127–30.

89. Sheila Rowbotham, (1972), 'Women's Liberation and the New Politics' in Wandor, ibid, p.18.

90. Nancy Chodorow, (1978), *The Reproduction of Mothering*, London, University of California Press; Luise Eichenbaum and Susie Orbach, (1982), *Outside In, Inside Out*, Harmondsworth, Penguin.

91. G. Staines et al., (1978), 'Wives' Employment Status and Marital Adjustment: Yet Another Look', *Psychology of Women Quarterly*, 3: pp.90–120.

92. Michael Lamb, Joseph Pleck and James Levine, (1987), 'Effects of increased paternal involvement on fathers and mothers' in McKee and O'Brien op.cit., p.112.

93. ibid, p.122.

94. Kathryn Backett, op.cit.

95. Ehrensaft, op.cit.

96. See Lynne Segal, (1987), *Is the Future Female?*, ch.4, London, Virago; or Sheila Rowbotham, (1989), *The Past is Before Us*, London, Pandora.

97. Cynthia Cockburn, (1981), 'The Material of Male Dominance' in *Feminist Review*, no.9.

98. Lorna McKee and Margaret O'Brien, (1982), 'The father figure: Some current orientations and historical perspectives', in McKee and O'Brien op.cit., p.29.

99. Carol Smart, (1987), 'There is of course the distinction dictated by nature': Law and the Problem of Paternity' in Michele Stanworth (ed.), *Reproductive Technologies*, Cambridge, Polity Press.

100. ibid, p.111.

101. Gillian Hanscombe and Jackie Forster, (1982), *Rocking the Cradle: Lesbian Mothers*, p.69, London, Sheba Press.

102. ibid.

103. See Sheila Rowbotham, (1989), op.cit.

104. Sue Allen and Lynne Harne, (1988), 'Lesbian mothers: the fight for child custody', in Bob Cant and Susan Hemmings (eds.), *Radical Records*, p.193, London, Routledge.

105. ibid.

106. Quoted in Lynne Harne, (1984), 'Lesbian Custody and the new myth of fatherhood', in *Trouble and Strife*, no.3, p.14.

107. Judith Williamson, (1987), *New Statesman*, 12 February, p.24.

108. See, for example, Patricia Beezley Mrazek and Arnon Bentovim, (1981), 'Incest and the Dysfunctional Family System' in Mrazek and Kempe (eds.), *Sexually Abused Children and their Families*, Oxford, Pergamon Press; Arnon Bentovim et al. (eds.), (1988), *Child Sexual Abuse Within the Family*, London, Wright.

109. See David Will, (1989), 'Feminism, Child Sexual Abuse, and the Demise of Systems Mysticism', in *Context: A News Magazine of Family Therapy*, Spring, vol.19, no.1.

110. Mary McIntosh, (1988), 'Family Secrets: Child Sexual Abuse' in *The Chartist*, January.

111. Mary MacLeod and Esther Saraga, (1988), 'Challenging the Orthodoxy: Towards a Feminist Theory and Practice', in *Feminist Review*, no.28.

112. Linda Gordon, (1989), *Heroes of Their Own Lives*, London, Virago.

113. Mary McIntosh, op.cit.

114. *The Observer*, January 17, 1988, p.1; *The Guardian*, January 18, p.1.

115. Michelle Stanworth, (1987), 'The Deconstruction of Motherhood', in *Reproductive Technologies*, op.cit., p.33.

116. Jeff Hearn, (1987), *The Gender of Oppression*, p.150, Brighton, Wheatsheaf.

117. Yvonne Roberts, (1984), op.cit., p.13.

118. Anne Machung, (1989), 'Talking Career, Thinking Job: Gender Differences in Career and Family Expectations of Berkeley Seniors' in *Feminist Studies*, p.53, vol.15, no.1, Spring.

119. ibid, p.54.

3. *Shrinking the Phallus: Contemporary Research on Masculinity (I)*

1. Quoted in Elaine Showalter, (1987), 'Critical Cross-Dressing; Male Feminists and the Woman of the Year', in Alice Jardine and Paul Smith (eds.), *Men in Feminism*, p.120, London, Methuen.

2. Compare, Sigmund Freud, (1933), 'Femininity' reprinted in *Standard Edition*, vol.22, London, Hogarth Press; Jacques Lacan, quoted in Stephen Heath, (1987), 'Male Feminism' in *Men in Feminism*, p.13, London, Methuen; Freud's question appears in a letter to Marie Bonaparte as quoted in Ernest Jones, (1955), *Sigmund*

Freud: Life and Work, vol.2, p.468, London, Hogarth Press.

3. Yvette Walczak, (1988), *He and She*, p.1, London, Routledge.

4. See J.E. Gerai and A. Sheinfeld, (1968), 'Sex Differences in Mental and Behavioural Traits', *Genetic Psychological Monographs*, no.77; J. Archer, (1976), 'Biological explanations of psychological sex differences'. In B. Lloyd and J. Archer (eds.), *Exploring Sex Differences*, London, Academic Press.

5. See, for example, Naomi Weisstein, (1971), 'Psychology Constructs the Female' in Vivian Gornick and Barbara Moran (eds.), *Woman in Sexist Society*, New York, Basic Books; Judith Bardwick and Elizabeth Douvan, (1971), 'Ambivalence: The Socialization of Women', in Gornick and Moran, ibid; Michele Hoffnung Garskoff (ed.), (1971), *Roles Women Play*, California, Cole Publishing Company.

6. Walczak, op.cit. p.37. Interestingly, even in the early days of sex-difference research there were just a few women psychologists, like Jessie Taft in the US in the 1930s, who found little evidence of difference and attributed what there was mainly to social circumstances, to what she referred to as women's 'cultural marginalisation'. See R.W. Connell, (1987), *Gender and Power*, p.30, London, Polity Press.

7. Eleanor Maccoby and Carol Jacklin, (1975), *The Psychology of Sex Differences*, London, Oxford University Press.

8. For example, Corinne Hutt, (1972), *Males and Females*, Harmondsworth, Penguin; Jeffrey A. Gray and A.W.H. Buffery, (1971), 'Sex differences in emotional and cognitive behaviour including man: adaptive and neural bases', *Acta Psychologica*, 35, pp.89–111.

9. Camilla Benbow and Julian Stanley, (1980), 'Sex differences in mathematical ability: Fact or artifact?' *Science*, 210, pp.1262–4.

10. Hugh Fairweather, (1976), 'Sex differences in cognition', *Cognition*, 4, pp.231–80.

11. Janet Sayers, (1986), *Sexual Contradictions: Psychology, Psychoanalysis, and Feminism*, pp. 6–10, London, Tavistock.

12. R.W. Connell, (1987), op.cit., p.170.

13. Stephen Katz, (1988), 'Sexualization and the lateralized Brain: From Craniometry to Pornography', in *Women's Studies International Forum*, vol.11, no.1, pp.29–41.

14. See Jerre Levy, (1978), 'Lateral differences in the human brain in cognition and behavioral control' in P. Buser and A. Rougeul-Buser (eds.), *Cerebral correlates of Conscious Experience*, New York, North London Publishing.

15. Hugh Fairweather, (1982), 'Sex Differences: Little Reason for Females to Play Midfield', in J.G. Beaumont (ed.), (1985), *Divided Visual Field Studies of Cerebral Organisation*, London, Academic Press.

16. A.W.H. Buffery and Jeffrey A. Gray, (1972), 'Sex differences in the development of spatial and linguistic skills' in C. Ounstead and D.C. Taylor (eds.), *Gender Differences: Their Ontogeny and Significance*, Edinburgh, Churchill Livingstone.

17. Katz, op.cit., p.36.

18. Ruth Bleier, (1984), *Science and Gender: A critique of biology and its theories on women*, p.94, London, Pergamon Press.

19. Lynne Segal, (1987), *Is the Future Female*, p.186, London, Virago.

20. Kate Soper, (1979), Marxism, Materialism and Biology', in John Mepham and D.H. Ruben, *Issues in Marxist Philosophy*, p.73, vol.2.

21. Talcott Parsons, (1942), 'Age and Sex in the Social Structure of the United States' in *American Sociological Review*, 7, pp.604–16; T. Parsons and R.F. Bales, (1956), *Family*

Socialization and Interaction Process, London, Routledge & Kegan Paul.

22. D.H.J. Morgan, (1975), *Social Theory and the Family*, pp.43–7, London, Routledge & Kegan Paul.

23. See R.W. Connell, (1983), *Which Way Is Up? Essays on Class, Sex and Culture*, pp.189–284, London, Allen & Unwin.

24. See Parsons and Bales, op.cit.

25. Mary McIntosh, (unpub.), Notes on gender.

26. For example, W. Miller, (1958), 'Lower-Class Culture as a Generating Milieu for Gang Delinquency', in *Journal of Social Issues*, 14, pp.5–19; Thomas Pettigrew, (1964), *A Profile of the Negro American*, New Jersey, Van Nostrand.

27. A. Bandura, (1965), 'Influence of Model Reinforcement Contingencies on the Acquisition of Imitative Response' in *Journal of Personality and Social Psychology*, 1, pp.589–95; D.W. Birnbaum and W.L.Croll, (1984), 'The Etiology of Children's Stereotypes about Sex Differences in Emotionality', in *Sex Roles*, vol.10, no.9/10, pp.677–91; K. Durkin, (1985), *Television, Sex Roles and Children: A Developmental Social Psychological Account*, Milton Keynes, Open University Press.

28. See Sayers, (1986), op.cit., p.25.

29. Ann Oakley, (1972), *Sex, Gender and Society*, London, Temple Smith.

30. Robert Stoller, (1968), *Sex and Gender*, London, Hogarth Press.

31. Ann Oakley, op.cit.

32. P. Rosenkrantz et al., (1968), 'Sex role stereotypes and self-concepts in college students', *Journal of Consulting and Clinical Psychology*, vol.32, pp.287–95.

33. See A. Constantinople, (1979), 'Sex Role Acquisition: In Search of the Elephant' in *Sex Roles*, vol.5, no.2, pp.121–33.

34. Sandra Bem, (1974), 'The Measurement of Psychological Androgyny' in *Journal of Consulting and Clinical Psychology*, vol.42, no.2, pp.155–62.

35. ibid.

36. ibid.

37. Constantinople op.cit; R.W. Connell, (1987), op.cit., p.171–5.

38. Sandra Bem, (1981), 'Gender schema theory: a cognitive account of sex typing' in *Psychological Review*, 66, pp.354–64; see also Margaret Wetherell, (1986), 'Linguistic Repertoires and Literary Criticism: New Directions for a Social Psychology of Gender' in *Feminist Social Psychology*, Sue Wilkinson (ed.), Milton Keynes, Open University Press.

39. See chapter 10 for a fuller discussion of the politics of men's liberation.

40. Herb Goldberg, (1976), *The Hazards of Being Male*, New York, Nash.

41. For example, see Joseph Pleck and Jack Sawyer (eds.), (1974), *Men and Masculinity*, Englewood Cliffs, Prentice Hall.

42. ibid, p.95.

43. Joseph Pleck, (1981), *The Myth of Masculinity*, Cambridge, MA, MIT Press.

44. ibid.

45. Tim Carrigan, Bob Connell and John Lee, (1987), 'Towards a New Sociology of Masculinity' in Harry Brod (ed.), *The Making of Masculinities: The New Men's Studies*, p.78, London, Allen & Unwin.

46. ibid, p.79.

47. See R.W. Connell, (1983), op.cit., p.195.

48. Sigmund Freud, (1900), *The Interpretation of Dreams, Standard Edition of the Complete Psychological Works*, vols. 4–5, London, Hogarth; (1933), *New Introductory Lectures on Psycho-Analysis, Standard Edition*, vol. 22, London, Hogarth.

49. Sigmund Freud, (1925), 'Some Psychical Consequences of the Anatomical

Distinction Between the Sexes', *Standard Edition*, vol.21, London, Hogarth; (1931), 'Female Sexuality', *Standard Edition*, vol.21, ibid.

50. Sigmund Freud, (1905), *Three Essays on the Theory of Sexuality, Standard Edition*, vol.7, London, Hogarth.

51. Sigmund Freud, (1909), 'Analysis of a Phobia in a Five-Year-Old Boy' *Standard Edition*, vol.10, London, Hogarth; T.J. Carrigan and R.W.Connell (1984), *Freud and Masculinity*, Sydney, Macquarie University.

52. Sigmund Freud, (1905), op.cit. 145n.

53. Sigmund Freud, 'From the History of an Infantile Neurosis' in *Standard Edition*, vol.17, London, Hogarth.

54. ibid, p.118.

55. D.W. Winnicott, (1986), 'This Feminism', in *Home is Where We Start From*, Harmondsworth, Penguin.

56. ibid, p.186.

57. Sigmund Freud, (1925), op.cit.

58. Ralph Greenson, (1968), 'Dis-Identifying from Mother: Its Special Importance for the Boy' in *International Psycho-Analytic Journal*, vol.49, p.270.

59. ibid, p.271.

60. Gregorio Kohon (ed.), *The British School of Psychoanalysis: The Independent Tradition*, pp.19–23, London, Free Association Books; Stephen Frosch, (1987), *The Politics of Psychoanalysis: An Introduction to Freudian and Post-Freudian Theory*, pp.96–107, London, Macmillan.

61. Kohon, ibid, p.22.

62. Frosch, ibid, p.109.

63. Arnold Cooper, (1986), 'What Men Fear: The Facade of Castration Anxiety', in Gerald Fogel et al., *The Psychology of Men: New Psychoanalytic Perspective*, p.129, New York, Basic Books.

64. Gerald Fogel, (1986), 'Being a Man', in Fogel et al., ibid, p.6.

65. ibid, p.9.

66. John Munder Ross, (1986), 'Beyond the Phallic Illusion: Notes on Man's Heterosexuality', in ibid.

67. Ethel S. Person, (1986), 'The Omni-Available Woman and Lesbian Sex', ibid, p.84.

68. ibid.

69. Personal communication from several Kleinian therapists.

70. Jane Temperley, (1984), 'Our Own Worst Enemies: Unconscious Factors in Female Disadvantage' in *Free Associations*, (Pilot Issue), p.29.

71. ibid.

72. Joyce McDougall, (1986), *Theatres of the Mind: Illusion and Truth on the Psychoanalytic Stage*, p.xi, London, Free Association Books.

73. Joel Kovel, (1981), *The Age of Desire: Case Histories of a Radical Psychoanalyst*, p.17, New York, Basic Books.

74. George Stade, (1986), 'Dracula's Women, and Why Men Love to Hate Them' in Fogel, op.cit., p.25.

75. Ross, op.cit., p.50.

76. ibid.

77. Dorothy Dinnerstein, (1978), *The Rocking of the Cradle*, p.102, London, Souvenir Press.

78. Nancy Chodorow, (1978), *The Reproduction of Mothering: Psychoanalysis and the Sociology of Gender*, London, University of California Press.

79. ibid, p.181.

80. ibid.

81. Nancy Chodorow, (1980), 'Gender, Relation, and Difference in Psychoanalytic Perspective', in Hester Eisenstein and Alice Jardine (eds.), *The Future of Difference*, p.14, Boston, MA, G.K. Hall & Co.

82. Chodorow, (1978), op.cit., p.218.

83. Andy Metcalfe and Martin Humphries (eds.), (1985), *The Sexuality of Men*, pp.13–14, London, Pluto Press.

84. Vic Siedler, 'Fear and Intimacy', in ibid, p.157.

85. Tom Ryan, 'Roots of Masculinity', in ibid, p.27.

86. Peter Bradbury, 'Desire and Pregnancy', in ibid, p.149.

87. Chodorow, (1978), op.cit. p.218; Luise Eichenbaum and Susie Orbach, (1984), *What Do Women Want?*, p.193, London, Fontana.

88. Lynne Segal, (1987), *Is the Future Female?*, pp.156–61, London, Virago.

89. ibid, p.144.

90. Jessica Benjamin, (1986), 'A Desire of One's Own: Psychoanalytic Feminism and Intersubjective Space' in Teresa de Lauretis (ed.), *Feminist Studies: Critical Studies*, p.81, Bloomington, Indiana University Press.

4. Asserting Phallic Mastery: Contemporary Research on Masculinity (II)

1. Richard Dyer, (1982), 'Don't Look Now – The Male Pin-Up' in *Screen*, vol.23, no.3–4, Sept/Oct, p.71.

2. Sherry Turkle, (1979), *Psychoanalytic Politics: Freud's French Revolution*, p.98, and pp.106–8, London, Andre Deutsch.

3. Jane Gallop, (1982), *Feminism and Psychoanalysis: The Daughter's Seduction*, p.18, London, Macmillan.

4. Juliet Mitchell, (1974), *Psychoanalysis and Feminism*, p.96, London, Allen Lane.

5. See Jacqueline Rose, (1982), 'Introduction 11' in Juliet Mitchell and Jacqueline Rose (eds.), *Feminine Sexuality: Jacques Lacan and the Ecole Freudienne*, p.41, London, Macmillan.

6. Jacques Lacan, (1977), *Ecrits: A Selection*, p.67, London, Tavistock.

7. Jacques Lacan, (1982), [Paper presented 1958] 'The Meaning of the Phallus', in Mitchell and Rose, op.cit., p.82.

8. Quoted in David Macey, (1988), *Lacan in Context*, p.137, London, Verso.

9. ibid, p.175.

10. Mitchell and Rose, op.cit. p.84; Stephen Heath, 'Male Feminism', in Alice Jardine and Paul Smith (eds.), *Men in Feminism*, p.8, London, Methuen.

11. Mandy Merck, (1987), 'Difference and Its Discontents', in 'Deconstructing Difference', *Screen*, vol.28, no.1, Winter, p.3.

12. Bice Benvenuto and Roger Kennedy, *The Works of Jacques Lacan: An Introduction*, p.186, London, Free Association Books.

13. Jacques Lacan, (1982), [First published as Seminar XX in *Encore*, lectures given 1972–3], 'God and the *Jouissance* of Woman. A Love Letter', in Mitchell and Rose op.cit., pp.137–60.

14. See Mitchell and Rose, ibid, p.30.

15. Lacan, (1977), op.cit., p.61.

16. Benvenuto and Kennedy, op.cit., p.61.

17. See Colin MacCabe, (1978), *James Joyce and the Revolution of the Word*, pp.49–50, and pp.108–9, London, Macmillan.

18. Mitchell and Rose, op.cit., p.44.

19. Lacan quoted in David Macey, (1978), 'Review Article: Jacques Lacan' in *Ideology & Consciousness*, no.4, p.126.

20. Mitchell and Rose, op.cit., p.45.

21. Richard Dyer, op.cit.

22. Margaret Walters, (1979), *The Male Nude*, Harmondsworth, Penguin.

23. Dyer, op.cit., p.67.

24. ibid, p.72.

25. Francoise Gadet, (1989), *Saussure and Contemporary Culture*, p.136, London, Hutchinson Radius. See also Macey, (1988), op.cit. pp.121–77; John Bird (1982) 'Jacques Lacan – The French Freud', in *Radical Philosophy*, no.30, Spring.

26. Peter Dews, (1987), *Logics of Disintegration: Post Structuralism and the Claims of Critical Theory*, ch.2, London, Verso.

27. ibid.

28. See Macey, (1988), p.200.

29. Dews, op.cit., p.106.

30. Quoted in Dews, p.106.

31. ibid.

32. See Deborah Cameron, (1985), *Feminism & Linguistic Theory*, pp.122–9, London, Macmillan.

33. Lynne Segal, (1987), op.cit., pp.132–4.

34. Luce Irigaray, (1985), *The Sex Which Is Not One*, p.28, New York, Cornell University.

35. Mary McIntosh, (unpub.), 'The Concept of Gender'.

36. Margaret Wetherell, (1986), 'Linguistic Repertoires and Literary Criticism: New Directions for a Social Psychology of Gender', in Sue Wilkinson (ed.), *Feminist Social Psychology*, Milton Keynes, Open University Press; Valerie Walkerdine, (1988), *The Mastery of Reason*, London, Methuen.

37. Wendy Hollway, (1984), 'Gender Difference and the Production of Subjectivity' in Julian Henriques et al., *Changing the Subject: Psychology, Social Regulation and Subjectivity*, ch.10, London, Methuen.

38. ibid.

39. Parveen Adams, (1979), 'A Note on Sexual Division and Sexual Differences', in *m/f*, no.3, p.52.

40. Andrew Tolson, (1977), *The Limits of Masculinity*, London, Tavistock.

41. ibid, p.25.

42. Paul Willis, (1977), *Learning to Labour*, p.159, Farnborough, Saxon House.

43. R.W. Connell, (1987), *Gender and Power*, Cambridge, Polity Press.

44. ibid, pp.99–107.

45. For example, Sheila Rowbotham, (1973), *Women's Consciousness, Man's World*, Harmondsworth, Penguin.

46. Connell, op.cit. pp.107–11; Cynthia Cockburn, (1986), *Machinery of Dominance*, London, Pluto Press.

47. For example, Elizabeth Wilson, (1977), *Women and the Welfare State*, London, Tavistock; Mary McIntosh, (1978), 'The State and the Oppression of Women' in Annette Kuhn and Anne-Marie Wolpe (eds.); *Feminism and Materialism*, London, Routledge & Kegan Paul.

48. Barbara Rogers, (1988), *Men Only: An Investigation into Men's Organisations*, London, Pandora.

49. Lynne Segal, op.cit., p.168.

50. Joan Smith, (1989), *Misogynies*, London, Faber.

51. Michelle Stanworth, (1987), 'Reproductive Technologies and the Deconstruction of Motherhood', in Michelle Stanworth (ed.), *Reproductive Technologies: Gender, Motherhood and Medicine*, Cambridge, Polity Press.

52. Tim Carrigan et al., (1987), 'Towards a New Sociology of Masculinity' in Harry Brod (ed.), *The Making of Masculinities*, p.93, London, Allen & Unwin.

53. See 'Women and Work', *The Guardian*, January 18, 1989.

54. For example, the increasing success of feminist publishers – Virago, Women's Press, Sheba Press in Britain.

55. Andrew Hacker, (1982), 'Farewell to the Family?', in *New York Review of Books*, vol. xxIx, no.4, March 18, p.37.

56. Andrew Cherlin, (1982), *Marriage Divorce Remarriage*, Boston, Harvard University Press.

57. Hacker, op.cit., p.44.

58. Connell, (1987), op.cit., pp.111–16.

59. Edmund White, (1982), *A Boy's Own Story*, p.172, London, Picador.

60. ibid, p.118.

61. See chapter 6.

62. Joel Kovel, (1981), *The Age of Desire*, p.47, New York, Pantheon.

63. Daniel Levinson, (1978), *The Seasons of a Man's Life*, New York, Ballantine; R. Bell, (1981), *Worlds of Friendship*, California, Sage.

64. Antony Easthope, (1985), *What A Man's Gotta Do*, p.166, London, Paladin.

5. Competing Masculinities (I): Manliness – The Masculine Ideal

1. Leonore Davidoff and Catherine Hall, (1987), *Family Fortunes: Men and Women of the English Middle Class, 1780–1850*, p.29, London, Hutchison.

2. Norman Mailer, (1959), *Advertisements for Myself*, p.222, New York, Putnam.

3. Norman Mailer, (1971), *Prisoner of Sex*, p.168, Boston, Little, Brown & Co.

4. Michael Kimmel, (1987), 'Teaching a Course on Men' in Michael Kimmel (ed.), *Changing Men: New Directions in Research on Men and Masculinity*, p.280, London, Sage Publications.

5. See J.A. Mangan and James Walvin (eds.), (1987), *Manliness and Morality*, Manchester, Manchester University Press; Christine Heward, (1988), *Making a Man of Him*, London, Routledge; Davidoff and Hall, op.cit.

6. Norman Vance, (1985), *The sinews of the spirit*, Cambridge, Cambridge University Press; Mangan and Walvin, op.cit.

7. Davidoff and Hall, op.cit.

8. ibid, p.21.

9. Quoted in ibid, p.111.

10. ibid, p.28 and p.399.

11. Walter Houghton, (1957), *The Victorian Frame of Mind*, p.197, London, Yale University Press.

12. Quoted in Vance, op.cit., p.93.

13. ibid, p.104.

14. Quoted in Houghton, p.203.

15. Vance, op.cit., p.195.

16. James Walvin, (1987), 'Symbols of Moral Superiority: Slavery, Sport and the Changing World Order 1800–1950', in Mangan and Walvin (eds.), op.cit. note 2.

17. Jeffrey Hantover, (1980), 'The Boy Scouts and the Validation of Masculinity' in Elizabeth Pleck and Joseph Pleck (eds.), *The American Man*, New Jersey, Englewood Cliffs.

18. ibid.

19. Jeffrey Weeks, (1981), *Sex, Politics and Society: The Regulation of Sexuality Since 1800*, p.40, London, Longman.

20. Edward Carpenter, (1948), [First edition 1896], *Love's Coming of Age*, p.34, London, George Allen & Unwin.

21. See Vance, op.cit., p.70.

22. Christine Heward, op.cit. p.55; J.A. Mangan, (1987), 'Social Darwinism and Upper-Class Education in Late Victorian and Edwardian England' in Mangan and Walvin, op.cit. p.152; Brian Simon, (1965), *Education and the Labour Movement 1870–1918*, p.109, London, Lawrence & Wishart.

24. Simon, ibid, p.110.

25. Vance, op.cit., p.190.

26. Simon, op.cit., p.111.

27. Roberta Park, (1987), 'Biological thought, athletics and the formation of "the man of character": 1830–1900' in Mangan and Walvin, op.cit.

28. Quoted in Timothy Ashplant, (unpub.), 'Autobiography, Identity and Gender'.

29. ibid.

30. Vance, op.cit., p.206.

31. In Danny Danziger (ed.), (1988), *Eton Voices*, p.198, London, Viking.

32. ibid, p.265.

33. ibid, p.261.

34. Keith McClelland, (1989), 'Some Thoughts on Masculinity and the "Representative Artisan" in Britain, 1850–1880', in *Gender and History*, vol.1, issue no.2, Summer.

35. See Keith McClelland, (1987), 'Time to Work, Time to Live: Some Aspects of Work and the Re-formation of Class in Britain, 1850–1880' in Patrick Joyce (ed.), *The Historical Meaning of Work*, Cambridge, Cambridge University Press.

36. Vance, op.cit., p.139.

37. J. Springhall, (1987), 'Building Character in the British Boy: The Attempt to Extend Christian Manliness to Working-Class Adolescents, 1880–1914' in Mangan and Walvin, op.cit.

38. Geoffrey Pearson, (1983), *Hooligan: A History of Respectable Fears*, p.75, London, Macmillan.

39. ibid, p.110.

40. ibid, p.112.

41. Quoted in Kenneth Lynn, (1987), *Hemingway*, p.648, London, Simon & Schuster.

42. ibid, p.399.

43. ibid, p.107.

44. Ernest Hemingway, (1987), *The Garden of Eden*, p.12, London, Grafton Books.

45. Kenneth Lynn, op.cit., p.533.

46. ibid, p.515.

47. Quoted in ibid, p.476.

48. ibid, p.27.

49. ibid, p.110.

50. Quoted in ibid, p.391.

51. Quoted in ibid, p.286.

52. See Peter Schwenger, (1984), *Phallic Critiques*, chapter 1, London, Routledge & Kegan Paul.

53. See ibid, chapter 3.

54. Theodore Adorno, (1978), [first published 1951], *Minima Moralia*, p.45, London, Verso.

55. ibid, p.46.

56. Theodore Adorno, et al. (1964), *The Authoritarian Personality*, New York, John Wiley.

57. ibid.

58. Sheila Ruth, (1983), 'A Feminist Analysis of the New Right' in *Women's Studies International Forum*, vol.6, no.4.

59. A similar argument is advanced by Cynthia Cockburn, (1988), in 'Masculinity, the Left and Feminism' in Rowena Chapman and Jonathan Rutherford, (eds.), *Male Order*, London, Lawrence & Wishart.

60. Klaus Theweleit, (1987), *Male Fantasies*, vol.1, p.27, Cambridge, Polity Press.

61. ibid, chapter 1.

62. ibid, chapter 2.

63. ibid, p.45.

64. ibid, p.61 and p.196.

65. ibid, p.367.

66. ibid, p.414.

67. ibid, vol.2, p.298.

68. ibid, p.17.

69. Lutz Niethammer, (1979), 'Male Fantasies: an Argument for and with an Important New Study in History and Psychoanalysis' in *History Workshop*, no.7.

70. Barbara Ehrenreich, Foreword to Theweleit, op.cit., p.xvi.

71. Theweleit, ibid, p.37.

72. ibid, p.377.

73. ibid, p.379.

74. ibid.

75. Claudia Koonz, (1988), *Mothers in the Fatherland*, London, Methuen.

76. ibid, p.56.

77. ibid, p.14.

78. ibid, p.512.

79. ibid, pp.416–17.

80. ibid, p.65.

81. Quoted ibid, p.66.

82. See, for example, Jill Stephenson, (1980), *The Nazi Organization of Women*, New York, Barnes & Noble.

83. Quoted, ibid, p.110.

84. Yvonne Roberts, (1984), *Man Enough: Men of 35 Speak Out*, p.185, London, Chatto & Windus.

85. ibid, p.184.

86. R.W. Connell, (unpub.), 'An Iron Man: The body and some contradictions of hegemonic masculinity'.

87. ibid, p.5.

88. Derek Hatton, (1988), *Inside Left*, p.117, London, Bloomsbury.

89. ibid, p.xiii.

90. ibid, p.6.

91. ibid, p.13.

92. ibid.

93. ibid, p.20.

94. ibid, p.xiv, p.61.

95. ibid, p.34.
96. ibid, p.91.
97. ibid, p.38.
98. ibid, p.76.
99. ibid. p.113.
100. Quoted in Bruce Woodcock, (1984), *Male Mythologies: John Fowles and the Myth of Masculinity*, p.11, Sussex, Harvester Press.
101. ibid.
102. ibid, p.18.
103. John Fowles, (1976), [first published 1965], *The Magus*, London, Cape, (1977), *Daniel Martin*, London, Grafton.
104. *Daniel Martin*, ibid, p.255.
105. ibid, p.289.
106. ibid.
107. Sarah Benton, (1983), talks to novelist John Fowles in 'Adam and Eve' *New Socialist*, no.11, May/June, p.19.
108. John Fowles, (1963), *The Collecter*, London, Pan.
109. ibid, p.252.
110. Quoted Woodcock, op.cit., p.16.
111. In Benton, op.cit., p.19.
112. John Fowles, (1964), *Aristos*, p.15, London, Grafton.
113. John Fowles, *The Magus*, op.cit., p.31.
114. Woodcock, op.cit., p.76.
115. Ray Raphael, (1988), *The Men from the Boys: Rites of Passage in Male America*, p.3, London, University of Nebraska Press.
116. ibid.
117. Robert Ardrey, (1977), *The Hunting Hypothesis*, London, Fontana; George Gilder, (1975), *Sexual Suicide*, New York, Bantam.
118. Raphael, op.cit., p.138.
119. ibid, p.118.
120. ibid, p.124.
121. See B.S. Johnson (ed.), (1973), *All Bull: The National Servicemen*, London, Quartet.
122. David Morgan, (1987), *It Will Make a Man of You: Notes of National Service, Masculinity and Autobiography*, p.2, Studies in Sexual Politics, no.17, Manchester, Manchester University.
123. ibid, p.38.
124. ibid, p.48.
125. ibid, p.79.
126. ibid, p.81.
127. ibid.

6. *Competing Masculinities (II): Traitors to the Cause*

1. Angus Suttie, (1976), 'From Latent to Blatant: a Personal Account' in *Gay Left*, no.2, Spring, p.5.
2, ibid, p.7.
3. In Yvonne Roberts, (1984), *Man Enough: Men of 35 Speak Out*, p.170, London, Chatto & Windus.
4. See Dennis Altman, (1983), *The Homosexualization of America*, p.4, Boston, Beacon Press; Jeffrey Weeks, (1977), *Coming Out: Homosexual Politics in Britain from the Nineteenth Century to the Present*, p.2, London, Quartet. Both Altman and Weeks

describe Benkert, it has since emerged inaccurately, as a doctor. For debate about the significance of this issue see Frederic Silverstolpe, (1987), 'Benkert was not a doctor: On the non medical origins of the homosexual category in the nineteenth century', in *Homosexuality, Which Homosexuality*, International Conference on Gay and Lesbian Studies, vol.I, Amsterdam, Free University.

5. Randolph Trumbach, (1989), 'Gender and the Homosexual Role in Modern Western Culture: the 18th and 19th Centuries Compared', in D. Altman et al., *Which Homosexuality?: Essays from the International Scientific Conference on Lesbian and Gay Studies*, p.156, London, GMP.

6. Weeks, (1977), op.cit., p.12.

7. Michel Foucault, (1979), *The History of Sexuality*, p.43, London, Allen Lane.

8. Weeks, (1977), op.cit., p.3.

9. Silverstolpe, op.cit. Trunbach, op.cit.

10. Silverstolpe, op.cit. p.216.

11. Anja van Kooten Niekerk, Theo van der Meer, (1989), Introduction to D. Altman et al., op.cit.

12. Silverstolpe, op.cit.

13. Jonathan Dollimore, (1986), 'Homophobia and Sexual Difference' in *Sexual Difference, Oxford Literary Review*, vol.8, nos.1–2, p.5.

14. For example, Kenneth Plummer (ed.), (1981), *The Making of the Modern Homosexual*, London, Hutchinson.

15. Mary McIntosh, (1968), 'The Homosexual Role', in *Social Problems*, vol.16, no.2.

16. ibid.

17. Kenneth Plummer, (1975), *Sexual Stigma: An Interactionist Account*, London, Routledge & Kegan Paul.

18. Jeffrey Weeks, (1981), 'Discourse, Desire and Sexual Deviance' in Plummer, (1981), op.cit. p.83.

19. ibid.

20. Jeffrey Weeks, (1980), 'Capitalism and the Organisation of Sex' in Gay Left Collective, (ed.) *Homosexuality: Power and Politics*, p.15, London, Allison & Busby.

21. ibid.

22. John Marshall, (1981), 'Pansies, Perverts and Macho Men: changing conceptions of male homosexuality', in Plummer, (1981), op.cit.

23. ibid, p.153.

24. Eve Kosofsky Sedgwick, (1985), *Between Men: English Literature and Male Homosexual Desire*, New York, Columbia University Press.

25. Craig Owen, (1987), 'Outlaws: Gay Men in Feminism', in Alice Jardine and Paul Smith (eds.), *Men in Feminism*, London, Methuen.

26. Quoted in Jeffrey Weeks, (1981), op.cit., p.111.

27. Jeffrey Weeks, (1977), op.cit., p.21.

28. Jeffrey Weeks, (1981), op.cit., p.117.

29. ibid, p.114.

30. ibid.

31. ibid, p.220.

32. Marshall, op.cit., p.149.

33. Quoted in ibid, p.148.

34. Alfred Kinsey et al., (1948), *Sexual Behaviour in the Human Male*, pp.614–15, p.623, and pp.636–8, Philadelphia, W.B. Saunders.

35. Tony Gould, (1983), *Inside Outsider: The Life and Times of Colin MacInnes*, pp.97–8, London, Chatto & Windus.

36. John Marshall, (1980), 'The Politics of Tea and Sympathy' in Gay Left Collective, (ed.), op.cit., p.78.

37. John D'Emilio and Estelle Freedman, (1988), *Intimate Matters: A History of Sexuality in America*, p.294, New York, Harper Row.

38. Barbara Ehrenreich, (1983), *The Hearts of Men*, p.26, 24, London, Pluto Press.

39. G.A. Studdert Kennedy, (1989), 'Passing the Love of Women', in Martin Taylor, (ed.), *Lads: Love Poetry of the Trenches*, p.148, London, Constable; See also Paul Fussell, (1975), *The Great War in Modern Memory*, ch.VIII, London, Oxford University Press.

40. Sedgwick, op.cit., p.89.

41. Trevor Royle, (1986), *The Best Years of Their Lives*, p.117, London, Michael Joseph.

42. David Morgan, (1987), 'It Will Make a Man of You', pp.34–5, *Studies in Sexual Politics*, no.17, Manchester, Manchester University.

43. ibid, p.53.

44. Quoted in ibid, p.54.

45. ibid.

46. Quoted in Ray Raphael, (1988), *The Men from the Boys*, p.134, London, University of Nebraska Press.

47. ibid.

48. Michel Foucault, op.cit., p.43.

49. ibid, p.101.

50. Christopher Isherwood, (1954), *The World in the Evening*, pp.125–6, London, Methuen.

51. Jack Babuscio, (1977), 'Camp and Gay Sensibility', in *Gays and Film*, p.40, London, British Film Institute.

52. Derek Cohen and Richard Dyer, (1980), 'The Politics of Gay Culture' in Gay Left Collective, (eds.), pp.176–7.

53. David Fernbach, (1981), *The Spiral Path*, p.206, London, Gay Men's Press.

54. Richard Dyer, (1979), *Stars*, pp.67–8, London, British Film Institute.

55. Babuscio, op.cit., p.41.

56. Andrew Britton, (1978/9), 'For Interpretation – Notes Against Camp', p.11, *Gay Left*, no.7.

57. ibid.

58. Jeffrey Weeks, (1980), op.cit., p.19.

59. Simon Watney, (1980), 'The Ideology of GLF' in Gay Left Collective (ed.), op.cit., p.73.

60. G.L.F. Manifesto, (1971), *Principles of GLF*, p.15.

61. Simon Watney, op.cit., p.72.

62. Quoted ibid, p.70.

63. D'Emilio and Freedman, op.cit., p.319.

64. For example, see David Fernbach, op.cit., p.20.

65. ibid, p.83, p.197.

66. ibid, p.199.

67. ibid, p.100.

68. G.L.F. Manifesto, pp.8–9.

69. See for example Keith Birch, (1980), 'The Politics of Autonomy' in Gay Left Collective (ed.) op.cit. or Sheila Rowbotham et al. (1980), *Beyond the Fragments: Feminism and the Making of Socialism*, London, Merlin.

70. Gay Left Collective, (1976), Editorial *Gay Left*, 2, Spring, p.1.

71. Jeffrey Weeks, (1979), 'Personal Politics – Ten Years On', in *Gay Left*, 8, Summer, pp.7–8.

72. Information from 'Nothing Personal', unpublished notes written by gay men and women who at the time of these events belonged to the International Marxist Group (IMG).

73. David Fernbach, op.cit., p.198.

74. Dennis Altman, (1983), op.cit., p.211.

75. ibid, p.1.

76. Martin Humphries, (1985), in Andy Metcalfe and Martin Humphries (eds.), *The Sexuality of Men*, p.72, London, Pluto Press.

77. Quoted in George Stambolian, (1984), *Male Fantasies/Gay Realities: Interviews with Ten Men*, New York, Sea Horse Press.

78. Dennis Altman, op.cit., p.56.

79. ibid, p.58.

80. Richard Dyer, (1981), 'Getting Over the Rainbow' in George Bridges and Rosalind Brunt (eds.), *Silver Linings*, p.61, London, Lawrence & Wishart.

81. In Yvonne Roberts, op.cit., pp.165–6.

82. ibid.

83. ibid, p.169.

84. George Stambolian, op.cit., p.155.

85. ibid, p.11.

86. ibid, p.154.

87. ibid, pp.159–60.

88. Dennis Altman, op.cit., p.180.

89. Shere Hite, (1981), *The Hite Report on Male Sexuality*, London, MacDonald; Nancy Friday, (1981), *Men in Love: Men's Sexual Fantasies*, London, Arrow Books.

90. Dennis Altman, op.cit., p.193.

91. See Scott McIntosh, in Yvone Roberts op.cit. or 'A Masochist', in George Stambolian, op.cit.

92. Dennis Altman, op.cit., p.195.

93. ibid, p.197.

94. ibid, p.198.

95. Richard Dyer, (1983), 'Coming to Terms', in *Jump Cut*, 30, p.27.

96. ibid.

97. ibid, p.29.

98. Martin Humphries, op.cit., p.85.

99. Nigel Young, (1979), 'Past Present', in *Gay Left*, 8, Summer, p.35.

100. Quoted in Dennis Altman, op.cit., p.18.

101. Edmund White, (1980), *States of Desire*, p.259, New York, E.P. Dutton.

102. See Michael Smith (ed.), (1983), *Black Men/White Men: A Gay Anthology*, San Francisco, Gay Sunshine Press; Joseph Beam (ed.), (1986), *In the Life: A Black Gay Anthology*, Boston, Alyson Publications Inc.

103. Joe DeMarco, (1983), 'Gay Racism' in Michael Smith, ibid, p.111.

104. ibid, p.118.

105. Quoted in Altman, op.cit., p.177.

106. Ellen Willis, (1981), *Beginning to See the Light*, p.163, Boston, South End Press.

107. Andrew Hacker, (1982), 'Farewell to the Family? *New York Review of Books*, vol.xxix, 4, March 18, p.37.

108. ibid.

109. ibid and also Neil Kinnock, (1983), 'A Labour viewpoint' in Family Policy:

alternative viewpoints in *Poverty: Child Poverty Action Group Journal*, 55, August.

110. Martin Weinberg and Colin Williams, (1975), *Male Homosexuals*, p.20, New York, Penguin Books.

111. John D'Emilio and Estelle Freedman, op.cit, chapter 15.

112. Gayle Rubin, (1987), 'Thinking Sex: Notes for a Radical Theory of the Politics of Sexuality', in Carol Vance, (1984), *Pleasure and Danger*, p.271, London, Routledge & Kegan Paul.

113. George Weinberg, (1972), *Society and the Healthy Homosexual*, p.4, New York, St Martin's Press. See also Martin Hoffman, (1968), *The Gay World*, pp.181–2, New York, Basic Books.

114. Dennis Altman, op.cit., p.65.

115. Sigmund Freud, (1933), 'Some Neurotic Manifestations in Jealousy, Paranoia and Homosexuality', in *Complete Works*, vol.18, p.232, London, Hogarth.

116. Andrew Kopkind, (1979), 'The Boys in the Barracks', in Karla Jay and Allen Young (eds.), *Lavender Culture*, New York, Jove HBJ; Dennis Altman, op.cit., p.61.

117. Paul Hoch, (1979), *White Hero, Black Beast*, p.85, London, Pluto Press.

118. David Morgan, op.cit.

119. Dennis Altman, op.cit., p.62.

120. 'The Vilest Men in Britain', headlines in *Sunday People*, 25 May, 1975.

121. In Altman, op.cit. p.173.

122. ibid, p.198.

123. Gay Left Collective (1978/9), 'Happy Families?': Paedophilia Examined' in *Gay Left*, 7, Winter, p.2.

124. ibid, p.5.

125. Roger Jowell and Colin Airey, (1984), *British Social Attitudes: the 1984 Report*, pp.136–43, London, Gower.

126. Quoted in Jeffrey Weeks, (1987), 'Love in a Cold Climate' in *Marxism Today*, January, p.13.

127. Richard Goldstein, (1985), 'The Uses of Aids' in *Village Voice*, December 5, p.27.

128. Jeffrey Weeks, (1987), op.cit., p.13.

129. Elizabeth Wilson, (1989) in *The Guardian*, March 14, p.21.

130. Lesley Dike, (1987), 'AIDS: What women should know' in *Outwrite*, 54, January, pp.10–11; Lynne Segal (1989) 'Lessons from the Past: Feminism, Sexual Politics and the Challenge of Aids', in Erica Carter and Simon Watney (eds.), *Taking Liberties: Aids and Cultural Politics*, London, Serpent's Tail.

131. *The Economist*, August 23, 1986, p.33.

132. Cindy Patton, (1988), 'AIDS: Lessons from the Gay Community' in *Feminist Review*, no.30, Autumn, p.108.

133. Dennis Altman, (1986), *AIDS And The New Puritanism*, London, Pluto Press.

134. ibid.

135. Simon Watney, (1987), *Policing Desire*, London, Comedia.

136. Bill Thorneycroft, Jeffrey Weeks and Mark Stevens, (1988), 'The Liberation of Affection', in Bob Cant and Susan Hemmings (eds.), *Radical Records: Thirty Years of Lesbian and Gay History*, p.167, London, Routledge.

137. Jeffrey Weeks, in ibid, p.168.

138. Leaflets from the Terrence Higgins Trust.

139. David Rampton, (1986), in *You: Mail on Sunday*, November 26.

140. *The Economist*, August 23, 1986, p.33.

141. Cindy Patton, op.cit., p.106.

142. ibid.

143. ibid.

144. Sylvia Strauss, (1982), *"Traitors to the Masculine Cause": The Men's Campaigns for Women's Rights*, London, Greenwood Press.

145. Edward Carpenter, (1948), [First edition 1896] *Love's Coming of Age*, London, Allen & Unwin.

146. See Jeffrey Weeks, (1977), op.cit., p.75.

147. ibid.

148. Sheila Rowbotham, (1977), 'Edward Carpenter: Prophet of the New Life' in Sheila Rowbotham and Jeffrey Weeks, *Socialism and the New Life: The Personal and Sexual Politics of Edward Carpenter and Havelock Ellis*, London, Pluto Press.

149. ibid.

7. Competing Masculinities (III): Black Masculinity and the White Man's Black Man

1. James Baldwin, as quoted in Fern Maya Eckman, (1968), *The Furious Passage of James Baldwin*, pp.32–3, London, Michael Joseph.

2. Joseph Conrad, (1986), [First published 1902], *Heart of Darkness*, p.105–6, Harmondsworth, Penguin.

3. Chinua Achebe, (1988), *Hopes and Impediments: Selected Essays 1965–87*, p.11, London, Heinemann.

4. Quoted in Dorothy Hammond and Alta Jablow, (1970), *The Africa That Never Was: Four Centuries of British Writings About Africa*, p.23, New York, Twayne Press.

5. William Blake, (1965), [First published 1789], 'The Little Black Boy' in (ed.), Max Plowman, *William Blake: Poems and Prophecies*, p.10, London, Everyman.

6. Hammond and Jablow, op.cit., p.26.

7. Patrick Brantlinger, (1987), 'Victorians and Africans: The Geneology of the Myth of the Dark Continent' in Henry Louis Gates Jr (ed.), *Race, Writing and Difference*, p.186, London, Univ. of Chicago Press.

8. Robin Blackburn, (1988), *The Overthrow of Colonial Slavery 1776–1848*, p.436, London, Verso.

9. See Brantlinger, op.cit., pp.186–92.

10. James Walvin, (1987), 'Symbols of Moral Superiority: slavery, sport and the changing world order, 1800–1950' in J.A. Mangan and James Walvin (eds.), *Manliness and Morality*, London, Manchester University Press.

11. Rudyard Kipling.

12. Walvin, op.cit., p.243.

13. Quoted in Brantlinger, op.cit., p.192.

14. Quoted ibid, p.187.

15. Quoted in Hammond and Jablow, op.cit., p.54.

16. Men like Alfred W. Cole and W. Winrood Reade were part of the former group, and men like Sir William Harris a part of the latter group of men. ibid, p.45.

17. ibid.

18. As quoted in Catherine Hall, (1989), 'The Economy of Intellectual Prestige: Thomas Carlyle, John Stuart Mill and the Case of Governor Eyre' in *Cultural Critique*, Summer.

19. See Hall, ibid.

20. Thomas Huxley, quoted in Brantlinger, op.cit. p.203; Mary Kingsley, quoted in Hammond and Jablow, op.cit., p.98.

21. ibid, p.98.

22. ibid.

23. Ronald Robinson et al., (1961), *Africa and the Victorians: The Official Mind of*

Imperialism, pp.465–75, London, Macmillan. Britain had entered the 'Scramble' for Africa to defend existing free trade relations in Africa, Egypt and Asia against the growing strength of competing European nations now threatening her former easy world dominance, alongside other threats arising from uprisings in Egypt, South Africa and Ireland.

24. H.R. Haggard, (1979) [First published 1885], *King Solomon's Mines* from *King Solomon's Mines, She, Allan Quatermain*, London, Octopus Press.

25. ibid, p.14.

26. Hammond and Jablow, op.cit., p.108.

27. Brantlinger, op.cit., p.211.

28. Quoted ibid.

29. Joel Kovel, (1988), [First published 1970], *White Racism: A Psycho-history*, p.xcix, London, Free Association Books.

30. Achebe, op.cit., p.2.

31. Conrad, op.cit., p.16.

32. ibid, p.50.

33. Graham Greene, (1948), *Journey Without Maps*, London, Pan.

34. ibid, p.114.

35. ibid, p.33.

36. Hammond and Jablow, op.cit., p.182.

37. Mrinalini Sinha, (1987), 'Gender and Imperialism: *Colonial Policy and the Ideology of Moral Imperialism in late nineteenth-century Bengal*' in Michael Kimmel (ed.), *Changing Men*, London, Sage.

38. ibid, p.226.

39. Rudie Bleys, 'The geography of perversion/desire: 18th and 19th century interpretations of primitive homosexuality' in International Scientific Conference of Gay and Lesbian Studies, *Homosexuality, Which Homosexuality?*, vol.1, (History), p.13, Amsterdam, Free University Amsterdam.

40. James Baldwin, (1985), [First published 1963], *The Fire Next Time* in *The Price of the Ticket*, p.375, London, Michael Joseph.

41. Quoted in Robert Altman, (1981), *Coming Out in the Seventies*, p.158, Boston, Alyson Publications; Robert Altman, (1981), *Coming Out in the Seventies*, p.158, Boston, Alyson Publications.

42. Frantz Fanon, (1970), [First published 1952], *Black Skins, White Masks*, p.118, London, Paladin.

43. Roger Bastide, (1972), 'Dusky Venus, Black Apollo' in Paul Baxter and Basil Sansom (eds.), *Race and Social Difference*, p.187, Harmondsworth, Penguin.

44. James Baldwin, (1985), [First published 1961], 'The Black Boy Looks at the White Boy', op.cit., p.290.

45. James Baldwin, (1985), [First published 1972], 'No Name in the Street', ibid, p.482.

46. James Baldwin, (1985), 'Here Be Dragons', ibid, pp.684–5.

47. James Baldwin, (1985), 'No Name in the Street', op.cit., p.477.

48. Geoffrey Summerfield, (1984), Introduction to Richard Wright, *Black Boy*, p.v, London, Longman.

49. B.W. Beacroft and M.A. Smale, (1982), *The Making of America*, p.104, London, Longman.

50. Quoted in Hazel Carby, (1987), '"On the Threshold of Women's Era": Lynching, Empire, and Sexuality in Black Feminist Theory', in Gates, op.cit., p.307.

51. Quoted in Jane Gaines, (1988), 'White Privilege and Looking Relations: Race and Gender in Feminist Film Theory' in *Screen*, vol.29, 4, p.24.

52. ibid.

53. See Helen Taylor, '*Gone With The Wind*: the mammy of them all' in Jean Radford (ed.), *The Progress of Romance: The Politics of Popular Fiction*, p.125, p.130, London, Routledge & Kegan Paul.

54. Robert Staples, (1982), *Black Masculinity: The Black Male's Role in American Society*, p.62, San Francisco, Black Scholar Press.

55. Quoted in Baldwin, op.cit., p.299.

56. Norman Mailer, (1960), 'The White Negro', in *Protest*, p.304, London, Panther.

57. ibid, p.291.

58. Fanon, op.cit.

59. Kobena Mercer, (1988), 'Racism and the Politics of Masculinity' in Kobena Mercer and Isaac Julien, 'Race, Sexual Politics and Black Masculinity: A Dossier', in Rowena Chapman and Jonathan Rutherford (eds.), *Male Order*, p.112, London, Lawrence & Wishart.

60. Bastide, op.cit., p.191.

61. See Johnson, op.cit., p.18.

62. ibid, p.19.

63. Lynne Segal, (1987), *Is the Future Female?: Troubled Thoughts on Contemporary Feminism*, chapter 1, London, Virago.

64. Johnson, op.cit., p.19.

65. Segal, op.cit., p.198.

66. Segal, op.cit., chapter 1.

67. Eldridge Cleaver, (1969), *Soul on Ice*, p.125, London, Cape.

68. Mtutuzeli Matshoba, (1979), *Call Me Not a Man*, p.18, London, Rex Collings.

69. ibid.

70. Quoted in Johnson, op.cit., p.119.

71. Richard Wright, (1984), op.cit., p.209.

72. ibid, p.222.

73. Chester Himes, (1986), [First published 1945], *If He Hollers Let Him Go*, p.2, p.4, London, Pluto Press.

74. ibid, p.35.

75. Kenneth Clark, (1965), *Dark Ghetto*, p.64, New York, Harper.

76. William Grier and Price Cobbs, (1968), *Black Rage*, p.149, New York, Bantam Books.

77. Charles Silberman, (1964), *Crisis in Black and White*, p.155, New York, Random House.

78. ibid, p.189.

79. ibid, p.235.

80. Daniel Moyniham, (1965), *The Negro Family: The Case for National Action*, Washington, U.S. Department of Labor.

81. Quoted in David Widgery, (1979), 'Baldwin' in *Achilles Heel*, 3, p.34.

82. Robert Staples, op.cit., p.88.

83. ibid, p.136.

84. ibid, p.2.

85. ibid, p.8.

86. ibid, p.13, emphasis added.

87. ibid.

88. ibid, p.68.

89. ibid, p.69.

90. ibid, p.80.

91. ibid, p.143.

92. Lillian Rubin, (1987), *Quiet Rage*, p.242, London, Faber & Faber.

93. Bell Hooks, *Talking Back: Thinking Feminist – Thinking Black*, p.242, London, Sheba.

94. ibid, p.178.

95. Staples, op.cit., p.89.

96. Greer and Cobb, op.cit., p.179.

97. Rubin, op.cit., p.242.

98. William Strickland, (1989), 'Sleaze: How Bipartisan Racism Defiled the 1988 Presidential Campaign', in *Zeta Magazine*, Jan. p.10.

99. Rubin, op.cit., p.38.

100. ibid, p.249.

101. ibid, p.104.

102. Bobby Seale, (1970), *Seize the Time: The Story of the Black Panther Party*, London, Arrow Books.

103. Joel Kovel, op.cit., p.cix.

104. LeRoi Jones, (1966), *Home*, p.164, New York, William Morrow & Co.

105. Quoted in Eckman, op.cit., p.136.

106. LeRoi Jones, op.cit., p.110.

107. Johnson, op.cit., p.85.

108. LeRoi Jones, op.cit., p.188.

109. Quoted in Eckman, op.cit., p.23.

110. Stuart Hall et al., (1978), *Policing the Crisis*, London, Macmillan.

111. ibid, p.357.

112. Dick Hebdige, (1979), *Subculture: The Meaning of Style*, p.37, London, Methuen.

113. Paul Gilroy, (1987), *There Ain't No Black in the Union Jack*, pp.164–5, London, Hutchinson.

114. ibid, p.171.

115. ibid, p.241.

116. ibid.

117. Beverley Bryan, Stella Dadzie and Suzanne Scafe, (1985), *The Heart of the Race: Black Women's Lives in Britain*, p.219, London, Virago.

118. Ken Pryce, (1979), *Endless Pressure*, p.53, Bristol, Bristol Classical Press.

119. Errol Lawrence, (1982), 'In the Abundance of Water the Fool is Thirsty: Sociology and Black Pathology', in CCCS (eds.), *The Empire Strikes Back*, London, Hutchinson; Paul Gilroy and Errol Lawrence, 'Two-Tone Britain: White and Black Youth and the Politics of Anti-Racism' in Philip Cohen and Harwant Bains (eds.), *Multi-Racist Britain*, London, Macmillan.

120. Toni Cade, (1970), 'On the Issue of Roles', in Toni Cade (ed.), *The Black Woman*, p.102, New York, Signet.

121. ibid, p.103.

122. ibid, p.106.

123. Toni Cade Bambara, (1972), *Gorilla, My Love*, New York, Random House; (1977), *The Sea Birds are Still Alive*, New York, Random House; and (1980), *The Salt Eaters*, New York, Random House.

124. Toni Cade, op.cit., p.268.

125. Paule Marshall, (1981), [First published 1959], *Brown Girl, Brownstones*, New

York, The Feminist Press.

126. Paule Marshall, (1970), 'Reena' in Cade, op.cit.

127. Toni Morrison, (1971), 'What the Black Woman thinks About Women's Lib' in *The New York Times Magazine*, August 22.

128. Zora Neale Hurston, (1986), [First published 1937], *Their Eyes Were Watching God*, XIII, London, Virago; Elaine Feinstein, (1985), *Bessie Smith*, p.97, London, Viking.

129. Rubin, op.cit., p.242.

130. Quoted in Johnson, p.109.

131. Alice Walker, (1970), *The Third Life of Grange Copeland*, London, Women's Press, p.94.

132. Alice Walker, (1982), *The Colour Purple*, London, Women's Press.

133. Michele Wallace, (1979), *Black Macho and The Myth of the Superwoman*, London, John Calder.

134. ibid, p.109.

135. ibid, p.32, p.48.

136. Eldridge Cleaver, op.cit., p.49.

137. LeRoi Jones, op.cit., p.227.

138. Wallace, op.cit., chapter 1.

139. Audre Lorde, (1983), 'My Words Will Be There', in (ed.) Mari Evans, *Black Women Writers*, p.267, London, Pluto.

140. Combahee River Collective, (1983), 'Collective Statement' in Barbara Smith (ed.), *Home Girls: A Black Feminist Anthology*, New York, Kitchen Table/Women of Color Press.

141. Ntozake Shange, (1980), 'comin to terms' in Mary Helen Washington (ed.), *Midnight Birds*, p.254, New York, Anchor Books.

142. Lauretta Ngcobo (ed.), *Let It Be Told: Black Women Writers in Britain*, p.31, London, Virago Press.

143. ibid, p.30.

144. Rhonda Cobham and Merle Collins, (1986), *Watchers and Seekers: Creative Writings by Black Women in Britain*, p.30, London, Women's Press.

145. Joan Riley, (1985), *The Unbelonging*, London, Women's Press.

146. Grace Nicholls, (1986), 'Even Tho', in Cobham and Collins, op.cit., p.65.

147. Beverley Bryan et al., op.cit., p.214.

148. Washington, op.cit., p.xvi.

149. Staples, op.cit., p.159.

150. Ishmael Reed, (1989), *Reckless Eyeballing*, London, Allison & Busby.

151. Johnson, op.cit., p.107.

152. Langston Hughes, (1986), [First published 1940], *The Big Sea: An Autobiography*, London, Pluto Press; James Baldwin, (1984), [First published 1962], *Another Country*, London, Black Swan.

153. Joseph Beam, (1986), 'Brother to Brother: Words From the Heart', in Joseph Beam (ed.), p.239, *In the Life: A Black Gay Anthology*.

154. Kobena Mercer and Isaac Julien, op.cit., p.99.

155. ibid.

156. ibid, p.105.

157. ibid, pp.139–40.

158. ibid, p.141.

159. Richard Pryor, (1971), *In Concert*, (Video).

160. See, for example, Lenny Henry, (1989), 'My Hero: Lenny Henry on Richard

Pryor', *The Independent Magazine*, 22 July, p.54.

161. Isaac Julien, *Looking For Langston*, Film shown on ITV Channel 4 as part of the series *Out on Tuesday*, (March 27 1989).

162. Hughes, op.cit., p.156.

163. Stuart Hall, (1987), 'Minimal Selves' in *Indentity: The Real Me*, London, I.C.A. Documents 6; Stuart Hall, (1987), 'New Ethnicities in *Black Film British Cinema*, p.27, London, I.C.A. Documents.

164. Essex Hemphill, (1986), *Conditions: Poem by Essex Hemphill*, Washington, BeBop Books.

165. Isaac Julien, (1988), 'Gary's Tale', in Mercer and Julien, op.cit., p.128.

8. *The Belly of the Beast (I): Sex as Male Domination?*

1. Nancy Friday, interview in *Spare Rib*, p.45, February 1976.

2. Dale Spender, (1984), 'NO MATTER WHAT ... Theoretical Issues in Contemporary Feminism, in Joy Holland (ed.), *Feminist Action*, pp.11–12, London, Battle Axe Books.

3. Catherine Stimpson, (1987), Foreword to Harry Brod (ed.), *The Making of Masculinities*, p.xl, London, Allen & Unwin.

4. Anon. (circe 1971), *Why Miss World?*, Pamphlet, London (n.d.).

5. See Michelene Wandor (ed.), (1972), *The Body Politic: Writings from the Women's Liberation Movement in Britain 1969–72*, London, Stage One.

6. See Sheila Rowbotham, (1989), *The Past is Before Us: Feminism in Action Since the 1960s*, p.64, London, Pandora.

7. See Lynne Segal, (1987), *Is the Future Female? Troubled Thoughts on Contemporary Feminism*, chapter 2, London, Virago Press.

8. Catherine MacKinnon, (1982), 'Feminism, Marxism, Method and the State', in *Signs*, vol.7, 3, p.529.

9. Catherine MacKinnon, (1984), Comments in *Signs*, vol.10, 1, p.182

10. Roger Scruton, (1983), in *The Observer*, 22 May.

11. Roger Scruton, (1983), *The Times*, 15 February.

12. Quoted in Jeffrey Weeks, (1985), *Sexuality and Its Discontents*, p.69, London, Routledge & Kegan Paul.

13. Quoted in Peter Schwenger, (1984), *Phallic Critiques*, p.76, London, Routledge & Kegan Paul.

14. Alberto Moravia, (1972), *The Two of Us*, p.111, London, Secker & Warburg.

15. Randy Thornhill et al., (1986), 'The Biology of Rape', in Sylvana Tomaselli and Roy Porter (eds.), *Rape*, p.113, Oxford, Basil Blackwell.

16. Rosalind Coward, (1984), 'The Sex Life of Stick Insects', in *Female Desire*, London, Paladin.

17. Barbara Ehrenreich et al., (1986), *Re-Making Love: The Feminization of Sex*, p.203, New York, Anchor Press.

18. For example, according to studies of New Guinea Highlands societies a person's gender 'does not lie locked in his or her genitals but can flow and change with contact as substances seep into and out of his or her body'. This quotation is cited in Fitz John Porter Poole, 'Transforming "natural" woman' in Sherry Ortner and Harriet Whitehead (eds.), (1981), *Sexual Meanings*, p.118, Cambridge, Cambridge University Press. See also G. Eichinger Ferro-Luzzi, (1980), 'The Female Lingam', in *Current Anthropology*, vol.21, 1; Shirley Ardener, (1987), 'A note on gender iconography: the vagina' in (ed.) Pat Caplan, *The Cultural Construction of Sexuality*; Olivia Harris, (1981), 'The power of signs: gender, culture and the wild in

the Bolivian Andes' in MacCormack and Strathern (eds.), *Nature, Culture and Gender*, Cambridge, Cambridge University Press. For one of the most recent anthropological texts assessing universalist fallacies surrounding Western notions of men, women and 'gender' see Marilyn Strathern, (1989), *The Gender of the Gift: Problems with Women and Problems with Society in Melanesia*, California, University of California Press.

19. Quoted in Andrew Tolson, (1977), *The Limits of Masculinity*, p.60, London, Tavistock.

20. Ethel Spector Person, (1980), 'Sexuality as the Mainstay of Identity: Psychoanalytic Perspectives', in *Signs*, vol.5, 4, p.619.

21. Gad Horowitz and Michael Kaufman, (1987), 'Male Sexuality: Toward A Theory of Liberation' in Michael Kaufman (ed.), *Beyond Patriarchy*, Toronto, Oxford University Press.

22. Norman Mailer, (1972), *The Prisoner of Sex*, p.12, London, Sphere.

23. ibid, p.126.

24. ibid, p.127.

25. See, for example, H.R. Hays, (1964), *The Dangerous Sex*, New York, Putnam; Wolfgana Lederer, (1968), *The Fear of Women*, New York, Harcourt Brace; Mervyn Meggitt, (1976), 'A Duplicity of Demons', in *Man and Woman in the New Guinea Highlands*, Special publication, American Anthropological Association, no.8.

26. Ian McEwan, (1978), *In Between the Sheets*, pp.19–21, London, Pan.

27. Nancy Friday, (1980), *Men in Love: Men's Sexual Fantasies*, p.471, New York, Arrow Books.

28. Eileen McLeod, (1982), *Women Working: Prostitution Now*, p.59, London, Croom Helm.

29. ibid, p.69.

30. ibid, p.70.

31. British and US figures quoted in ibid, pp.70–72.

32. David Feintwick, (1979), 'Men's Lives: extract from an autobiography' in *Achilles Heel*, 2, p.38.

33. Friday, op.cit.

34. Wendy Hollway, (1984), 'Women's Power in Heterosexual Sex' in *Women's Studies Int. Forum*, vol.7, 1, pp.63–8.

35. ibid, pp.65–6.

36. ibid, p.68.

37. Carole Vance and Ann Snitow, (1984), 'Towards a Conversation about Sex in Feminism', in *Signs*, vol.10, 1, p.131.

38. Editorial collective, (1979), 'Notes from the collective' in *Achilles Heel*, 3, p.5.

39. London Feminist History Group, (1983), *The Sexual Dynamic of History*, p.4, London, Pluto Press.

40. Angela Carter, (1979), *The Sadeian Woman*, p.14, London, Virago Press.

41. Andy Moye, (1985), 'Pornography' in Andy Metcalfe and Martin Humphries (eds.), *The Sexuality of Men*, p.63, London, Pluto Press.

42. ibid, pp.59–60.

43. Jeffrey Fracher and Michael Kimmel, (1987), 'Hard Issues and Soft Spots: Counselling Men About Sexuality', in Murray Scher et al. (eds.), *Handbook of Counselling & Psychotherapy with Men*, London, Sage.

44. ibid, p.84.

45. ibid, p.89.

46. ibid.

47. Leonore Tiefer, (1987), 'The Pursuit of the Perfect Penis: The Medicalization of Male Sexuality' in Michael Kimmel (ed.), *Changing Men*, p.170, London, Sage.

48. ibid, p.166.

49. Sheila Jeffreys, (1983), 'Sex reform and anti-feminism in the 1920s' in London History Group, op.cit., p.187.

50. ibid, p.193.

51. Deirdre English, (1980), 'The Politics of Porn: Can Feminists Walk the Line?' in *Sex, Porn and Male Rage*, San Francisco, Mother Jones Reprint.

52. Henry Schipper, 'Filthy Lucre: A Tour of America's Most Profitable Frontier', in ibid.

53. ibid.

54. Caroline Harris and Jennifer Moore, (1988), 'Altered Images', in *Marxism Today*, November, p.25.

55. Nan Hunter, (1986), 'The Pornography Debate in Context: a Chronology of sexuality, media and violence issues in feminism', in Kate Ellis et al., (eds.), *Caught Looking: feminism, pornography and censorship*, p.26, New York, Caught Looking Inc.

56. Andrea Dworkin in *Pornography and Sexual Violence: Evidence of Links*, (Public Hearings Minneapolis City Council), p.11, London, Everywoman.

57. Andrea Dworkin, (1981), *Pornography: Men Possessing Women*, London, Women's Press.

58. ibid, p.128.

59. As quoted in John Forrester, (1985), 'Rape, Seduction and Psychoanalysis' in Tomaselli and Porter, op.cit., p.62.

60. See Nancy Friday, (1980), op.cit., Lynne Segal, (1983), 'Sensual Uncertainty, or Why the Clitoris is Not Enough', in Sue Cartledge and Joanna Ryan (eds.), *Sex and Love*, London, Women's Press.

61. See Lynne Segal, (1987), *Is the Future Female? Troubled Thoughts on Contemporary Feminism*, chapter 3, London, Virago.

62. Richard Green, (1986), testimony as reported in Philip Nobile and Eric Nadler, *United States of America vs Sex*, pp.89–92, New York, Minotaur Press.

63. Michael Goldstein and Harold Kant, (1973), *Pornography and Sexual Deviance*, p.73, Berkeley, University of California Press.

64. Robert Staples, (1986), Commentary written for Nobile and Nadler, op.cit., p.363.

65. Lori Onstenk, (1980), addendum to English, op.cit.

66. See N. Malamuth and E. Donnerstein (eds.), (1984), *Pornography and Sexual Aggression*, Orlando, Academic Press; Edward Donnerstein and Daniel Linz, (1987), 'Mass-Media Sexual Violence and Male Viewers: Current Theory and Research' in Kimmel, op.cit.

67. Evidence given in *Pornography and Sexual Violence: Evidence of Links*, op.cit., p.16.

68. Quoted in Nobile and Nadler, op.cit., p.83.

69. Daniel Linz, Edward Donnerstein and Steven Penrod, (1987), 'Sexual Violence in the Mass Media: Social Psychological Implications' in Phillip Shaver and Clyde Hendrick (eds.), *Sex and Gender*, p.118, London, Sage.

70. Donald Mosher, (1970), 'Psychological Reactions to Pornographic Films' in *Technical Reports of the Commission on Obscenity and Pornography*, vol.8, Washington, U.S. Government Report; Mosher, (1986), Quoted in Nobile and Nadler, op.cit., p.93.

71. See Kate Ellis et al., (1986), *Caught Looking*, op.cit., p.26.

72. Larry Baron and Murray Straus, (1986), Commentary in Nobile and Nadler, op.cit., pp.351–353.

73. Quoted in Ellis et al., op.cit., p.65.

74. Ellen Levine, (1986), Commentary in Nobile and Nadler, op.cit., p.311.

75. Lisa Duggan, (1986), 'Censorship in the Name of Feminism' in Ellis et al., p.67.

76. Everywoman, (1988), Introduction to *Pornography and Sexual Violence: Evidence of Links*, op.cit.; Catherine Itzin, (1987), in *London Daily News*, April 20. For further arguments for and against promoting a Minneapolis Ordinance in Britain see Gail Chester and Julienne Dickey (eds.), (1988), *Feminism and Censorship*, London, Prism Press.

77. Quoted in Ellis, et al., op.cit., p.77.

78. Andrea Dworkin, (1987), *Right-Wing Women: The Politics of Domesticated Females*, London, Women's Press.

79. See Judith Ennew, (1986), *The Sexual Exploitation of Children*, pp.145–7, Cambridge, Polity Press.

80. See Seph Weene, (1981), 'Venus' in *Sex Issues: Heresies*, no.2, who discusses her feelings of power when she is performing; or Nickie Roberts, (1986), *The Front Line: Women in the Sex Industry Speak*, London, Grafton Books, who describes her decision, like that of other women she interviews, to escape the unhealthy dreary jobs awaiting her for work as a stripper; or Judith Walkovitz, (1984), 'Male Vice and Female Virtue: Feminism and the Politics of Prostitution in Nineteenth-Century Britain', in Ann Snitow et al. (eds.), *Powers of Desire: The Politics of Sexuality*, London, Virago, for historical tensions between prostitutes and their would-be feminist liberators.

81. Ann Snitow et al., (1975). op. cit., p. 460.

82. Ann Snitow, (1986), 'Retrenchment Vs Transformation: the politics of the anti-pornography movement' in Ellis et al., op.cit., p.12.

83. For example, see Tony Eardley, (1980), 'Pin-Ups Come Down on Building Sites', in *Achilles Heel*, 4.

84. Deirdre English, op.cit., p.46.

85. Pat Califia, (1986), 'Among Us, Against Us: the New Puritans' in Ellis et al., op.cit., p.20.

86. Mariana Valverde, (1985), *Sex, Power and Pleasure*, p.138, Toronto, Women's Press.

87. ibid, p.140.

88. Susan Brownmiller, (1976), *Against Our Will*, p.359, (emphasis original), Harmondsworth, Penguin.

89. Ellen Willis, (1985), 'Feminism, Moralism and Pornography' in Snitow et al., *Powers of Desire*, op.cit., p.462.

9. *The Belly of the Beast (II): Explaining Male Violence*

1. Susan Griffin, (1971), Reprint from 'Rape: The All-American Crime', *Ramparts*, September, pp.26–35.

2. ibid.

3. ibid, p.35.

4. Shulamith Firestone, (1971), *The Dialectic of Sex*, London, Paladin; Kate Millet, (1972), *Sexual Politics*, London, Abacus.

5. Germaine Greer, (1970), *The Female Eunuch*, London, MacGibbon & Kee.

6. Sheila Rowbotham, (1973), *Women's Consciousness, Man's World*, Harmonds-

worth, Penguin; Juliet Mitchell, (1971), *Woman's Estate*, Harmondsworth, Penguin.

7. Susan Brownmiller, (1976), *Against Our Will: Men, Women and Rape*, Harmondsworth, Penguin.

8. Elizabeth Stanko, (1985), *Intimate Intrusions: Women's Experience of Male Violence*, London, Routledge & Kegan Paul.

9. For example, see Rape Crisis Centre, (1977), *First Annual Report*, London, Rape Counselling and Research Project.

10. Susan Griffin, op.cit., p.22.

11. Brownmiller, op.cit., p.14.

12. For example, as portrayed in the British film, *Distant Voices, Still Lives*, Terrence Davies, 1988.

13. Brownmiller, op.cit., p.209.

14. ibid, p.15.

15. See John Forrester, (1985), 'Rape, Seduction and Psychoanalysis' in Tomaselli and Porter (eds.), *Rape*, p.62, Oxford, Basil Blackwell.

16. See Alfred Kinsey et al., (1953), *Sexual Behaviour in the Human Female*, p.410, pp.116–22, Philadelphia, W.B. Saunders.

17. Peggy Reeves Sanday, (1985), 'Rape and the Silencing of the Feminine' in Tomaselli and Porter, op.cit., p.85.

18. Margaret Mead, (1935), *Sex and Temperament in Three Primitive Societies*, London, Routledge & Kegan Paul.

19. For these and other examples see Julia Schwendinger and Herman Schwendinger, (1983), *Rape and Inequality*, London, Sage.

20. Roy Porter, (1985), 'Rape – Does it Have a Historical Meaning?' in Tomaselli and Porter, op.cit.

21. ibid, p.223.

22. Barbara Lindemann, (1984), '"To Ravish and Carnally Know": Rape in Eighteenth-Century Massachusetts', in *Signs*, Autumn, vol.10, 1.

23. ibid, p.72.

24. ibid, p.81.

25. Ellen Ross, (1982), '"Fierce Questions and Taunts": Married Life in Working-class London, 1870–1914', in *Feminist Studies*, vol.8, 3, Fall.

26. ibid, p.596.

27. Figures quoted in Donald West, (1984), 'The Victim's Contribution to Sexual Offences' in June Hopkins (ed.), *Perspectives on Rape and Sexual Assault*, p.2, London, Harper & Row. See also Jennifer Temkin, (1987), *Rape and the Legal Process*, p.9, London, Sweet & Maxwell.

28. Porter, op.cit., p.223.

29. Brownmiller, op.cit., p.9.

30. Ruth Hall et al. (1981), *The Rapist Who Pays the Rent: Evidence Submitted by Women Against Rape, Britain to the Criminal Law Revision Committee*, Bristol, Falling Wall Press; Ruth Hall, (1985), *Ask Any Woman: A London Inquiry into Rape and Sexual Assault*, Bristol, Falling Wall Press.

31. Ann Snitow, (1985), 'Retrenchment Vs Transformation: the politics of the anti-pornography movement' in Kate Ellis et al., *Caught Looking*, New York, Caught Looking Inc.

32. Menachim Amir, (1971), *Patterns in Forcible Rape*, Chicago, University of Chicago Press.

33. ibid, p.320.

34. ibid.

35. Diana Russell, (1984), *Sexual Exploitation – Rape, Child Sexual Abuse and Workplace Harassment*, pp.34–48, Beverley Hills, Sage.

36. Tempkin, op.cit., p.11.

37. Ruth Hall, (1985), op.cit.

38. Brian MacLean, (1985), Review of *Ask Any Woman* in *British Journal Criminology*, vol.25, p.390.

39. ibid, p.391.

40. Hall, (1985), op.cit.

41. Ian Blair, (1985), *Investigating Rape: A New Approach for Police*, London, Croom Helm; Harry O'Reilly, (1984), 'Crisis Intervention with Victims of Forcible Rape: A Police Perspective', in Hopkins (ed.), op.cit.

42. See, for example, Susan Edwards, (1981), *Female Sexuality and the Law*, ch.2, Oxford, Martin Roberts; Carol Smart, (1976), *Women, Crime and Criminology*, London, Routledge & Kegan Paul.

43. Jalna Hanmer and Mary Maynard (eds.), (1987), *Women, Violence and Social Control*, p.11, London, Macmillan.

44. Elizabeth Stanko, (1985), op.cit., p.1.

45. Liz Kelly, (1988), *Surviving Sexual Violence*, p.1, Cambridge, Polity Press.

46. ibid, p.27.

47. ibid.

48. P.H. Gebhard et al., (1965), *Sexual Offenders: An Analysis of Types*, London, Heinemann; Amir, op.cit.; Schwendinger and Schwendinger, op.cit.; Barbara Toner, (1982), *The Facts of Rape*, London, Arrow.

49. Robert Staples, (1982), *Black Masculinity*, San Francisco, Black Scholar Press.

50. Richard Wright, (1980), *The English Rapist, New Society*, 17 July, p.124.

51. Robert Staples, (1985), Commentary in Philip Nobile and Eric Nadler (eds.), *United States of America Vs Sex*, p.363, New York, Minotaur Press.

52. Amir, op.cit.

53. Porter, op.cit., p.235.

54. Ken Plummer, (1984), 'The Social Uses of Power: Symbolic Interaction, Power and Rape', in Hopkins (ed.), op.cit., p.46.

55. West, (1984), in ibid, p.41.

56. A.M. Scacco Jr (1975), *Rape in Prison*, Springfield, Illinois, Charles C. Thomas.

57. ibid, p.86.

58. Plummer, op.cit., p.49.

59. Paul Wilson, (1978), *The Other Side of Rape*, St Lucia, University of Queensland Press.

60. ibid.

61. West, op.cit., p.11.

62. As reported in Kelly, op.cit., p.53.

63. West, op.cit., p.11.

64. ibid, p.13.

65. ibid, p.11.

66. Maria Balinska, (1989), 'Australian Rules' in *The Guardian*, 17 January, p.17.

67. In a recent British survey the Women's Committee of the South East Region of the TUC (SERTUC) reports: 'Roughly a decade since the issue was first raised in union circles it finally seems to be universally accepted as a serious concern – as evidenced by the number of publications on the subject and its profile on union

courses in both female and male dominated unions.' SERTUC Women's Committee, (1988), *Still Moving Towards Equality*, (no page no.), London, SERTUC.

68. D.J. West, C. Roy and Florence Nichols, (1978), *Understanding Sexual Attacks*, London, Heinemann; Sylvia Levine and Joseph Koenig (eds.), *Why Men Rape*, (1983), London, Star.

69. Levine and Koenig, ibid, p.3.

70. West et al., op.cit., p.35.

71. Levine and Koenig, p.41.

72. ibid, p.50.

73. Reported in Deborah Cameron and Elizabeth Frazer, (1987), *The Lust to Kill*, p.69, Cambridge, Polity Press.

74. Gordon Burn, (1984), *Somebody's Husband, Somebody's Son: The Story of the Yorkshire Ripper*, p.99, London, Pan Books.

75. Nicole Ward Jouve, (1986), *'The Streetcleaner': The Yorkshire Ripper Case on Trial*, p.149, London, Marion Boyars.

76. ibid, p.72.

77. ibid, p.100.

78. ibid, p.102.

79. Burn, op.cit., pp.58–9.

80. Quoted in Wendy Hollway, (1981), '"I Just Wanted to Kill a Woman". Why? The Ripper and Male Sexuality' in *Feminist Review*, no.9, Autumn, p.39.

81. Quoted in Eileen Fairweather, (1982), 'Leeds: Curfew on Men' in Marsha Rowe (ed.), *Spare Rib Reader*, p.441, Harmondsworth, Penguin.

82. Quoted in David Robins, (1984), *We Hate Humans*, p.110, Harmondsworth, Penguin.

83. Judith Walkovitz, (1982), 'Jack the Ripper and the Myth of Male Violence' in *Feminist Studies*, vol.8, 3, Fall, p.570.

84. A recent survey by Granada Television found that nearly 70% of women said they either would not go out alone after dark or would go out only if absolutely necessary. 34% of these women had been sworn at in the street, 18% had experienced unwelcome physical contact and 17% had been flashed at. (World In Action, Granada TV 9.1.89.)

85. Irene Hanson Frieze, (1983), 'Investigating the Causes and Consequences of Marital Rape' in *Signs*, vol.8, 3.

86. Jan Pahl, (1985), *Private Violence and Public Policy*, p.8, London, Routledge & Kegan Paul.

87. Richard Gelles, (1979), *Family Violence*, London, Sage.

88. William Goode, (1971), 'Force and Violence in the Family' in *Journal of Marriage and the Family*, vol.33, no.4; Murray Straus, (1980), 'A Sociological Perspective on the Prevention of Wife-beating' in Murray Strauss and Gerald Hotaling (eds.), *Social Causes of Husband-Wife Violence*, Minneapolis, University of Minneapolis Press.

89. Gelles, op.cit., p.139.

90. ibid, p.171.

91. Linda Gordon, (1988), *Heroes of Their Own Lives: The Politics and History of Family Violence*, p.291, New York, Viking.

92. Pahl, op.cit., p.47.

93. ibid.

94. ibid, p.48.

95. Bell Hooks, (1989), *Talking Back; Thinking Feminist – Thinking Black*, p.89,

London, Sheba.
96. ibid, p.87.
97. ibid, p.86.
98. Gordon, op.cit., p.8.
99. ibid, p.292.
100. ibid, p.286.
101. Linda Gordon, (1988b), 'The Politics of Child Sexual Abuse: Notes from American History' in *Feminist Review*, no.28, Spring, p.57.
102. S. Weinberg, (1955), *Incest Behaviour*, New York, Citadel Press; Norman Bell and Ezra Vogel (eds.), (1963), *A Modern Introduction to the Family*, New York, Free Press; Paul Gebhardt et al., (1965), *Sexual Offenders*, New York, Harper & Row.
103. Figures reported in Kelly, op.cit., p.89.
104. Figures adopted, for example, by Islington Council in London. See Margaret Boushel and Sara Noakes, (1988), 'Islington Social Services: Developing a Policy on Child Sexual Abuse', in *Feminist Review*, no.28, Spring, p.154.
105. Ruth Kempe and C. Henry Kempe, (1978), *Child Abuse*, London, Fontana/Open Books; Patricia Mrazek and C. Henry Kempe, (1981), *Sexually Abused Children and Their Families*, Oxford, Pergamon Press.
106. Kempe and Kempe, ibid, p.66.
107. Gordon, (1988a), p.288.
108. See, for example, Judith Williamson, (1986), 'Prisoner of Love', in *Consuming Passions*, London, Marion Boyars.
109. Gordon, (1988a), op.cit., p.290.
110. ibid, p.276.
111. ibid.
112. Sara Maguire, (1988), '"Sorry Love" – violence against women in the home and the state response' in *Critical Social Policy*, issue 23, Autumn, p.36.
113. ibid, p.37.
114. Gordon, (1988a), op.cit., p.288.
115. Anthony Giddens, (1984), *The Constitution of Society*, p.175, Cambridge, Polity Press.
116. Kathy Davis, (1987), 'The Janus-Face of Power: Some theoretical considerations involved in the study of gender and power', p.13. Paper presented at the symposium, *The Gender of Power*, Leiden.
117. See Pahl, op.cit.
118. Barbara Hart, (1986), in Kerry Lobel (ed.), *Naming the Violence: Speaking Out About Lesbian Battery*, p.9, Washington: Seal Press.
119. p.11.
120. in ibid, p.24.
121. ibid, p.46.
122. ibid, p.52.
123. Anne Campbell, (1981), *Girl Delinquents*, p.133, Oxford, Basil Blackwell.
124. ibid. p.150.
125. ibid. p.181.
126. ibid, p.196.
127. ibid, p.237.
128. David Robins, op.cit., p.95.
129. Andrew Tolson, (1977), *The Limits of Masculinity*, London, Tavistock.
130. Robins, op.cit., p.153.
131. ibid, p.152.

132. Peter Marsh, Elizabeth Rosser and Rom Harre, (1978), *The Rules of Disorder*, London, Routledge & Kegan Paul.

133. Eric Dunning, Patrick Murphy and John Williams, (1988), *The Roots of Football Hooliganism: An Historical and Sociological Study*, p.187, London, Routledge.

134. ibid, p.206.

135. Marsh et al., op. cit.

136. See Janet Sayers, (1986), *Sexual Contradictions: Psychology, Psychoanalysis, and Feminism*, p.142, London, Tavistock.

137. ibid, p.157; Jane Temperley, (1984), 'Our Own Worst Enemies: Unconscious Factors in Female Disadvantage' in *Free Associations*, Pilot Issue.

138. Temperley, ibid.

139. Sarah Benton, (unpub.), 'Notes on sex and violence'.

140. ibid.

141. Deborah Cameron and Elizabeth Frazer, op.cit., p.47.

142. David Morgan, (unpub.), Research Proposals for a Study of Masculinity and Violence.

143. Russel Dobash, R. Emerson Dobash, Sue Gutteridge, (1986), *The Imprisonment of Women*, p.86, p.147, Oxford, Blackwell.

144. Lynne Segal, (1987), *Is the Future Female?*, chapter 5, London, Virago.

145. Kum Kum Bhavnani, (1987), 'Turning the World Upside Down' in *Charting the Journey*, p.264, London, Sheba.

146. ibid, p.268.

147. Bell Hooks, (1989), 'Feminism and Militarism; A Comment' in Hooks, op.cit., p.93.

148. Morgan, op.cit.

149. Martin Walker, (1989), in *The Guardian*, January 16.

150. Spike Lee talks to Steve Goldman, (1989), 'Heat of the Moment' in *The Weekend Guardian*, June 24–5, p.15.

10. *Beyond Gender Hierarchy: Can Men Change?*

1. Elizabeth Janeway, (1982), *Cross Sections: from a decade of change*, p.17, New York, William Morrow & Co.

2. ibid, p.13.

3. ibid, p.19.

4. Ann Oakley, (1984), *Taking it Like a Woman*, London, Jonathan Cape.

5. ibid, p.78.

6. ibid, p.78, p.80.

7. ibid, p.116.

8. ibid, p.121.

9. ibid, p.13.

10. ibid, p.74.

11. ibid, p.156.

12. ibid, p.190.

13. ibid, p.201.

14. ibid, p.116.

15. Ann Barr Snitow, (1985), 'Mass Market Romance: Pornography for Women Is Different' in Ann Snitow et al. (eds.), *Powers of Desire: The Politics of Sexuality*, New York, Monthly Review Press.

16. See Lynne Segal, (1983), 'Smash the Family?' in Lynne Segal (ed.), *What is to be done about the family?* Harmondsworth, Penguin.

17. See, for example, Angela Hamblin, (1972), 'The Suppressed Power of Female Sexuality' in *Shrew: Women's Liberation Workshop Paper*, vol.4, 6, December.

18. Sheila MacLeod, (1988), 'A Fairy Story', in Sara Maitland (ed.), *Very Heaven*, p.182, London, Virago.

19. Angela Carter, (1988), 'Truly, It Felt Like Year One' in ibid, p.214.

20. Quoted in ibid, p.4.

21. Sara Maitland, (1988), '"I Believe in Yesterday" – An Introduction' in ibid, p.15.

22. Marsha Rowe, (1988), 'Up from Down Under' in ibid, p.166.

23. See, for example, the reflections of journalist and agony aunt Carol Lee, (1989), *The Blind Side of Eden*, pp.6–7, London, Bloomsbury.

24. Alix Kates Shulman, (1988), 'Sex and Power: Sexual Bases of Radical Feminism' in *Signs*, vol.5, 4, p.604.

25. Shere Hite, (1981), *The Hite Report on Male Sexuality*, London, MacDonald.

26. Wendy Cope, (1987), *Making Cocoa for Kingsley Amis*, p.39, London, Faber.

27. Shere Hite, (1988), *Women and Love*, p.xxvi, London, Viking.

28. ibid, p.4.

29. ibid, p.5.

30. ibid, p.125.

31. ibid, p.867, p.10.

32. ibid, p.654.

33. Sara Maitland, (1988), 'And two for tea', review of Shere Hite *Women and Love* in *New Statesman*, 26 February, p.21.

34. ibid.

35. Shere Hite, op.cit., back cover.

36. ibid, p.42.

37. Naomi Weisstein, (1988), 'The Hite Reports: Charting an Ideological Revolution in Progress' in ibid, p.xlii.

38. Hite, op.cit., p.458.

39. ibid, p.431.

40. ibid, p.457.

41. ibid, p.761.

42. Richard Sennett, (1976), *The Fall of Public Man*, p.28, London, Faber & Faber.

43. Sheila Rowbotham, (1987), 'Feminism and its discontents', in *New Socialist*, 53, December, p.40.

44. As heard on BBC1, Sue Lawley on 'Wogan', 28 September 1988.

45. Jon Snodgrass, (1977), 'Introduction: Men and the Feminist Movement' in Jon Snodgrass (ed.), *For Men Against Sexism*, p.7, Albion, California, Times Change Press.

46. From a report by the Islington Men's Group written in 1974, published in Dalston Men's Group (eds.), *Men's News*, 5 May 1977, p.12.

47. Dalston Men's Group, 'A History' in ibid. p.2.

48. South London Men Against Sexism, (1974), 'Why Men's Liberation?' in *Brothers Against Sexism*, Spring 3, p.7.

49. John Rowan, (1987), *The Horned God*, p.17, London, Routledge & Kegan Paul.

50. Heard at the Islington Socialist Centre Christmas party, December 1978.

51. In Interview by East London Men's group of Islington Men's Group (unpub.).

52. Conversations with various feminists.

53. Danny Cohen, (1978), '"Men Against Sexism" or "Men's Liberation"' in *Men*

Against Sexism National Conference, 2nd Newsletter, p.2. Similar arguments describing all men as 'the enemies of women' were made by many other men against sexism, for example, Brad Kress, (1975), 'Chosing' [sic] in *Men Against Sexism or The Pig's Last Grunt*, Spring, p.15.

54. Report by Islington Men's Group, op.cit., p.13.

55. South London Men Against Sexism, (1974), 'Where do we go from here?' in *Brothers Against Sexism*, Spring, no.3, p.3.

56. Nigel Armistead, (1975), 'Men's Liberation and Men Against Sexism', in *Men Against Sexism or The Pig's Last Grunt*, op.cit., p.6.

57. Interview by East London Men's Group of Islington Men's Group, op.cit.

58. Steve Gould, (1978), *The London Men's Conference* in *Islington Gutter Press*, May, p.8.

59. John Rowan, op.cit., p.21.

60. Martin Humphries, (1987), 'Choosing with Care: working with non-gay men', in Gillian Hanscombe and Martin Humphries (eds.), *Heterosexuality*, p.90, London, Gay Men's Press.

61. Jan Bradshaw, (1982), 'Now What Are They Up To? Men in the "Men's Movement"!', in Scarlet Friedman and Elizabeth Sarah (eds.), *On the Problem of Men*, p.184, London, Women's Press.

62. Armistead, op.cit., p.6.

63. Jeff Hearn, (1987), *The Gender of Oppression: Men, Masculinity and the Critique of Marxism*, p.171, Brighton, Wheatsheaf.

64. ibid.

65. See, *Can I stop being a tree soon?*, an account of men minding 200 children at the 1977 Women's Liberation Conference, London, Men's Free Press.

66. Harry Brod, 'The Case for Men's Studies' in Harry Brod (ed.), *The Making of Masculinities*, p.51, London, Allen & Unwin.

67. Hearn, op.cit., p.173.

68. Sue O'Sullivan, (1988), 'From 1969', in Amanda Sebestyen (ed.), *'68, '78, '88: From Women's Liberation to Feminism*, London, Prism.

69. Andrew Tolson, (1977), *The Limits of Masculinity*, p.143, London, Tavistock.

70. Reported in *Men Against Sexism*, Spring, 1975.

71. ibid.

72. See editorial, *Achilles Heel*, no.3, p.4.

73. *Achilles Heel*, published articles about sexual politics and socialism.

74. Keith Motherson, (1979), 'Developing Our Power' in *Anti-Sexist Men's Newsletter*, 5, pp.3–4.

75. Dan Muir, (1975), 'Review of *The Dangerous Sex* by H.R. Hayes' in *Men Against Sexism*, Spring.

76. Editorial, (1978), in *Achilles Heel*, 1, Summer, p.5.

77. Martin Humphries, op.cit., p.88.

78. Editorial, (circe 1980), *Achilles Heel*, 5, p.1.

79. ibid.

80. Tolson, op.cit., p.144.

81. Kevin Devaney, (circa 1982), 'Mining – A World Apart' in *Achilles Heel*, 6&7, p.12.

82. ibid, p.13.

83. ibid, p.14.

84. Vic Seidler, (circa 1980), 'Raging Bull' in *Achilles Heel*, 5, pp.8–9.

85. R.W. Connell, (1987), *Gender and Power*, p.234, Cambridge, Polity Press.

86. R.W. Connell, (1983), *Which Way is UP?: Essays on Class, Sex and Culture*, p.22, London, Allen & Unwin.

87. See J. Kagan and H.A. Moss, (1962), *Birth to Maturity*, New York, Wiley; Daniel Levinson et al., (1978), *The Seasons of a Man's Life*, New York, Ballantine; Alison Thomas, (1988), 'Men's Accounts of Their "Gender Identity": A Constructionist Approach', Paper presented to the annual conference of the Social Psychology Section of the British Psychological Society, University of Kent, at Canterbury 23–25 September.

88. For example, Thomas, ibid.

89. ibid.

90. There are no regularly appearing national Men Against Sexism publications in Britain today. There are some regional newsletters, for example, *Men For Change*, in Nottingham. Information collected from discussion with Jeff Hearn and various other men still active in men against sexism activities.

91. See A Roundtable Discussion, (1988), 'Mending the broken heart of Socialism' in Rowena Chapman and Jonathan Rutherford (eds.), *Male Order: Unwrapping Masculinity*, London, Lawrence & Wishart.

92. For example, Tony Eardley et al., (1983), *About Men*, Broadcasting Support Services, London.

93. See Linkman, (British Newsletter on Men's Studies), Harry Gray, Department of Educational Research, Cartmel College, University of Lancaster, UK.

94. See Don Long, (1987), 'Working With Men Who Batter' in Murray Scher et al. (eds.), *Handbook of Counselling & Psychotherapy with Men*, London, Sage.

95. Hearn, op.cit., p.178.

96. Frank Mort, (1988), 'Boys Own? Masculinity, Style and Popular Culture' in Chapman and Rutherford (eds.), op.cit., p.193.

97. ibid, p.194.

98. Prince, (1988), Anna Stesia, *LoveSexy*, New York, Paisley Park Records.

99. See, for example, John Fiske et al., (1987), *Myths of Oz: Reading Australian Popular Culture*, London, Allen & Unwin.

100. Mirra Komarovsky, (1976), *Dilemmas of Masculinity: A study of college men*, New York, Norton; Joseph Pleck, (1987), 'The Contemporary Man' in Murray Scher et al. (eds.), op.cit.; Thomas, op.cit.

101. Pleck, ibid; Graeme Russell, (1983), *The Changing Role of Fathers*, Queensland, University of Queensland Press.

102. Yvonne Roberts, (1984), *Man Enough: Men of 35 Speak Out*, p.11, London, Chatto & Windus.

103. Pleck, op.cit., p.20.

104. ibid, p.24.

105. Cynthia Cockburn, (1988), 'Masculinity, the Left and Feminism' in Chapman and Rutherford (eds.), op.cit., p.308.

106. See 'Women & Work' in *The Guardian*, January 18, 1989. In the US in 1988 the Boss of the Year was a woman; in the UK the owner of the Body Shop chain of stores, a woman, was named Businessman of the Year at around that time. For the rising number of middle-class women in the US moving into professional and middle-management jobs (including the judiciary), and the rapid growth in businesses owned by women, see Sara Rix (ed.) (for the Women's Research & Education Institute of the Congressional Caucus for Women's Issues), (1989), *The American Woman 1987–88; A Report in Depth*, pp.187–8, London, W.W. Norton.

107. Rowena Chapman and Jonathan Rutherford, (1988), in ibid, p.13.

108. Quoted in Hilary Land, (1980), 'The Family Wage' in *Feminist Review*, no.6, p.161.

109. See Jane Humphries, (1981), 'Protective Legislation, the Capitalist State, and Working-Class Men: The Case of the 1842 Mines Regulation Act' in *Feminist Review*, no.7.

110. Sarah Boston, (1987), *Women Workers and the Trade Unions*, p.25, London, Lawrence & Wishart.

111. ibid, p.28.

112. Martha May, (1982), 'The Historical Problem of the Family Wage: The Ford Motor Company and the Five Dollar Day' in *Feminist Review*, vol.8, no.2, Summer.

113. See Boston, op.cit., p.24.

114. Anne Phillips and Barbara Taylor, (1980), 'Sex and Skill: Notes Towards a Feminist Economics' in *Feminist Review*, no.6.

115. Quoted in ibid.

116. Paul Thompson, (1983), *The Nature of Work: An Introduction to Debates on the Labour Process*, pp.203–6, London, Macmillan.

117. For example, Ruth Cavendish, (1982), *Women on the Line*, London, Routledge & Kegan Paul.

118. Anna Pollert, (1981), *Girls, Wives, Factory Lives*, p.84, London, Macmillan.

119. Ruth Milkman, (1987), *Gender at Work: The Dynamics of Job Segregation by Sex during World War II*, p.6, Chicago, University of Illinois Press.

120. Boston, op.cit., p.25.

121. ibid, p.74.

122. ibid, p.40.

123. ibid.

124. ibid, p.81.

125. Women in the early years of the trade union movement organised themselves separately from men in the Women's Trade Union League, the National Federation of Women Workers and the Women's Co-operative Guild. See Boston, op.cit.

126. See Lynne Segal, (1989), 'Slow Change or No Change: Feminism, Socialism and the Problem of Men' in *Feminist Review*, no.31, Spring.

127. See Ruth Elliot, (1984), 'How Far Have We Come? Women's Organization in the Unions in the United Kingdom' in Cockburn (ed.), 'Trade Unions and the Radicalizing of Socialist Feminism' in *Feminist Review*, no.16.

128. Ruth Elliot, ibid, p.69, p.71.

129. ibid, p.72.

130. Inez McCormack, in Roundtable Discussion, in Chapman and Rutherford, op.cit., p.258.

131. Jenny Beale, (1982), *Getting It Together: Women as Trade Unionists*, p.86, London, Pluto Press.

132. ibid, p.92.

133. ibid, p.89.

134. Cynthia Cockburn, (1987), *Women, Trade Unions and Political Parties*, p.9, London, Fabian Research Series, no.349.

135. SERTUC Women's Committee, (1989), *Still Moving Towards Equality: A survey of progress towards equality in trade unions*, London, SERTUC.

136. Andrew Parker, (1984), 'Opinion' in *British Printer*, July, p.5.

137. Jack Dromey, in Roundtable Discussion, in Chapman and Rutherford, op.cit., p.256.

138. Linda Burnham, (1985), 'Has Poverty Been Feminized in Black America?' in *The Black Scholar*, March/April, p.15.

139. ibid, p.16.

140. Quoted in 'Women and Work' in *The Guardian*, January 18, 1989.

141. Richard Dyer, (1989), 'Old briefs for new' in *New Statesman and Society*, 24 March, p.43.

142. Sheila Rowbotham, (1989), *The Past is Before Us*, p.107, London, Pandora.

143. Pippa Norris, (1987), *Politics and Sexual Equality: The Comparative Position of Women in Western Democracies*, p.11, Brighton, Wheatsheaf.

144. ibid, p.126.

145. ibid, p.129.

146. Anette Borchorst and Birte Siim, (1987), 'Women and the advance of the welfare state – a new kind of patriarchal power?' in Anne Showstack Sassoon (ed.), *Women and the State*, p.137, London, Hutchinson.

147. Helena Norberg, (1988), 'Women on the Move in Trade Unions within the Public Sector', Paper presented at the European Socialist Feminist Forum, Manchester, United Kingdom, November.

148. Pippa Norris, op.cit., p.61.

149. Mary Ruggie, (1984), *The State and Working Women*, Princeton, Princeton University Press.

150. Norris, op.cit., p.153.

151. Parents – of either sex – are entitled to 12 months leave, 9 months paid at 90 per cent of earnings, 3 months paid at a lower, fixed rate. In addition either parent of a child under 12 is entitled to 60 days paid leave to care for a sick child. Parents of pre-school children are entitled to work a 6-hour day, but without compensation for loss of earnings.

152. Norris, op.cit., p.116.

153. ibid, p.103.

154. The clauses of the Swedish Marriage Act assert: 'Spouses shall jointly care for home and the children and promote the well-being of the family on the basis of joint consultation' ... 'Spouses shall share the expenses and discharge of household duties'. In The Working Party for the Role of the Male, (1986), 'The Changing Role of the Male', Stockholm.

155. Hilda Scott, (1982), *Sweden's "Right to be Human"*, p.148, London, Allison & Busby.

156. Norris, op.cit., p.134.

157. The Working Party for the Changing Role of the Male, op.cit.

158. Scott, op.cit.

159. Karin Sandqvist, (1987), 'Swedish family policy and the attempt to change paternal roles' in Charlie Lewis and Margaret O'Brien (eds.), *Reassessing Fatherhood*, p.149, London, Sage.

160. ibid, p.151.

161. ibid, p.152.

162. ibid.

163. ibid, p.151.

164. See Lynne Segal, (1987), *Is the Future Female?*, chapters 1, 2, London, Virago.

165. Sarah Perrigo, (1988), 'Notes on the problem of organizing effectively in the British Labour Party'. Paper given at the European Socialist Feminist Forum, Manchester, November.

166. Di Parkin and Irene Breugel, (1988), 'Entering the Structures: Socialist

Feminism in Britain and the Local State'. Paper given at European Socialist Feminist Forum, ibid.

167. Kathryn Harriss, (1989). 'New Alliances: Socialist Feminism in the Eighties' in *Feminist Review*, no.31, Spring.

168. Ruth Elliot, (1988), 'Women, Restructuring and Union Strategies' in *Women and the Economy*, London, Women's Studies Unit, Polytechnic of North London. Another paper in this collection, Jenny Hurstfield, 'Sex Inequalities and Pay', provides figures on low pay. In April 1987, 2.37 million men in Britain worked full time for very low wages (less than £3.50 an hour), accompanying the 2.66 million women working full time on very low pay.

169. Harriss, op.cit., p.51.

170. Derek Hatton, (1988), *Inside Left*, p.170, London, Bloomsbury.

171. Quoted in Michele Barrett and Jeffrey Weeks, (1987), 'Labouring Over Love: Can a traditional family party cope with gay and lesbian sexuality?' in *New Socialist*, 49, May, p.22.

172. From various positions taken in *New Statesman* editorials around April/May, 1987, just before the last general election in Britain. Also at that time Andrew Lumsden, the *New Statesman*'s then only out gay reporter, was sacked.

173. Elizabeth Wilson, (1989), 'In a Different Key' in Katherine Gieve (ed.), *Balancing Acts: On Being a Mother*, p.15, London, Virago.

174. ibid.

175. Diane Ehrensaft, (1987), *Parenting Together: Men and Women Sharing the Care of their Children*, New York, Free Press.

176. ibid.

177. Jennifer Uglow, (1989), 'Medea and Marmite Sandwiches' in Gieve, op.cit., p.146.

178. Jean Radford, (1989), 'My Pride and Joy' in Gieve, ibid, pp.141–2.

Bibliography

Franklin Abbot (ed.) (1987), *New Men, New Minds*, The Crossing Press/Freedom, Canada.

Chinua Achebe (1988), *Hopes and Impediments: Selected Essays 1965–87*, Heinemann, London.

Parveen Adams (1979), 'A Note on Sexual Division and Sexual Differences' in *m/f*, 3.

Theodore Adorno (1978), [first published 1951], *Minima Moralia*, Verso, London.

Theodore Adorno *et al.* (1964), *The Authoritarian Personality*, John Wiley, New York.

Sheila Allen *et al.* (1986) *The Experience of Unemployment*, Macmillan, London.

Sue Allen and Lynne Harne (1988), 'Lesbian Mothers: the Fight for Child Custody' in Bob Cant and Susan Hemmings (eds.), *Radical Records*, Routledge, London.

Kenneth Allsop (1964), *The Angry Decade*, Peter Owen, London.

Walter Allen (1960), 'Review of *Lucky Jim*' in Feldman and Gartenberg, *op.cit.*.

Robert Altman (1981), *Coming Out in the Seventies*, Alyson Publications, Boston.

Dennis Altman (1983), *The Homosexualization of America*, Beacon Press, Boston.

Dennis Altman (1986), *AIDS and the New Puritanism*, Pluto Press, London.

D. Altman et al. (1989), *Which Homosexuality?: Essays from the International Scientific Conference on Lesbian and Gay Studies*, GMP, London.

Menachim Amir (1971), *Patterns in Forcible Rape*, University of Chicago Press, Chicago.

Anon. (circa 1971), *Why Miss World?* Pamphlet, London.

J. Archer (1976), 'Biological Explanations of Psychological Sex Differences' in B. Lloyd and J. Archer (eds.), *Exploring Sex Differences*, Academic Press, London.

Shirley Ardener (1987), 'A Note on Gender Iconography: the Vagina' in Pat Caplan (ed.), *The Cultural Construction of Sexuality*, Tavistock Publications, London.

Robert Ardrey (1977), *The Hunting Hypothesis*, Fontana, London.

Nigel Armistead (1975), 'Men's Liberation and Men Against Sexism' in *Men Against Sexism or The Pig's Last Grunt*.

Timothy Ashplant (unpub), 'Autobiography, Identity and Gender'.

Jack Babuscio (1977), 'Camp and Gay Sensibility' in *Gays and Film*, BFI, London.

Kathryn Backett (1982), *Mothers and Fathers*, Macmillan, London.

Maria Balinska (1989), 'Australian Rules' in *The Guardian* (17 January).

James Baldwin (1957), *Giovanni's Room*, Michael Joseph, London.

James Baldwin (1963), *Another Country*, Michael Joseph, London.

James Baldwin (1985), *Price of the Ticket*, Michael Joseph, London.

Toni Cade Bambara (1972), *Gorilla, My Love*, Random House, New York.

Toni Cade Bambara (1977), *The Sea Birds are Still Alive*, Random House, New York.

Toni Cade Bambara (1980), *The Salt Eaters*, Random House, New York.

Judith Bardwick and Elizabeth Douvan (1971), 'Ambivalence: The Socialization of Women' in Gornick and Moran (eds.), *op.cit.*.

Michele Barrett and Jeffrey Weeks (1987), 'Labouring Over Love: Can a Traditional Family Party Cope with Gay and Lesbian Sexuality'? in *New Socialist*, 49, May.

Roger Bastide (1972), 'Dusky Venus, Black Apollo' in Paul Baxter and Basil Sansom, *Race and Social Difference*, Penguin, Harmondsworth.

Jenny Beale (1982), *Getting it Together: Women as Trade Unionists*, Pluto Press, London.

Joseph Beam (ed.) (1986), *In the Life: A Black Gay Anthology*, Alyson Publications Inc., Boston.

Joseph Beam (1986), 'Brother to Brother: Words From the Heart' in Joseph Beam (ed.), *In the Life: A Black Gay Anthology, op.cit.*.

Lou Becker (1987), 'An Older Father's Letter to his Young Son' in Abbot (ed.), *op.cit.*.

Colin Bell et al. (1983), *Fathers, Childbirth and Work*, Equal Opportunities Commission, 46, Manchester.

Norman Bell and Ezra Vogel (eds.) (1963), *A Modern Introduction to the Family*, Free Press, New York.

R. Bell (1981), *Worlds of Friendship*, Sage, California.

Sandra Bem (1974), 'The Measurement of Psychological Androgyny' in *Journal of Consulting and Clinical Psychology*, vol. 42, 2, pp.155–62.

Sandra Bem (1981), 'Gender Schema Theory: A Cognitive Account of Sex Typing' in *Psychological Review*, pp.354–64.

Camilla Benbow and Julian Stanley (1980), 'Sex Differences in Mathematical Ability: Fact or Artifact?', *Science* 210, pp.1262–4.

Jessica Benjamin (1986), 'A Desire of One's Own: Psychoanalytic Feminism and Intersubjective Space' in Teresa de Lauretis (ed.), *Feminist Studies: Critical Studies*, Indiana University Press, Bloomington.

Sarah Benton (unpub) 'Notes on Sex'.

Sarah Benton (1983), talks to novelist John Fowles in 'Adam and Eve' in *New Socialist*, 11, May/June.

Arnon Bentovim et al. (eds.) (1988), *Child Sexual Abuse Within the Family*, Wright, London.

Bice Benvenuto and Roger Kennedy (1987), *The Works of Jacques Lacan: An Introduction*, Free Association Books, London.

Kum Kum Bhavnani (1987), 'Turning the World Upside Down' in *Charting the Journey*, p.264, Sheba, London.

Keith Birch (1980), 'The Politics of Autonomy' in Gay Left Collective (eds.), *Homosexuality: Power and Politics*, Alison & Busby, London, *op.cit.*.

Caroline Bird (1979), *The Two-Paycheck Marriage*, Pocket Books, New York.

John Bird (1982), 'Jacques Lacan – the French Freud' in *Radical Philosophy*, 30, Spring.

D.W. Birnbaum and W.L. Croll (1984), 'The Etiology of Children's Stereotypes about Sex Differences in Emotionality' in *Sex Roles*, vol. 10, 9/10, pp.677–91.

Peter Biskind (1983), *Seeing is Believing*, Pantheon, New York.

Robin Blackburn (1988), *The Overthrow of Colonial Slavery 1776–1848*, Verso, London.

Ian Blair (1985), *Investigating Rape: A New Approach for Police*, Croom Helm, London.

Ruth Bleier (1984), Science and Gender: A Critique of Biology and its Theories on Women, Pergamon Press, London.

Rudie Bleys (1988), 'The Geography of Perversion/Desire: 18th and 19th Century Interpretations of Primitive Homosexuality' in International Scientific Conference of Gay and Lesbian Studies, *Homosexuality, Which Homosexuality?*, vol 1 (History), Free University Amsterdam, Amsterdam.

Anette Borchorst and Birte Siim (1987), 'Women and the Advance of the Welfare State – a New Kind of Patriarchal Power?' in Anne Showstack Sassoon (ed.), *Women and the State*, Hutchison, London.

Elizabeth Bott (1967), *Family and Social Network*, Tavistock, London.

Sarah Boston (1987), *Women Workers and the Trade Unions*, Lawrence & Wishart, London.

Margaret Boushel and Sara Noakes (1988), 'Islington Social Services: Developing a Policy on Child Sexual Abuse' in *Feminist Review*, 28, Spring.

Peter Bradbury (1985), 'Desire and Pregnancy' in Andy Metcalfe and Martin Humphries (eds.), *The Sexuality of Men*, Pluto Press, London.

Tony Bradman (1985), *The Essential Father*, Unwin Paperbacks, London.

Jan Bradshaw (1982), 'Now What Are They Up To? Men in the "Men's Movement"!' in Scarlet Friedman and Elizabeth Sarah (eds.), *On the Problem of Men*, Women's Press, London.

Patrick Brantlinger (1987), 'Victorians and Africans: The Geneology of the Myth of the Dark Continent' in Henry Louis Gates Jr *Race, Writing and Difference*, University of Chicago Press, London.

Andrew Britton (1978/9),'FOR Interpretation – Notes Against Camp' in *Gay Left*, 7.

Harry Brod, 'The Case for Men's Studies' in Harry Brod (ed.), *The Making of Masculinities*, Allen & Unwin, London.

Susan Brownmiller (1976), *Against Our Will: Men, Women and Rape*, Penguin, Harmondsworth.

Beverly Bryan, Stella Dadzie and Suzanne Scafe (1985), *The Heart of the Race: Black Women's Writing in Britain*, Virago, London.

Rebecca Bryson et al. (1978), 'Family Size, Satisfaction, and Productivity in Dual-Career Couples' in *Psychology of Women Quarterly*, 3, pp.167–77.

A.W.H. Buffery and Jeffrey A. Gray (1972), 'Sex Differences in the Development of Spatial and Linguistic Skills' in C.Ounstead and D.C. Taylor (eds.), *Gender Differences: Their Ontogeny and Significance*, Churchill Livingstone, Edinburgh.

Gordon Burn (1984), *Somebody's Husband, Somebody's Son: The Story of the Yorkshire Ripper*, Pan Books, London.

Linda Burnham (1985), 'Has Poverty Been Feminized in Black America?' in *The Black Scholar*, March/April.

Toni Cade (1970), 'On the Issue of Roles' in Toni Cade (ed.), *The Black Woman*, Signet, New York.

Pat Califia (1986), 'Among Us, Against Us: the New Puritans' in Ellis, *op.cit.*.

Bebe Moore Campbell (1988), *Successful Women, Angry Men*, Arrow Books, London.

Anne Campbell (1981), *Girl Delinquents*, Basil Blackwell, Oxford.

Deborah Cameron (1985), *Feminism & Linguistic Theory*, Macmillan, London.

Deborah Cameron and Elizabeth Frazer (1987), *The Lust to Kill*, Polity Press, Cambridge.

Pat Caplan (ed.) (1987), *The Cultural Construction of Sexuality*, Tavistock, London.

Hazel Carby (1987), '"On the Threshold of Women's Era": Lynching, Empire, and Sexuality in Black Feminist Theory' in Gates, *op.cit.*.

Edward Carpenter (1948), [First edition 1896] *Love's Coming of Age*, Allen & Unwin, London.

Tim Carrigan, Bob Connell and John Lee (1987), 'Towards a New Sociology of Masculinity' in Harry Brod (ed.), *The Making of Masculinities: The New Men's Studies*, p. 78, Allen & Unwin, London.

Angela Carter (1979), *The Sadeian Woman*, Virago, London.

Angela Carter (1983), 'Sugar Daddy' in Ursula Owen (ed.), *Fathers: Reflections by Daughters*, p. 25, Virago, London.

Angela Carter (1988), 'Truly, It Felt Like Year One' in Maitland (1988a), *op.cit.*.

Erica Carter, Simon Watney (eds.), *Taking Liberties: Aids and Cultural Politics*, Serpent's Tail, London.

Ruth Cavendish (1982), *Women on the Line*, Routledge & Kegan Paul, London.

Rowena Chapman and Jonathan Rutherford (eds.) (1988), *Male Order: Unwrapping Masculinity*, Lawrence & Wishart, London.

Gail Chester and Julienne Dickey (eds.) (1988), *Feminism and Censorship*, Prism Press, London.

Andrew Cherlin (1982), *Marriage Divorce Remarriage*, Harvard University Press, Boston.

Nancy Chodorow (1978), *The Reproduction of Mothering: Psychoanalysis and the Sociology of Gender*, University of California Press, London.

Nancy Chodorow (1980), 'Gender, Relation, and Difference in Psychoanalytic Perspective' in Hester Eisenstein and Alice Jardine (eds.), *The Future of Difference*, G.K. Hall & Co., Boston MA.

Kenneth Clark (1965), *Dark Ghetto*, Harper, New York.

Eldridge Cleaver (1969), *Soul on Ice*, Cape, London.

Rhonda Cobham and Merle Collins (1986), *Watchers and Seekers: Creative Writing By Black Women in Britain*, Women's Press, London.

Cynthia Cockburn (1981), 'The Material of Male Dominance' in *Feminist Review*, 9.

Cynthia Cockburn (1987), *Women, Trade Unions and Political Parties*, Fabian Research Series No. 349, London.

Cynthia Cockburn (1988), 'Masculinity, the Left and Feminism' in Chapman and Rutherford (eds.), *op.cit.*.

Derek Cohen and Richard Dyer (1980), 'The Politics of Gay Culture', in Gay Left Collective (eds.), *op.cit.*.

Combahee River Collective (1983), 'Collective Statement' in Barbara Smith (ed.), *Home Girls: A Black Feminist Anthology*, Kitchen Table/Women of Color Press, New York.

Joseph Conrad (1986), [First published 1902], *Heart of Darkness*, Penguin, Harmondsworth.

R.W. Connell (1983), *Which Way is UP?: Essays on Class, Sex and Culture*, Allen & Unwin, London.

R.W. Connell (1987), *Gender and Power*, Polity Press, Cambridge.

R.W. Connell (unpub), 'An Iron Man: The body and some contradictions of hegemonic masculinity'.

A. Constantinople (1979), 'Sex Role Acquisition: In Search of the Elephant' in *Sex Roles*, vol. 5, 2.

David Cooper (1964), 'Sartre on Genet', *New Left Review*, no 25, May/June.

Wendy Cope (1987), *Making Cocoa for Kingsley Amis*, Faber, London.

Rosalind Coward (1984), *Female Desire*, Paladin, London.

Dalston Men's Group (eds.) (1977), *Men's News*, 5, May.

Danny Danziger (ed.) (1988), *Eton Voices*, Viking, London.

Leonore Davidoff and Catherine Hall (1987), *Family Fortunes: Men and Women of the English Middle Class 1780–1850*, Hutchison, London.

John D'Emilio and Estelle Freedman (1988), *Intimate Matters: A History of Sexuality in America*, Harper & Row, New York.

N. Dennis, F. Henriques and C. Slaughter (1969), *Coal is Our Life*, Tavistock, London.

Kevin Devaney (circa 1982), 'Mining – a World Apart' in *Achilles Heel*, 6&7.

Peter Dews (1987), *Logics of Disintegration: Post-Structuralism and the Claims of Critical Theory*, Verso, London.

Lesley Dike (1987), 'AIDS: What Women Should Know' in *Outwrite*, 54, January.

Dorothy Dinnerstein (1978), *The Rocking of the Cradle*, Souvenir Press, London.

Russell Dobash, R. Emerson Dobash and Sue Gutteridge (1986), *The Imprisonment of Women*, Blackwell, Oxford.

Edward Donnerstein and Daniel Linz (1987), 'Mass-Media Sexual Violence and Male Viewers: Current Theory and Research' in Kimmel, *op.cit.*.

Edward Donnerstein and Steven Penrod (1987), 'Sexual Violence in the Mass Media: Social Psychological Implications' in Phillip Shaver and Clyde Hendrick (eds.), *Sex and Gender*, Sage, London.

Jonathan Dollimore (1983), 'The Challenge of Sexuality' in Alan Sinfield (ed.), *Society and Literature 1945–1970*, Methuen, London.

Jonathan Dollimore (1986), 'Homophobia and Sexual Difference' in *Sexual Difference, Oxford Literary Review*, vol. 8, 1–2.

Stephanie Dowrick and Sibyl Grundberg (eds.) (1980), *Why Children?*, Women's Press, London.

Lisa Duggan (1986), 'Censorship in the Name of Feminism' in Ellis, *op.cit.*.

Eric Dunning, Patrick Murphy and John Williams (1988), *The Roots of Football Hooliganism: An Historical and Sociological Study*, Routledge, London.

K. Durkin (1985), *Television, Sex Roles and Children: A Developmental Social Psychological Account*, Open University Press, Milton Keynes.

Andrea Dworkin (1981), *Pornography: Men Possessing Women*, Women's Press, London.

Andrea Dworkin (1987), *Right-Wing Women: The Politics of Domesticated Females*, Women's Press, London.

Richard Dyer (1979), *Stars*, British Film Institute, London.

Richard Dyer (1981), 'Getting Over the Rainbow' in George Bridges and Rosalind Brunt (eds.), *Silver Linings*, Laurence & Wishart, London.

Richard Dyer (1982), 'Don't Look Now – The Male Pin-Up' in *Screen*, vol. 23, 3–4, Sept/Oct.

Richard Dyer (1986), 'Coming to Terms' in *Jump Cut*, 30.

Tony Eardley, Martin Humphries and Paul Morrison (1983), *About Men*, Broadcasting Support Services, London.

Antony Easthope (1985), *What a Man's Gotta Do*, Paladin, London.

Fern Maya Eckman (1968), *The Furious Passage of James Baldwin*, Michael Joseph, London.

Susan Edwards (1981), *Female Sexuality and the Law*, Martin Robertson, Oxford.

Barbara Ehrenreich et al. (1986), *Re-Making Love: The Feminization of Sex*, Anchor Press, New York.

Barbara Ehrenreich (1983), *The Hearts of Men*, Pluto Press, London.

Diane Ehrensaft (1987), *Parenting Together: Men and Women Sharing the Care of their Children*, Free Press, New York.

Luise Eichenbaum and Susie Orbach (1982), *Outside In, Inside Out*, Penguin, Harmondsworth.

Luise Eichenbaum and Susie Orbach (1984), *What Do Women Want?*, Fontana, London.

G. Eichinger Ferro-Luzzi (1980), 'The Female Lingam' in *Current Anthropology*, vol. 21, 1.

Ruth Elliot (1984), 'How Far Have We Come? Women's Organization in the Unions in the United Kingdom' in Cockburn (ed.), 'Trade Unions and the Radicalizing of Socialist Feminism' in *Feminist Review*, 16.

Ruth Elliot (1988), 'Women, Restructuring and Union Strategies' in *Women and the Economy*, Women's Studies Unit, Polytechnic of North London, London.

Kate Ellis et al. (1986), *Caught Looking: Feminism, Pornography and Censorship*, Caught Looking Inc., New York.

Deirdre English (1980), 'The Politics of Porn: Can Feminists Walk the Line?' in *Sex, Porn and Male Rage*, Mother Jones Reprint, San Francisco.

Judith Ennew (1986), *The Sexual Exploitation of Children*, Polity Press, Cambridge.

Everywoman (1988), *Pornography and Sexual Violence: Evidence of Links*, London.

Eileen Fairweather, (1982), 'Leeds: Curfew on Men' in Marsha Rowe (ed.), *Spare Rib Reader*, Penguin, Harmondsworth.

Eileen Fairweather (1983), 'The Man in the Orange Box' in Owen, *op.cit.*.

Hugh Fairweather (1976), 'Sex Differences in Cognition', *Cognition*, 4.

Hugh Fairweather (1982), 'Sex Differences: Little Reason for Females to Play Midfield' in J.G. Beaumont (ed.) (1985), *Divided Visual Field Studies of Cerebral Organisation*, Academic Press, London.

Frantz Fanon (1970), [First published 1952] *Black Skin, White Masks*, Paladin, London.

Margo Farnham (1986), 'In the Name of the Father – Fathers and Class' in *Trouble and Strife*, 8.

Elaine Feinstein (1985), *Bessie Smith*, Viking, London.

Dave Feintwick (1979), 'Men's Lives: Extract from an Autobiography' in *Achilles Heel*, 2.

Gene Feldman and Max Gartenberg (eds.) (1960), *Protest*, Panther, London.

David Fernbach (1981), *The Spiral Path*, Gay Men's Press, London.

Shulamith Firestone (1971), *The Dialectic of Sex*, Paladin, London.

John Fiske et al. (1987), *Myths of Oz: Reading Australian Popular Culture*, Allen & Unwin, London.

Gerald Fogel et al. (1986), *The Psychology of Men*, Basic Books, New York.

John Forrester (1985), 'Rape, Seduction and Psychoanalysis' in Tomaselli and Porter (eds.), *Rape*, Blackwell, Oxford.

Michel Foucault (1979), *The History of Sexuality*, Allen Lane, London.

David Ford and Jeff Hearn (1988), *Studying Men and Masculinity: A Sourcebook of*

Literature and Materials, Applied Social Studies, University of Bradford.

John Fowles (1963), *The Collector*, Pan, London.

John Fowles (1964), *Aristos*, Grafton, London.

John Fowles (1976), *Daniel Martin*, Grafton, London.

John Fowles (1977), *The Magus*, Cape, London.

Jerry Fracher and Michael Kimmel (1987), 'Hard Issues and Soft Spots: Counselling Men about Sexuality' in Murray Scher et al. (eds.), *Handbook of Counselling & Psychotherapy with Men*, Sage, London.

Nancy Friday (1980), *Men in Love: Men's Sexual Fantasies*, Arrow Books, New York.

Irene Hanson Frieze (1983), 'Investigating the Causes and Consequences of Marital Rape' in *Signs* vol 8, 3.

Sigmund Freud (1900), *The Interpretation of Dreams, Standard Edition of the Complete Psychological Works*, vols. 4–5, Hogarth, London.

Sigmund Freud (1905), *Three Essays on the Theory of Sexuality, Standard Edition*, vol. 7, Hogarth, London.

Sigmund Freud (1909), 'Analysis of a Phobia in a Five-Year-Old Boy', *Standard Edition*, vol. 10, Hogarth, London.

Sigmund Freud (1925), 'Some Psychical Consequences of the Anatomical Distinction Between the Sexes' *Standard Edition*, vol. 21, Hogarth, London.

Sigmund Freud (1933), 'From the History of an Infantile Neurosis' in *Standard Edition*, vol. 17, Hogarth, London.

Sigmund Freud (1933), 'Some Neurotic Manifestations in Jealousy, Paranoia and Homosexuality' in *Complete Works*, vol. 18, Hogarth, London.

Sigmund Freud (1933), 'Female Sexuality', *Standard Edition*, vol. 21, Hogarth, London.

Sigmund Freud (1933), 'Femininity' reprinted in *Standard Edition*, vol. 22, Hogarth, London.

Sigmund Freud (1933), *New Introductory Lectures on Psycho-Analysis, Standard Edition*, vol. 22, Hogarth, London.

Stephen Frosch (1987), *The Politics of Psychoanalysis: An Introduction to Freudian and Post-Freudian Theory*, Macmillan, London.

Paul Fussell (1975), *The Great War in Modern Memory*, Oxford, London.

Francoise Gadet (1989), *Saussure and Contemporary Culture*, Hutchinson Radius, London.

Jane Gallop (1982), *Feminism and Psychoanalysis: The Daughter's Seduction*, Macmillan, London.

Michele Hoffnung Garskoff (ed.) (1971), *Roles Women Play*, Cole Publishing Company, California.

Jane Gaines (1988), 'White Privilege and Looking Relations: Race and Gender in Feminist Film Theory' in *Screen*, vol. 29, 4.

Henry Louis Gates, Jr (1986), *Race, Writing and Difference*, University of Chicago, London.

Henry Louis Gates, Jr (1987), *Figures in Black*, Oxford University Press, Oxford.

Gay Left Collective (1978/9), 'Happy Families?: Paedophilia Examined' in *Gay Left*, 7 Winter.

Paul Gebhard et al. (1965), *Sexual Offenders: An Analysis of Types*, Heinemann, London.

Richard Gelles (1979), *Family Violence*, Sage, London.

J.E. Gerai and Sheinfield (1968), 'Sex Differences in Mental and Behavioural

Traits', in *Genetic Psychological Monographs*, 77.

Anthony Giddens (1984), *The Constitution of Society*, Polity Press, Cambridge.

Kathrine Gieve (1989), *Balancing Acts: On Being a Mother*, Virago, London.

Paul Gilroy (1987), *There Ain't No Black in the Union Jack*, Hutchison, London.

Paul Gilroy and Errol Lawrence (1989), 'Two-Tone Britain: White and Black Youth and the Politics of Anti-Racism' in Philip Cohen and Harwant Bains (eds.), *Multi-Racist Britain*, Macmillan, London.

Herb Goldberg (1976), *The Hazards of Being Male*, Nash, New York.

Richard Goldstein (1985), 'The Uses of Aids', in *Village Voice*, December 5.

William Goode (1971), 'Force and Violence in the Family' in *Journal of Marriage and the Family*, vol.33, 4.

Linda Gordon (1988), 'The Politics of Child Sexual Abuse: Notes from American History' in *Feminist Review*, 28, Spring.

Linda Gordon (1989), *Heroes of Their Own Lives: The Politics and History of Family Violence*, Virago, London.

Geoffrey Gorer (1955), *Exploring English Character*, Nelson, London.

Vivian Gornick and Barbara Moran (1971), *Woman in Sexist Society: Studies in Power and Powerlessness*, Basic Books, New York.

Ray Gosling (1960), 'Dream Boy', *New Left Review* May/June, 3.

Tony Gould (1983), *Inside Outsider: The Life and Times of Colin MacInnes*, Chatto & Windus, London.

Jeffrey A. Gray and A.W.H. Buffery (1971), 'Sex Differences in Emotional and Cognitive Behaviour including Man: Adaptive and Neural Bases', *Acta Psychologica* 35.

Graham Greene (1948), *Journey Without Maps*, Pan, London.

Ralph Greenson (1968), 'Dis-Identifying from Mother: Its Special Importance for the Boy' in *International Psycho-Analytic Journal*, vol.49.

Germaine Greer (1970), *The Female Eunuch*, MacGibbon & Kee, London.

Nigel Grey (1974), *The Silent Majority – A Study of the Working Class in Post-War British Fiction*, Vision Critical Studies, London.

William Grier and Price Cobbs (1968), *Black Rage*, Bantam Books, New York.

Susan Griffin (1971), Reprint from 'Rape: The All-American Crime', *Ramparts*, September.

Andrew Hacker (1982), 'Farewell to the Family?,' *New York Review of Books*, vol. xxix, 4, March 18.

Helen Hacker (1957), 'The New Burdens of Masculinity' in *Marriage and Family Living*, 19.

H.R. Haggard (1979), [First published 1885], *King Solomon's Mines; She; Allan Quatermain*, Octopus Press, London.

Ruth Hall *et al.* (1981), *The Rapist Who Pays the Rent: Evidence Submitted by Women Against Rape, Britain to the Criminal Law Revision Committee*, Falling Wall Press, Bristol.

Ruth Hall (1985), *Ask Any Woman: A London Inquiry into Rape and Sexual Assault*, Falling Wall Press, Bristol.

Stuart Hall *et al.* (1978), *Policing the Crisis*, Macmillan, London.

Stuart Hall (1987), 'Minimal Selves' in *Identity: The Real Me*, I.C.A. Documents 6, London.

Stuart Hall (1987), 'New Ethnicities' in *Black Film British Cinema*, I.C.A. Documents, London.

Stuart Hall (1989), *Out of Apathy*, Verso, London.

Angela Hamblin (1972), 'The Suppressed Power of Female Sexuality' in *Shrew: Women's Liberation Workshop Paper*, vol. 4, 6, December.

Dorothy Hammond and Alta Jablow (1970), *The Africa That Never Was: Four Centuries of British Writings About Africa*, Twayne Press, New York.

Jalna Hanmer and Mary Maynard (eds.) (1987), *Women, Violence and Social Control*, Macmillan, London.

Gillian Hanscombe and Jackie Forster (1982), *Rocking the Cradle: Lesbian Mothers*, Sheba Press, London.

Jeffrey Hantover (1980), 'The Boy Scouts and the Validation of Masculinity' in Elizabeth Pleck and Joseph Pleck (eds.), *The American Man*, Englewood Cliffs, New Jersey.

Lynne Harne (1984), 'Lesbian Custody and the New Myth of Fatherhood' in *Trouble and Strife*, 3.

Caroline Harris and Jennifer Moore (1988), 'Altered Images' in *Marxism Today*, November.

Olivia Harris (1981), 'The Power of Signs: Gender, Culture and the Wild in the Bolivian Andes' in MacCormack and Strathern (eds.), *Nature, Culture and Gender*, Cambridge University Press, Cambridge.

Olivia Harris (1984), 'Heavenly Father' in Owens *op.cit.*

Fraser Harrison (1985), *A Father's Diary*, Fontana, London.

Kathryn Harriss (1989), 'New Alliances: Socialist Feminism in the Eighties' in *Feminist Review*, 31, Spring.

Derek Hatton (1988), *Inside Left*, Bloomsbury, London.

H.R. Hays (1964), *The Dangerous Sex*, Putnam, London.

Jeff Hearn (1987), *The Gender of Oppression: Men, Masculinity and the Critique of Marxism*, Wheatsheaf, Brighton.

Stephen Heath (1987), 'Male Feminism' in Jardine and Smith (eds.), *op.cit.*.

Dick Hebdige (1979), *Subculture: The Meaning of Style*, Methuen, London.

Ernest Hemingway (1987), *The Garden of Eden*, Grafton Books, London.

Essex Hemphill (1986), *Conditions: Poems by Essex Hemphill*, BeBop Books, Washington.

Melanie Henwood, Lesley Rimmer and Malcom Wicks (1987), *Inside the Family: Changing Roles of Men and Women*, Family Policy Studies Centre, London.

Rosanna Hertz (1986), *More Equal Than Others: Women and Men in Dual-Career Marriages*, University of California Press, London.

Christine Heward (1988), *Making a Man of Him*, Routledge, London.

Chester Himes (1986), [First published 1945] *If He Hollers Let Him Go*, Pluto Press, London.

Shère Hite (1981), *The Hite Report on Male Sexuality*, MacDonald, London.

Shere Hite (1988), *Women and Love*, Viking, London.

Tony Hipgrave (1982), 'Lone Fatherhood: A Problematic Status' in McKee and O'Brien (eds.), *op.cit.*.

Paul Hoch (1979), *White Hero, Black Beast*, Pluto Press, London.

Martin Hoffman (1968), *The Gay World*, Basic Books, New York.

Richard Hoggart (1957), *The Uses of Literacy*, Penguin, Harmondsworth.

Wendy Hollway (1981), '"I Just Wanted to Kill a Woman". Why? The Ripper and Male Sexuality' in *Feminist Review*, 9, Autumn.

Wendy Hollway (1984), 'Gender Difference and the Production of Subjectivity' in

Julian Henriques et al., *Changing the Subject: Psychology, Social Regulation and Subjectivity*, Methuen, London.

Wendy Hollway (1984), 'Women's Power in Heterosexual Sex' in *Women's Studies International Forum*, vol. 7, 1.

Bell Hooks (1989), *Talking Back: Thinking Feminist – Thinking Black*, Sheba, London.

Jane Hope (1957), *Happy Event*, Frederick Muller, London.

June Hopkins (ed.) (1984), *Perspectives on Rape and Sexual Assault*, Harper & Row, London.

Walter Houghton (1957), *The Victorian Frame of Mind*, Yale University Press, London.

Gad Horowitz and Michael Kaufman (1987), 'Male Sexuality: Toward A Theory of Liberation' in Michael Kaufman (ed.), *Beyond Patriarchy*, Oxford University Press, Toronto.

Judith Hubback (1957), *Wives Who Went to College*, Heinemann, London.

Langston Hughes (1986), [First published 1940], *The Big Sea: An Autobiography*, Pluto Press, London.

Jane Humphries (1981), 'Protective Legislation, the Capitalist State, and Working-Class Men: The Case of the 1842 Mines Regulation Act' in *Feminist Review*, 7.

Martin Humphries (1987), 'Choosing with Care: Working with non-gay men' in Gillian Hanscombe and Martin Humphries (eds.), *Heterosexuality*, Gay Men's Press, London.

Nan Hunter (1986), 'The Pornography Debate in Context: A chronology of Sexuality, Media and Violence Issues in Feminism' in Kate Ellis, *op.cit.*.

Zora Neale Hurston (1986), [First published 1937] *Their Eyes Were Watching God*, Virago, London.

Corinne Hutt (1972), *Males and Females*, Penguin, Harmondsworth.

Christopher Isherwood (1954), *The World in the Evening*, Methuen, London.

Luce Irigaray (1985), *The Sex Which Is Not One*, Cornell University, New York.

Catherine Itzin, (1987), in *London Daily News*, April 20.

Brian Jackson (1983), *Fatherhood*, Allen & Unwin, London.

Elizabeth Janeway (1982), *Cross Sections: From a Decade of Change*, William Morrow & Co., New York.

Alice Jardine and Paul Smith, *Men in Feminism*, Methuen, London.

Sheila Jeffreys (1983), 'Sex Reform and Anti-Feminism in the 1920s' in London History Group, *op.cit.*.

B.S. Johnson (ed.) (1973), *All Bull: The National Servicemen*, Quartet, London.

Charles Johnson (1988), *Being & Race: Black Writing Since 1970*, Serpent's Tail, London.

Ernest Jones (1955), *Sigmund Freud: Life and Work*, vol. 2, Hogarth Press, London.

LeRoi Jones (1966), *Home*, William Morrow & Co., New York.

Nicole Ward Jouve (1986), *'The Streetcleaner': The Yorkshire Ripper Case on Trial*, Marion Boyars, London.

Roger Jowell and Colin Airey (1984), *British Social Attitudes: the 1984 Report*, Gower, London.

Isaac Julien (1988), 'Gary's Tale' in Mercer and Julien, *op.cit.*

Stephen Katz (1988), 'Sexualization and the Lateralized Brain: From Craniometry to Pornograpy' in *Women's Studies International Forum*, vol. 11, 1.

Liz Kelly (1988), *Surviving Sexual Violence*, Polity Press, Cambridge.

Ruth Kempe and C. Henry Kempe (1978), *Child Abuse*, Fontana/Open Books, London.

Michael Kimmel (1987), 'Teaching a Course on Men' in Michael Kimmel (ed.), *Changing Men: New Directions in Research on Men and Masculinity*, Sage Publications, London.

Alfred Kinsey et al. (1948), *Sexual Behaviour in the Human Male*, W.B. Saunders, Philadelphia.

Alfred Kinsey et al. (1953), *Sexual Behaviour in the Human Female*, W.B. Saunders, Philadelphia.

Gregorio Kohon (ed.) (1986), *The British School of Psychoanalysis: The Independent Tradition*, Free Association Books, London.

Mirra Komarovsky (1976), *Dilemmas of Masculinity: A Study of College Men*, Norton, New York.

Claudia Koonz (1988), *Mothers in the Fatherland*, Methuen, London.

Anja van Kooten Niekerk and Theo van der Meer (1989), Introduction in Altman et al. (1989), *op.cit.*.

Andrew Kopkind (1979), 'The Boys in the Barracks' in Karla Jay and Allen Young *Lavender Culture*, Jove, New York.

Joel Kovel (1981), *The Age of Desire: Case Histories of a Radical Psychoanalyst*, Basic Books, New York.

Joel Kovel (1988), [First published 1970] *White Racism: A Psychohistory*, Free Association Books, London.

Jacques Lacan (1977), *Ecrits: A Selection*, Tavistock, London.

Jacques Lacan (1982), [Paper presented 1958] 'The Meaning of the Phallus' in Mitchell and Rose, *op.cit.*.

Jacques Lacan (1982), [First published as Seminar XX in *Encore*, lectures given 1972–3] 'God and the *Jouissance* of Woman. A Love Letter' in Mitchell and Rose, *op.cit.*.

Michael Lamb, Joseph Pleck and James Levine (1987), 'Effects of Increased Paternal Involvement on Fathers and Mothers' in Lewis and O'Brien (eds.), *op.cit.*.

Hilary Land (1980), 'The Family Wage' in *Feminist Review*, 6.

Errol Lawrence (1982), 'In the Abundance of Water the Fool is Thirsty: Sociology and Black Pathology' in CCCS (eds.), *The Empire Strikes Back*, Hutchinson, London.

Wolfgana Lederer (1968), *The Fear of Women*, Harcourt Brace, New York.

Carol Lee (1989), *The Blind Side of Eden*, Bloomsbury, London.

Spike Lee talks to Steve Goldman (1989), 'Heat of the Moment' in *The Weekend Guardian*, June 24–5.

Doris Lessing (1972), *The Golden Notebook*, Panther, St Albans.

Sylvia Levine and Joseph Koenig (eds.) (1983), *Why Men Rape*, Star, London.

Daniel Levinson (1978), *The Seasons of a Man's Life*, Ballantine, New York.

Jerre Levy (1978), 'Lateral Differences in the Human Brain in Cognition and Behavioral Control' in P. Buser and A. Rougeul-Buser (eds.), *Cerebral Correlates of Conscious Experience*, North London Publishing, New York.

Charlie Lewis (1982), 'The Observation of Father-Infant Relationships: An "Attachment" to Outmoded Concepts' in McKee and O'Brien (eds.), *op.cit.*.

Charlie Lewis (1986), *Becoming a Father*, Open University Press, Milton Keynes.

Charlie Lewis and Margaret O'Brien (eds.) (1987), *Reassessing Fatherhood*, Sage, London.

Peter Lewis (1978), *The Fifties*, Heinemann, London.

Barbara Lindemann (1984), '"To Ravish and Carnally Know": Rape in Eighteenth-Century Massachusetts' in *Signs*, Autumn, vol.10, 1.

Linkman (British Newsletter on Men's Studies), Harry Gray, Department of Educational Research, Cartmel College, University of Lancaster, UK.

Danial Linz, Edward Donnerstein and Steven Penrod (1987), 'Sexual Violence in the Mass Media: Social Psychological Implications' in Phillip Shaver and Clyde Henrick (eds.), *Sex and Gender*, Sage, London.

Kerry Lobel (ed.), *Naming the Violence: Speaking Out About Lesbian Battery*, Seal Press, Washington.

David Lodge (1982), *Ginger You're Barmy*, Penguin, Harmondsworth.

London Feminist History Group (1983), *The Sexual Dynamic of History*, Pluto Press, London.

Don Long (1987), 'Working with Men who Batter' in Murray Scher *et al.* (eds.), *op.cit.*.

Audre Lorde (1983), 'My Words Will Be There' in Mari Evans (ed.), *Black Women Writers*, Pluto Press, London.

Kenneth Lynn (1987), *Hemingway*, Simon & Schuster, London.

Colin MacCabe (1978), *James Joyce and the Revolution of the Word*, Macmillan, London.

Eleanor Maccoby and Carol Jacklin (1975), *The Psychology of Sex Differences*, Oxford University Press, London.

David Macey (1988), *Lacan in Context*, Verso, London.

Colin MacInnes (1959), *Absolute Beginners*, MacGibbon & Kee, London.

Colin MacInnes (1966), 'Pacific Warriors' in *New Society*, 30 June.

Anne Machung (1989), 'Talking Career, Thinking Job: Gender Differences in Career and Family Expectations of Berkeley Seniors' in *Feminist Stuides*, vol.15, Spring.

Catherine MacKinnon (1982), 'Feminism, Marxism, Method and the State' in *Signs*, vol.7, 3.

Catherine MacKinnon (1984), Comments in *Signs*, vol.10, 1.

Brian MacLean (1985), Review of *Ask Any Woman* in *British Journal Criminology*, vol.25.

Mary MacLeod and Esther Saraga (1988), 'Challenging the Orthodoxy: Towards a Feminist Theory and Practice in *Feminist Review*, 28.

Sheila MacLeod (1988), 'A Fairy Story' in Maitland (ed.), 1988, *op.cit.*.

Sara Maguire (1988), '"Sorry Love" – Violence against Women in the Home and the State Response' in *Critical Social Policy*, 23, Autumn.

Norman Mailer (1959), *Advertisements for Myself*, Putnam, New York.

Norman Mailer (1960), 'The White Negro' in *Protest*, Panther, London.

Norman Mailer (1971), *Prisoner of Sex*, Little, Brown & Co., Boston.

Sara Maitland (1984), 'Two for the Price of One' in Owen, *Fathers: Reflections by Daughters*, *op. cit.*.

Sara Maitland (ed.) (1988a) *Very Heaven: Looking Back at the 1960s*, Virago, London.

Sara Maitland (1988b), 'And Two for Tea', review of Shere Hite *Women and Love* in *New Statesman*, 26 February.

N. Malamuth and E. Donnerstein (eds.) (1984), *Pornography and Sexual Aggression*, Academic Press, Orlando.

J.A. Mangan and James Walvin (eds.) (1987), *Manliness and Morality*, Manchester University Press, Manchester.

J.A. Mangan (1987), 'Social Darwinism and Upper-Class Education in late Victorian and Edwardian England' in Mangan and Walvin (eds.), *op.cit.*.

Peter Marsh, Elizabeth Rosser and Rom Harre (1978), *The Rules of Disorder*, Routledge & Kegan Paul, London.

John Marshall (1980), 'The Politics of Tea and Sympathy' in Gay Left Collective (ed.), *op.cit.*.

John Marshall (1981), 'Pansies, Perverts and Macho Men: Changing Conceptions of Male Homosexuality' in Plummer, *op.cit.*.

Paule Marshall (1981), [First published 1959], *Brown Girl, Brownstones*, The Feminist Press, New York.

Paule Marshall (1970), 'Reena' in Cade, *op.cit.*.

Mtutuzeli Matshoba (1979), *Call Me Not a Man*, Rex Collings, London.

Martha May (1982), 'The Historical Problem of the Family Wage: The Ford Motor Company and the Five Dollar Day' in *Feminist Studies*, vol.8, 2, Summer.

Keith McClelland (1987), 'Time to Work, Time to Live: Some Aspects of Work and Re-formation of Class in Britain, 1850–1880' in Patrick Joyce (ed.), *The Historical Meaning of Work*, Cambridge University Press, Cambridge.

Keith McClelland (1989), 'Some Thoughts on Masculinity and the "Representative Artisan" in Britain, 1850–1880', *Gender and History*, vol.1, 2, Summer.

Jean McCrindle (1982), 'Reading The Golden Notebook in 1962' in Jenny Taylor (ed.), *Notebooks/Memoirs/Archives: Reading and Re-reading Doris Lessing*, Routledge & Kegan Paul, London.

Jean McCrindle (1987), 'The Left as Social Movement' talk given at *Out of Apathy* Conference, Oxford, 14 November.

Joyce McDougall (1986), *Theatres of the Mind: Illusion and Truth on the Psychoanalytic Stage*, Free Association Books, London.

Eileen McLeod (1982), *Women Working: Prostitution Now*, Croom Helm, London.

Ian McEwan (1978), *In Between the Sheets*, Pan, London.

Ian McEwan (1987), *The Child in Time*, Jonathan Cape, London.

Mary McIntosh (1968), 'The Homosexual Role' in *Social Problems*, vol.16, 2.

Mary McIntosh (1978), 'The State and the Oppression of Women' in Annette Kuhn and Anne-Marie Wople (eds.), *Feminism and Materialism*, Routledge & Kegan Paul, London.

Mary McIntosh (1988), 'Family Secrets: Child Sexual Abuse' in *The Chartist*, January.

Lorna McKee (1987), 'Fathers' in *The Guardian*, 19th January, p.12.

Lorna McKee and Colin Bell (1986), 'His unemployment, Her Problem' in Allen et al., *op.cit.*.

Lorna McKee and Margaret O'Brien (1982), 'The Father Figure: Some Current Orientations and Historical Perspectives' in McKee and O'Brien, *op.cit.*.

Lorna McKee and Margaret O'Brien (1982), *The Father Figure*, Tavistock, London.

Lorna McKee (1982), 'Fathers' Participation in Infant Care: A critique', in McKee and O'Brien, *op.cit.*.

Margaret Mead (1935), *Sex and Temperament in Three Primitive Societies*, Routledge & Kegan Paul, London.

Mervyn Meggitt (1976), 'A Duplicity of Demons' in *Man and Woman in the New Guinea Highlands*, American Anthropological Association, 8.

Kobena Mercer (1988), 'Racism and the Politics of Masculinity' in Kobena Mercer and Isaac Julien, 'Race, Sexual Politics and Black Masculinity: A Dossier' in Chapman and Rutherford, *op.cit.*.

Mandy Merck (1987), 'Difference and Its Discontents' in *Deconstructing 'Difference': Screen*, vol.28, 1.

Andy Metcalfe and Martin Humphries, *The Sexuality of Men*, Pluto Press, London.

Ruth Milkman (1987), *Gender at Work: The Dynamics of Job Segregation by Sex During World War II*, University of Illinois Press, Chicago.

D.W. Miller (1958), 'Lower-Class Culture as a Generating Milieu for Gang Delinquency' in *Journal of Social Issues*, vol.14, pp.5–19.

Kate Millet (1972), *Sexual Politics*, Abacus, London.

Juliet Mitchell (1971), *Woman's Estate*, Penguin, Harmondsworth.

Juliet Mitchell (1974), *Psychoanalysis and Feminism*, Allen Lane, London.

Juliet Mitchell and Jacqueline Rose, *Feminine Sexuality: Jacques Lacan and the Ecole Freudienne*, Macmillan, London.

Donald Mosher (1970), 'Psychological Reactions to Pornographic Films' in *Technical Reports of the Commission on Obscenity and Pornography*, vol.8, U.S. Government Report, Washington.

Alberto Moravia (1972), *The Two of Us*, Secker & Warburg, London.

D.H.J. Morgan (1975), *Social Theory and the Family*, Routledge & Kegan Paul, London.

David Morgan (1987), *It Will Make a Man of You*, Studies in Sexual Politics, no.17, Manchester University, Manchester.

David Morgan (unpub.), Research Proposals for a Study of Masculinity and Violence.

Toni Morrison (1971), 'What the Black Woman Thinks About Women's Lib', in *The New York Times Magazine*, August 22.

Toni Morrison (1979), *The Bluest Eye*, Grafton Books, London.

Frank Mort (1988), 'Boys Own? Masculinity, Style and Popular Culture' Chapman and Rutherford (eds.), *op.cit.*.

Peter Moss and Julia Brannen (1987), 'Fathers and Employment' in Lewis and O'Brien (eds.), *op.cit.*.

Peter Moss and Julia Brannen (1987), 'Fathers and Employment' in Lewis and O'Brien (eds.), *op.cit.*.

Keith Motherson (1979), 'Developing Our Power' in *Anti-Sexist Men's Newsletter*, 5.

Andy Moye (1985), 'Pornography' in Metcalf and Humphries (eds.), *op.cit.*.

Daniel Moyniham (1965), *The Negro Family: The Case for National Action*, U.S. Department of Labor, Washington.

Patricia Beezley Mrazek and Arnon Bentovim (1981), 'Incest and the Dysfunctional Family System' in Mrazek and Kempe (eds.), *Sexually Abused Children and their Families*, Pergamon Press, Oxford.

Dan Muir (1975), 'Review of *The Dangerous Sex*, by H.R. Hayes' in *Men Against Sexism*, Spring, *op.cit.*.

Alva Myrdal and Viola Klein (1956), *Women's Two Roles*, Routledge & Kegan Paul, London.

John and Elizabeth Newson (1963), *Patterns of Infant Care in an Urban Community*, Allen & Unwin, London.

Lauretta Ngcobo (1988), *Let It Be Told: Black Women Writers in Britain*, Virago, London.

Grace Nichols (1986), 'Even Tho', in Cobham and Collins, *op.cit.*.

Lutz Niethammer (1979), 'Male Fantasies: an Argument for and with an Important New Study in History and Psychoanalysis' in *History Workshop*, 7.

Philip Nobile and Eric Nadler, *United States of America Vs Sex*, Minotaur Press, New York.

Helen Norberg (1988), 'Women on the Move in Trade Unions within the Public Sector' paper presented at the European Socialist Feminist Forum, Manchester, United Kingdom, November.

Pippa Norris (1987), *Politics and Sexual Equality: The Comparative Position of Women in Western Democracies*, Wheatsheaf, Brighton.

Ann Oakley (1972), *Sex, Gender and Society*, Temple Smith, London.

Ann Oakley 1984), *Taking it Like a Woman*, Jonathan Cape, London.

John Osborne (1960), 'Sex and Failure' in Gene Feldman & Max Gartenberg (eds.), *Protest*, Panther, London.

Sue O'Sullivan (1988), 'From 1969' in Amanda Sebestyen (ed.), *'68, '78, '88: From Women's Liberation to Feminism*, Prism, London.

Craig Owen (1987), 'Outlaws: Gay Men in Feminism' in Jardine and Smith (eds.), *op.cit.*.

Ursula Owen (ed.) (1983), *Fathers: Reflections by Daughters*, Virago, London.

Oxford University Socialist Discussion Group (1988), *Out of Apathy: Voices of the New Left 30 Years On*, Verso, London.

Jan Pahl (1985), *Private Violence and Public Policy*, Routledge & Kegan Paul, London.

Roberta Park (1987), 'Biological Thought, Athletics and the Formation of "the Man of Character": 1830–1900' in Mangan and Walvin (eds.), *op.cit.*.

Ross Parke (1981), *Fathering*, Fontana Paperbacks, London.

Andrew Parker (1984), 'Opinion' in *British Printer*, July.

Di Parkin and Irene Breugel (1988), 'Entering the Structures: Socialist Feminism in Britain and the Local State'. Paper given at European Socialist Feminist Forum, Manchester, November.

Talcott Parsons (1942), 'Age and Sex in the Social Structure of the United States' in *American Sociological Review*, 7.

T. Parsons and R.F. Bales (1956), *Family Socialization and Interaction Process*, Routledge & Kegan Paul, London.

Cindy Patton (1988), 'AIDS: Lessons from the Gay Community' in *Feminist Review*, 30, Autumn.

Geoffrey Pearson (1983), *Hooligan: a History of Respectable Fears*, Macmillan, London.

Sarah Perrigo (1988), 'Notes on the Problem of Organizing Effectively in the British Labour Party'. Paper given at the European Socialist Feminist Forum, Manchester, November.

Ethel Spector Person (1980), 'Sexuality as the Mainstay of Identity: Psychoanalytic Perspectives' in *Signs*, vol.5, 4.

Ethel S. Person (1986), 'The Omni-Available Woman and Lesbian Sex' in Fogel et al., *op.cit.*.

Thomas Pettigrew (1964), *A Profile of the Negro American*, Van Nostrand, New Jersey.

Anne Phillips and Barbara Taylor (1980), 'Sex and Skill: Notes Towards a Feminist Economics' in *Feminist Review*, 6.

Joseph Pleck (1981), *The Myth of Masculinity*, MIT Press, Cambridge, Mass.

Joseph Pleck (1987), 'The Contemporary Man' in Murray Scher et al. (eds.), *op.cit.*.

Joseph Pleck and Jack Sawyer (eds.), *Men and Masculinity*, Prentice Hall, Englewood Cliffs.

Kenneth Plummer (1975), *Sexual Stigma: An Interactionist Account*, Routledge & Kegan Paul, London.

Kenneth Plummer (ed.) (1981), *The Making of the Modern Homosexual*, Hutchinson, London.

Ken Plummer (1984), 'The Social Uses of Power: Symbolic Interaction, Power and Rape' in Hopkins (eds.), *op.cit.*.

Anna Pollert (1981), *Girls, Wives, Factory Lives*, Macmillan, London.

Roy Porter (1985), 'Rape – Does it have a Historical Meaning?' in Tomaselli and Porter (eds.), *op.cit.*.

Fitz John Porter Poole (1981) 'Transforming "natural" Woman' in Sherry Ortner and Harriet Whitehead (eds.) (1981), *Sexual Meanings*, Cambridge University Press, Cambridge.

Ken Pryce (1979), *Endless Pressure*, Bristol Classical Press, Bristol.

Peter Rabe (1957), *From Here to Maternity*, Frederic Muller, London.

Jean Radford (1989), 'My Pride and Joy' in Gieve *op.cit.*.

David Rampton (1986), in *You: Mail on Sunday*, November 26.

Rape Crisis Centre (1977), *First Annual Report*, Rape Counselling and Research Project, London.

Ray Raphael (1988), *The Men from the Boys: Rites of Passage in Male America* University of Nebraska Press, London.

Rhona Rapoport and Robert Rapoport (1971), *Dual-Career Families*, Penguin, Harmondsworth.

Rhona Rapoport and Robert Rapoport (1976), *Dual-Career Families re-Examined*, Harper & Row, New York.

Ishmael Reed (1989), *Reckless Eyeballing*, Allison & Busby, London.

Denise Riley (1983), *War in the Nursery*, Virago, London.

Joan Riley (1985), *The Unbelonging*, Woman's Press, London.

Sara Rix (ed.) (for the Women's Research & Education Institute of the Congressional Caucus for Women's Issues) (1989), *The American Woman 1987–88: A Report in Depth*, W.W. Norton, London.

Yvonne Roberts (1984), *Man Enough: Men of 35 Speak Out*, Chatto & Windus, London.

David Robins (1984), *We Hate Humans*, Penguin, Harmondsworth.

Ronald Robinson et al. (1961), *Africa and the Victorians: The Official Mind of Imperialism*, Macmillan, London.

Barbara Rogers (1988), *Men Only: An Investigation into Men's Organisations*, Pandora, London.

P. Rosenkrantz et al. (1968) 'Sex-role Stereotypes and Self Concepts in College Students' in *Journal of Consulting and Clinical Psychology*, vol. 32.

Ellen Ross (1982), '"Fierce Questions and Taunts": Married Life in Working-Class London, 1870–1914' in *Feminist Studies*, vol.8, 3, Fall.

John Munder Ross (1986), 'Beyond the Phallic Illusion: Notes on Man's Heterosexuality' in Fogel *et al.*, *op.cit.*.

Sheila Rowbotham (1972), 'Women's Liberation and the New Politics' in Michelene Wandor (ed.), *op.cit.*.

Sheila Rowbotham (1973), *Women's Consciousness, Man's World*, Penguin, Harmondsworth.

Sheila Rowbotham (1977), 'Edward Carpenter: Prophet of the New Life in Sheila Rowbotham and Jeffrey Weeks *Socialism and the New Life: The Personal and Sexual*

Politics of Edward Carpenter and Havelock Ellis, Pluto Press, London.
Sheila Rowbotham (1984), 'Our Lance' in Ursula Owen (ed.), *op.cit.*.
Sheila Rowbotham (1987), 'Feminism and its discontents' in *New Socialist*, 53, December.
Sheila Rowbotham (1989), *The Past is Before Us: Feminism in Action Since the 1960s*, Pandora, London.
Sheila Rowbotham, Lynne Segal, Hilary Wainwright (1980), *Beyond the Fragments: Feminism and the Making of Socialism*, Merlin, London.
Marsha Rowe (1988), 'Up from Down Under' in Maitland (ed.), *op.cit.*.
B. Seebohm Rowntree and G.R. Lavers (1951), *English Life and Leisure*, Longmans, London.
Trevor Royle (1986), *The Best Years of their Lives*, Michael Joseph, London.
Gayle Rubin (1975), 'The Traffic in Women: Notes on the "Political Economy" of Sex' in R. Reita (ed.), *Towards an Anthropology of Women*, Monthly Review Press, New York.
Gayle Rubin (1987), 'Thinking Sex: Notes for a Radical Theory of the Politics of Sexuality' in Carol Vance (ed.), *op.cit.*.
Lillian Rubin (1987), *Quiet Rage*, Faber & Faber, London.
Mary Ruggie (1984), *The State and Working Women*, Princeton University Press, Princeton.
Diana Russell (1982), *Rape in Marriage*, Macmillan, New York.
Diana Russell (1984), *Sexual Exploitation – Rape, Child Sexual Abuse and Workplace Harassment*, Sage, Beverley Hills.
Graeme Russell (1983), *The Changing Role of Fathers*, University of Queensland Press, London.
Graeme Russell (1987), 'Problems in Role-Reversed Families' in Lewis and O'Brien (eds.), *op.cit.*.
Sheila Ruth (1983), 'A Feminist Analysis of the New Right' in *Women's Studies International Forum*, vol.6, 4.
Jonathan Rutherford (unpub), 'Dads can do it'.
Tom Ryan, 'Roots of Masculinity' in Metcalfe and Humphries (eds.), *op.cit.*.
J.D. Salinger (1951), *The Catcher in the Rye*, Penguin, Harmondsworth.
Anthony Sampson (1962), *Anatomy of Britain*, Hodder & Stoughton, London.
Raphael Samuel (1987), 'Class and Classlessness'. Talk given at *Out of Apathy* Conference, Oxford, November.
Peggy Reeves Sanday (1985), 'Rape and the Silencing of the Feminine' in Tomaselli and Porter (eds.), *op.cit.*.
Karin Sandqvist (1987), 'Swedish Family Policy and the Attempt to Change Paternal Roles' in Lewis and O'Brien (eds.), *op.cit.*.
Janet Sayers (1986), *Sexual Contradictions: Psychology, Psychoanalysis, and Feminism*, Tavistock, London.
A.M. Scacco Jr (1975), *Rape in Prison*, Charles C. Thomas, Springfield, Illinois.
H.R. Schaffer and P. Emerson (1964), *The Development of Social Attachment in Infancy*, Monograph No 29, Society for Research in Child Development.
Henry Schipper (1980), 'Filthy Lucre: A Tour of America's Most Profitable Frontier' in English, *op.cit.*.
Julia Schwengdinger and Herman Schwengdinger (1983), *Rape and Inequality*, Sage, London.
Peter Schwenger (1984), *Phallic Critiques*, Routledge & Kegan Paul, London.

Hilda Scott (1982), *Sweden's "Right to be Human"*, Allison & Busby, London.

Bobby Seal (1970), *Seize the Time: The Story of the Black Panther Party*, Arrow Books, London.

Eve Kosofsky Sedgwick (1985), *Between Men: English Literature and Male Homosexual Desire*, Columbia University Press, New York.

Vic Seidler (circa 1980), 'Raging Bull' in *Achilles Heel*, 5.

Vic Seidler (1984), 'Fear and Intimacy' in Metcalfe and Humphries (eds.), *op.cit.*.

Lynne Segal (1983), 'Sensual Uncertainty, or Why the Clitoris is Not Enough' in Sue Cartledge and Joanna Ryan (eds.), *Sex & Love*, Women's Press, London.

Lynne Segal (1983), 'Smash the Family' in Lynne Segal (ed.), *What is to be Done About the Family?*, Penguin, Harmondsworth.

Lynne Segal (1987), *Is the Future Female? Troubled Thoughts on Contemporary Feminism*, Virago, London.

Lynne Segal (1989), 'Lessons from the Past: Feminism, Sexual Politics and the Challenge of Aids', in Erica Carter and Simon Watney (eds.), *op.cit.*.

Richard Sennett (1976), *The Fall of Public Man*, Faber & Faber, London.

SERTUC Women's Committee (1988), *Still Moving Towards Equality*, SERTUC, London.

Ntozake Shange (1980), 'comin to terms' in Mary Helen Washington (ed.), *Midnight Birds*, Anchor Books, New York.

Sue Sharpe (1985), *Double Identity*, Penguin, Harmondsworth.

Elaine Showalter (1987), 'Critical Cross-Dressing; Male Feminists and the Woman of the Year' in Jardine and Smith (eds.), *op.cit.*.

Alix Kates Shulman (1988), 'Sex and Power: Sexual Bases of Radical Feminism' in *Signs*, vol.5, 4.

Charles Silberman (1964), *Crisis in Black and White*, Random House, New York.

Alan Sillitoe (1960), *Saturday Night and Sunday Morning*, Pan, London.

Alan Sillitoe (1961), 'What Comes on Monday' in *New Left Review*, 4.

J. Silverman and S. Dinitz (1974), 'Compulsive Masculinity and Deliquency' in *Criminology*, pp.499–515.

Frederic Silverstolpe (1987), 'Benkert was not a Doctor: On the Non Medical Origins of the Homosexual Category in the Nineteenth Century' in *Homosexuality, Which Homosexuality* International Conference on Gay and Lesbian Studies, vol.1, Free University, Amsterdam.

Madeleine Simms and Christopher Smith (1982), 'Young Fathers: Attitudes to Marriage and Family Life' in McKee and O'Brien (eds.), *op.cit.*.

Brian Simon (1965), *Education and the Labour Movement 1870–1918*, Lawrence & Wishart, London.

Alan Sinfield (ed.) (1983), *Society and Literature 1945–1970*, Methuen, London.

Mrinalini Sinha (1987), 'Gender and Imperialism: Colonial Policy and the Ideology of Moral Imperialism in late nineteenth-century Bengal' in Michael Kimmel (ed.), *Changing Men*, Sage, London.

Carol Smart (1976), *Women, Crime and Criminology: A Feminist Critique*, Routledge & Kegan Paul, London.

Carol Smart (1987), 'There is of course the Distinction Dictated by Nature': Law and the Problem of Paternity' in Michelle Stanworth, *op.cit.*.

Gavin Smith (1987), 'The Crisis of Fatherhood' in *Free Associations*, 9.

Joan Smith (1989), *Misogynies*, Faber, London.

Michael Smith (1983), *Black Men/White Men: A Gay Anthology*, Gay Sunshine

Press, San Francisco.

Ann Barr Snitow (1985), 'Mass Market Romance: Pornography for Women is Different', in Snitow *et al.*, *op.cit.*.

Ann Barr Snitow et al., *Powers of Desire: The Politics of Sexuality*, Monthly Review Press, New York.

Ann Snitow (1985), 'Retrenchment Vs Transformation: the Politics of the Anti-Pornography Movement' in Kate Ellis, *op.cit.*.

Jon Snodgrass (1977), 'Introduction: Men and the Feminist Movement' in Jon Snodgrass (ed.), *For Men Against Sexism*, Times Change Press, Albion, California.

Kate Soper (1979), 'Marxism, Materialism and Biology' in John Mepham & D-H. Ruben, *Issues in Marxist Philosophy*, vol.2.

South London Men against Sexism (1974), 'Why Men's Liberation?' in *Brothers Against Sexism*, 3.

Dale Spender (1984), 'NO MATTER WHAT ... Theoretical Issues in Contemporary Feminism' in Joy Holland (ed.), *Feminist Action*, Battle Axe Books, London.

J. Springhall (1987), 'Building Character in the British Boy: the attempt to Extend Christian Manliness to Working-Class Adolescents, 1880-1914' in Mangan and Walvin (eds.), *op.cit.*.

George Stade (1986), 'Dracula's Women, and Why Men Love to Hate Them' in Fogel, *op.cit.*.

George Stambolian (1984), *Male Fantasies/Gay Realities: Interviews with Ten Men*, Sea Horse Press, New York.

Elizabeth Stanko (1985), *Intimate Intrusions: Women's Experience of Male Violence*, Routledge & Kegan Paul, London.

Michelle Stanworth (1987), *Reproductive Technologies: Gender, Motherhood and Medicine*, Polity Press, Cambridge.

Robert Staples (1982), *Black Masculinity: The Black Male's Role in American Society*, Black Scholar Press, San Francisco.

Jill Stephenson (1980), *The Nazi Organization of Women*, Barnes & Noble, New York.

Catherine Stimpson (1987), Foreword to Harry Brod (ed.), *op.cit.*.

Robert Stoller (1968), *Sex and Gender*, Hogarth Press, London.

Mary Stott (1987), *Women Talking – An Anthology from the Guardian Women's Page*, Pandora, London.

Marilyn Strathern (1989), *The Gender of the Gift: Problems with Women and Problems with Society in Melanesia*, University of California Press, Berkeley.

Murray Straus (1980), 'A Sociological Perspective on the Prevention of Wife-Beating' in Murray Straus and Gerald Hotaling (eds.), *Social Causes of Husband-Wife Violence*, University of Minneapolis Press, Minneapolis.

Sylvia Strauss (1982), *"Traitors to the Masculine Cause": The Men's Campaigns for Women's Rights*, Greenwood Press, London.

William Strickland (1989), 'Sleaze: How Bipartisan Racism Defiled the 1988 Presidential Campaign', in *Zeta Magazine*, January.

Angus Suttie (1976), 'From Latent to Blatant: a Personal Account' in *Gay Left*, 2, Spring.

Helen Taylor (1986), 'Gone With the Wind: The mammy of them all' in Jean Radford (ed.), *The Progress of Romance: The Politics of Popular Fiction*, Routledge & Kegan Paul, London.

Martin Taylor (ed.) (1989) *Lads: Love Poetry and the Trenches*, Constable, London.

Jennifer Temkin (1987), *Rape and the Legal Process*, Sweet & Maxwell, London.

Jane Temperley (1984), 'Our Own Worst Enemies: Unconscious Factors in Female Disadvantage' in *Free Associations* (Pilot Issue).

Klaus Theweleit (1987), *Male Fantasies*, vol.1, Polity Press, Cambridge.

Alison Thomas (1988), 'Men's Accounts of Their "Gender Identity": A Constructionist Approach'. Paper presented to the annual conference of the Social Psychology Section of the British Psychological Society, University of Kent at Canterbury, 23–25 September.

Paul Thompson (1983), *The Nature of Work: An Introduction to Debates on the Labour Process*, Macmillan, London.

Betty Thorne (1987), 'Life in Our Street [1960]', in Mary Stott (ed.), *op.cit.*.

Randy Thornhill et al. (1986), 'The Biology of Rape', in Tomaselli and Porter (eds.), *op.cit.*.

Bill Thorneycroft, Jeffrey Weeks and Mark Stevens (1988), 'The Liberation of Affection' in Bob Cant & Susan Hemmings (eds.), *Radical Records: Thirty Years of Lesbian and Gay History*, Routledge, London.

Leonore Tiefer (1987), 'The Pursuit of the Perfect Penis: The Medicalization of Male Sexuality', in Kimmel (ed.), *op.cit.*.

Andrew Tolson (1977), *The Limits of Masculinity*, Tavistock, London.

Sylvana Tomaselli and Roy Porter (eds.) (1986), *Rape*, Blackwell, Oxford.

Barbara Toner (1982), *The Facts of Rape*, Arrow, London.

Polly Toynbee (1987) 'The Incredible, Shrinking New Man in *The Guardian*, April 6.

Randolph Trumbach (1989), 'Gender and the Homosexual Role in Modern Western Culture: the 18th and 19th Centuries Compared' in D. Altman et al., *op.cit.*.

Jonathan Trustram (1985), 'A Co-Operative Creche' in Caroline New and Miriam David (eds.), *For the Children's Sake*, Penguin, Harmondsworth.

Sherry Turkle (1979), *Psychoanalytic Politics: Freud's French Revolution*, André Deutsch, London.

Jennifer Uglow (1989), 'Mede and Marmite Sandwiches', in Gieve, *op.cit.*.

Carol Vance (ed.) (1984), *Pleasure and Danger: Exploring Female Sexuality*, Routledge & Kegan Paul, London.

Carole Vance and Ann Snitow (1984), 'Towards a Conversation about Sex in Feminism', in *Signs*, vol.10, 1.

Norman Vance (1985), *The Sinews of the Spirit*, Cambridge University Press, Cambridge.

Mariana Valverde (1985), *Sex, Power and Pleasure*, Women's Press, Toronto.

Alice Walker (1970), *The Third Life of Grange Copeland*, Women's Press, London.

Alice Walker (1982), *The Color Purple*, Women's Press, London.

Judith Walkowitz (1982), 'Jack the Ripper and the Myth of Male Violence', in *Feminist Studies*, vol.8, 3, Fall.

Judith Walkowitz (1984), 'Male Vice and Female Virtue: Feminism and the Politics of Prostitution in Nineteenth-Century Britain', in Ann Snitow *et al.* (eds.), *Desire: The Politics of Sexuality*, Virago, London.

Michele Wallace (1979), *Black Macho and the Myth of the Superwoman*, John Calder, London.

James Walvin (1987), 'Symbols of Moral Superiority: Slavery, Sport and the Changing World Order, 1800–1950' in J.A. Mangan and James Walvin (eds.), *Manliness and Morality*, Manchester University Press, London.

Yvette Walczek (1988), *He and She: Men in the Eighties*, Routledge, London.

Valerie Walkerdine (1988), *The Mastery of Reason*, Methuen, London.
Ken Walpole (1983), *Dockers and Dectectives*, Verso, London.
Margaret Walters (1979), *The Male Nude*, Penguin, Harmondsworth.
Micheline Wandor (ed.) (1972), *The Body Politic: Writings from the Women's Liberation Movement in Britain 1969–72*, Stage One, London.
Simon Watney (1980), 'The Ideology of GLF' in Gay Left Collective (ed.), *op.cit.*.
Simon Watney (1987), *Policing Desire*, Comedia, London.
Jeffrey Weeks (1977), *Coming Out: Homosexual Politics in Britain from the Nineteenth Century to the Present*, Quartet, London.
Jeffrey Weeks (1980), 'Capitalism and the Organisation of Sex' in Gay Left Collective, (ed.) *Homosexuality: Power and Politics*, Allison & Busby, London.
Jeffrey Weeks (1981), 'Discourse, desire and sexual deviance' in Plummer (ed.), *op.cit.*.
Jeffrey Weeks (1981), *Sex Politics and Society: The Regulation of Sexuality Since 1800*, Longman, London.
Jeffrey Weeks (1985), *Sexuality and its Discontents*, Routledge & Kegan Paul, London.
Jeffrey Weeks (1987), 'Love in a Cold Climate' in *Marxism Today*, January.
Seph Weene (1981), 'Venus', in *Sex Issues: Heresies*, 2.
Naomi Weisstein (1971), 'Psychology Constructs the Female', in Gornick and Moran (eds.), *op.cit.*.
Naomi Weisstein (1988), 'The Hite Reports: Charting an Ideological Revolution in Progress' in Hite, *op.cit.*.
Ellen Willis (1985), 'Feminism, Moralism and Pornography' in Snitow et al., *Powers of Desire, op.cit.*.
Fay Weldon (1971), *Down Among the Women*, Penguin, Harmondsworth.
Fay Weldon (1975), *Female Friends*, Pan, London.
George Weinberg (1972), *Society and the Healthy Homosexual*, St Martin's Press, New York.
Martin Weinberg and Colin Williams (1975), *Male Homosexuals*, Penguin Books, New York.
S. Weinberg (1955), *Incest Behaviour*, Citadel Press, New York.
D.J. West, C. Roy and Florence Nichols (1978), *Understanding Sexual Attacks*, Heinemann, London.
Margaret Wetherell (1986), 'Linguistic Repertoires and Literary Criticism: New Directions for a Social Psychology of Gender' in *Feminist Social Psychology*, Sue Wilkinson (ed.), Open University Press, Milton Keynes.
Edmund White (1980), *States of Desire*, E.P. Dutton, New York.
Edmund White (1982), *A Boy's Own Story*, Picador, London.
David Widgery (1979), 'Baldwin' in *Achilles Heel*, 3.
David Will (1989), 'Feminism, Child Sexual Abuse, and the Demise of Systems Mysticism' in *Context: A News Magazine of Family Therapy*, Spring, vol. 19, 1.
Sue Wilkinson (ed.), (1986), *Feminist Social Psychology*, Open University Press, Milton Keynes.
Judith Williamson (1986), 'Prisoner of Love', in *Consuming Passions*, Marion Boyars, London.
Ellen Willis (1981), *Beginning to See the Light*, South End Press, Boston.
Paul Willis (1977), *Learning to Labour*, Saxon House, Farnborough.
Colin Willock (1958), *The Man's Book*, Edward Hulton, London.

Elizabeth Wilson (1977), *Women and the Welfare State*, Tavistock, London.

Elizabeth Wilson (1989), 'In a Different Key', in (ed.) Kathrine Gieve, *op.cit.*.

Elizabeth Wilson (1989), in *The Guardian*, March 14.

Paul Wilson (1978), *The Other Side of Rape*, Univ. of Queensland Press, St. Lucia.

D.W. Winnicott (1986), 'This Feminism', in *Home Is Where we Start From*, Penguin, Harmondsworth.

Bruce Woodcock (1984), *Male Mythologies: John Fowles and the Myth of Masculinity*, Harvester Press, Sussex.

Rochelle Wortis (1972), 'Child-Rearing and Women's Liberation', in Wandor, *op.cit.*.

Richard Wright (1980), *'The English Rapist' New Society* 17 July.

Michael Young and Peter Willmont (1962), *Family and Kinship in East London*, Penguin, Harmondsworth.

Nigel Young (1979), 'Past Present', in *Gay Left*, 8, Summer.

Index

Other Virago Books of Interest

IS THE FUTURE FEMALE?
Troubled Thoughts on Contemporary
Feminism

Lynne Segal

In one of the most provocative books for many years, Lynne Segal challenges many of the current feminist orthodoxies — on female sexuality, pornography, war and peace, psychoanalysis and sociobiology. She argues against the exponents — Mary Daly, Andrea Dworkin and Dale Spender among them — of the new apocalyptic feminism, which says that men wield power over women through terror, greed and violence and that only women because of their essentially greater humanity, can save the word from social, ecological and nuclear disaster. She urges that to base the politics of feminism on innate and essential differences between men and women is mistaken, dangerous, and basically a counsel of despair, since its logical conclusion is that nothing can change. Things emphatically *have* changed for women, she asserts, and we must build on these changes, combining autonomy with alliances to alter power relations and forge a new future for women *and* men.

THE BONDS OF LOVE
Psycholanalysis, Feminism and the Problems of Domination

Jessica Benjamin

'*The Bonds of Love* gives us Benjamin at her best, and psycho-analytic social theory at its best, as she demonstrates brilliantly the complex intertwining of familial, gender and social domination' — *Nancy Chodorow*

Why do people submit to authority and even derive pleasure from the power others have over them? What is the appeal of domination and submission, and why are they so prevalent in erotic life? Why is it so difficult for men and women to meet as equals? Why indeed do they continue to recapitulate the positions of master and slave?

Jessica Benjamin makes use of feminist reinterpretations of psychoanalytic theory to consider anew the problem of domination, of individual development, gender difference and authority. Domination is revealed as a complex psychological process which ensnares both parties in bonds of complicity, and one which underlies our family life, social institutions and especially sexual relationships, in spite of our conscious commitment to equality and freedom. In her questioning of gender polarities in which woman is object to the male subject she argues for a change which she describes as both 'modest and utopian' — in disentangling the bonds of love we seek a mutual recognition of equal subjects which would lead to both personal and social transformation.

TOMORROW'S CHILD
Reproductive Technologies in the 90s

Lynda Birke,
Susan Himmelweit
and Gail Vines

The first 'test-tube' babies are now adolescents. Yet, at the mere mentions of in vitro fertilisation, surrogate mothering or pre-natal diagnosis, arguments rage. What is the controversy really about? Should research on embryos be permitted? Should fetuses carrying genetic diseases be aborted? Are women's rights of paramount and overriding importance? Much feminist writing on the subject expresses a complete rejection of reproductive technologies based on fear: fear that we are witnessing a takeover by scientists of women's reproductive role. The authors recognise the origin of this fear but do not agree with the conclusion. They argue that technological solutions are not always bad for women. Therefore women have to be informed if they are to make choices. *Tomorrow's Child* is a lucid and concerned book that tells you what these technologies are — the hazards and the benefits, how they work and how they are likely to develop; it discusses the ethical dilemmas, and the assumptions they make about fetuses and women; and above all it contributes to the debate by suggesting strategies by which women can take control.

DEMOCRACY IN THE KITCHEN
Regulating Mothers and Socialising Daughters

Valerie Walkerdine and Helen Lucey

How are daughters raised, how are mothers made to be 'proper' mothers and what does all this have to do with democracy? From the post-war period, with its emphasis on expanding educational possibilities for all children, to equal opportunities in the 1970s and '80s, the prevailing notion has been that 'natural' mothering (for how could it be otherwise?) would produce 'normal' children, fit for the new democratic age. These ideas have become commonsense ones, but at what cost to the lives of women? Valerie Walkerdine and Helen Lucey explore these effects by examining a well-known study of four-year-olds with their mothers, and in doing so, they tell us a different story about the divides of class and gender and the consequent social inequalities. The authors argue that, although ideas from developmental psychology are held to be progressive, they serve to support the view that there is something wrong with working-class mothering which could be put right by making it more middle-class. But nor is the middle-class home one of happy normality: in both classes, women are differently but oppressively, regulated. In this provocative book, the authors call for a new feminist engagement with class and gender socialisation to constitute a new politics of difference.

Lynne Segal was born in Sydney, Australia. She came to London with her 14-month-old son in 1970, having received a doctorate in psychology from Sydney University. Since arriving in London she has taught psychology at Middlesex Polytechnic and has been involved in feminist and socialist politics; she is a member of the *Feminist Review* collective and participated in the launching of the national Socialist Society. Her previous works include *Is the Future Female? Troubled Thoughts on Contemporary Feminism* (Virago 1987) and *Beyond the Fragments*, with Sheila Rowbotham and Hilary Wainwright (1980). She lives in London.

Following the enormous success of her controversial *Is the Future Female?*, Lynne Segal's latest book tackles the prevailing feminist pessimism about men and male power. Challenging the notion of masculinity as a monolithic entity, she points out the contradictory and competing nature of its different forms: tough guys and martial men, super-macho, camp, gay, black-macho and anti-sexist men, all are carefully scrutinised in this provocative study. Men's resistance to change is not simply due to psychic obstinacy or incapacity – men can and do change. If we are to move on, argues Lynne Segal, it is vital that we recognise, and build on, these changes – and construct a vision of a future non-repressive sexual agenda for both men and women.